Michael Egan

11 1605

THE POLITICAL ECONOMY OF FOREIGN POLICY IN SOUTHEAST ASIA

D1053966

The Political Economy of Foreign Policy in Southeast Asia

Edited by

David Wurfel
Professor of Political Science
University of Windsor, Ontario

and

Bruce Burton
Associate Professor of Political Science
University of Windsor, Ontario

St. Martin's Press   New York

© David Wurfel and Bruce Burton 1990

All rights reserved. For information, write:
Scholarly and Reference Division,
St. Martin's Press Inc., 175 Fifth Avenue,
New York, N.Y. 10010

First published in the United States of America in 1990

Phototypeset by Input Typesetting Ltd, London
Printed in Hong Kong

ISBN 0-312-03612-4 cloth
ISBN 0-312-03611-6 paper

Library of Congress Cataloging-in-Publication Data

The Political Economy of Foreign Policy in Southeast Asia/edited by
 David Wurfel and Bruce Burton.
   p.   cm. — (International Political Economy Series)
 Includes index.
 ISBN 0-312-03612-4. — ISBN 0-312-03611-6 (pbk.)
 1. Asia, Southeastern — Foreign economic relations — Case studies.
 2. International division of labor — Case studies.   I. Wurfel,
 David.   II. Burton, Bruce.   III. Series.
 HF1591.P65   1990
 337.59 — dc20   89-34720
                                                            CIP

Contents

List of Figures and Tables

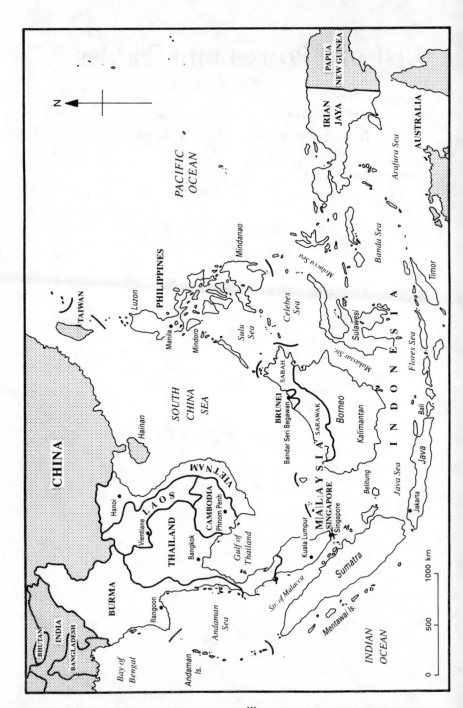

viii

Acknowledgements

This volume has been very much a collaborative undertaking. First drafts of most of the chapters were presented at the Conference on 'Managing the External Environment: the Political Economy of Foreign Policy in Southeast Asia' held in June 1987 at the University of Windsor. Many months of exchange of drafts between editors and individual chapter authors followed, and we are indebted to the contributors for their patience during this extended process. We very much hope that between us we have realized our joint objective of providing a comprehensive, up-to-date analysis of the foreign policies of a region of continuing salience in world politics.

The Windsor Conference was supported by grants from the Social Science and Humanities Research Council of Canada, the Canadian Institute for International Peace and Security, the University of Toronto-York University Joint Centre for Asia Pacific Studies, and the President and the Dean of Social Science of the University of Windsor. We also benefitted from the administrative support of our own Department of Political Science, and in particular from the secretarial assistance we received from Barbara Faria and Lea Wilkinson. Able organizational assistance for the Conference was cheerfully provided by Margaret Beddoe, Iris Kohler and Brad Zubyk, and in the later stages of the project Jiang Hongkuan furnished efficient editorial assistance.

We also gratefully acknowledge the scholarly insights provided by Peter Bell, David Dewitt, Don Emmerson, Paul Evans, John Girling, Gérard Hervouet, Huynh Kim Khanh, Charles Lindsey, R. S. Milne, and Martin Rudner during the course of the extensive discussions that took place at the Windsor Conference. While their contributions have undoubtedly enhanced the quality of the subsequent book, neither they nor anyone else but editors and contributors are responsible for any inadequacies in the content of what follows.

We would like to thank the Asia Pacific Foundation of Canada for the generous grant it awarded to assist in the preparation and publication of this book. And we would also like to express our appreciation to Timothy Shaw, for agreeing to include the volume in the Macmillan International Political Economy Series of which he is the General Editor, and to Timothy Farmiloe, Editorial Director at Macmillan, for his forbearance over the delay in producing the final version of the manuscript of this collective enterprise.

Finally, we owe a very special debt of gratitude to our wives and children for their indispensable support and encouragement throughout this undertaking.

David Wurfel
Bruce Burton
May 1989, Windsor, Ontario

Notes on the Contributors

John Badgley is Curator of the John Echols Collection on Southeast Asia of the Cornell University Library. Previously a professor of political science at Miami University of Ohio and The Johns Hopkins' School of Advanced International Studies, Dr Badgley authored *Politics Among Burmans* (1970) and *Asian Development: Problems and Prognosis* (1971), and contributed to *Politics towards China: Views from Six Continents* (1965) as well as two dozen articles on Burma in journals and several other books.

Bruce Burton was educated at Oxford and The Hague, is currently an Associate Professor of Political Science and Co-ordinator of the International Relations Programme at the University of Windsor, Ontario. He is the author of numerous scholarly articles on Asian and international affairs and has travelled extensively in the region.

Nayan Chanda has served with the *Far Eastern Economic Review* since 1974, mostly in Southeast Asia, but also as Washington Bureau Chief. Educated at Presidency College and Jadavpur University in Calcutta, as well as at the University of Paris, he has contributed chapters to *Confrontation or Coexistence: the Future of ASEAN-Vietnam Relations* (1985) and *Contemporary Laos* (1982) and authored the major work on post-1975 Indochina, *Brother Enemy: The War after the War* (1986).

K. J. Holsti, PhD (Stanford) 1961, is presently Professor of Political Science, University of British Columbia in Vancouver. His books include *International Politics: A Framework for Analysis* (5th edn., 1988), *Why Nations Realign* (1982), and *The Dividing Discipline: Hegemony and Diversity in International Theory* (1985). He has been a visiting professor at McGill University, Kyoto University, the Hebrew University of Jerusalem, the Australian National University, and the International University of Japan. He is a past-president of the Canadian Political Science Association and of the International Studies Association.

Dwight King, PhD (Chicago, 1978) is Associate Professor of Political Science at Northern Illinois University. He has spent about five years, cumulatively, conducting research and consulting in Indonesia since 1972. Among his previous publications are a monograph, *Interest Groups and Political Linkage in Indonesia, 1800–1965*, and contributions to *Comparative Political Studies* (1981), Anderson and Kahin (eds), *Interpreting Indonesian Politics* (1982), *Public Administration and Development* (1988) and *Asian Survey* (1988).

Bahgat Korany is Professor of Political Science and Director of the Arab studies programme at the University of Montreal. He has been visiting professor at Laval University, Carleton University and the University of Dakar, and a Fellow of the Center for International Affairs, Harvard University. He is the author of *Social Change, Charisma and International Behavior* (1976), with Ali Dessouki, *The Foreign Policies of Arab States* (1984), and is editor and co-author of *How Foreign Policy Decisions are Made in the Third World: A Comparative Analysis* (1986).

Linda Y. C. Lim, PhD (Michigan) is an economist from Singapore who teaches international business and Asian studies at the University of Michigan, and runs its Southeast Asia Business Program. Her research interests focus on foreign investment, export manufacturing, and the political economy of development in Southeast Asian countries, especially Singapore. She has just completed a jointly-authored volume on *Foreign Investment and Industrial Restructuring in Newly-Industrializing Asian Countries*, and is editing a collected volume on *The Political Economy of Industrialization in Southeast Asia*.

Clark D. Neher is Professor of Political Science at Northern Illinois University. He has written extensively on politics in Thailand, politics in Southeast Asia, and women's political roles in Southeast Asia. He has lived in Thailand and the Philippines carrying out research sponsored by the Fulbright Foundation, Ford Foundation and National Science Foundation. Professor Neher has served as President of the Council on Thai Studies and the Midwest Asian Association, and has served as chairman of the Southeast Asia Council and as a member of the Board of Directors of the Association for Asian Studies.

Gareth Porter PhD (Cornell) is Academic Director for Peace and Conflict Resolution, Washington Semester Program, The American

University. He has published articles on Indochina and Southeast Asia in *Foreign Affairs, Pacific Affairs,* and *Problems of Communism*, as well as other academic journals. His books include *A Peace Denied: The United States, Vietnam and the Paris Agreement*, and *Vietnam: A History in Documents*. He is now completing a book on the Vietnamese political system.

Timothy M. Shaw is Professor of Political Science, Director of the Centre for African Studies and Director of International Development Studies at Dalhousie University, Halifax, Nova Scotia. He is author of numerous articles on Africa and *Towards a Political Economy of Africa: the dialectics of dependence*. He is also co-editor of various works including *Africa Projected, Political Economy of African Foreign Policy* and *Regional Development in Africa and Canada*.

Martin Stuart-Fox is Reader in History at the University of Queensland, Brisbane, Australia. He was formerly a correspondent for United Press International in Laos and Vietnam. In addition to numerous articles in scholarly journals, Dr Stuart-Fox is the editor of a collection of studies entitled *Contemporary Laos*, and author of *The Murderous Revolution* on Kampuchea, and *Laos: Politics, Economics and Society* in the series on world Marxist regimes.

Richard Stubbs is currently Associate Director, Joint Centre for Asia Pacific Studies, University of Toronto-York University and Visiting Associate Professor, Department of Political Science, University of Toronto. He has published widely on Southeast Asian politics and the international commodity trade. His latest book is *Hearts and Minds in Guerrilla Warfare: The Malayan Emergency, 1948–60*.

David Wurfel received his PhD from Cornell and has been a Professor of Political Science at the University of Windsor, Ontario since 1969. He has taught previously at the universities of Michigan, Missouri, Singapore and the International Christian University at Tokyo. Among his books on the region are *Philippine Foreign Policy* (1983) and *Filipino Politics* (1988). He has also contributed to *Governments and Politics in Southeast Asia* (1964), *The Philippines after Marcos* (1985) and *Government and Rebellion in SE Asia* (1985) among others. He is a past president of the Canadian Asian Studies Association.

1 Introduction: A Foreign Policy Framework for Southeast Asian States

David Wurfel and Bruce Burton

The comparative study of foreign policy, which lagged in the 1970s, has been revived in recent years by a new focus on Third World states, with a leading role taken by specialists on Africa and the Middle East (Shaw and Aluko, 1983; Shaw and Aluko, 1984; Korany and Dessouki, 1984). The present volume is an attempt to bring to another region, Southeast Asia, the same combination of area studies and concern for frameworks of analysis.

Our book has been inspired by a view similar to that found in some other recent work, that rather than narrowing the focus to discover truth – which already by the end of the 1960s had produced several distinct schools of foreign policy analysis (Knorr and Rosenau, 1969) – the time has come to be more inclusive. The rising importance of economic considerations in all studies of the Third World has led some to approach foreign relations as merely a function of economics – which may be accurate for some countries in certain periods. But others have continued to look at foreign policy as essentially a question of security concerns. We would like to encompass both approaches.

We have chosen to place our approach to foreign policy analysis within the framework of 'political economy', which Staniland has characterized as 'a long-standing intellectual enterprise concerned with understanding the relationship of politics and economics' (Staniland, 1985: ix). As others have noted, 'The definition of political economy may itself raise questions, because of the variety of approaches. . . .' (Leyton-Brown and Ruggie, 1987: 3). For many, political economy implies a particular theory, of which there are several, but we do not align ourselves with any one – though authors of some chapters may adopt the assumptions of one theoretical orientation or another. We do assert, however, the importance of economic phenomena – for example, social classes, multinational corporations or world markets – as independent, intervening or

1

dependent variables in the understanding of foreign policy, a role we also ascribe to 'politics'; for instance, intra-élite competition, ethnic rebellion, or the nature of political institutions. Thus any hypotheses that might be derived from these case studies would likely fall in the 'interactive' category (Staniland, 1985: 7). This approach involves the difficulty of trying to relate what is rational, and quantifiable with that which is neither – but this variance exists within the traditional bounds of political science in any case.

This political economy framework, therefore, is not meant to exclude examination of elements in the foreign policy process which have been the concern of writers in the field of comparative foreign policy for many years. Elite images, security threats, military capabilities – these all remain potentially important. But we believe that economic dimensions are much more important than has heretofore been recognized in the comparative foreign policy tradition. A few writers have gone so far as to apply a political economy framework to foreign policy that is explicitly materialist, emphasizing 'substructure' rather than 'superstructure' (see Shaw and Aluko, 1984: 10), but this would be too restrictive for Southeast Asia.

There are three reasons why non-economic factors need to be given a prominent place in the comparative analysis of Southeast Asian countries, thus making inappropriate a more economistic version of political economy, even though it might fit the circumstances of Africa or Latin America. (1) The strength of the pre-colonial legacy: pre-colonial political institutions and cultures were older and more highly developed in Southeast Asia than in most parts of the Third World. Furthermore, the earlier tradition was not almost totally destroyed, as in Peru or Mexico. Most modern states were preceded by traditional kingdoms whose institutions and cultures have left powerful legacies for the present (with the Philippines being the obvious exception). Thus national self-images, perceptions of external threat and decision-making styles all have pre-colonial roots, despite the impact of economic exploitation in the colonial era. (2) The importance of political and cultural, as well as economic, factors in explaining the level of autonomy: because of the vigor of anti-colonial nationalism, especially in Burma, Indonesia, and Indo-China, and because of the innovations and hard work of Chinese entrepreneurs, especially in Singapore the dependence created by colonialism has been substantially reduced in some countries. (At the same time Indo-China has adopted a new dependency pattern, for political reasons.) And (3) at present the greatest direct military presence of both superpowers in any Third World region; in fact, only five Southeast Asian states have been able to avoid that presence. This has heightened the salience of military/strategic considerations.

The effort to formulate a new foreign policy framework for application in Southeast Asia is justified primarily by the fact that there is no work which attempts rigorous comparison of all the states in the region. A decade ago Charles Morrison and Astri Suhrke dealt with six of the ten Southeast Asian states in *Strategies of Survival: The Foreign Policy Dilemmas of Smaller Asian States*. Several useful studies have recently appeared focusing on one dimension of the foreign policies of Southeast Asian states or on the foreign policy of one country, such as Sheldon Simon, *The ASEAN States and Regional Security*; Donald Crone, *The ASEAN States: Coping with Dependence*; Jayaratnam Saravanamuttu, *The Dilemma of Independence: Two Decades of Malaysia's Foreign Policy*; and Michael Leifer, *Indonesia's Foreign Policy*. But not all of these efforts devoted much attention to economic phenomena. More recent studies that have used sophisticated political economy frameworks have not encompassed the full range of foreign policy, but have focused on the treatment of multinational corporations. Thus in covering all of Southeast Asia and in adopting a fresh multi-dimensional political economy framework, our book will be making its own special contribution. A set of case studies in a comparative framework is not the same as theory building, but will provide the necessary empirical base for any attempt to formulate hypotheses.

Yet some would argue that Southeast Asia has such diversity that it is less amenable to comparative study than other Third-World regions. The diversity of both states and societies – and foreign policies – in Southeast Asia cannot be denied. There are mini-states as well as the world's fifth largest. All major world religions are represented. The richest state has average per capita income more than a hundred times the poorest. Political regimes range from liberal democratic to military authoritarian to monarchical to Communist. Foreign policies can be found which are either pro-US, pro-Soviet or neutralist. With such diversity some find it difficult to conceive of Southeast Asia as a 'region', even though a large part of it is now covered by an increasingly active regional organization.

The diversity of Southeast Asia does indeed make it difficult to hold very many variables constant in the attempt to discern what best explains foreign policy. It is unlikely that we will discover a

'Southeast Asian type'. But, on the other hand, this diversity makes Southeast Asia more representative of the Third World as a whole and thus hypotheses derived from its study are more generally applicable.

Our case studies are not as sharply focused as might be desirable for some kinds of theory building; concentration on policy toward a particular power (already attempted by Halpern, 1965) or a single issue area would logically be the 'second book'. An attempt to characterize policies more broadly and their trends over time would seem to have the first priority. This will make it possible to distinguish between strategy and tactic, between structural and contingent factors, and between word and deed. This historical survey would also make possible the identification of a pattern of 'restructuring' (Holsti, 1982), or other important changes should they exist.

A book with country chapters implies that the state is still the primary actor in international affairs of the region, even though we recognize an important role for other entities, for instance, the MNLF, the Khmer Rouge, the IMF or transnational corporations. In fact, some non-state actors may be stronger than certain states at a particular point in time. But for some in the *dependencia* school, even this admission would not be enough; they would deny the existence of the Third-World state as an autonomous actor on the world scene. This is one point at which 'inclusiveness' in our approach would deter rather than facilitate useful analysis. We must reassert the possibility of state autonomy, even when trade, investment or credit dependence is well documented. Those states, clearly not autonomous, which are too weak to achieve 'dependency reversal' in a particular time frame, may still retain that potential. In any case, the autonomy or dependence of any particular state is to be empirically demonstrated, not assumed.

Dependencia in its most extreme formulation, 'the development of underdevelopment', was a hopeless determinism that could hardly be integrated into an open-ended empirical study of foreign policy. But a dependency approach that calls attention to the severe constraints placed on Third-World states by the operation of the world capitalist system, both through semi-public institutions, for instance, the IMF and World Bank, and through private corporations, is a valuable contribution to our understanding of foreign policy options available to such states. When dependency analysts also point out how these constraints have sometimes become internalized by Third-World élites who share interest and perspectives with centres of world capitalist power, then the sophistication of our analysis is still further improved. But while there is almost universal agreement now on the significance of quantifiable dependence through trade, investment and credit, the establishment of linkages between these economic phenomena and foreign policy decisions in the dependent state is a difficult research task and the consequences of those linkages are still a topic of some disagreement among analysts.

Domestic and foreign policies are seen as distinctions along a continuum. Foreign policy, our focus here, is the sum of statements and actions by a state's policy-makers to promote or control the impact of changes in the external environment. Traditionally that environment was made up of policies, attitudes and actions of other states, but we must now add the role of non-state actors. Though we will often speak of the impact of foreign policy on the domestic political economy – regime survival, economic development, or counter-insurgency efforts – the first target of that policy is by definition a foreign actor, even though the outcome of policy implementation may have major domestic consequences, and the expectation of those consequences may have been the primary motivation of policy-makers in the first place.

In recent years the scope of 'foreign' policy has expanded, including more phenomena economic in character, for example, the category 'acquiring foreign economic resources for development' listed under outputs. In fact, for Third World countries extractions from the external environment – in a manner quite different from imperialists, of course – have been more important than inputs into it, though the latter has been the focus of traditional foreign policy studies. Recognizing the reality of dependence, and of 'soft', penetrable, states, we may need to push the concept of foreign policy just a bit further. If penetration is the active expression of dominance in a dependency relationship (penetration of a particular sub-culture or interest group may also take place outside of general dependency, for instance, that by an Islamic organization) and even a dependent state may not have lost its desire for autonomy, then regulating, or attempting to stop certain kinds of penetration is an important aspect of 'managing the external environment' (Clapham, 1985: 113). (Attempting to regulate flows of interactions across state borders has been called 'management', but for many Third World states, and several in Southeast Asia, this conjures up an image of successful manipulation which is probably not justified, thus 'coping' with the external environment would seem to be a more modest, and more accurate, phrase.)

The framework developed by the editors to guide the writing of country chapters has no pretensions of being a 'model', that is, a package of interrelated hypotheses adequate to explain all, or even most, foreign policy behavior. But if any existing hypothesis is to be strengthened, or any new one to emerge – in the 'middle range' or higher – certain common questions must be addressed and certain comparable data must be provided.

Each author first of all describes the nature of the national society, the economy and the regime, indicating whether any important changes have taken place over time. The foreign policy-makers and their interests and values are then identified and the foreign policy process explored, with attention to the degree to which it has been institutionalized.

Attention is then given to domestic resources (or 'capabilities') such as administrative and diplomatic skills, military and economic strength, degree of regime legitimacy, and to domestic constraints, such as ethnic or religious conflict in the population or lack of natural resources.

Next to be examined are constraints and opportunities in the external environment. The geographic location of the state, any territorial or boundary disputes, great power interventions in the region, or the role of international organizations can be potent influences on a country's foreign policy outputs, as can be the various forms of economic dependence. Likewise, the policy-makers' *perceptions* of threats, constraints and opportunities emanating from the international environment have a decisive impact on actual policy decisions and actions.

Finally, foreign policy outputs are accorded systematic treatment. In order to facilitate comparative analysis, each author was requested to employ the following categories when discussing the main objectives of foreign policy: security (encompassing territorial integrity as well as state survival), maximizing autonomy (including the ability to monitor and control foreign penetration), regime maintenance, national welfare/development (especially the acquisition of foreign resources for development purposes), and nation-building (defined as the process of promoting and strengthening national integration and national identity) and state-building. National strategies employed in the pursuit of these objectives and basic foreign policy orientations are also examined. Since policy-makers will differ in the priority they accord the five main objectives from country to country and from period to period within the same country, authors were asked to assist the process of comparative analysis by ranking the various objectives according to their importance for the particular country and/or time period being analyzed. Contributors were invited to conclude with an evaluation of the degree of success that policy-makers have had in realizing objectives, and a determination as to whether their country of specialization had ever experienced a restructuring of foreign policy, that is, a fundamental change in foreign policy orientation.

While the country studies naturally form the core of this book, the editors felt that the analysis would be enhanced by an examination of the external environment for Southeast Asian foreign policies generally and by the inclusion of three chapters placing the case studies in wider analytical perspective. The first looks at the comparative analysis of foreign policy in general, the second discusses current approaches to the study of Third-World foreign policies, and the third assesses African foreign policy, suggesting some comparisons with Southeast Asia. The conclusion develops intra-regional and extra-regional comparisons of Southeast Asian foreign policies and explores possible causal relationships.

BIBLIOGRAPHY

Calvert, Peter, *The Foreign Policy of New States* (Brighton: Wheatsheaf, 1986).
Clapham, Christopher, *Third World Politics: An Introduction* (Madison: University of Wisconsin Press, 1985), esp. ch. 6, 'Managing the External Political Arena'.
Crone, Donald K., *The ASEAN States: Coping with Dependence* (New York: Praeger, 1983).
Doran, Charles, George Modelski and Cal Clark (eds), *North/South Relations: Studies of Dependency Reversal* (New York: Praeger, 1983).
Halpern, A. M. (ed), *Policies Toward China: Views from Six Continents* (New York: McGraw-Hill, 1965).
Hermann, Charles F., Charles W. Kegley, Jr. and James N. Rosenau (eds), *New Directions in the Study of Foreign Policy* (Boston: Allen & Unwin, 1987).
Holsti, K. J., *The Dividing Discipline: Hegemony and Diversity in International Theory* (Boston and London: Allen & Unwin, 1985).
Holsti, Kal (ed.), *Why Nations Realign: Foreign Policy Restructuring in the Post-War World* (London: Allen & Unwin, 1982).

Knorr, Klaus and James Rosenau (eds), *Contending Approaches to International Politics* (Princeton: Princeton University Press, 1969).

Korany, Bahgat (ed.), *How Foreign Policy Decisions Are Made in the Third World: A Comparative Analysis* (Boulder: Westview, 1986).

Korany, Bahgat and Ali Dessouki, *The Foreign Policies of Arab States* (Boulder: Westview Press, with American University in Cairo Press, 1984).

Leifer, Michael, 'Southeast Asia', in C. Clapham (ed.), *Foreign Policy-Making in Developing States* (New York and London: Praeger, 1977).

Leifer, Michael, *Indonesia's Foreign Policy* (London and Boston: Allen & Unwin, 1983).

Leyton-Brown, David and John Gerard Ruggie, 'The North American Political Economy in the Global Context: An Analytical Framework', *International Journal* XLII (Winter 1986–87) 3–24.

McCloud, Donald G., *System and Process in Southeast Asia: The Evolution of a Region* (Boulder: Westview, 1986).

Morrison, Charles and Astri Suhrke, *Strategies of Survival: The Foreign Policy Dilemmas of Smaller Asian States* (New York: St Martin's Press, 1979).

Saravanamuttu, Jayaratnam, *The Dilemma of Independence: Two Decades of Malaysia's Foreign Policy, 1957–1977* (Penang: Penerbit Universiti Sains Malaysia, 1983).

Staniland, Martin, *What is Political Economy? A Study of Social Theory and Underdevelopment* (New Haven: Yale University Press, 1985).

Shaw, Timothy M. and Olajide Aluko (eds), *Nigerian Foreign Policy* (London: Macmillan, 1983).

Shaw, Timothy M. and Olajide Aluko (eds), *The Political Economy of African Foreign Policy: Comparative Analysis* (New York: St Martin's Press, 1984).

Shaw, Timothy M., *Towards a Political Economy for Africa: The Dialectics of Dependence* (London: Macmillan, 1985).

Simon, Sheldon W., *The ASEAN States and Regional Security* (Stanford: Hoover Institution Press, 1982).

Snyder, Richard, H. W. Bruck and Burton Sapin (eds), *Foreign Policy Decision-Making* (New York: Free Press, 1962).

Tilman, Robert, *The Enemy Beyond: External Threat Perceptions in the ASEAN Region* (Singapore: Institute of Southeast Asian Studies, 1984).

Weinstein, Franklin, *Indonesian Foreign Policy and the Dilemma of Dependence* (Ithaca: Cornell University Press, 1976).

Wurfel, David, 'The Pattern of Southeast Asian Response to International Politics' in William Henderson (ed.), *SE Asia: Problems for US policy* (Cambridge, Mass.: MIT Press, 1963).

Wurfel, David, 'Southeast Asian Alignments', *International Journal*, XXIX:3 (Summer 1974), 441–77.

2 The Comparative Analysis of Foreign Policy: Some Notes on the Pitfalls and Paths to Theory

K. J. Holsti

This volume is important because, aside from offering the first focused comparative analyses of all the countries in Southeast Asia, it provides an opportunity to evaluate progress in an area of inquiry that, according to James Rosenau (1980), is neither a fad nor a fantasy, but is an established subfield of political science and international relations. My purpose is not to present a review of the field, as others have already done this (East, 1987; Hill and Light, 1985). Rather, I would like to take this opportunity to examine critically some of the problems that have appeared in attempts to develop a coherent, cumulative, comprehensive, and comparative field.

One way to approach the problem is to ask what should be the essential contours of a field of inquiry. It would be presumptuous for any individual to suggest that his or her preferred criteria are authoritative or exhaustive. The comments below are therefore suggestive and open to argument. Whatever their merit, however, I believe it is important to think about them because they will at least provide benchmarks against which to measure progress, and perhaps offer a sense of direction for future research. I would list the following among my set of preferences:

(1) A consensus on critical questions to ask (the criterion of centrality).
(2) Agreement on major analytical categories and how to connect them (the criterion of conceptual consensus).
(3) Examination of a sufficiently large number of cases, that is,

9

countries' foreign policies, over time (the criterion of representativeness).

(4) Using concepts, categories and typologies that foster rather
than hinder comparative analysis (the criterion of comparability).

Most disciplines converge on, or are derived from, a few critical
normative and/or scientific questions. In the case of international
relations, for example, virtually all work of enduring value can be
traced to questions about the source of war and the conditions for
peace/order, and stability. Questions of equity, justice, and distribution of welfare values and public goods are at the core of international political economy.

It is not clear that foreign policy analysis of the comparative sort
has a central intellectual puzzle to solve. Presumably we want to
describe how states, typically and untypically, act toward the external
environment, and somehow to account for both patterned and highly
idiosyncratic behaviors. But it is easier to state that this is *the* core
problem than to demonstrate that we have made much progress in
elaborating sets of independent and dependent variables around such
key concerns. Because we do not have a consensus regarding the
problems that should animate research, individual studies are likely
to be idiosyncratic and hence not easily amenable to comparative
analysis.

Do we have a reasonable consensus on key analytical categories
and concepts? In foreign policy analysis the literature reveals considerable convergence on such concepts as decision-making, bureaucratic politics, capabilities, crisis, deterrence, compellance, and
coercion. We can isolate decisions and actions, and researchers have
developed an extensive list of their sources. But the critical question
of what we are trying to explain remains contentious. There is no
consensus on what the concept of foreign policy includes or excludes,
or what are its essential and non-essential indicators. Our field lacks
a carefully delineated dependent variable.

The problem of bias, parochialism, and unrepresentativeness
plagues the field, although there are welcome signs of improvement.
The vast majority of studies that have some theoretical and comparative content to them are authored by Americans, and implicitly or
explicitly use the United States as a model for others. For example,
the model of bureaucratic politics (Allison, 1971) supposedly of
universal applicability, derived from an experience of the United

States in a crisis situation. To what extent can this situation be considered typical? As Kim Nossal (1984) has pointed out, the Westminster model of a parliamentary system has important implications for foreign policy-making in other countries. We certainly need to be alert to the possibility that policy is the result of bureaucratic pulling and tugging, but in no sense can Allison's model claim to provide a 'paradigm' of foreign policy in general.

The Foreign Policy Course Syllabus Project of the International Studies Association's Comparative Foreign Policy Section has collected a number of syllabi of undergraduate and graduate courses in American universities. Even those labelled 'Comparative Foreign Policy' include almost no non-American authored works, and the comparative content is almost non-existent. A course syllabus 'Foreign Policy Decision-Making' at the University of Texas lists 123 different required and suggested readings for the students. Of these, only nine are authored by non-Americans, seven of whom are Canadian. The course examines foreign policy decision-making in only two countries, the United States and Israel. The problem of parochialism and bias is acute and needs to be addressed seriously before we can claim that the subfield even begins to meet the criterion of representativeness.

While dependency theory provides some highly suggestive insights of a non-American perspective, and while no doubt persisting economic structures do provide constraints and limit some nations' freedom of action, the theory is unsatisfactory as a comprehensive guide for comparative foreign policy analysis because it cannot account for the great variations of foreign policy practice that prevail in the Third World. On most important indicators, Burma's foreign policy, for example, is fundamentally different from Egypt's; Kenya, Zambia, and Tanzania have demonstrated significantly different orientations, roles, and actions over the past decades, although each shares the various characteristics of the dependency syndrome. Moreover, reducing political choices and actions to economic phenomena is to overlook a host of essentially non-economic issues which create a variety of foreign policy problems for all states in the system.

There is, of course, no dearth of excellent country studies (for example, Weinstein, 1972; Saravanamuttu, 1983) that contain theoretical content, but most of these are not cast in frameworks that easily lend themselves to comparative analysis. The self-consciously comparative efforts are mostly of very recent vintage (Korany and

Dessouki, 1984); it remains to be seen if they can serve as models for the work of others.

The fourth desideratum is employing concepts, categories, and typologies that foster rather than hinder comparative analysis. Since academics in North America appear to place considerable emphasis on novelty, this is a difficult criterion to meet. Each researcher is likely to develop a vocabulary and roster of concepts for his or her own work, not mindful of the desirability of using concepts and categories that others have used, and which can be used in future work. The result is a predictable accumulation of country studies that are largely incomparable.

Lest this listing of weaknesses and impediments in the field appear overly pessimistic, let me acknowledge that in the areas of individual behaviour, as in decision-making studies and the techniques of influence, we have observed very substantial progress over the past decades. The works of Brecher, Jervis, George, Ole Holsti, Lebow, Stein, Steinbruner, Tanter, and others has been largely cumulative and self-critical. Models of decision-making have become increasingly complex, and an impressive array of historical and simulation researchers have uncovered many fascinating and significant findings. But there is one caveat: these are studies of how policy-makers come to decisions, or at least how they array their preferences, usually in crisis situations. The decisions are highly constrained in the sense that an immediate situation has to be dealt with on an emergency basis. These incidents, while of obvious importance, do not tell us much about the broader foreign policy purposes of individuals and governments. Foreign policy cannot be reduced to crises alone.

Comparative studies on the instruments of foreign policy and techniques of influence have been no less impressive. For example, the works by George and Smoke (1974), and George, Hall, and Simons (1971) employing an explicit methodology of 'focused comparison' provide numerous generalizations about the employment of coercive and deterrent strategies in foreign policy.

The literature on a particular type of foreign policy – imperialism – has developed to the point where it has considerable theoretical content (the search for explanations), numerous case studies, and generalizations that transcend the particular activities of individual states. It is in this area, of course, that the Marxist tradition has made the greatest contribution. But that contribution has been predominantly in the form of insights. In the realm of logic and provision of testable hypotheses regarding a general form of foreign policy behavior, the tradition has been the subject of telling criticism (Waltz, 1979; Reynolds, 1981).

What of numerous quantitative studies employing events data? Here, too, we can see significant advances in terms of explicit theoretical work, rigorous methodology, and cumulation, all important hallmarks of a theoretical enterprise. But as an approach to the study of foreign policy, patterns of events have serious limitations. They are useful for mapping transactions between nations, usually classified in terms of typologies of co-operation, conflict, threats, rewards, and the like. They can also inform us of the ups and downs of hostility and friendship between governments. But events data are not a very good indicator of foreign policy, if by that term we mean purposive behavior directed toward changing or sustaining a particular state of affairs at home or abroad. We cannot infer motive, purpose, aspiration, and long-range objectives from discrete events and actions (cf., Callahan, 1982).

SKETCHES FOR A CONCEPT OF FOREIGN POLICY

The comments that follow concentrate on the persisting problem of the dependent variable – foreign policy. In the realist tradition, states are power maximizers. Foreign policy is thus reduced to the problems deriving from the 'security dilemma'. At the systemic level, foreign policy is seen predominantly as the activities states take to erect, preserve, or destroy balances of power. These activities are of only two types: mobilizing domestic capabilities, and forming alliances.

However adequate this view of foreign policy may have been as a shorthand description of diplomacy in the eighteenth and nineteenth centuries, it is clearly inadequate today. It is overly simplistic and fails to acknowledge many other types of problems that concern governments in their foreign relations.

This model, however, has the virtue of portraying policy-makers as goal-achievers. Governments have *objectives* which they seek to achieve; foreign policy behavior is purposive behavior. It is also rational behavior in that governments typically attempt to fit ends to means, and make calculations about the relative costs and advantages of various policy options. Foreign policy, then, is the total of the decisions and actions taken to achieve stated objectives. As the framework proposed by the editors suggests, the purpose of foreign policy analysis is to identify the objectives and the strategies and

actions fashioned to maximize goal-achievement. This model under-
lies a significant part of the literature on foreign policy and international politics. It has the virtue of compensating for the simplicities
of the power-maximizing school by suggesting that there are numerous things governments, through their policy-makers, aspire to, and
that actions cannot be reduced to the mobilization of domestic capabilities and allies. The concepts of objectives, strategies, and actions
are not difficult to operationalize, and they are certainly comparable.

The model of the goal-achiever, however, may be overly specific,
with the result that the analyst will tend to concentrate on behavior
that is unique and largely context-determined. To compensate for
this problem, we can ask: what 'problems' do all governments share
vis-à-vis the external environment? followed by the question, what
sorts of objectives or purposes are unique to each state?

Foreign policy analysis can thus take the perspective of *problem-
solving* as its base, and add to it elements of the goal-oriented model.
The concepts of problems and objectives are not mutually exclusive,
nor are the distinctions between them entirely clear. What I have in
mind is a distinction of magnitude rather than quality. Governments,
as I will suggest, face a set of common problems. They cope, adapt,
solve, control or manage them in different ways. Within the problem
areas, they seek to achieve or defend specific objectives. Most objectives, then, are components of an overall problem. Other objectives,
however, are unique. One example may clarify the distinction. The
Soviet Union, like all states, has a security problem which it manages
or resolves by developing weapons and deploying them in a certain
fashion, by maintaining alliances, and possibly by engaging in arms
control negotiations. Within each of these policy sectors, decision-
makers seek to achieve certain specific objectives, such as an advantageous arms control agreement. In addition, however, the Soviet
Union has historically pursued a set of objectives that deals with
ideological preferences, namely the promotion of revolution abroad.
These objectives *do not* derive from the problems that all states
typically face. They are largely unique to the Soviet Union. To put
it succinctly, the problem category encompasses activities that are
essential to the survival of states. This is the realm of necessity.
Other purposes or objectives are in the realm of choice, expressing
aspirations and changes in the international environment that may
be important, but are not essential.

I believe there are four clusters of problems that all governments
face, irrespective of size, location, technology level, population and

many other attributes. They are (1) autonomy; (2) welfare; (3) security; and (4) regime maintenance. For many developing countries, a fifth category is state- and/or nation-building. This list is not exhaustive, nor are the categories mutually exclusive. The dividing line between them is obviously fuzzy and, as I have suggested elsewhere (K. Holsti, 1986), the 'guns versus butter' dichotomy is not always clearcut. The links between security and autonomy are even closer.

Every state faces some sort of problem about its autonomy. One meaning of autonomy is the ability to monitor and control foreign penetration and/or transnational processes. However, the problem is not equally acute for all states. It is a continuum in which, for example, the United States has much less to worry about than does Canada or the Ivory Coast. Foreign policy analysis can, on a comparative basis, examine how states control, adapt, or succumb to external constraints and/or penetration. Policies can range from highly exclusionist, such as those of Albania, Burma, or Iran, to rules and decisions that exclude only certain kinds of foreign penetration (for instance, American regulations about foreign ownership of defense-related industries, and support for the domestic computer chip industry). Autonomy may also refer to the many ways governments avoid international arrangements that seriously compromise their freedom of action.

Until the nineteenth century, national welfare was often synonymous with the welfare of dynasties; indeed, even some regimes in the twentieth century have appeared to place a much higher priority on the aggrandizement of ruling families than on the welfare of the average citizen. The names Trujillo, Somoza, Duvalier, and Marcos, come to mind. These of course are exceptions. Most contemporary governments are to some degree committed to enhancing and protecting public welfare, often defined in terms of employment, income, health, and production levels. Since most economies are entrenched in global productive, financial, and trade networks, the provision of welfare goods is highly dependent upon global trends and decisions made abroad. Every government must seek to maximize opportunities abroad, and to limit the impact of injurious policies by others. The second major problem of foreign policy, then, is to promote, guide, steer, monitor and control those processes and decisions that relate to national welfare. And in so far as some regimes make explicit ties between commercial and political questions, the welfare problematic can be closely linked to issues in the autonomy and security domains. National trade policy, for example, can be a significant component of national security policy. But for analytical purposes, they can be kept distinct. On the assumption that governments seek to maximize welfare values, comparative analysis can focus on constraints and opportunities, and on the particular mix of externally-directed policies governments choose to deal with the problem.

Every state also has a security 'problem'. There is of course no solution in the sense that any particular set of policies will make the problem go away. But by manipulating such variables as strategic doctrine, the size, location, deployment, and armaments of military forces, and/or alliance commitments, governments try to minimize externally-derived threats, either immediately or in the long run. Some (fortunate) states do not appear to face any immediate danger from abroad, but even these commit valuable resources to the creation and maintenance of armed forces, either for reasons of internal security and regime maintenance, or as insurance for the future.

Presently-available textbooks and monographs on defense policies generally eschew comparative analysis, focusing instead on the particular dispositions of forces, hardware, and strategic doctrines of the governments they cover. Our fetish for describing the properties of various weapons systems – particularly ballistic missiles – in the Soviet-American competition has monopolized much of the postwar literature on defense matters. Let us start with the assumption that all states have an actual or potential security problem, and then compare how they cope with it, placing hardware questions in that larger context.

For purposes of this sketch, our final common problem is regime maintenance, that is, the various ways that governments maintain constitutional orders, parties, and personnel in place. Many governments, of course, do not see this as a foreign policy problem, but the literature on linkage politics (Rosenau, 1969) suggests that domestic political issues and foreign policy concerns cannot be neatly separated. Just as foreign trade policy is often linked to security policy, so domestic political arrangements are heavily influenced by events and trends in the external environment. Some governments, particularly in Africa, earn more than 10 per cent of their Gross National Product (GNP) through aid transfers. A regime may well survive or collapse depending on whether it can augment or sustain such levels of foreign largesse. A comparative analysis would thus focus on the various ways that governments 'use' foreign policy issues and external relationships to help them remain in office.

For some states, nation creation and state building became central foreign policy concerns. In seventeenth-century Europe wars created states, and states went to war to establish recognized boundaries, to create central administrative systems capable of extracting resources to fund further wars, and to create and sustain national and/or dynastic political units. In the post-1945 world, liberation movements and international legislation have created a raft of new states, many of which lack the empirical ingredients of statehood (defined territory, government control, and coincidence between the territorial state and actual political communities). Though the comparison is stretched, a number of the new states resemble fifteenth- and sixteenth-century European political organizations more than their twentieth-century successors. Torn by secessionist movements, border disputes, minority rebellions, local warlords and the like, many of the new states are compelled to use foreign policy as just one of many instrumentalities for creating viable political orders that coincide more or less with the territorial boundaries bequeathed to them by the colonial powers. The attempt to overcome dependency, for example, cannot be divorced from efforts to transform weak, conditionally viable entities into genuine international actors. For some countries, then, foreign policy and nation/state-building are inextricably linked.

These are, then, four universal problems of foreign policy. The fifth problem – nation and state building – confronts mostly developing countries in Asia, Africa and the Middle East. All governments face these four 'problematics', although obviously not in equal degrees of importance or urgency. If this proposition is valid, then we have moved toward comparative analysis, because no state can be seen as having policies that are entirely unique and therefore incomparable. We can search for commonalities, describing policies not so much in their specifics, but as *types*. For example, for the security problematic, policies can be of the coalition-building types (alliances), non-alignment and neutrality, or isolation, buttressed by various configurations of military deployment. Viewed through the lenses of a problem-solving (or coping) approach, and a typology of policies, comparative analysis becomes relatively easy.

But as the goal-oriented model suggests, many states also *do* have unique aspirations; not all policy can be subsumed under the five problematics. Libya's commitment to the Palestinian cause has little to do with any of them; some would argue that the American government's fascination or obsession with the Sandinista regime was unre-

lated to American autonomy, welfare, security concerns, or maintenance of the Reagan presidency. Many other examples could be cited.
They all point to the fact that many governments – though by no
means all – develop sets of objectives as diverse as promotion of
human rights abroad, imperialism on a regional or global scale,
protection of ethnic kin abroad, and many other forms of international activity. Comparative analysts should try to identify and
classify as many of these as possible, and then ask why questions.
A goal-oriented model, as developed by the editors of this volume,
describing objectives, strategies, decisions, and actions would seem
most appropriate.

One final problem remains: change. Most monographic literature
on foreign policy, even that small segment which is formally comparative, is static. A writer composes, in effect, a 'photo' of country
X's foreign policy, usually within a prescribed time frame. This sort
of descriptive account is obviously necessary to obtain the essential
facts. But as suggested in our discussion of the four problematics,
governments tend to experiment with different bundles of policies
for each problem. Some work, some fail, in other instances, circumstances at home and abroad change sufficiently so that the policies
that are appropriate for one period become obsolete. Change is
more than just keeping up with the latest facts. It entails a number
of interesting questions. If country A and country B have similar
foreign policies, why does one change, while the other does not?
What constitutes significant change, and how do we measure it?
(Holsti, 1982). Does a change in regime, even a revolutionary
change, result in significant modifications of foreign policy? If so, it
suggests personalities matter; if not, it suggests situations are compel-
ling (Hagan, 1987).

CONCLUSION

The thoughts in this essay do not constitute a solution or set of
solutions to the many problems confronting the subfield of comparative foreign policy analysis. However, I have identified several areas
that require attention. The first priority must be to develop some
conceptual consensus on the notion of foreign policy. Despite numerous attempts to come to grips with this problem (cf. Callahan, 1982),
researchers continue to go their own ways, thus rendering comparison difficult. Second, individual country studies must be cast in

frameworks that are inherently comparable. The concerns of the area expert, where facts and description are based on the sole justification of being 'interesting', should be expanded to include a theoretical justification. Third, researchers must be sensitized to the problems of parochialism. Models and frameworks implicitly or explicitly based on the experience of a single country must be approached with caution, and most importantly, we need to expand significantly the roster of countries whose foreign policy activities come under rigorous scrutiny. To date, the criterion of representativeness has not been met, although there are hopeful signs that the situation is improving.

These sketches might at least point us in a rewarding direction as regards some of the criteria. Models of foreign policy based on events and/or goals are appropriate for some types of analysis, but they fail to pick up certain kinds of behavior. An approach emphasizing problems that all governments face enhances comparative possibilities, and provides numerous opportunities for those whose interests are both empirical *and* theoretical.

BIBLIOGRAPHY

Allison, Graham T. (1971), *The Essence of Decision* (Boston: Little, Brown).

Callahan, Patrick (1982), 'Event Data and the Study of Policy', in Linda P. Brady and, Margaret G. Hermann (eds), *Describing Foreign Policy Behavior* (Beverly Hills, Calif.: Sage) 293–305.

East, Maurice A. (1987), 'Assessing the Field of Comparative Foreign Policy', paper presented at the 28th Annual Meeting of the International Studies Association, 14–18 April, Washington, DC.

George, Alexander, David K. Hall, and William R. Simons (1971), *The Limits of Coercive Diplomacy* (Boston: Little, Brown).

George, Alexander A. and Richard Smoke (1974), *Deterrence in American Foreign Policy: Theory and Practice* (New York: Columbia University Press).

Hagan, Joe (1987), 'Regime Change and Foreign Policy Restructuring: The Third World in the Postwar Era', paper presented at the 28th Annual Meeting of the International Studies Association, 14–18 April, Washington, DC.

Hermann, Charles F., Charles W. Kegley, Jr. and James N. Rosenau (eds) (1987), *New Directions in the Study of Foreign Policy* (Boston: Allen & Unwin).

Hill, Christopher and Margot Light (1985), 'Foreign Policy Analysis', in Margot Light and A. J. R. Groom (eds), *International Relations: A Handbook of Current Theory* (London: Frances Pinter).

Holsti, K. J. *et al.* (1982), *Why Nations Realign: Foreign Policy Restructuring in the Postwar World* (London: Allen & Unwin).

Holsti, K. J. (1986), 'Politics in Command: Foreign Trade as National Security Policy', *International Organization*, 40 (Summer) 645–71.

Korany, Bahgat and Ali Hillal Dessouki (1984), *The Foreign Policies of Arab States* (Boulder, Col.: Westview Press).

Nossal, Kim Richard (1984), 'Bureaucratic Politics and the Westminster Model', in Robert O. Matthews, Arthur G. Rubinoff, and Janice Stein (eds), *International Conflict and Conflict Management* (Scarborough, Ont.: Prentice-Hall of Canada) 12–27.

Reynolds, Charles (1981), *Modes of Imperialism* (Oxford: M. Robertson).

Rosenau, James N. (1975), *Comparing Foreign Policies: Theories, Findings, Methods* (Beverly Hills, Calif.: Sage).

Rosenau, James N. (ed.) (1969), *Linkage Politics* (New York: The Free Press).

Rosenau, James N. (1966), 'Pre-Theories and Theories of Foreign Policy', in R. Barry Farrell (ed.), *Approaches to Comparative and International Politics* (Evanston, Ill.: Northwestern University Press).

Rosenau, James N. (1980), *The Scientific Study of Foreign Policy* (London: Frances Pinter).

Saravanamuttu, Jaya (1983), *The Dilemma of Independence: Two Decades of Malaysia's Foreign Policy, 1957–1977* (Penang: Penerbit Universiti Sains Malaysia).

Waltz, Kenneth (1979), *Theory of International Politics* (Reading, Mass.: Addison-Wesley).

Weinstein, Franklin (1972), 'The Use of Foreign Policy in Indonesia: An Approach to the Analysis of Foreign Policy in Less Developed Countries', *World Politics*, 24, 356–82.

3 Analyzing Third-World Foreign Policies: A Critique and a Reordered Research Agenda
Bahgat Korany

INTRODUCTION: THE PROBLEM

At present, Third-World foreign policy analysis (FPA) is experiencing a dynamism similar to that in comparative politics. Specifically relevant for our purposes is the debate between, on the one hand, area specialists (of Africa, Asia or Latin America) and, on the other, social science generalists. The former emphasize the importance of case studies and in-depth historically-oriented analysis; the latter collect data on a large number of cases and use cybernetic or psychological concepts and quantitative techniques to establish general laws.

Many area specialists tend to equate the latter activity with ivory-tower abstraction, an academic industry that avoids facing up to the substantive issues worthy of our attention. It has to be admitted that the American-based behavioral persuasion (Ricci, 1984: 133–75) which inspires this brand of theorization often encourages such allergic reactions. The movement's overdose of jargon, its predilection for abstraction, and endless discussion of precision in quantification, led to excesses and an extreme form of methodologism.

However, such excesses of a certain brand of theorizing should not push us to the other extreme of shunning all forms of conceptualization and methodological rigor – thereby throwing out the baby with the bath water. Indeed, stock-taking, the sorting-out of FPA propositions and the evaluation of their relevance to Third-World countries are mandatory. Such endeavors are prerequisites for – indeed could condition – any advance in both foreign policy theory-building generally and the study of Third-World foreign policies in particular. In this respect, one is struck at the outset by the dearth of material on the subject.

In two recent surveys of foreign policy studies on 17 selected countries of the Middle East and North Africa, I documented the dearth of systematic empirical knowledge (Korany and Dessouki, 1984 for tables, comments, sources covered and procedures followed; Korany, 1987 for extension of the survey data). Two conclusions should be recalled:

(1) For the 20 year period 1965–85 for these 17 Arab-Islamic countries, the average available was not even one study per country/per year.

(2) An obvious characteristic of the data was its uneven distribution. Egypt seemed to be relatively over-published, possessing 60 times as many items as Mauritania or Somalia, and ten times as many as Morocco (an influential African power with a strategic location on both the Mediterranean and the Atlantic) or Tunisia, the headquarters of the Arab League since 1979. On the other hand, Libya – whose population is about an eighth that of Morocco – had three times as many studies on its foreign policy.

In the absence of uniform criteria for country selection, one could see that many countries were chosen because they happened to be newsworthy, and this tainted many studies with an air of sensationalism. Consequently, the majority of studies were dominated by the exigencies of the specific moment and lacked in-depth analysis. Factual accounts did not obey rigorous methodological rules and conclusions were not linked to the conceptual literature. In short, there was information but not data. Are these quantitative and qualitative shortcomings in the state of the literature on Third World foreign policies due to empirical barriers: for example, difficulties in data accessibility and conducting field work? Those conducting field research in the Third World know only too well the obstacles: a narrow concept of security, barriers to interviews, local political and social taboos. But then, why have researchers of other so-called closed systems still fared well in meeting these data problems? Moreover, our colleagues in comparative politics have managed to produce thoroughly-documented Third-World studies on party transformation (for instance, Bienen, 1967), élite structure and circulation (for example, Quandt, 1969; Waterbury, 1971; Zartman *et al.*, 1982) or even the mechanism and personnel of a military coup (Luckham 1971). The fact that solid empirical research and systematic data-collection could be achieved in other areas of Third-World studies directs attention to barriers emanating from foreign policy theory itself. This is why we must start by surveying the conceptual loop-holes in both the 'Classical' and 'Scientific' foreign policy approaches. Our critical evaluation reverses the customary order in dealing with components of foreign policy analysis. It starts with discussing the output, then the inputs or determinants, and lastly the transform-ation of inputs into outputs: the decision-making process. The con-clusion reiterates the advantages of this suggested reordering of our research agenda. But we start with a synthesis of the characteristics of the two main schools of thought in FPA: the classical versus the scientific.

SCHOOLS OF FOREIGN POLICY: SO MUCH MOVEMENT BUT NO SIGNIFICANT ADVANCE

Some forms of FPA are quite old, such as a body of theory in the so-called traditional or classical approach to international relations known as 'Realism' (Holsti, 1985, and Korany, 1984 for a synthesis). In a nutshell, this classical approach synthesized the myriad of foreign policy determinants into two basic concepts, the state's search for power and national interest. It thus brought order to the com-plexity of foreign policy as expounded by diplomatic historians and commentators on international affairs. The approach also expressed its ideas in straightforward language supposedly based on the 'lessons of history' as extracted from the experiences of ancient Greece and the work of Thucydides. Emphasizing the age-old wisdom and ideas of such figures as Machiavelli or Hobbes, the approach is identified not only with common sense but also with 'good sense'.

A closer look, however, reveals serious deficiencies in this approach. The drawbacks are due to its simplicity and the parochial nature of its historical samples – its ethnocentrism. The approach's limitations can be dealt with under two headings: the vagueness of the concept of national interest, and the artificiality of its model of rational-unitary actor.

The Vagueness of the National Interest Concept

Who would dispute that any foreign policy should have as its *raison d'être* what Winston Churchill called 'national interest?' However, in order to understand foreign policy the analyst has to go beyond this general level and break the concept into some specific components. The literature seems to emphasize three points, a sort of 'holy trinity': physical survival, economic well-being, and freedom of action or manoeuvrability at the international level (Pearson and Rochester, 1984: 145–81). But this is where the problem starts:

(1) The concept of national interest is extremely vague because the components are not operationalized: for instance, does economic well-being mean economic self-sufficiency or does it rather follow the neo-classical trade theory of comparative advantage? Should economic well-being dictate expansion beyond one's borders or rather co-operation and sharing of advantages?

(2) The components can be incompatible as some current debates clearly show: for example, 'guns versus butter' or 'better red than dead'. Consequently, trade-offs are mandatory, yet the policy-maker has no yardstick to scale priorities among the components and hence not all decision-makers rank foreign policy goals in a uniform way.

(3) How does one integrate into the national interest trinity a foreign policy objective such as prestige, an objective which seems to be part and parcel of many countries' foreign policy?

(4) There is also the ambiguity of delimitation between a state's national interest and the 'legitimate' demands of its international environment. Thus, when does national interest stop and international interest start? Would not the ambiguity of the frontier in this case encourage the development of unlimited national interest as some states' goal, leading to a collision of national interests, the breakdown of the balance of power, and Hobbes' war of all against all? In an age of balance of terror, would not such a war-prone system be the negation of each and every national interest?

(5) At a less dramatic but equally basic level: whose national interest are we talking about within the state? For given the vagueness of the concept, each government or élite group will tend to 'interpret' the country's national interest. Such an

interpretation may benefit the nation as a whole or – most probably the case – privilege one social segment more than another. For instance, a defense programme might find its effects trickling down to some of the unemployed, the rural population or the marginalized urbans. However, the programme's prime benefits would go to the military within the country or to an external firm, in addition to speculators or commission-mongers. And among the 250 ethnic groups of Nigeria, for instance, whose national interest does the Federal government stand for?

This neglect of the conceptualization of social groups within the state hits at the foundation of the classical approach and brings us to the second major criticism: the approach's model of the state as an undifferentiated unitary-rational actor.

The Artificiality of the State as a Unitary-Rational Actor

Though almost all of us use shorthand expressions like 'the USSR', 'Jakarta' or 'India' decided 'A' because the country wanted 'B', the rational-unitary actor model goes beyond this to attribute super-human qualities to a collectivity. Of course, a state does not exist apart from its population and is manned by human beings as decision-makers. However, the model ignores the nation's social dynamics and even underestimates the human qualities (for example, the fickleness, occasional mistakes) of the decision-maker. As Krueger (1973: 93) affirmed after reviewing the 'social origins of recent American foreign policy': 'most American historians view diplomacy as the outcome of decisions made by rational men in pursuit of the national interest'. Indeed, the model is so ingrained in the thinking of laymen and most analysts that it has rarely been recognized. As Allison (1971: 13) says, '. . . to explain an occurrence in foreign policy simply means to show how the government could have rationally chosen that action. In this sense, the frame of reference can be called the classical.'

The model's basic unit of analysis is a choice. This choice is more – almost at leisure – by a national actor: a *rational, unitary decision-maker* with one set of specified goals, perceived options and a single estimate of the consequences that follow from each alternative. This choice in the strategic market place is based on a static selection, that is, a steady-state choice among alternative outcomes (rather than, for example, a large number of partial choices in a dynamic stream). This presupposes that a government's goals and objectives are not only explicit and clearly set but also consensual, that options and their different consequences are easily identifiable, compared, evaluated and ranked in terms of preference, and that the final choice is value-maximizing (Allison, 1971: 10–31).

Thus the analyst adopting this unitary-rational actor model has 'explained' the 1962-installation of Soviet missiles in Cuba by showing how this action was reasonable given Soviet strategic objectives. Consequently, 'predispositions about what a nation will do or would have done are generated by calculating the rational thing to do in a certain situation, given specified objectives' (Allison, 1971: 5; and for a detailed application of the model to the USA-USSR cases in the context of the Cuban crisis, 39–66).

As a result, this mental map excluded the various characteristics of the state, the complexity of state-society relations and the different aspects of a decision-making process. Moreover, if this rational approach were really applied by each and every decision-maker, no decision would fail. For, according to this model, each state has crystal clear concepts of its national objectives, their consequences, as well as the means-end trajectory to maximize gains and minimize losses.

But we can see now that the 'real world' which the classical approach prided itself on reflecting is indeed different:

> How many people are capable of viewing the world in a totally objective, unbiased manner? How many undertake the efforts to spell out goals and to come to grips with the often agonizing choices between equally desired but mutually incompatible benefits? How many have the time to ponder all conceivable options, or possess the complete information with which to arrive at the very best solution? (Pearson and Rochester, 1984: 192–3).

These deficiencies explain why the decision-making model of Snyder *et al.* (1962) achieved such a major breakthrough in the subfield of FPA (Korany, 1974: 76–102 for a synthesis and evaluation). This decision-making model initiated and accelerated what would be called by the mid-1960s the scientific schools or 'comparative foreign policy (CFP) movement' in foreign policy analysis (Brecher, 1972, 1974; Rosenau, 1980, 1984). These schools – despite their variety of variables, concepts and methods – all emphasize the importance of rigor and cumulativeness (for detailed critical evaluation, Korany,

1986a: 39–60). If any one basic assumption tied all these conceptual frameworks together, it was the emphasis on the role of the man at the top in shaping foreign policy. (For a comparative testing, including an Asian case, see Korany, 1986c.)

It is true that the vast majority of Third World countries have only weak institutions, that policy processes are personalized, and that regimes change without changing the type of *monarchie presidentielle* so dominant. The influence of the man at the top should not then be overlooked (Korany, 1986c). But we should also avoid extremes and not fall into the trap of a 'great man theory of history'. Such psychological reductionism equates the most visible with the most important and substitutes the man at the top for the analysis of social dynamics.

EVALUATING THE ASSETS AND LIABILITIES

Other difficulties of these schools appear in the following critical evaluation which is organized around the four main questions in any foreign policy theory-building: foreign policy output (the 'What' question), foreign policy inputs or determinants (the 'Why' question), the conversion of inputs into outputs or the decision-making process (the 'How' question), and fourth – the question of 'method' followed in conducting the research to completion.

The 'What' Question: that which needs to be explained

The classical approach left the foreign policy output amorphous, and the 'what' question itself was not really raised. This is where the CFP movement was most innovative, classifying the output into issue-areas, concentrating on either decisions or, more frequently, concrete acts – identified as foreign policy behavior (East *et al.*, 1978, Rosenau, 1980). The problem of operationalization was thus tackled and partially solved. A price, however, was paid for this:

(1) The CFP school, obsessed with the measurable and qantifi-able, went to the other extreme by neglecting the verbal aspects of foreign policy, the country's general objectives, strategy and international orientation.
(2) By being narrowly positivistic and numerological and concentrating on the measurable, the approach deprived itself of the

country's normative and verbal patterns that situate dispersed
acts in their context and give them meaning, that is, to identify
a meaningful body of foreign policy rather than merely an
agglomeration of state actions.

(3) By concentrating only on acts, this scientific approach could
not identify or deal with a very intriguing characteristic of the
foreign policy output of many states: a gap between foreign
policy declarations and foreign policy acts, between the verbal
and the behavioral, between 'say' and 'do'. Yet such a gap is
characteristic of many foreign policies, especially those of
Third-World states who may lack the needed resources to
carry their declarations into action.

(4) It follows that the CFP movement could not identify some
basic aspects of a country's foreign policy role-conflict, the
possibility of foreign policy crises or failures, and the necessity
of change or restructuring in the actor's foreign policy. The
school became unduly static, emphasizing continuity rather
than change.

(5) Even if we accept the movement's lop-sidedness (namely,
limiting foreign policy only to its behavioral or measurable
level of acts), the movement was indeed even more parochial
since it continued the established tradition of being attentive
to only so-called 'high politics' narrowly defined, that is, questions of war and peace. But for almost all Third-World countries, with the crises of development, the stagnation of the
North/South dialogue, and the stalling of different distribution
strategies, economic issues are not only important, they are
indeed 'high politics'. The increasing acuteness of the debt
problem, and the negotiations with the World Bank or the
IMF over the tricky questions of subsidies, are often literally
survival issues.

So to summarize the advantages/disadvantages of the comparative
CFP movement regarding the 'What' question, one can indeed see
an advance in its tackling, identification and precise definition of
foreign policy behavior. There is noticeable progress compared to
the classical approach which did not even raise the 'What' question.
However, the CFP school remained atomistic, static and traditional
– despite claims to the contrary. Worse still, when the movement
tried to be innovative, it got bogged down in endless frustrating
debates about problems of precision and measurement, and the

respective merits of quantitative techniques (that is, events data), while the *raison d'être* of the debate – foreign policy behavior itself – seemed to be buried in the dust of the controversy.

The 'Why' Question: Foreign Policy Determinants

The search for causality is the primordial and final objective for understanding Third-World foreign policies, and foreign policy theory-building in general. In all sciences, explanation (that is, linking cause to effect) is a complicated process. The classical approach emphasized geo-politics and single-factor explanation: the search for power, defense of the national interest. Despite its deceptive clarity and seeming relevance in relation to 'reality' and practice, the approach suffered from a series of ambiguities and fell prey to partiality. The CFP movement shunned single-factor explanation as too simplistic. Moreover, it surveyed traditional international relations analyses and works of diplomatic history (which so frequently but unsystematically speculated on foreign policy sources) to extract the different determinants and put order in them – as the attempts by both Rosenau and Brecher do show. (Korany, 1986a for the synthesis – in a diagrammatic form – of these theories.) The CREON project (East *et al.*, 1978) which had been influenced by Rosenau's pre-theory, and the IBA (Inter-State Behavior Analysis) of Wilkenfeld *et al.* (1980), show the elements of continuity between the classical and CFP approaches, despite the latter's use of data-banks, regression and factor analysis.

Though a nascent sub-school is increasingly trying to investigate the impact of type; of regime on foreign policy (Salmore in East *et al.*, 1978; Hagen, 1987, Hermann, 1987); the CFP neglected the *structural* dimension of societal factors. More importantly, external determinants of foreign policy have been terribly under-analysed. In the case of 'subordinate' and 'periphery' countries that interest us here, this is indeed a fatal deficiency. The combination of these two major drawbacks led to a neglect of the characteristics of the Third-World state and historical patterns of state-formation. If any specificity was emphasized for Third World countries, it was the insistence on the importance of the top leader in decision-making. This seemed indeed to be the bottom line, the super-determinant in the explanation of the foreign policy of the international periphery. This was not only an *a priori* determination of determinants but it tended also to blur the lines between the analysis of foreign policy determinants proper and the analysis of decision-making.

The 'How' Question: the Decision-making Process

The analysis of foreign policy outputs and inputs by the different schools may be deficient, but the analysis of the Third-World decision-making process is virtually non-existent. Here the black box has not been – to all intents and purposes – opened.

The dominant proposition – implicit or explicit in the few studies available – is the emphasis on psychological factors of one individual (the king, president or prime minister), and the search, for instance, for signs of stress (for example, analysis of the leader's verbal and non-verbal material, with emphasis on indicators such as 'ah' repetitions and other voice characteristics, as well as gestures of stress like nose-rubbing and head-scratching) (Hermann in Hopple, 1982). The time-consuming nature and high cost of such techniques apart, the question should be raised as to how such gestures can explain the anatomy of a decision when the state is facing a series of imposing internal or external constraints that eliminate most choices, when the leader at the top is not really a decision-maker but only a decision-taker.

As a result, the CFP movement fell into the trap of formalistic and marginal analysis. Indeed, psychological variables tended to be substitutes for the analysis of social complexity, political fragmentation (for example, intra-élite cleavages or ethnic conflicts) and external networks.

Method of Generalization and Theory-building

Though method is essentially instrumental, it is a prerequisite to rigorous analysis and may indeed bias the findings, that is, the substantive issue. Except in an intuitive or primitive sense, methodological consciousness was virtually absent in the classical approach. Based primarily on diplomatic history, the information used by this approach was selective and inspired by judgement. The result is that heated debates on major substantive issues continue to be open-ended, for example, origins of the First World War, of the Second, or of the Cold War.

More reflective of this methodological insouciance of the classical approach is the sample of cases as the basis of generalization. Not only was the historian's case study preferred with its particularistic tendency, but also no attempt was made to choose representative or typical case studies so that the conclusions would reflect the characteristics of a wider number of cases. As a result, the model of the European nation-state was thoughtlessly generalized to other and different international actors who shared with the genotype little other than the name.

The CFP approach reacted to this methodological sloppiness and almost went to the other extreme. Its writings are loaded with discussion of criteria of rigorous definition, specification of variables and their indicators, and the merits and demerits of various quantification techniques. Its emphasis and even *raison d'être* was comparison. However, this insistence on the comparative method was not equalled by a grasp of the intricacies of that method or the adoption of an explicit strategy: for instance, comparing most similar or most different actors, whole or partial systems, and adopting a synchronic or diachronic mode of analysis. Instead, we were faced with a large number of cases supported by tables of correlation or factor analysis.

As the French say, '*comparaison n'est pas raison*', and the manipulation of numbers and figures cannot replace the sorting out of differences and similarities among different cases and their types. The CFP's selection of a large number of cases to produce the needed tables of so-called comparison, in fact, substituted breadth for depth and looked like a search for security in numbers. Consequently, instead of thoughtful use of quantification to illuminate social phenomena and build substantive generalizations on a solid basis, we ended with a concentration on number-crunching and an analysis out of context. Thus, for instance, foreign policy behavior was sometimes reduced to one indicator – UN votes and roll-call analysis (Richardson, 1978; Moon, 1985), an extremely meager reflection of the complexity and richness of a country's foreign policy.

CONCLUSION: SUGGESTIONS FOR A WAY OUT OF THE BLIND ALLEY

In a standard survey of the foreign policy field Cohen and Harris remark (1975: 381–432): 'When scholars characterize the study of foreign policy as in a primitive theoretical stage, and when they feel compelled to insist that our first steps be the definition and classification of foreign policy, those over fifty may be swept by

despair, while those under thirty may sense unlimited opportunity.'
What about those between the two age brackets, one might ask.
'. . . (T)here is still a third frame of mind . . . : a mildly optimistic
sense of movement at last, akin to one's first responses as a traffic
jam unlocks and the cars begin, hesitantly and tentatively, to pick
up forward speed.'

Indeed, problems of data-collection are being seriously confronted. We are also outgrowing some false dilemmas. Rather than
choosing between, on the one hand, social science conceptual sophistication that might be inapplicable and, on the other, rich area
specialization that is conceptually pedestrian, many analysts are com-
bining the assets of the two approaches. Thus, instead of an 'either
. . . or' research strategy of either a large number of cases that can
lead to superficial analysis and numerology or a traditional case study
approach that is hyperfactual, many analysts are closing the gap of
each and producing comparative case studies (Allison, 1971;
Weinstein, 1976). But some crucial problems still exist.

To start with we have to be more conscious of our basic assumptions, since international actors have become so structurally diverse.
Foreign policy 'theories', mostly 'made in the USA' do not seem to
take this diversity into consideration. Moreover, these 'theories'
are of one ideological brand, privileging the 'superstructure' and
neglecting 'infrastructural' dimensions of polity and economy. Thus,
despite some recent emphases (McGowan and Kegley, 1983; Moon
1987; Shaw, 1986; Korany, 1986a), political economy (Staniland,
1985 for a straightforward survey and definition) is still under-
analyzed in FPA. This is a serious drawback in dealing with underdeveloped countries and dependent societies. Both this book's analytical framework and the case studies deal with this aspect. Consequently, what needs to be emphasized is how some specific aspects
of political economy contribute to foreign policy theory-building: for
instance, how patterns of state-formation and levels of development
influence the different components of the foreign policy system
(inputs, outputs and the decision-making process); how the new
international division of labour and the increasing stratification
within the South itself impinge on the foreign policies of the 'many
Third Worlds' (Deyo, 1987; Korany, 1986b); and how a change in
international status – up or down – may or may not lead to foreign
policy restructuring (Holsti *et al.*, 1982) and how this takes place.
Most importantly, these questions should be part of an applicable
and relevant research strategy.

In this respect and to cope with the conceptual problems emphasized in the evaluative part, I reiterate a suggestion already implied in my discussion of the various FPA schools: start the analysis with the foreign policy output. This output embraces both 'say' and 'do' in a country's foreign policy. It can be divided into three operational components: (1) general objectives and verbal strategy that provide the rationale for the country's global postures and orientation; (2) routine actions: for instance, economic transactions, cultural agreements or pattern of diplomatic representation; and (3) turning-point decisions, in the areas of international conflict or co-operation: for instance, to impose an economic boycott, to launch a war, to recognize a new government, or to federate with another state.

This reversal of the research strategy in foreign policy analysis is contrary to what the great majority of studies – both 'theory' and application, classical and scientific – have been doing all along. Indeed, such reordering of research questions might require some psychological adjustment given the weight of established tradition. However, the potential payoffs more than compensate for the effort of adjustment:

(1) In answering the basic question 'what aspects of X's foreign policy should be emphasized?' the researcher would be guided by what the country itself identifies as its own priorities: at the bilateral, regional or global levels, and in the economic, cultural, military or diplomatic issue-areas. In dealing with this complexity, the researcher gets help from an 'indigenous' focus rather than imposing his own premises and normative lenses. The danger of the analyst's subjectivity and 'misperception' of his object of analysis is thus greatly reduced.

(2) By emphasizing at the outset the three above-mentioned components of the foreign policy output, the analyst could immediately identify anomalies or inconsistencies between 'say' and 'do', and at what level and in what issue-area of the country's foreign policy they exist. Having identified them, the way is thus paved for their explanation.

(3) Once the output problematique is clearly identified from the start, it becomes easier to select and possibly rank the myriad of foreign policy inputs or determinants accordingly. Instead of listing them automatically and leaving the reader with the difficult task of sorting out the elusive input–output linkage, the reader could see why, for instance, an economic dimen-

sion, a geographic primacy or historical conditioning is crucial and for what issue area.

(4) Once the linkage problem is concretely tackled, the analyst's attention is directed to what factors, groups and persons do *in fact* influence the foreign policy process. Instead of being overwhelmed by the difficulties of opening the black-box, a small light guides him as to the actors and factors that do influence the country's decision-making.

With such reordering of our research agenda, we reduce the weight of the *a priori*s as a focus of explanation, whether they are the 'national interest', the 'rational actor', or the great man at the top. We become less biased in conceptual analysis and more relevant to the case at hand. We become indeed like the doctor who starts with the 'observable' concrete symptoms, traces them back to their origin in the structure and history of the case under scrutiny, and reaches findings accordingly, that is, according to this case's characteristics and not to the preferences of the analyst himself. With such reversal of the research procedure, not only is epistemological-conceptual bias greatly reduced, but relevance itself is assured.

BIBLIOGRAPHY

Allison, G. (1971), *Essence of Decision* (Boston: Little Brown).

Bienen, H. (1967), *Tanzania: Party Transformation and Economic Development* (Princeton: Princeton University Press).

Brecher, M. (1974), *Decisions in Israel's Foreign Policy* (London: Oxford University Press).

Brecher, M. (1972), *The Foreign Policy System of Israel* (London: Oxford University Press).

Cohen, B. and S. Harris (1975), 'Foreign Policy', in F. Greenstein and N. Polsby (eds), *Handbook of Political Science* (Reading, Mass.: Addison-Wesley), Vol. VI, 381–437.

Delancey, M. (1981), *African International Relations: An Annotated Bibliography* (Boulder, Col.: Westview Press).

DeRivera, J. (1968), *The Psychological Dimension of Foreign Policy* (Columbus, Ohio: Merrill).

Deyo, F. (1987) (ed.), *The Political Economy of the New Asian Industrialism* (Ithaca and London: Cornell University Press).

East, M. *et al.* (1978), *Why Nations Act: Theoretical Perspectives for Comparative Foreign Policy* (Beverly Hills and London: Sage).

Evans, P. *et al.* (1985), *Bringing the State Back In* (Cambridge: Cambridge University Press).

George, A. (1980), *Presidential Decision-Making in Foreign Policy* (Boulder, Col.: Westview Press).

Hermann, C. (1987), 'Political Opposition as Potential Agents of Foreign Policy Change: Developing a Theory', paper, International Studies Association meeting, Washington, DC, 1987.

Hermann, M. G. (1982), 'A Look Inside the "Black Box": Building on a Decade of Research', in G. Hopple, 1–36.

Hollist, W. L. and J. Caporaso (1985), 'International Political Economy Research', in W. L. Hollist and F. L. Tullis (eds), *An International Political Economy* (Boulder, Col.: Westview Press) (International Political Economy Yearbook) Vol. I, 27–49.

Holsti, K. J. (1985), *The Dividing Discipline* (London: Allen & Unwin).

Holsti, K. J. *et al.* (1982), *Why Nations Realign* (London: Allen & Unwin).

Holsti, O. (1962), 'The Belief System and National Images: A Case Study', *Journal of Conflict Resolution*, 6, 244–52.

Hopple, G. (ed.) (1982), *Biopolitics, Political Psychology and International Politics* (New York: St Martin's).

Korany, B. (1987), 'Biased Science or Primitive Art? The State of the Art in Foreign Policy Analysis', in T. Ismael (ed.), *The State of the Art in Middle Eastern Studies*.

Korany, B. (with contributors) (1986a), *How Foreign Policy Decisions Are Made in the Third World* (Boulder, Col.: Westview Press).

Korany, B. (1986b), 'Stratification Within the South: In Search of Theory', *Third World Affairs Yearbook*, Vol. II (London: Third World Foundation for Social and Economic Affairs).

Korany, B. (1986c), 'When and How Do Personality Factors Influence Foreign Policy?' *Journal of South Asian and Middle Eastern Studies*, Vol. IX, No. 3, 35–60.

Korany, B. (1984), 'Une, deux ou quatre . . . Les écoles de Relations internationales', in B. Korany (sous la direction de) 'La crise des relations internationales: vers un bilan', *Etudes Internationales* (numéro spécial), Vol. XV, No. 4, 699–723.

Korany, B. (1974), 'Modèles de politique étrangère et leur pertinence empirique aux pays du tiers monde: une critique et contre-proposition', *Revue internationale de sciences sociales*, Vol. 26, No. 1, 74–102.

Korany, B. and A. Dessouki *et al.* (1984a), *The Foreign Policies of Arab States* (Boulder, Col.: Westview Press).

Korany, B., J. Balladier and J. B. Gauthier (1984b), *Dépendance et Politique Etrangère au Monde Arabe*, Vol. 5 (Montréal: Etudes Arabes).

Krueger, T. (1973), 'The Social Origins of Recent American Foreign Policy', *Journal of Social History*, Vol. 7, No. 3.

Luckham, R. (1971), *The Nigerian Military* (Cambridge: Cambridge University Press).

McGowan, P. and H. Shapiro (1973), *The Comparative Study of Foreign Policy* (Beverly Hills, Calif.: Sage).

McGowan, P. and C. Kegley (eds) (1983), *Foreign Policy and the Modern*

World System (Beverly Hills, Calif.: Sage International Yearbook of Foreign Policy Studies, Vol. 8).

McGowan, P. and C. Kegley (eds) (1981), *The Political Economy of Foreign Policy Behaviour* (Beverly Hills, Calif.: Sage International Yearbook of Foreign Policy Studies, Vol. 6).

Merle, M. (1985), 'La politique étrangère', in M. Grawitz et J. Lecas (sous la direction de) *Traité de science politique* (Paris: Presses universitaires de France) Vol. 4, 467–633.

Moon, B. (1987), 'Political Economy Approaches to the Comparative Study of Foreign Policy', in Charles Hermann *et al.* (eds), *New Directions in the Study of Foreign Policy* (Boston: Allen & Unwin, 1987).

Pearson, F. and J. Rochester (1984), *International Relations* (Reading, Mass.: Addison-Wesley).

Quandt, W. (1969), *Revolution and Political Leadership, Algeria 1954–1968* (Cambridge, Mass.: MIT Press).

Ricci, D. (1984), *The Tragedy of Political Science: Politics, Scholarship and Democracy* (New Haven and London: Yale University Press).

Rosenau, J. (1984), 'A Pre-Theory Revisited: World Politics in an Era of Cascading Inter-dependence', *International Studies Quarterly*, 28/3 (Sept.), 245–305.

Rosenau, J. (1980), *The Scientific Study of Foreign Policy* (London: Francis Pinter).

Shaw, T. M. (1983), *Africa's International Affairs: An Analysis and a Bibliography* (Halifax, N.S.: Centre for Foreign Policy Studies, Dalhousie University).

Shaw, T. M. (1986), 'Peripheral Social Formations in the New International Division of Labour: African States in the Mid–1980s', *The Journal of Modern African Studies*, Vol. 24, No. 3, 489–508.

Snyder, R. *et al.* (1962), *Foreign Policy Decision-Making* (New York: The Free Press).

Staniland, M. (1985), *What is Political Economy?* (New Haven: Yale University Press).

Stein, J. (1978), 'Can Decision-Makers Be Rational and Should They Be?' *Jerusalem Journal of International Affairs* 3 (Winter-Spring), 316–39.

Strange, S. (ed.) (1984), *Paths to International Political Economy* (London: Allen & Unwin).

Sylvan, D. and S. Chan (eds) (1984), *Foreign Policy Decision-Making: Perception, Cognition and Artificial Intelligence* (New York and London: Praeger).

Thurow, L. (1983), *Dangerous Currents: The State of Economics* (New York: Random House).

Walker, S. (ed.) (1987), *Role Theory and Foreign Policy Analysis* (Durham: Duke University Press).

Waterbury, J. (1970), *The Commander of the Faithful: Morocco's Political Elite* (New York: Columbia University Press).

Weinstein, F. (1976), *Indonesian Foreign Policy and the Dilemma of Dependence* (Ithaca, New York: Cornell University Press).

Wilkenfeld, J. *et al.* (1980), *Foreign Policy Behavior: The Interstate Behavior Analysis Model* (Beverly Hills and London: Sage).

Zartman, I. W. *et al.* (1982), *Political Elites in Arab North Africa* (New York and London: Longman).

4 Foreign Policy and the New International Division of Labor in the Late–1980s: the African Dimension
Timothy M. Shaw

Foreign policy in Africa as both practice and analysis has changed dramatically in the 1980s with important implications for comparative *praxis*. The confident, consensual decade of the 1960s, when personality and ideology were assumed to be primary, yielded to a conflictual stand-off in the 1970s between diplomacy and dependency, followed by a novel agenda in the 1980s: debt, devaluation, privatization and ecology. These moods of analysts and modes of analysis reflect the mixed fortunes of the continent as the postwar Bretton Woods order yielded to a New International Division of Labor in which Africa was marginal and vulnerable in economic and strategic terms, respectively. They may be contrasted in terms of intensity and implication with moods and modes elsewhere in the so-called Third World (Korany, 1986).

TOWARDS POLITICAL ECONOMY AS FACTOR AND/OR MODE OF ANALYSIS

Africa's new maturity in diplomacy stands in contrast to its marginality in economy and vulnerability in security. Africa at the end of the 1980s contains more 'Fourth World' least-developed states than any other region; it is the only southern continent with no apparent Newly Industrializing Countries (NICs) (Carlsson and Shaw, 1988). As the Brundtland Commission recognizes in *Our Common Future* (1987: 71):

The international community must realise that Africa cannot pull itself out of the planet's·most serious economic and ecological crisis without much more long-term assistance than is currently envisioned . . . greatly increased external financing for development must be accompanied by policy changes that recognise the need to avoid environmental degradation.

The unpromising legacy of Africa's first quarter-century of recaptured independence poses problems of both enquiry and policy not only for the continent but also for comparable regions. Unfortunately, Africa's crisis has usually been treated as *sui generis* rather than as one aspect of the global transition from United States' hegemony (Zwingina, 1987) to a mix of nuclear bipolarity with economic multipolarity.

Africa's difficulties are not merely a coincidence; rather they are structurally related to the concentration of productive, financial and energy resources in OECD, NICs and OPEC (Mwanag'onze, 1987). This redefinition of 'trilateralism' effectively excludes African and other Fourth-World political economies and challenges prevailing assumptions about the continent's reform, recovery and re-emergence (Adedeji and Shaw, 1985). In this setting the agendas of African states and/or African studies at the end of the 1980s are very distinctive, especially when contrasted either with African states and studies at the end of the 1960s (Shaw, 1985) or with other Third-World states and studies in the 1980s (Shaw, 1986). The interrelated issues identified in *Our Common Future* (1987: 290) put a unique emphasis on the environment:

The links between environmental stress and developmental disaster are most evident in sub-Saharan Africa. Per capita food production, declining since the 1960s, plummeted during the drought of the 1980s. . . . Human overuse of land and prolonged drought threaten to turn the grasslands of Africa's Sahel region into desert. No other region more tragically suffers the vicious cycle of poverty leading to environmental degradation, which leads in turn to even greater poverty (*Our Common Future*, 1987: 31).

The declining condition of the continent which transformed the United Nations' and other international agendas in the early 1960s, 20 years later resulted in a special General Assembly on its crisis. But if political economy rather than orthodox diplomacy and security has now become the preoccupation of African leaders and policy-makers concerned with the continent, it has yet to dominate academe, which is resistant to an espousal of non-traditional preoccupations. Likewise, in studies of other Third-World regions, the focus is often still on orthodox notions of security and development rather than the contemporary issues of debt, devaluation, deregulation, environment, gender and the informal sector. Yet the African crisis compels a longer-term, structural analysis of the continent's contradictions and directions which are in part a function of extra-continental conditions and constraints; hence, the imperative for a critical, comparative and contextual treatment of Africa's foreign policy and political economy.

Historically, Third-World comparative foreign policy could treat ideology and personality as factors; more recently, alternative development directions and regime changes were highlighted along with regional conflicts and organizations. But the post-Bretton Woods and post-OPEC period is distinctive: the foreign policy of debt negotiations, state contraction, and negative development. Regrettably, few scholars have yet begun to recognize let alone to analyze the new agenda despite the fact that it facilitates inter-regional comparisons. Large oil-exporting (Nigeria and Indonesia) and oil-importing (Ethiopia and Vietnam) and small industrial (Zimbabwe and Malaysia) and agricultural (Côte d'Ivoire and Thailand) states can be compared along with states in postwar difficulty (Mozambique and Laos) or still at war (Angola and Kampuchea). But there are limits to such an approach: Africa has no Singapore or South Korea, while Asia has no Chad or Uganda. Clearly the reasons for such non-comparable cases – NICs and anarchy, respectively – lie in national, regional and global political economy.

Social and strategic choices are always framed and made within structural limits of history and economy, society and diplomacy. To treat political economy as a factor in the analysis of foreign relations would seem to be both desirable and inevitable in the contemporary period given the continuing salience of 'development' and the new imperatives of debt and 'reform', especially if changes in the global economy cannot be contained or neutralized through policies of self-reliance. Indeed, the latter begin to appear in the current era of the New International Division of Labor to be *passé*: impossibilities in a period of structural adjustment.

By contrast to political economy as factor, its adoption as mode of analysis is more controversial: the recognition that questions of production, distribution, accumulation and reproduction are central.

Yet, most of the extant perspectives – psychological, realist, idealist and *dependentista* (Shaw, 1985 and 1986) – have been discredited over time so that any alternative is to be welcomed, especially for small, weak, underdeveloped states in a period of transition (Bryan, Greene and Shaw, 1990. The issue of mode of analysis is compounded by the existence of several varieties of political economy, particularly the materialist and non-materialist. Both treat the inter-relationships between economics and politics at several levels as central to explanation but in the former, unlike the latter, relations of production are taken to be primary and dialectical. Non-materialist political economy has generated notions of inter-dependence, even dependence, whereas the more Marxist variant has focused on modes of production such as capitalism and on class formations, forces and factions. Despite their common label, then, these two different and distinct genres really have divergent theoretical roots – Marxism and liberalism, respectively – so that debates between this pair may be as intense as those between them and non-political economy forms of analysis.

The materialist variety tended to be overlooked in studies of international relations in the postwar world given economic expansion and political and strategic revolutions. The non-materialist strand become popularized in the 1970s as economic contraction and strategic stalemate focused attention on 'transnational' relations. The materialist genre in turn was reinvigorated with the demise of *dependencia* and the recognition that the interplay between national and global relations of production was a dynamic feature of differentiation and accumulation. In short, the shifting global and national hierarchies of the last decade or so have served to renew interest in neo-Marxist scholarship: the on-going dialectic of politics and economics.

Political economy as approach seems to be particularly attractive because of its compatibility with foreign policy and area studies. Comparative foreign policy has already proven to be fruitful for area specialists as it advances comparisons among a group of proximate state actors who typically share a history of regional conflict and co-operation. In turn, such regions can be contrasted with each other as in the 'subordinate state system' framework. Whilst cultures and leaders have often been treated as primary in such exercises, contemporary issues have of necessity drawn attention towards economic resources and performances. The exponential differentiation among regions, states and peoples in an era of fluctuating exchange rates, debt reschedulings and structural adjustments has served to advance this trend so that by the mid-1980s even classical foreign policy studies had come to pay some attention to economics, if not to the political economy of policies, positions and potentials.

The juxtaposition, if not integration, of insights drawn from these three inter-related approaches of foreign policy, area studies and political economy is apparent in this as in other collections, even if it is not yet always recognized at the level of the field as a whole. Furthermore, this juxtaposition can be enhanced by identifying particular periods and conjunctures as a means of recognizing change. And clusters of factors can be compared across regions as well as within them, such as between, say, Indonesia and Nigeria, or Malaysia and Côte d'Ivoire. At the subsystemic level, the only parallels to Vietnam's regional role are perhaps those of Libya and South Africa while Africa remains more distant from great power presences than does Southeast Asia, with China on its borders. But such inter-regional comparisons logically succeed intra-regional and must also be placed in global and historical context: the constellation of international and national classes, companies and capitals.

The 'new' international divisions of labor and power pose considerable challenges for analysis as well as response. After a quarter-century of comparative foreign policy and area studies we have yet to reach a satisfactory state of synthesis. But if an agreed 'paradigm' remains elusive, something of a consensus does exist over the parameters of comparison: political economy is accepted as subject matter if not mode of analysis and the connections among different sectors and levels of relations are treated as givens. This foundation offers some promise for future comparative analyses in the remaining decade of this century: capitalisms and corporatisms, militarisms and democracies, regionalisms and coalitions (Shaw, 1987).

In this venture, as in others, comparisons among Third World areas – South-South intellectual exchanges – may be particularly illuminating given divergent histories and experiences. For once, in part because of its proliferation of states, Africa may contribute more than it receives from such an exchange. The sociology of knowledge in this as other fields is fascinating in its own right – the evolution of universities, institutes, projects and publications – yet the intellectual history of Africa has so far proven to be in the vanguard of Third-World comparative foreign policy and political economy (Korany, 1983 and 1984). Whether it will remain so, given the spill-over of the continent's economic difficulties into a decline of academe, remains to be seen. The graduation of NICs and near-NICs in all other regions of the world economy except Africa may yet be reflected in the advance of their scholarship in this as other fields (Carlsson and Shaw, 1988).

AFRICA'S FOREIGN POLICY IN COMPARATIVE PERSPECTIVE

The African continent's foreign policy has, then, a considerable vintage – including pre-colonial and pre-capitalist external relations of marginal nation-states (Shaw, 1979) – but its contemporary contributions have been concentrated in the post-colonial period. Since the halcyon independence days of the early 1960s, the practice and analysis of Africa's foreign policy have evolved from a concentration on personality and ideology through an indecisive era in the 1970s, when realist and *dependencia* perspectives vied for dominance (see Mazrui, 1977 and Nnoli, 1978) to the 1980s: a decade of novel official agendas and related analytic approaches. The orthodoxies of the 1960s and uncertainties of the 1970s have thus been superseded by a concentration on political economy as both factor and mode (see Ake, 1981 and Freund, 1984). To be sure, the former is more widely recognized than the latter, but when mode of analysis embraces non-materialist as well as materialist forms it is more popular than ever. And political economy can be rendered compatible with analyses of security issues (Arlinghaus, 1984 and Thom, 1984) as well as of ideology and diplomacy. More than 20 years ago, however, such perspectives were absent: they have only become widespread and recognized in the late 1970s and early 1980s as idealism and optimism evaporated.

The post-OPEC crises of drought and debt have compelled a fundamental re-evaluation of Africa's development and foreign policies (Shaw, 1983). Coming in the wake of the transnational and interdependence perspectives in the North and of *dependencia* and disengagement approaches in the South, the new issues of environment and renegotiation serve to reinforce the trend towards political economy. Thus the continent's economic marginalization has coincided with its analytic maturation. The latter has enhanced its relevance as a comparable region while the former has attracted further external attention. In turn, broader debates about types of political economy have intersected with more parochial African(ist) discourses: more or less materialist definitions and conceptions. Together these have superseded the simplistic notions of *dependencia* popularized in the 1970s; many African jurisdictions do not feature in current corporate or financial maps of the world. Thus the African studies' and states' agendas have been transformed during the present decade; in a 'post-neocolonial' period alternative modes of explanation and prescription are imperative.

The new 'African diplomacy' is thus distinct from the 'old' (that is, pre- and post-colonial protocols) because of its emphasis on (1) economic as well as political factors, (2) developmental as well as diplomatic issues, and (3) novel conceptions of security and democracy (Mwang'onze, 1987). First, then, such 'radical' studies locate the causes of foreign policy in political economy rather than in ideology of leadership or institution: the external dimension of 'peripheral social formations'. Second, they treat issues of development – Basic Human Needs (BHN) of food, welfare, infrastructure, and the like – as integral aspects of foreign relations: the external aspect of changes in relations and patterns of production, distribution and accumulation. And third, a recent and not yet so frequent reformulation in African diplomacy has been in the area of 'strategic studies' and regime changes: redefinitions of security and democracy in economic as well as strategic or formal terms, respectively.

As reflections of the continent's new marginality and maturity, analyses of African diplomacy have become increasingly sophisticated and sustained, unlike the rather superficial and ephemeral descriptions of the initial post-independence period. The continuing crisis has concentrated the minds of states-persons and scholars alike (Bender, Coleman and Sklar, 1985 and Zartman, 1985).

Further, both indigenous and expatriate analysts are beginning to go beyond superstructure to examine substructure: modes and relations of production, distribution and accumulation. Korany, Dessouki *et al.* (1984) in their long-awaited collection on *The Foreign Policies of Arab States* have begun to transcend the established assumption, common to students of 'old' and 'new' states alike, that foreign relations consist only of policy, diplomacy and strategy or even of dependency. Instead, particularly for dependent and vulnerable states, there is a new recognition that economic relations are central and that indigenous social forces are integral to both external interests and foreign policy: the reconsideration and reconceptualization of 'national interest'.

Dessouki and Korany go beyond not only several layers of analysis

– the interaction among as well as separation of national, regional and global levels – but also point to the salience of treating Third-World social formations as more than mere 'dependent' peripheries, but rather as complex and contradictory political economies. In their conclusion, they call for 'more comparative and cumulative studies on the foreign policies of developing countries, either within one region or interregional' (Korany and Dessouki, 1984: 329). Hence the salience of the present collection, which does both.

Such a direction points not only towards case studies of countries, policies, decisions and institutions, but also towards consideration of the characteristics and dialectics of peripheral (and semi-peripheral) political economies: social connections and contradictions. In particular, it suggests two types of comparative analyses: (1) comparisons among similar *social forces* in different states (for example, technocratic, military, comprador or national bourgeois fractions in several peripheral political economies) and (2) comparisons between similar *state actors* in different periods (for instance, before, during and after the successive 'oil shocks' of the early and late 1970s or the debt traumas of the mid-1980s).

The balance of political, technocratic, military and religious forces in Algeria and Saudi Arabia is quite comparable, for example, to that in Indonesia and Nigeria. Such novel varieties of social coalitions or 'triple alliances' (Evans, 1979: 11 and 313) in oil-rich states in the post-OPEC order have led, according to Korany and Dessouki, to distinctive diplomatic postures and initiatives; for instance, Algeria over NIEO and Saudi Arabia over Israel. Such proposals were far more than reflections of individual psyches or national values: they reflected real social contradictions within as well as between states. In short, the particular expressions of 'national interests' in Arab and Sub-Saharan Africa are not aberrations – the assumption of distinctive 'African' mores and laws – but rather reflections of constraints and contradictions at the (semi-) periphery in a changing global order.

AFRICA AND THE GLOBAL POLITICAL ECONOMY

The prerequisites for any critical and convincing analysis of African states befitting the post-neocolonial order are, then, to go beyond not only strategic conflicts and national interests but also (1) the artificial internal-international divide, (2) the diversion of dependence, (3) the assumption that leaders are 'compradors', and (4) the over-concentration on super- rather than sub-structure. In other words, to situate peripheral (and semi-peripheral) social formations in the context of a changing international division of labor in which a cluster of transnational relations over technology and ideology have begun to create new patterns of articulation.

Reflective of the salience of this new juxtaposition – with its emphasis on inequalities within and between African states rather than further repetition of the old shibboleths about Africa's homogeneity and equality (Korany, 1986) – is a remarkably non-dogmatic collection of East European Africanist scholarship on *African Countries' Foreign Policy* assembled by Anatoly Gromyko (1983) of Moscow's Institute of African Studies. This volume emphasizes sub- rather than super-structure, whilst appreciating the limits of economic determinism and the resilience of politics on the continent: 'Differentiation – on a class not a national basis – is becoming increasingly typical of African foreign policy' (Gromyko, 1983: 197).

It also nicely situates the dialectic between continental integration and global marginalization as Africa confronts the changing international division of labor:

> Any analysis of the foreign policy pursued by independent African countries should take into consideration two simultaneous processes in inter-African affairs. First, the trend toward unity, concerted action and comprehensive cooperation on the continental scale. Second, the socio-economic and political polarization of these countries. . . . These centrifugal and centripetal trends affect the policies of each independent African country. . . . The dialectical contradiction between consolidation and differentiation. . . .
> (Gromyko, 1983: 75)

Curiously, Africanists in the other superpower, still preoccupied by bipolar Cold War issues, have focused more narrowly on the linkage between regional conflicts on the continent and domestic disputes in the US. *African Crisis Areas and US Foreign Policy* is thus as much about bureaucratic and political debates and coalitions in the US as about African contradictions: a reflection of US parochialism. In a revival of realist and superpower preoccupations, Bender, Coleman and Sklar (1985: 11) argue that 'the internationalization of Africa's crisis areas is a function of the disposition and capacity of the United States and the Soviet Union to penetrate them'. So they focus on Southern Africa, the Horn, Zaire and the Sahara rather than on either Africa's economic crisis or the roots of its vulnerability; they concentrate on great power and diplomatic inequalities rather than on differentiation inside and around Africa (cf. Korany, 1986), whilst appreciating that 'Ideology has been grossly exaggerated in past explanations of the international relations of African states' (Bender, Coleman and Sklar, 1985: 9).

Differentiation in Africa can be seen to be increasing from the perspective of international political economy in at least four often interrelated ways: between states, between classes, within classes and between genders (Shaw, 1985). The first division is based on very uneven and exponential patterns of growth: the minority of Third and majority of Fourth World countries. The second contradiction is founded on different relations to the means of production (and decision): more versus less bourgeois. The third tension exists within such classes: national, bureaucratic-technocratic, comprador or military fractions within the indigenous bourgeoisie; more versus less aristocratic within the proletariat; and big or small fractions within the peasantry. And finally, the 'gender gap' is both growing and increasingly recognized as women's role in agriculture as well as in the household becomes especially crucial in a period of economic decline. Taken together, these distinctions throw up a variety of new challenges for both African scholars and statespersons: how to go beyond established assumptions about inequalities and ideologies.

Novel patterns of differentiation have produced, then, a variety of new relationships and *problématiques* for Africa at the levels of analysis and *praxis*, which exist below or beyond those of orthodox state-centrism. Amongst the more central and controversial are: (1) the definition of the post-neocolonial state in both theory and diplomacy; (2) the prospects for African capitalism based on the national fraction of the indigenous bourgeoisie; (3) the potentials for class coalitions – African corporatism – as well as contradictions in a period of economic contraction; (4) the possibilities for re-evaluations of gender relations given the imperatives of agricultural revival and population control; (5) the identification of alternative development strategies – self-reliance or reincorporation, informal sectors or reindustrialization – based on new international, national and sexual divisions of labor; and (6) the redefinitions of security and democracy as basic human needs and human rights become eroded under the pressures of structural adjustment.

The first of these *problématiques*, the decline if not demise of the neo-colonial state through a mix of internal decay and external conditionality, has undermined the bases of African foreign policy. If the national regime cannot pay its bills let alone its debts, then it is unlikely to wield international influence. As the New International Division of Labor has moved away from manufacturing based on Third-World commodities to service and communications industries based on First-World technologies so the Fourth World has suffered declining terms of trade and currency rates. The rise of the informal sector, from petty trade to drug smuggling, is a corollary of state decay. Unfortunately, the decline of national regimes has not yet been formally recognized by African intellectuals and institutions despite the apparent 'high politics' of debt.

Second, both historical pressures and World Bank preferences are leading towards the rehabilitation of capitalism in Africa: the release of market forces in agricultural production, commodity exchange, and foreign currency levels. Hitherto forbidden capitalist issues like devaluation, deregulation and privatization have come to dominate the new agenda of 'reform', largely defined by the World Bank (1981 and 1986), in its series of reports in the 1980s. In turn, the stand-off between the IBRD/IMF and ECA has generated a series of debates and proceedings which treat the sub- as well as super-structure of Africa's condition (Adedeji and Shaw, 1985). Although this genre is cast within the economic development rather than foreign policy mold, it does serve to highlight the new emphases and bases of international relations: debt renegotiations, currency alignments, parastatal reform and agricultural revival. Thus foreign policy has shifted away from the old 'high' politics of military security to the hitherto 'low' politics of economic security, in which central banks, treasuries and economic institutions predominate rather than foreign offices. As Thomas M. Callaghy (1987: 154) notes, 'Both Paris and London club reschedulings are increasingly important in the foreign relations of African states. Repeat reschedulings are now the norm for Africa, which is by far the most rescheduled region in the world.'

African capitalism is more likely to emerge and prosper in semi-peripheral political economies where the social bases are supportive: strong national and technocratic rather than comprador fractions. The diverse patterns of capital in the new global order enhance the space for national bourgeoisies, if they control viable national economies.

Third, by contrast African corporatism – exclusive social coalitions, institutions and accumulation (Nyang'oro and Shaw, 1989) – is most likely to emerge in those Fourth World states in decline: the response of bureaucratic and military fractions to economic contraction and political tension. In such cases, capital, whether national or international, will be disinterested as the periphery is further marginalized, abandoning ex-neo-colonies to their hapless fate, except when occasional strategic (for example, US bases in Somalia) or diplomatic (for example, recognition of Western Sahara) imperatives dictate otherwise. This is particularly so for the myriad island and enclave states long since discarded as their utility declined with shifts in merchant capital. Such peripheral states will, alas, be most vulnerable to aberration (for instance, Nguema's Equatorial Guinea and Bokassa's Central African Empire) and anarchy (for example, the disintegration of Chad, Sudan or Uganda). By contrast, the relatively expansive capitalisms of Côte d'Ivoire and Nigeria in West Africa or Kenya and Zimbabwe in Eastern Africa will attract further investment, assistance and migrants, despite increasingly unequal economies. Growth at least perpetuates false hopes; decline serves only to smash them. Yet out of decay can emerge a renaissance as well as anarchy, particularly if informal economies have sustained and redirected communities in the interim.

Fourth, as many African regimes have lost the means and abilities to govern effectively so the prospects for an informal sector, peasants and women improve. Typically women have endured patriarchal structures throughout the continent whilst simultaneously, noticeably in West Africa, they have carved out niches for themselves. Just as class relations have continued to evolve under World Bank reforms and structural adjustments in favor of national bourgeoisies and peasantries, so gender relations have also been transformed, encouraged by transnational feminist pressures. Overall, Africa needs more food and less people. Given women's crucial role in both these issues, the future of African international relations ignores the gender question at its own peril.

Fifth, orthodox dichotomous development choices – capitalism or socialism – have been superseded by a pair of distinct options – structural adjustment or self-reliance. Fear of the latter is one reason for compliance with the former. This rather starkly-drawn debate gains strength from the ongoing IBRD-ECA stand-off, in which the former seeks reincorporation on any terms and the latter self-reliance whatever the price (Adedeji and Shaw, 1985 and Ravenhill, 1986). Such options are also posed for national regimes.

Finally, sixth, the survival of African societies over the last decade under extremely adverse environmental and financial regimes has drawn attention once again to the redefinition of security and democracy in part as responses to the prospects of militarism. The former is becoming conceived in terms of basic human needs and rights, while the latter has been revived in terms of popular participation: the abilities of smaller-scale communities, outside the reach of the central authority, sometimes stretching across apparent 'national' boundaries, to establish their own democratic structures (Chazan and Shaw, 1988). This mix of appropriate technologies, processes and life-styles should not be overly romanticized – it is a necessary response to adversity and reproduction – yet it does afford a timely antidote to images of helpless and hapless Africans. The proximate demise of the state under the twin pressures of internal contractions and external conditions has compelled creative responses with interesting foreign policy implications: will weak states be able to sustain external relations on an ongoing basis? And will local communities, sometimes with NGO encouragement, have to establish their own, relatively autonomous, transnational relations? In short, by the end of the 1980s will the established African state system begin to fragment so that the borders bequeathed by the Berlin treaty of over a century ago begin to disappear and are redefined altogether?

There is one further set of analyses which serves to round-out the renaissance of African foreign policy, at least in its more structural form: studies of regionalism, a central element in ECA proposals but a neglected strand in IBRD prognostications. To be sure, regionalism in Africa as elsewhere has received some comparative attention since independence but general studies blossomed again in the early 1980s and Southern African studies only in the mid-1980s.

Thus, while the African continent is apparently faced with a stormy future, it is one which will continue to command some analytic, diplomatic and strategic attention. The region with the most states, particularly that with the most impoverished states, cannot be completely dismissed, in either academic or economic terms, even if it is increasingly marginal. On closer inspection, then, the relevance of 'African' corporatism and capitalism for Asia is apparent: how one region responded to ongoing external pressures and internal changes to generate a different and distinctive political economy. Culture and religion may seem to camouflage relations of political economy yet in reality are largely determined by them.

In conclusion, the myriad states, regimes and issues of the African continent since independence throw up a series of pointers for comparative foreign policy analysis elsewhere; Africa continues to be a veritable social laboratory. However, there is one conceptual question which has yet to be addressed directly here, on which Ronaldo Munck (1984) provides so usefully in his *Politics and Dependence in the Third World* for Latin America: periodization of social forces and state types. The new genre of African political economy points to the salience of such distinctions as the continent has moved from nationalism to post-neocolonialism, expansion to contraction, and optimism to pessimism. As modes of production have evolved so have their social relations and formations. Hence the need for a new 'comparative politics' of both internal and international 'regimes', which treats political economy and focuses on changing class constellations: the succession of class coalitions and policy directions. Munck's (1984: 64) periodization of 'late capitalism' in Latin America may not fit perfectly for Africa or Southeast Asia. But the focus on distinctive forms of political economy which are 'neither classically democratic, nor fascist, nor Communist revolutionary' may be *apropros* for domestic politics and foreign policies alike throughout the Third World.

BIBLIOGRAPHY

Adedeji, Adebayo and Timothy M. Shaw (eds) (1985), *Economic Crisis in Africa: African perspectives on development problems and potentials* (Boulder: Lynne Reinner).

Arlinghaus, Bruce (1984), *Military Development in Africa: the political and economic risks or arms transfers* (Boulder: Westview).

Ake, Claude (1981), *A Political Economy of Africa* (London: Longman).

Bender, Gerald J., James S. Coleman and Richard L. Sklar (eds) (1985), *African Crisis Areas and US Foreign Policy* (Berkeley: University of California Press).

Berg, Robert J. and Jennifer Seymour Whitaker (eds) (1986), *Strategies for African Development* (Berkeley: University of California Press).

Bryan, Anthony T., J. Edward Greene and Timothy M. Shaw (eds) (1990), *Peace, Development and Security in the Caribbean: perspectives to the year 2000* (London: Macmillan).

Carlsson, Jerker (ed.) (1983), *Recession in Africa* (Uppsala: Scandinavian Institute of African Studies).

Carlsson, Jerker and Timothy M. Shaw (eds) (1988), *Newly Industrializing Countries and the Political Economy of South-South Relations* (London: Macmillan).

Callaghy, Thomas M. (1987), 'Between Scylla and Charybdis: the foreign relations of Sub-Saharan African states', *The Annals* 489, January: 148–63.

Chazan, Naomi and Timothy M. Shaw (eds) (1988), *Coping with Africa's Food Crisis* (Boulder: Lynne Reinner).

Evans, Peter (1979), *Dependent Development: the alliance of multi-national, state and local capital in Brazil* (Princeton: Princeton University Press).

Freund, Bill (1984), *The Making of Contemporary Africa* (London: Macmillan).

Gromyko, Anatoly *et al.* (1983), *African Countries' Foreign Policy* (Moscow: Progress).

Hanlon, Joseph (1986), *Beggar Your Neighbours: apartheid power in Southern Africa* (London: James Currey).

Johnson, Phyllis and David Martin (eds) (1986), *Destructive Engagement: Southern Africa at war* (Harare: Zimbabwe Publishing House).

Korany, Bahgat (1983), 'The Take-off of Third World Studies? The case of foreign policy', *World Politics* 35(3), April: 465–87.

Korany, Bahgat (1984), 'Foreign policy in the Third World: an introduction', *International Political Science Review* 5(1): 7–20.

Korany, Bahgat (1986), 'Hierarchy within the South: in search of theory', *Third World Affairs 1986* (London: Third World Foundation) 85–100.

Korany, Bahgat, Ali E. Hillal Dessouki *et al.* (1984), *The Foreign Policies of Arab States* (Boulder: Westview).

Mazzeo, Domenico (ed.) (1984), *African Regional Organizations* (Cambridge: Cambridge University).

Msabaha, Ibrahim S. R. and Timothy M. Shaw (eds) (1987), *Confrontation and Liberation in Southern Africa: regional directions after the Nkomati Accord* (Boulder: Westview).

Munck, Ronaldo (1984), *Politics and Dependency in the Third World; the case of Latin America* (London: Zed).

Mwanag'onze, E. H. B. (1987), 'JAM – 5 years later', *Journal of African Marxists* 10, June: 8–17.

Nnoli, Okwudiba (1978), *Self-Reliance and Foreign Policy in Tanzania* (New York: NOK).

Nyang'oro, Julius and Timothy M. Shaw (eds) (1988), *Corporatism in Africa: comparative analysis and practice* (Boulder: Westview).

Onwuka, Ralph I. and Amady Sesay (eds) (1985), *The Future of Regionalism in Africa* (London: Macmillan).

Onwuka, Ralph I. and Timothy M. Shaw (eds) (1989), *Africa and World Politics: into the 1990s* (London: Macmillan).

Ravenhill, John (ed.) (1986), *Africa in Economic Crisis* (London: Macmillan).

Shaw, Timothy M. (1979), 'The Actors in African International Politics' in Timothy M. Shaw and Kenneth A. Heard (eds), *Politics of Africa: dependence and development* (London: Longman) 357–96.

Shaw, Timothy M. (1983), *Africa's International Affairs: an analysis and bibliography* (Halifax: Centre for Foreign Policy Studies).

Shaw, Timothy M. (1985), *Towards a Political Economy for Africa: the dialectics of dependence* (London: Macmillan).

Shaw, Timothy M. (1986), *Southern Africa in Crisis: an analysis and bibliography* (Halifax: Centre for Foreign Policy Studies).

Shaw, Timothy M. (1986), 'Peripheral social formations in the new international division of labour: African states in the mid-1980's', *Journal of Modern African Studies* 24(3), September, 489–508.

Shaw, Timothy M. (1987), 'The Future of the Great Powers in Africa: towards a political economy of intervention' in Olajide Aluko (ed.), *Africa and the Great Powers in the 1980s* (Lanham: University Press of America) 289–332.

Our Common Future: the World Commission on Environment and Development (1987) (Oxford: OUP).

Thom, William G. (1984), 'Sub-Saharan Africa's Changing Military Environment', *Armed Forces and Society* 11(1), Fall: 32–58.

World Bank (1981), *Accelerated Development in Sub-Saharan Africa: an agenda for action* (Washington).

World Bank (1986), *Financing Adjustment with Growth in Sub-Saharan Africa* (Washington).

Zartman I, William, (1985), *Ripe for Resolution: conflict and intervention in Africa* (New York: Oxford University Press).

Zwingina, Jonathan S. (1987), 'The Crisis of Hegemonic Decline: US disinterest in Africa', *Review of African Political Economy* 38, April: 71–7.

5 The External Environment for Southeast Asian Foreign Policy

Nayan Chanda

The foreign policy of a country is inevitably influenced by the external environment – the policies as well as economic and military power of its neighbors. (A country's domestic ambitions and fears *vis-à-vis* its neighbors complete the broad matrix in which policies are determined.) In Southeast Asia, however, more than the regional equation, big-power rivalry has proved to be a significant determinant of foreign policy.

Nothing perhaps better demonstrates the dramatic change in the external environment for Southeast Asian foreign policy in the 1980s than four events that occurred late in the decade. In May 1987 China signed a military supply agreement with Thailand – its first with a non-Communist Southeast Asian country. In February 1989 Indonesia announced its plan to restore diplomatic ties with China, frozen since 1965. In March 1989 Australian Prime Minister Bob Hawke floated the idea of forming a trade and economic grouping of the Pacific Basin countries, but initially excluded the United States from the core group because of reluctance of some Southeast Asian countries as well as Australia's own displeasure with US trade policies. In May 1989 Soviet President and Party Secretary General Mikhail Gorbachev travelled to China for a summit meeting with China's supreme leader Deng Xiaoping – the first such visit in 30 years. These developments took place against the backdrop of trade tensions with the United States and doubts about its commitment to the region. The significance of these events can be grasped only if one remembers that for nearly four decades Southeast Asian policy-makers considered China to be the principal threat to the region and the Soviet Union another subversive power to be kept at arms length. China, to be sure, still arouses fear in some countries in the region and the Soviet Union is still treated with deep suspicion, but they have now emerged as important external actors on the stage that once was virtually monopolized by the United States.

This chapter attempts to analyze the threats and opportunities offered by external powers to policy-makers in Southeast Asia in the postwar years. While its focus is primarily on the post-Vietnam War years, it nevertheless starts with the evolution of the policies of outside powers prior to the end of the Second Indo-China War.

THE ERA OF AMERICAN DOMINANCE (1945–68)

At the end of the Second World War while France, Holland and Great Britain still clung to their colonial possessions it was the United States, a some time anti-colonialist with its newly proven nuclear might, which dominated the Southeast Asian scene. Although in July 1946 the US granted independence to the Philippines, thanks to the Bell Trade Act (1946) and later the Laurel-Langley Agreement (1955), it had retained a privileged economic position in the country. The Military Bases Agreement signed in 1946 also provided the United States with two large air and naval bases that would prove to be the pillars of America's military preponderance in Southeast Asia (Schirmer and Shalom, 1987: 87–103). As the Cold War lines were drawn in Europe the new task of US power in Asia was defined by Communist victory in China and its advance in Indo-China and the Korean peninsula.

On the eve of the proclamation of the People's Republic of China in 1949 a National Security Council study warned that 'the extension of Communist authority in China represents a grievous political defeat for us; if Southeast Asia also is swept by Communism we shall have suffered a major political rout the repercussion of which will be felt throughout the rest of the world' (*Pentagon Papers*, 1971: I, 37). The very existence of Communist China was seen to hold the threat of overt aggression against its neighbors, but also feared was domination through subversion proceeding in chain-reaction. As another NSC study in June 1952 put it:

> The loss of any of the countries of Southeast Asia to communist aggression as a consequence of overt or covert Chinese communist aggression would have critical psychological, political and economic consequences. In the absence of effective and timely counter-

action, the loss of any single country would probably lead to relatively swift submission to or an alignment with communism by the remaining countries of this group (*Pentagon Papers*, 1971, I, 384–90).

The Domino Theory emerges

The fall of one Southeast Asian country under Communism, it was believed, would not only weaken the political will of other countries but would also deliver a blow to the West's access to natural resources that these countries produced – tin, rubber, rice, copra, iron ore, tungsten and oil. Washington policy-makers argued that if the West and especially Japan became dependent on resources in the Southeast Asian countries that fell under Communist domination then they would have to seek accommodation with Communism (Kolko, 1985: 76). The triple concern of stopping Chinese expansionism or Beijing-sponsored guerrilla war, preventing loss of vital resources to the West and damage to American credibility drove US policy in the region for nearly three decades after the war.

One of the first tests of US policy came in 1950 as France sought desperately to regain its control over Indo-China. The US offered massive military and economic support to France in its war against the Vietminh but, chastened by the experience of the Korean War, it refrained from direct intervention (Kahin, 1986: 42–4; see also Kolko, 1985: 81–2). Washington was unable to stop the French from conceding half of Vietnam to the Democratic Republic of Vietnam at the Geneva conference – the first Communist state in Southeast Asia. But in the post-Geneva period the US developed a three-pronged approach – bolster anti-Communist regimes in South Vietnam, Thailand and the Philippines, give covert support to anti-Communist groups in other countries and erect a security alliance – the Southeast Asia Treaty Organization (SEATO), embracing the Philippines and Thailand. The treaty was designed more as a scarecrow for the Communist countries than a hair-trigger device for intervention. The only SEATO member to which the US was prepared to make a firm commitment was the Philippines, a former colony that formed part of US Pacific defense plans. But despite Thai requests, the US refused to commit its forces to the treaty area as a whole.

However, that shortcoming of SEATO was made up by a bilateral mutual defense agreement signed in 1962 by US Secretary of State

Dean Rusk and Thai Foreign Minister Thanat Khoman. In March 1947 the US had already signed a military assistance agreement with the Philippines and three years later it did the same with Thailand. The Joint US Military Advisory Group (JUSMAG) in the Philippines and Thailand emerged as key US instruments in maintaining the pro-US orientation of the regimes by dispensing aid and advice. In the three decades after the 1947 agreement the US gave the Philippines over $400 million in military aid (see Schirmer and Shalom, 1987: 250; Buss, 1977: 127). Between 1951 and 1971 the US provided Bangkok with $935.9 million worth of military aid, which was equivalent to 59 per cent of the total Thai military budget for the same period (Girling, 1981: 236).

SEATO also offered its 'mantle of protection' to Cambodia and Laos, which had chosen to be neutral. The move served to warn the Communist countries without explicitly calling into question Laos and Cambodia's professed neutrality. The offer of protection was backed by military and economic aid to Laos and Cambodia. Between 1955 and 1964 Cambodia received over $400 million in US aid, of which nearly a fourth was in military assistance. However, aid to the governments was coupled with covert US intelligence efforts to encourage individuals and groups in these countries who would adopt a more openly anti-Communist stance and align with the US strategy in Asia. In 1959 Prince Norodom Sihanouk's government foiled a right-wing coup plot which was linked to the US embassy (Smith, 1965: 130). Eleven years later disgruntled Cambodian army and right-wing politicians successfully overthrew Sihanouk with tacit US backing. The US role in Laos was even less restrained. Along with providing military aid and training to the Royal Lao Army, the Central Intelligence Agency undertook to support a succession of right-wing politicians trying to seize power. In the course of a few years these covert efforts developed into a full-scale 'secret war' against the Pathet Lao and their North Vietnamese ally in which the US provided money, weapons, advisers and training and eventually committed American men and equipment (Brown and Zasloff, 1986: 64–100).

As the 'secret war' in Laos and the US involvement in South Vietnam grew, Thailand became the springboard for American operations in Indo-China. By 1968 some 45,000 US Air Force personnel were stationed in six bases in Thailand. Similarly the US bases in the Philippines, which in 1958 had been used for covert US operations in support of an anti-Communist rebellion in Indonesia, became important launch pads for the American war effort in Indo-China.

The predominant American position in Asia and its Cold War approach to Communism meant very limited foreign policy options for countries in the region. The Soviet Union, which had taken an interest in fomenting revolution in Southeast Asia in the late 1940s, seemed to have abandoned the colonial or 'neo-colonial' countries of the region to China's revolutionary care. Not surprisingly, very few of the newly emergent nations were attracted by Moscow. Until the mid-1960s Indonesia was the only country outside Indo-China to have ties with the Soviet Union. That relationship brought Soviet support for Indonesia at the United Nations and considerable economic and military aid.

China, the object of US containment policy, was a feared giant but had even less to offer in terms of assistance. The existence of some 15 million overseas Chinese in Southeast Asian countries, who were often viewed as Beijing's 'fifth column', also made regional countries apprehensive about China. Compared to massive US military power, the covert operations at its disposal, and the advantages of aid and trade that it offered (later joined by its ally Japan) Chinese and Soviet abilities were limited. So the Southeast Asian countries could either hitch their foreign policy to the US wagon (as did Thailand and the Philippines), maintain a non-allied but close relationship with the US (as did Singapore and Malaysia) or follow a non-aligned course.

Sihanouk tried to steer a neutral course for Cambodia by receiving US aid as well as seeking friendship and assistance from China and the Soviet Union, but had only limited success. Although China pledged its support for Cambodia against threats from pro-US neighbors, in view of physical distance and its limited military ability such pronouncements could only cause anger but not deter the hostile neighbors (see Armstrong, 1977: 186–97; also Smith, 1965 104–121).

Indonesia, which had appreciated US support for its independence struggle against the Dutch, and became a recipient of US aid, found itself at odds, however, with Washington's Cold War posture. Indonesia not only recognized the People's Republic of China but offered Beijing its first international forum at the Bandung Conference. The result of that policy was a favorable agreement with China over the status of the overseas Chinese. China also gave its backing to the Indonesian annexation of West Irian from the Dutch (1962) and its confrontation against Malaysia (1963) (see Weinstein, 1976:

70–5). The Soviet Union supplied Indonesia with weapons and an ageing fleet of ships, submarines and aircraft to support Sukarno's grand foreign policy in defiance of the West, while in 1964 the US cut off its economic aid to Indonesia to show displeasure over its confrontation with Malaysia.

The Chinese were the only other significant external political influence in the region. One constant objective in the Chinese approach to Southeast Asia has been an effort to prevent the emergence of any strong power close to its border and to maintain a balanced state system in a region that it viewed as within its general sphere of influence. It was out of its desire to deny Vietnam full control of Indo-China that China pushed Hanoi to make concessions at the Geneva Conference (see Joyaux, 1979: 231–323). And in order to keep the US away from its border China insisted on the neutrality of Cambodia and Laos. The same objectives led Beijing to offer aid and protection to Cambodia from the 1950 through the 1970s.

However, this basic policy went through some modifications as China's domestic policy and the external threat changed. Until 1957 China sought to break through the American containment by offering good neighborliness and aid to anyone who would recognize the PRC. China was ready to allay fears about the loyalty of the overseas Chinese community and to play down its proletarian internationalism. But in subsequent years Chinese foreign policy became increasingly militant in its opposition to 'US imperialism' and later 'Soviet revisionism'. By the time the Cultural Revolution was underway in China (1966) Beijing was not only calling for people's wars in all Southeast Asian countries, but was actively supporting guerrilla struggles in Thailand, Malaysia and Indonesia by broadcasting revolutionary propaganda and sending material support (Van Ness, 1970: 132–8). Following the abortive coup attempt by the pro-Beijing Communist Party of Indonesia (PKI) in September 1965 Jakarta broke its diplomatic ties with China. Ironically, however, as the threat from a revolutionary China loomed large in apparent fulfillment of earlier American prophecy the US view of Southeast Asian security was undergoing a subtle transformation.

THE ERA OF DECLINING AMERICAN POWER (1969–77)

The increasingly violent Sino-Soviet dispute and Washington's growing frustration with the course of the Vietnam War brought about significant modification in the US approach to Southeast Asia. While the Vietnam War was increasingly unsupportable at home and called for a reappraisal, the US saw opportunity in the growing Sino-Soviet hostility. Wooing China would not only weaken the Soviet global posture but could also pressure Hanoi into making concessions. The US disengagement from Asia announced in Guam in July 1969 thus marked a watershed in Southeast Asian diplomacy, opening the door for an active Chinese and Soviet role.

President Richard Nixon's Guam speech not only announced the beginning of US withdrawal from Vietnam but restricted America's self-appointed responsibility for assuring security in Asia. Nixon told a press conference that as far as international security was concerned, except for the threat of a major power involving nuclear weapons, the US expected that this problem would be 'increasingly handled by, and the responsibility for it taken by, the Asian nations themselves' (*New York Times*, 26 July 1969). Nixon also implicitly abandoned the domino theory by praising the economically strong non-Communist Southeast Asia for its ability to stand up to Communist threats and by stressing the limits that 'Red China's' internal problems were placing on its ability to export revolution. Soon the administration also made it clear that it no longer viewed a Chinese 'juggernaut type threat to its neighbors' as a likely prospect. With American threat perception radically altered, maintenance of US credibility became the major justification for continued US involvement in an Indo-China war which had also engulfed Cambodia from March 1970 (Colbert, 1987: 3). Even that credibility came under increasing question as the US began drawing down its involvement in Vietnam and changing its strategic course.

Within months of the Guam declaration the Philippines announced it was withdrawing its forces from Vietnam and publicly evoked the possibility of coexistence with China. Henry Kissinger's secret visit to China in 1971 and the announcement of Nixon's trip there the following year dramatically altered the foreign policy environment of Southeast Asia. Thailand was shocked by the China initiative taken by the US without any prior consultation. While the new American posture shook its allies in Asia, China's admission to the UN in October 1971 signalled the beginning of an era in which China would play a legitimate role in the region. Malaysia, which had begun contacts with China in May 1971, took the initiative in symbolically breaking the Association of Southeast Asian Nations (ASEAN) away from a pro-West alignment. The new objective of the organization, it was announced would be to seek international recognition and respect for Southeast Asia as a 'Zone of Peace, Freedom and Neutrality [ZOPFAN], free from any form or manner of interference by outside powers'. Malaysia, which had until 1971 relied on British military protection, saw the need to rely on diplomacy to strengthen its security in the new environment. As a Malaysian official put it while voting for China's entry to the UN in October 1971, 'We cannot ask Communist China to guarantee the neutrality of Southeast Asia and at the same time say we do not approve of her' (quoted in Morrison and Suhrke, 1978: 160).

The ripple effect of the changing power balance was immediately felt not only in the ASEAN declaration but in diplomatic initiatives by all member countries. In preparation for a time when the US would no longer be there to protect their security the countries began distancing themselves from the US war effort and preparing for a deal with the Communist countries. The decision of Thailand and Malaysia to establish relations with China was particularly striking as China was still actively engaged in supporting guerrilla war led by the Malayan Communist Party (MCP) and the Communist Party of Thailand (CPT). In the new international context, ties with the West and its counter-insurgency expertise alone were no longer seen as sufficient deterrence against Beijing-backed insurgency. Any lingering hope about the reliability of the US commitment to the region had been removed by the traumatic fashion in which the US forces withdrew from Cambodia and Vietnam.

The beginning of US disengagement from Asia came at a time of increasing tension between China and the Soviet Union – a tension that was soon to cast its shadow over Southeast Asia. In June 1969 Leonid Brezhnev had called for the creation of an Asian Collective Security system which would unite the countries on such noble principles as renunciation of use of force and non-interference in the internal affairs of others and pave the way for neutralization. The Soviet foreign ministry's Asia expert, Mikhail Kapitsa, who travelled through Laos, Thailand, Malaysia and Burma explaining the proposal, was received politely but found a total lack of interest. While China denounced the proposal as a design for a grand anti-China alliance other countries of the region were also wary of the new suitor. In subsequent years Thai and Malaysian officials visited Moscow and small trade and cultural contacts were initiated, but, fearful about getting embroiled in the Sino-Soviet rivalry, none of the ASEAN countries was ready for anything but very formal ties.

By 1975, when the curtain finally fell on the US involvement in Indochina, the rivalry between Beijing and Moscow had reached a new height. Beijing saw in the Vietnamese victory and precipitate American withdrawal an ominous sign for Soviet advances in Asia. Barely weeks after the collapse of South Vietnam China began issuing veiled warnings about the possibility of Soviet naval bases in Vietnam. It warned Southeast Asia against letting in the Soviet hegemonist 'tiger' by the back door after the American 'wolf' had left through the front door. The warnings were coupled with a new accommodating approach. China not only held up the possibilities of trade, particularly supply of Chinese oil at 'friendship prices' but also the prospect of easing Chinese support for insurgencies. China, which in 1967 had denounced ASEAN as an 'anti-Chinese and anti-Communist alliance' rigged by US imperialism and Soviet revisionism, was now inclined to support it as a possible barrier against Moscow's advance (de Beauregard, 1986: 223). The Soviet Union, which had quickly moved in to strengthen its ties with the newly emergent regimes in Vietnam and Laos, was also ready to embrace ASEAN. While it had very little with which to entice the countries of the region, Moscow began a propaganda campaign to warn Southeast Asia against China's expansionist designs and its overseas Chinese 'fifth column'.

While Beijing and Moscow stepped up their conflict, the one-time hegemon, the US, seemed ready to withdraw into an offshore posture. Symbolic attempts at shoring up American credibility during the Mayaguez episode in June 1975 only helped to underline the changing power balance. Strong Thai criticism of the unauthorized American use of Thai bases to attack Cambodia in a way marked the symbolic end of an American era. By July 1976 all American troops had been withdrawn from Thailand. The attempt by Washington to normalize relations with Vietnam (starting with the despatch of a presidential mission to Hanoi in March 1976) which appeared to be a high priority of the Carter administration, also generated doubt about the US commitment towards non-Communist Southeast Asia and strengthened the appeal for neutrality as the most desirable policy.

The fact that the Soviet Union was more interested in pursuing détente with the US rather than confrontation and that neither Moscow nor Beijing was in a dominating position also helped create an atmosphere suitable for neutrality. At the Bali summit in February 1976 – the first ever meeting of ASEAN heads of state – the concept of ZOPFAN was consecrated as the long-term goal of the organization. ASEAN also called for peaceful coexistence with Communist Indochina and urged Vietnam to join the group. The attendance of the United States, Australia and Japan at the summit and their support for the organization's objectives gave the group new confidence. That confidence was further boosted by the fact that both Beijing and Moscow were willing to endorse it as the best available guarantee against domination by the other power. The Bali summit and international endorsement of ASEAN symbolically ended the fluidity that had marked Southeast Asia since the enunciation of the Guam doctrine. In fact, the East Asian policy-makers of the Carter administration saw ASEAN fitting very well into a new American approach in Asia where American support for economic and social progress would replace the military security emphasis of the past (Colbert, 1987: 13). Japan, which steadily increased its trade and investment in non-Communist Southeast Asia but had been ambivalent towards ASEAN, took an active interest in promoting the organization after Bali. A Japan-ASEAN forum was set up in early 1977 to discuss the relations between the two and in August Japanese premier Takeo Fukuda went on a tour of ASEAN countries, in the course of which he announced $1.5 billion in aid to the group (Shibusawa, 1984: 105).

THE ERA OF SINO-AMERICAN ALLIANCE (1978–85)

The uneasy power balance around ASEAN and Indo-China did not last long. The intensification of conflict among the external powers and the emergence of open strife within Indo-China, nevertheless gave ASEAN unexpected new leverage in dealing with China and the Soviet Union, for a while.

The origins of the Sino-Vietnamese and Cambodian-Vietnamese conflict have been detailed elsewhere (see Chanda, 1986). For the purpose of this chapter, suffice it to note that a confrontational approach taken by the Khmer Rouge towards Vietnam and Vietnam's own strategic imperative in seeking a security parameter in Indochina set them on a warpath. That conflict soon became enmeshed with a deeper struggle between Vietnam and China and worsening Sino-Soviet relations. By the spring of 1978 Cambodia had broken its relations with Vietnam, and Beijing and Hanoi had come to open blows over the treatment of ethnic Chinese in Vietnam.

Although the growing public feud between Hanoi and Beijing and its Khmer Rouge allies raised the specter of war, it brought an unexpected diplomatic windfall for ASEAN. In the autumn of 1978, as both Beijing and Hanoi prepared for war, Vietnamese premier Pham Van Dong and Chinese vice-chairman Deng Xiaoping vied with each other in proffering their friendship to non-Communist Southeast Asia. Dong apologized to Malaysian leaders for past Vietnamese help to the Malaysian Communists and assured Thai leaders that Vietnamese support for the CPT had ended (Chanda, 1986: 318). Deng refused to give such public assurances, but Beijing made quiet arrangements to end Chinese backing for the Thai Communists. By the middle of 1979 China-based transmitters of the CPT fell silent. Hundreds of members of the CPT who were exiles in China began trickling back under an amnesty program arranged by the Thai government. Such arrangements aside, the conflict between their big brothers – China and Vietnam – as well as closure of CPT training camps in Cambodia run by the Khmer Rouge seriously demoralized the party members.

However, ASEAN could sit in the middle and enjoy the wooing by the Communist rivals and benefit from the security it brought only as long as there was a stalemate. Chinese support for the Khmer Rouge was welcome to ASEAN countries as it provided a counter to Vietnamese forays into Cambodia, which in turn were found useful if these diverted Khmer Rouge attention away from the Thai border. Thai premier Kriangsak Chomanond, in fact, quietly endorsed Vietnamese incursions into Cambodia.

But the signing of the Soviet-Vietnamese friendship treaty and the Vietnamese invasion of Cambodia in December 1978 suddenly altered the power balance in Southeast Asia. Some 180 000 Vietnamese troops in occupation of Cambodia not only posed a new security threat to Thailand and other ASEAN countries but, more seriously, established a dangerous precedent in Southeast Asia where the state system is still young and borders are far from being well established. For small states like Singapore surrounded by larger and more populous neighbors the sight of Vietnam intervening in a small neighboring country to install a regime of its own choosing was particularly portentous. The fact that Vietnam was backed by a massive flow of Soviet arms prior to the invasion was an additional matter of concern. Not surprisingly, one of the direct consequences of the invasion was a sharp increase in the defense expenditures of most ASEAN countries in mainland Southeast Asia.

China's punitive expedition into Vietnam in February 1979 brought only a limited satisfaction in ASEAN. While some were pleased to see Vietnam chastised, the implications of China acquiring the role of a regional gendarme were no cause for comfort. Countries like Indonesia and Malaysia, with significant Chinese populations, had watched warily China's angry response to Vietnam's treatment of the ethnic Chinese (see Godley, 1980: 41). China's seeming exercise of imperial power in 'teaching Vietnam a lesson' gave them some additional reasons for pause. Despite misgivings of some ASEAN states, unpublicized Sino-Thai military cooperation began in an effort to revive and organize a Khmer Rouge resistance to the Vietnamese. China, which had been Thailand's principal enemy for three postwar decades, was on the way to becoming its protector. Other ASEAN countries came around to accept Beijing as a valuable partner in their effort to remove the Vietnamese presence from Cambodia.

It soon became evident that advantages that seemed to accrue from the Sino-Soviet rivalry in the mid-1970s were overshadowed by the dangers this posed for the region. In the midst of the growing struggle over Cambodia the hope of working towards a zone of neutrality vanished. When in 1980 Indonesia and Malaysia tried to revive the concept of neutrality in the so-called 'Kuantan formula' it was greeted with embarrassed silence by other ASEAN partners. Meeting at Kuantan in Malaysia the leaders of the two countries – Premier Hussein Onn and President Suharto – had called for a Cambodian settlement that took into account Vietnam's security interests, and for withdrawal of foreign military presence from the region. In the light of the hard realities of China-ASEAN collaboration against Vietnam the idea was seen as a pipe-dream.

A direct consequence of the Sino-Vietnamese conflict was the emergence of the Soviet Union as a military power in Southeast Asia. Since March 1979, when the first Soviet naval contingent steamed into Cam Ranh Bay in Vietnam, the Soviet military presence has grown steadily. Although insignificant compared to the massive US presence in the Philippines, for the first time in history the Soviet Union came to possess a strike capability in Southeast Asia and also the ability to operate all the year round in the region's waters.

The emergence of China as a key power was helped by apparent US backing of China's role in opposing the Soviet Union and its allies. Contrary to expectations in Thailand, the US reaction to the developments in Cambodia was muted. The US accelerated delivery of weapons to Thailand and recalled that its security commitment to Thailand made under the Manila pact in 1954 was still in effect. The Thais, however, remained unconvinced that such reiteration meant any change in the basic US disinterest in Southeast Asia. They compared $14 million military aid given to Thailand to a $450 million package Washington offered to Pakistan facing the Soviets in Afghanistan as the measure of America's limited concern (Nair and Jeshurun, 1980: 133). The low-key American response to the military developments in the region was linked to Washington's support for China. It was clear to the regional powers that Washington blessed the Chinese military intervention in Vietnam. (The suspicion was later confirmed by Brzezinski, 1983: 410). A subsequent US decision to allow NATO allies to sell weapons to China and its own proclamation of support for China against the Soviet Union and its allies tended to bind them in a *de facto* alliance. Visiting China in August 1979, Vice-President Walter Mondale declared that Washington was committed to advance 'many parallel strategies and bilateral interests' it shared with China and warned that 'any nation which seeks to weaken or isolate you [China] in world affairs assumes a stance counter to American interests'. Many in non-Communist Southeast Asia concluded that Washington was eager to oppose the Soviets in the region mainly through the Chinese proxy. How close the Sino-American alliance had grown was demonstrated at the 'International Conference on Kampuchea' held at the UN in 1981. When ASEAN and Chinese representatives clashed over the formula for peace in Cambodia the former came under heavy American pressure to compromise. ASEAN also found that Japan refused to back them against American wishes. At least one bitter ASEAN diplomat cabled home about the lesson learned at the meeting: 'When the chips are down small countries cannot count on any friend' (Chanda, 1986: 456).

After 1981, when the US announced its decision to sell China lethal weapons, the Sino-American military relationship blossomed. A steady stream of high level American and Chinese visitors – from defense secretary and defense minister to service chiefs – have exchanged visits. Washington has progressively liberalized dual-use technology sales to China and has pressured the NATO agency for controlling exports to the Soviet bloc (COCOM) to relax its restrictions on technology transfers to China. Despite ASEAN misgivings and often public complaints, the US made commitments to sell over a billion dollars' worth of weapons and technology to China to modernize its armed forces (Ross, 1986). A new symbolic height was reached in 1986 when the US and Chinese navy ships held a 'passing exercise' in the South China Sea and a US fleet visited the Chinese port of Qingdao. Although the US has repeatedly assured ASEAN that it would not sell China weapons that would affect their security nor would it delegate to China the role of a gendarme in Southeast Asia, these assurances were taken with deep skepticism.

THE ERA OF TRIANGULAR COMPETITION (1986–)

While the year 1986 saw the high-water mark in US-China military co-operation it may also have signalled the beginning of a new era in Southeast Asia with the Sino-American collaboration against Moscow giving way to a triangular power balance between the West led by the US and Japan, China and the Soviet Union. Soviet party general secretary Mikhail Gorbachev's Asian initiative launched on 28 July in Vladivostok may be seen by future historians as the Soviet Union's long-delayed response to America's Guam Doctrine of 1969.

The Vladivostok speech, in which Gorbachev clearly staked out a Soviet claim to be an Asian and Pacific power, was a long time coming. Ever since 1983, when Moscow and Beijing had begun normalization tasks, relations between the two have slowly improved. But Gorbachev's decision to make an all-out effort to woo China and improve Soviet ties with non-Communist Southeast Asia has created a new situation. The Sino-Soviet summit held in Beijing in May 1989 formally ending the three-decades old hostility also conferred legitimacy on a Soviet role in the region. Indonesia's decision to restore ties with China and Indian Prime Minister Rajiv Gandhi's trip to Beijing were early recognition of the new reality. The effect of the Sino-Soviet détente was quickly felt in Indo-China. By the end of 1988 Laos, an ally of Moscow and Hanoi, had restored full diplomatic relations with China. Partly as a result of Soviet pressure Hanoi announced an early pullout of its forces from Cambodia (by 1 October 1989). In January 1989 a Vietnamese official travelled to Beijing for normalization talks. Even before the Beijing summit the emergence of the Soviet Union as a recognized power broker in the region was attested by a long line of ASEAN leaders who visited Moscow to solicit its support in seeking a settlement to the Cambodian problem. The eager welcome that was accorded to

Eduard Shevardnadze in Bangkok and Jakarta in March 1987 and the highly publicized visit to Moscow by Thai Foreign Minister Sitthi Sawetsila in May and that of Malaysian Prime Minister Mahathir Mohamad in July and of the Thai army chief General Chavalit Yongchaiyut in November underlined Moscow's growing importance in the region. Nothing perhaps helped more to dramatize Moscow's new stature in Southeast Asia than the high profile Soviet presence in Bangkok during the Thai king's 60th birthday celebrations in December 1987. The commander of the Soviet Land Forces was the highest ranking foreign official present at the ceremony.

Moscow seemed to accord special attention to Indonesia which had been the most vocal among ASEAN countries in calling for a nuclear weapons-free Southeast Asia, a proposal strongly opposed by the United States. On the occasion of the first anniversary of his Vladivostok speech Gorbachev granted an interview to the Indonesian paper *Merdeka* in which he announced Soviet acceptance of a 'zero option' on the Intermediate Nuclear Force (INF) treaty with the US that would eliminate SS–20 missiles in Asia and Europe and also expressed support for the Indonesian call for a Southeast Asia Nuclear Weapon-Free Zone (SEANFZ).

Although Washington was strongly opposed to the idea of SEANFZ and some member countries of ASEAN were cool, it was an indication of the changing times that during the third ASEAN summit (14–15 December 1987) the leaders agreed that 'ASEAN should intensify its efforts towards the early establishment of a Southeast Asia Nuclear Weapon-Free Zone'. They also agreed to explore 'possible relations with additional third countries' which would certainly include China, the Soviet Union, India and South Korea. The opening of institutionalized relationships with these countries would only underline the multipolar pattern emerging in the region.

The increased Chinese and Soviet interest in Southeast Asia has come at a time when US relations with its non-Communist Asian partners are facing strains over trade as well as security issues. Once the anchor of America's defense posture in mainland Southeast Asia, Thailand has grown increasingly critical of the US as a result of trade policies that affect Thailand's principal exports. Yet another irritant has been the US criticism of Thai handling of Indo-Chinese refugees. Bangkok's resentment over dwindling US military aid has been compounded by Washington's refusal to sell Thailand certain weapon systems out of fear that they might end up in China's hands.

The traditional patron-client relationship enjoyed by the US in the

Philippines also underwent change. Despite last minute US backing in the overthrow of the unpopular Marcos regime in the Philippines in February 1986, the dominant US position in the country was increasingly in question. As a result of a rising nationalism American bases in Clark airfield and Subic Bay were a source of tension and increasingly a potential source of discord as the base renegotiation in 1989 approached. Notwithstanding increased US grant aid to the Philippines in 1986, anti-US feeling has grown, especially among the urban élite; it was fuelled, among other factors, by a feeling that Washington cared only about the bases. Protectionist moves in the US that threatened major Philippines exports could only reinforce that view.

Although an increase in US aid to the Philippines in 1986 was an exception, declining US economic and military aid to the region and growing trade and trade-related friction provided the backdrop for the change in the strategic environment described above. After the initial shock of Communist victory in Indo-China and US military withdrawal from mainland Southeast Asia, the non-Communist countries of the region (with the exception of Marcos' Philippines) sought security principally through economic growth and the collective diplomacy of a regional political alliance while maintaining a steady defense build-up. Their economic growth, especially booming exports, has given them a new self-confidence, but it has also brought in its wake friction with their principal trading partner – the United States. In 1986 six ASEAN countries together constituted the seventh largest trading partner of the US. Twenty-three per cent of ASEAN's total exports went to the US. The fact that the United States ran a sizeable trade deficit with all of them resulted in increasing tension.

The US sale of tin from its strategic stockpile has brought angry protests from Malaysia, Indonesia and Thailand whose exports have suffered as a result. Reduced US sugar quotas for ASEAN countries and subsidized sugar exports to China adversely affected Philippine and Thai exports. Proposed US legislation designed to curb textile imports brought angry reaction from Southeast Asia. One of the most controversial pieces of US legislation in 1985 subsidized rice exports, which had the effect of knocking Thai rice out of certain markets. The measure, affecting some 23 million rice farmers in Thailand, was seen as a cruel blow from a treaty ally and a long-time protector. A leading Thai newspaper published a cartoon showing the Statue of Liberty holding a dagger pointed at a baby marked

'Thailand' in her arms. Washington had used the threat of ending its duty-free import advantage given to some ASEAN countries under the Generalized System of Preferences (GSP) to remove trade barriers and secure better copyright protection for US industry. But by the end of 1987, faced with an enormous trade deficit, the US seemed likely to withdraw that benefit at least from Singapore, and perhaps from Thailand as well. Although US anger at its growing trade deficit was understandable, ASEAN states noted that the trade figures did not take into account their considerable arms purchases from the US and expenditure of over half a billion dollars annually by more than 50 000 students from ASEAN in the United States.

While the strain in ASEAN-US trade relations was in danger of further aggravation, Japan was emerging as the dominant economic power in the region. It was not that ASEAN did not have trade complaints against Japan, which enjoyed a large trade surplus and whose imports from the region consisted mainly of raw materials and agricultural goods. But with its private investment and developmental aid surpassing that of the United States Japan gained paramount economic influence. In 1986 Japan's private direct investment in ASEAN amounted to $14 billion compared to $10 billion from the US. Japan's pre-eminence was underlined during the Third ASEAN Summit in Manila where Japanese premier Noburo Takeshita was the only senior foreign official present. He offered a new $2 billion soft loan to private investors in ASEAN.

Both China and the Soviet Union seemed eager to exploit difficulties faced by ASEAN in their relations with the US. For instance, Soviet officials visiting Thailand have offered to buy Thai rice that is hard to export due to US trade policy (FBIS APA, 27 April 1987, J3–5). China too has offered to help by buying Thai rice (FBIS APA, 20 April 1987, J1). Moscow has offered to launch Indonesian satellites at a lower cost after failure of the US shuttle program threatened to delay its launch. In the wake of the scrapping of a US-financed nuclear power station, Moscow has offered to build a $350 million coal-fired power plant in the Philippines which would save 3.6 million barrels of oil (FBIS APA, 6 April 1987, P1–2). In a move that held out economic benefits as well as possibilities of friction between the US and the Philippines, Moscow offered to have 80 ships serviced at a cost of $8 million at Philippine docks. A shipyard executive said he anticipated objections from the Americans, but was eager to do the work (FBIS APA, 23 April 1987, P1). The Philippines also showed interest in the Soviet proposal to hire Filipino guest workers to develop Siberia, an answer to the problem of the 'drying up' of the Middle East market (FBIS APA, 10 April 1987, P1).

However rich in symbolism the Soviet offers may have been, very little was actually achieved mainly because of the security concerns of ASEAN countries and the technological backwardness of the Soviet Union. While Moscow could increase its purchase of raw materials or manufactured products from ASEAN, it had precious little to offer for sale to these countries other than military equipment. The situation, however, could change considerably if the Soviet effort to develop eastern Siberia leads to an invitation for joint ventures with Asian industrialists.

Although China's trade with ASEAN has increased considerably since 1978 it too is constrained by the lack of complementarity. However, compared to Moscow, which has not succeeded in persuading ASEAN countries to buy Soviet hardware such as helicopters, China has made significant headway in breaking into the arms market – so long a Western preserve. In May 1987 Thailand concluded a deal to buy 30 T–69 tanks and 30 pieces of 37 mm anti-aircraft artillery from China at 'friendship prices' (FBIS APA, 4 May 1987, J3). Thailand was also reported to be considering the purchase of Chinese made armoured personnel carriers.

In many ways Thailand, the country standing at the border between the Communist and non-Communist worlds of Southeast Asia, has been the weather vane of the region. Thailand's efforts in the late 1980s to balance its deep-rooted security ties with the US by military and trade co-operation with China and improving ties with Moscow symbolize the changes in power-balance that have taken place in Southeast Asia. The growth of Soviet military power in the region, China's emergence as the second largest economy after Japan and the incipient economic decline of the US have combined to bring new challenges to ASEAN. While the weakening of the traditional alliance system has introduced uncertainty, it also offers the countries of the region a new freedom to chart an independent and balanced course.

BIBLIOGRAPHY

Armstrong, J. D. (1977), *Revolutionary Diplomacy: Chinese Foreign Policy and the United Front Doctrine* (Berkeley: University of California Press).

Brown, MacAlister and Joseph J. Zasloff (1986), *Apprentice Revolutionaries: The Communist Movement in Laos, 1930–1985* (Hoover Press).

Brzezinski, Zbigniew (1983), *Power and Principle: Memoirs of the National Security Adviser* (1977–81) (New York: Farrar Straus & Giroux).

Buss, Claude (1977), *The United States and the Philippines* (Washington: American Enterprise Institute).

Chanda, Nayan (1986), *Brother Enemy: The War After the War* (New York: Harcourt Brace Jovanovich).

Colbert, Evelyn (1987), 'The United States and Vietnam 1975–1987', paper presented at the symposium on Indochinese relationships, at the Foreign Service Institute, Washington DC, 10 March.

de Beauregard, P., *et al.* (1986), *La Politique Asiatique de la Chine* (Paris: Fondation Pour les Etudes de Défense Nationale).

Foreign Broadcast Information Service (FBIS)

Girling, J. L. S. (1981), *Thailand: Society and Politics* (Ithaca: Cornell University Press).

Godley, Michael (1980), 'Summer Cruise to Nowhere: China and the Vietnamese in Chinese Perspective', *The Australian Journal of Chinese Affairs*, July.

Joyaux, François (1979), *La Chine et le réglement du premier conflit d'Indochine, Genève 1954* (Paris: Publication de la Sorbonne, 1979).

Kahin, George McT. (1986), *Intervention: How America Became Involved in Vietnam* (New York: Alfred A. Knopf).

Kolko, Gabriel (1985), *Anatomy of A War: Vietnam, the United States and Modern Historical Experience* (New York: Pantheon Books).

Morrison, Charles E. and Astri Suhrke (1978), *Strategies of Survival: The Foreign Policy Dilemma of Smaller Asian States* (St Lucia: University of Queensland Press).

Nair, K. K. and Chandran Jeshurun (1980), *Southeast Asia and the Great Powers* (Kuala Lumpur: Malaysian Economic Association).

Pentagon Papers (1971), Gravel edn (Boston: Beacon Press).

Ross, Edward (1986), 'US-China Military Relations', paper presented at a Heritage Foundation conference, Washington DC, 28 January.

Schirmer, Daniel B. and Stephen Rosskamm Shalom (eds) (1987), *The Philippines Reader: A History of Colonialism, Neocolonialism, Dictatorship and Resistance* (Boston: South End Press).

Shibusawa, Masahide (1984), *Japan and the Asian Pacific Region* (London: Royal Institute of International Affairs).

Smith, Roger M. (1965), *Cambodia's Foreign Policy* (Ithaca: Cornell University Press).

Van Ness, Peter (1970), *Revolution and Chinese Foreign Policy: Peking's Support for Wars of National Liberation* (Berkeley: University of California Press).

Weinstein, Franklin B. (1976), *Indonesian Foreign Policy and the Dilemma of Dependence: From Sukarno to Soeharto* (Ithaca: Cornell University Press).

6 Indonesia's Foreign Policy
Dwight King

Indonesian foreign policy has displayed two sharply contrasting faces over the past 30 years. Sukarno, known for his flamboyant style, condemned the prevailing international system and aspired to leadership of an international anti-imperialist front. Under Suharto, in contrast, the anti-imperialist crusade has been abandoned in favor of a search for Western economic aid and capital investment. Nevertheless, foreign policy consistently reflects a strong sense of national identity and regional entitlement combined with a sense of vulnerability due to economic underdevelopment. Indonesians consider economic underdevelopment a legacy of colonialism and thus a symbol of the limitations on Indonesia's independence. Economic development, in other words, is a means of giving substance to independence. But this creates a dilemma: foreign aid and investment are needed for development, which causes dependence and results in vulnerability. Related to identity and entitlement is a further characteristic, the aspiration in recent years to become a major player in the international system, for instance as mediator in great power conflicts.

POLITY, ECONOMY, SOCIETY

Indonesia's ruling coalition since 1966, identifying itself as the New Order, has been dominated by the military, especially the Army. 'In contrast to the open competition between political parties during the liberal democratic period and the balance between rival political forces under the Guided Democracy regime, the military-dominated New Order government has virtually eliminated all non-military contenders for power in a system that is unambiguously authoritarian' (Crouch, 1984: 75). Over the past two decades of New Order rule, a single officer, General Suharto (ret.), has consolidated power, and the presidency, which he occupies, has become steadily more autonomous both from the Army as an institution and from other

74

élite groups. Yet because of the close links between Suharto's family, high government officials, and business groups, élite-level interests have easy access to policy-makers. The latter are relatively insulated from pressures from the mass-level, despite some nominally democratic procedures and institutions.

Although sovereignty is vested formally in the People's Representative Assembly (MPR), including selection and dismissal of the president and vice-president, the Assembly has been easily controlled by the New Order executive. About eight out of every ten were either directly appointed by the president or owed their membership to GOLKAR, Suharto's electoral organization. The New Order has sought to build its legitimacy in part through nominal adherence to constitutional principles and procedures, including general elections for the purpose of selecting members of People's Representative Councils at three levels of government (DPR, DPR–I, DPR–II). But these legislative institutions have only an advisory relationship to the executive.

Restrictions on political competition are substantial. Viewing the results of the 1971 election in which GOLKAR gleaned only 61 per cent of the vote as a mandate for political restructuring, New Order authorities required in 1973 that nine political parties merge into two composite parties, the Development Unity Party (PPP) and the Indonesian Democratic Party (PDI). This resulted in organizational conflicts that have kept the parties weak. Only leaders acceptable to New Order authorities have retained positions and these leaders have great influence over selection of party candidates. The parties have not been allowed to maintain a grass-roots political organization between elections. Their candidates were warned against certain campaign practices; for example, not to offend the dignity of the government and its officials; not to criticize policies of the government; and not to disrupt national unity by discussing ethnic, religious, racial, or class issues. Party leaders were required to send lists of potential candidates to New Order authorities for security clearance and suffered heavy losses from the screening process. There was prohibition on anyone who was a member or a close relative to a member of an organization once affiliated with the Communist Party, even if such affiliation occurred before Communist organizations were proscribed in 1965.

Other means of restricting political competition have been used as well. During anti-Communist hysteria in 1965–66, when hundreds of thousands of members of the Indonesian Communist Party (PKI) were massacred, many with the complicity of the military, about one-and-a-half million persons were detained. Although the great majority have been released, only about six out of every 10 000 ever had their cases examined in any judicial process, and most spent several years – many more than a decade – in detention under appalling circumstances. In recent years there has been a marked increase in the *scope* or number of different groups whose rights have been violated, although the *scale* or sheer numbers of political prisoners and political killings has probably not yet returned to the level of the late 1960s. In addition to suspected Communists, several thousand others, including Muslim activists, Timorese supporters of the dissident Fretilin organization, and stateless Chinese, have been detained without trial for extended periods (King, 1987; Thoolen, 1987).

The press has been tightly controlled. There was only one government-owned television station until 1988 when a private station in the capital city was scheduled to begin broadcasting. Radio stations are required to use news from the official wire service. Although there is no official censorship of print media, warnings have been issued frequently and occasionally newspapers and magazines are shut down and books banned. Editors operate on the principle that when there is any doubt, it is better not to publish.

The economic context is distinguished by the fact that Indonesia's economy is over twice the size of any other in Southeast Asia with a GDP of US$ 86 billion in 1985. In per capita terms, however, Indonesia and the Philippines are the poorest members of ASEAN, with GNPs per capita between US$ 500–600 in 1985. Despite the fact that about 60 per cent of Indonesia's labor force is employed in agriculture, mining (including petroleum and natural gas) contributes more to the GDP than either agriculture (25 per cent) or manufacturing (14 per cent) (World Bank, 1987). Nevertheless, New Order leaders are particularly proud of having enabled the country to feed itself. In 1978 Indonesia was the world's largest importer of rice, but by 1984 it had become self-sufficient.

The New Order's economic policies brought a period of sustained economic growth until the world economic slow-down in the early 1980s. For the 20 year period 1965–85, average annual growth was 4.8 per cent, the highest in Southeast Asia except for Singapore. But most observers would agree that this rate was inflated by windfall profits from petroleum exports after 1973 resulting from the efforts of the OPEC cartel of which Indonesia is a member. Oil and gas revenues, after being raised ten-fold during the 1970s by OPEC price manipulation, have been sluggish and on a downward trend since 1980. Since the government has been dependent on oil and gas for over half of its revenues and New Order authorities are committed to an overall 'balanced' budget, the austere economic realities have been reflected in the government budget since 1986 (Hainsworth, 1987).

The benefits of economic growth have not been felt evenly throughout the society. The main beneficiaries have been members of the élite – military officers and their bureaucratic and business associates – and a relatively small stratum, the urban middle class, composed of middle-level civil servants, managerial and administrative employees in the private sector, members of the professions, and some middle-level businessmen. Using data on occupation from the 1980 Census, the size of the urban middle class can be estimated at around 7 per cent of the population. The growing prosperity of this stratum has been an important factor enabling the New Order to consolidate its position. Although some progress has been made in reducing poverty, about a quarter of the urban population are still considered below the poverty line. But for the rural areas, where 70 per cent of the Indonesian people live, the figure jumps to over 40 per cent. Many Indonesians believe the gap between the rich and the poor is growing (Bonner, 1988: II. 79).

Nevertheless, the major and growing political contradiction within the New Order is that between the emerging factions of the urban middle class, who have benefitted from the economic policies of the New Order, and the New Order state itself. Human rights abuse has grown with the expansion of middle-class groups, who are beginning to challenge seriously the ideological assumptions and political prerogatives of the New Order élite.

At the time of independence Indonesians had little more in common than that they were all part of the Netherlands East Indies. There are some three hundred ethnic groups speaking more than 200 distinct languages. They are dispersed throughout an island archipelago spanning 3000 miles, although the majority, about 100 million, reside on the island of Java. Understandably, Indonesia has sometimes been on the verge of disintegration. Hence, many of the political élite, especially central government authorities, have an underlying fear that centrifugal forces could predominate.

Once the economy had stabilized and sustained economic growth was under way, the New Order became more concerned with ideology and shaping political culture. In an effort to create greater homogeneity, the government stimulated an intensive debate within Indonesia beginning in the late 1970s on the nature of *Pancasila*, the five principles of official state ideology, and its role in Indonesian society, launching in 1979 an extensive program of two-week seminars which were made obligatory first for all civil servants, and then gradually for many other groups, for example, prisoners and first-year university students. The role of *Pancasila*-based secular moral education became the focus of national discussion. In 1982 Suharto declared that all mass organizations – including reluctant Muslim groups – would be required to accept *Pancasila* as their single basic principle, a decree which was passed into law by the DPR in 1985.

Studies of the content of élite political culture suggest strong orientations towards consensus, compromise, non-violence, a hierarchical social order and a greater importance of personal ties than rational analysis for policy-making. Behavior codes in political life include a propensity for negotiation, conciliation and accommodation. And the style of political behavior is marked by circuitousness, innuendo, formalism and reliance on intermediaries. Thus, Suharto has preferred to pursue his foreign policy goals through informal negotiations and conventional diplomatic means. His style has been more congruent with the political culture than was Sukarno's flamboyant, coercive diplomacy.

Three historical experiences that get considerable attention in the political enculturation process are the Indonesian anti-colonial struggle for national independence, the Islamic-inspired regional rebellions, and the so-called GESTAPU (or G–30-S-PKI), which refers to the complex series of events that began the night of 30 September 1965 and culminated in the annihilation of the Communist Party and the overthrow of Sukarno's 'Old Order'. The memory of the national independence struggle has influenced perceptions and policy towards Vietnam. The memory of the regional rebellions is a reminder of the potential danger of political Islam and keeps the New Order wary of close ties with radical Islamic countries such as Iran and Libya. Due to CIA assistance to some of the rebel groups, remembering them also helps to instill a degree of xenophobia, especially within the military. And the memory of GESTAPU has influenced perceptions and policy towards China, which will be discussed below.

POLICY-MAKERS AND THE POLICY PROCESS

The makers of foreign policy have changed over time. In the liberal democracy of the 1950s, the Foreign Ministry was afflicted by inter-party contests for patronage and the making of foreign policy was greatly influenced by the open clash of domestic political forces. During the period of Guided Democracy, President Sukarno was the dominant voice, and professional standards of the ministry were subordinated by considerations of ideology as well as patronage.

Likewise under the New Order, President Suharto is the dominant foreign policy voice. But there has been a revival of professional standards, foreign ministers have been civilians, and the ministry enjoys a measure of political latitude. Legislators (MPR, DPR) have very little impact, except for periodically ratifying and thus helping to legitimize general policy guidelines. Ultimate sanction for the conduct of foreign policy comes from the military establishment. 'Its dominance is indicated by recurrent bypassing of the Foreign Ministry and in the filling of senior official and ambassadorial posts which has given rise to intra-bureaucratic tensions' (Leifer, 1983: xv). In 1986 half of the leading positions as well as most ambassadorships, including those to Indonesia's major partners: ASEAN, Australia, the EEC (except Belgium and France), Japan, and the USA, were held by ex-military men (MacDougall, 1986). (Distributing prestigious foreign service positions to senior military officers has been an important means through which Suharto has rewarded loyalty, neutralized critics and co-opted potential opponents.) Nevertheless, Leifer concludes, 'Although for practical purposes foreign policy was subject to the control of a military establishment a civilian face was presented to the outside world because of the importance of restoring international confidence' (1983: 131).

These circumstances resulted in competition for the ear and authority of President Suharto. Thus the policy process retained some particularistic aspects. Writing about Adam Malik, who served as foreign minister until 1978, Leifer observes:

> . . . although the Foreign Ministry was relegated to a secondary status vis-à-vis the Ministry of Defense and Security and various intelligence agencies, Malik, through his personal relationship with the President, was able to moderate a military propensity to regard foreign policy in terms of stark alternatives which were likely to frustrate or favour communism. (1983: 131–2)

In addition to the civilian-military cleavage, another has emerged in recent years over economic policy. The economic technocrats, who have held about a dozen portfolios in each of the last two cabinets, were in competition with the protectionists/nationalists/engineers (the so-called '*Mandiri*') group who have controlled the State Secretariat, and the Ministries of Industry, and Research and Technology. The technocrats have won some major policy debates, enabling them to keep up the momentum for deregulation and economic reform, but appeared to have lost ground in the implementation. Their credibility and position depended on their ability to continue to procure official foreign assistance and commercial loans.

Outside the government there were some élite groups that had influence on foreign policy. One was the Center for Strategic and International Studies (CSIS), a think-tank closely associated with one of the New Order founders, the late General Ali Murtopo, and GOLKAR. This group was generally an architect or supporter of pragmatism in foreign policy, especialy policies for attracting Western economic assistance. Another group advocated more nationalistic policies and expressed their views in the *Merdeka* daily newspaper. A third group could be identified whose influence was limited primarily to policies on Islamic affairs, including towards the states of the Middle East. During Professor Mochtar Kusumaatmadja's tenure as foreign minister, contracting by the government with major universities for research on foreign policy issues appeared to increase, which served the dual purpose of encouraging more input from the intellectual community and attempting to counter military influence.

Thus meaningful political competition occurred not in the representative assemblies, but among élites in the executive agencies. Since they lacked an autonomous political base and were dependent on the President for their appointment, their conflicts served to maximize Suharto's power as they competed for his attention and sought his agreement with their positions. The lack of co-operation and co-ordination among members of the Fourth Development Cabinet (1983–88) gave rise to a new acronym in Indonesian political discourse: KISS, 'to the Palace one by one' (*ke Istana sendiri-sendiri*).

Three decision-making models have been posited for describing the process by which Suharto chooses from among conflicting policy alternatives. One posits that he is forced by domestic political considerations to balance one faction against another. Here the substance of the policy is less important than the source of the proposal. The second model stresses Suharto's firm convictions that are deeply imbedded in his personality. He makes core foreign policy decisions that are consonant with his convictions, although power centers may incrementally affect policy-making at the periphery. The third model is a hybrid between the first two and likens the policy process to that in a traditional village council:

> The village headman listens impassively and at great length to the conflicting positions of the village elders, and when he feels that he has heard enough he pronounces the consensus of the council. In cases with the potential to be significantly disruptive, this consensus must mollify all major parties and defuse the issue, and here the headman's discretion is not unconstrained. However . . . in, many situations the 'village consensus' largely reflects the headman's personal preferences. (Tilman, 1987: 39)

In all three models, Suharto plays the dominant role.

A focus on the politics of decision-making in the bureaucracy and among the élite raises the question, to what extent have institutions emerged and spun webs of constraint around the arbitrary impulses of heads of state? Writing about the New Order in the early 1980s, Liddle argues that

> . . . [Suharto's] policies have been remarkably consistent and successful over two decades. . . . Though the New Order appears to have shifted from a system of personal rule to an institutionalized 'presidential-military-bureaucratic complex,' there is still much room for the idiosyncratic behavior of an incumbent president to shake the structure. (1985: 70–1)

Liddle postulates a 'close connection' between institutionalization and policy continuity, and finds evidence of continuity especially in Suharto's economic policies. But an argument could be made that continuity in economic policy was less related to institutionalization than to Suharto's appreciation of his continuing need for large injections of economic assistance from external donors/investors and his consequent sensitivity to their policy preferences and advice.

Focusing on élite images, 'definitions of the situation' and foreign policy goals, rather than style, or pattern of external alignments, Don Emmerson argues for *continuity* of international outlook between the Sukarno and Suharto regimes. There has been an abiding concern for the integrity of the state, a sense of regional entitlement and an interest in regional autonomy. Moreover, if one defines rationality in the instrumental sense, considered a property of the relationship between means and ends, then a case can also be made for considerable rationality in Sukarno's policies and thus continuity in foreign policy process between regimes (1986: 88–109).

Observers who argue for the greater rationality of foreign policies under the New Order commonly attribute rationality to those policies which have promoted economic growth, reduced absolute poverty, enlarged and co-opted an emergent middle class, and improved national defense. However, despite instances of overall rationality in foreign policy, there are also some outstanding elements of instrumental *irrationality* in the policies of the New Order. Some domestic policies, such as coercion of Islamic activists and critics, have tended to undercut the goal of national security, which was being pursued in particular foreign policies. In other words, domestic and foreign means to the same end undermined each other (Emmerson, 1986: 107).

The power of the economic technocrats to implement rational policies which conflicted with the interests of military-associated firms and of Suharto family businesses was very limited. The national oil company, Pertamina, and the rice trading agency, Bulog, were managed by army officers, trusted friends of Suharto, who largely avoided accountability to formally superordinate agencies (for example, the Ministry of Finance) – at least until Pertamina's financial crisis in 1975 – and who siphoned off funds for the patronage machine. The tendering of many important, often foreign assisted, development projects was fixed in favor of firms which often failed to meet the technical criteria but which had military or Suharto family connections. Foreign investments usually took the form of joint ventures in which the domestic partner had military or Suharto-family ties and influence so that regulations imposed by the technocrats were often waived in practice. In other words, the military's sense of political entitlement and the ideology of dual function (*dwifungsi*), their commercial activities, their preoccupation with political stability and governmental control, influenced perhaps by Javanese political traditions that stressed centralization and monopolization of power, intruded on the rationality and the institutionalization of the policy process. 'The scope for rational policy-making usually expanded only when the regime faced an economic crisis but always narrowed again once the crisis was passed' (Crouch, 1984: 83).

DOMESTIC RESOURCES AND CONSTRAINTS

With its vast and resource-rich archipelago, its 170 million people, most of whom now share a common language and intense love of their country, its strategic location astride the sea lanes connecting the Indian and Pacific oceans, and its respectable record of economic growth over the past 20 years, Indonesia has become a major Third-World power. Add to these assets its reputation for political stability. President Suharto has held power uninterruptedly for over 20 years, longer than any other Southeast Asian leader except Lee Kuan Yew, and enjoys the respect of most Indonesians. He is often viewed in Indonesia as a benevolent grandfather and has been christened the Father of Development.

Indonesia's military capacity increased substantially in the early 1980s. Due largely to the sharp rise in oil prices, Indonesia was awash with funds which the economy could not easily absorb. Military leaders saw a golden opportunity to modernize the armed forces and defense expenditure nearly doubled between 1979 and 1982. The air force acquired 15 F-5 fighters, 29 A-4 Skyhawk fighter-bombers, and 12 F-16s and the navy underwent considerable modernization as well. However, the mainstay of the Indonesian armed forces is the army which currently numbers about 230 000.

These important resources notwithstanding, constraints have exceeded resources. Even with this new capacity, Indonesia's air force is about half the size of Singapore's. The Indonesian navy's capacity to support a major external campaign against a strong enemy is still very limited (Crouch, 1986). The large size of the army relative to all others in Southeast Asia, except Vietnam, does not mean a correspondingly greater ability to project Indonesian power abroad. Like armies everywhere, a substantial proportion of Indonesian army personnel are employed in administrative and support duties. In addition, but unique to Indonesia with its doctrine of the dual function (*dwifungsi*) of the armed forces, the military is not limited to a defense-and-security function, but has an obligation to participate in all fields of national life, including the government. Since 1966, this second, political role has been the predominant one.

Another constraint is the absence of a single great cultural tradition, which is expressed in communal divisions that have determined the constituencies of political life. The most important division is that between devout and nominal Muslims, the latter considered a majority by most estimates. Both presidents, a large majority of military officers and high-ranking civil servants have been identified with the outlook and behavior of the latter group. In general the devout Muslim constituency has been least supportive of the pragmatic, pro-Western foreign policy of the New Order. But the increasing size of the devout group, stimulated by the world-wide Islamic resurgence, has kept New Order policy-makers sensitive to Muslim concerns. They have been obliged to balance carefully their external associations in order to appease domestic Islamic opinion without appearing to enhance its national standing in political terms.

Division was also apparent between Muslims and Christians. The difficulties the New Order experienced in its efforts to integrate East Timor and Irian Jaya into the Indonesian nation-state, and the attendant foreign policy problems with Portugal, Papua New Guinea, and Australia, cannot be well understood without taking this religious difference into account.

Indonesia's geographical configuration, combined with social diversity, has encouraged centrifugal political tendencies. During the Sukarno era, regional rebellions broke out on Sumatra and Sulawesi, traditionally considered part of the 'outer' islands – a way of distinguishing them from the heavily populated island of Java, the 'bureaucratic center' of the nation-state. Under the New Order, open expression of seccessionist sentiments in areas outside of Java have occasionally been heard and quickly suppressed. Nevertheless, development policy in the 1980s has reflected a concern over regional inequalities and a felt need to direct new investment disproportionately to outlying islands, especially those in eastern Indonesia. The transmigration or resettlement program has moved hundreds of thousands off Java into sparsely populated areas, including border areas considered to be relatively insecure. The unintended ecological damage caused by the program in some areas and conflict with indigenous Melanesians in Irian Jaya which fanned the Free Papua insurgency movement (OPM) enlarged and complicated the foreign policy agenda.

Indonesia's physical structure and location have nurtured two contradictory perspectives among policy-makers. Because it is an island nation with as much territorial water as territorial land, it was sometimes viewed as open, porous, and vulnerable. On the other hand, it could also be viewed as surrounded by a 'great moat' that provided protection. Its strategic location in the middle of several major sea arteries forces the country into the mainstream of international politics even if it should prefer to remain aloof (Tilman, 1987: 40).

The ethnic Chinese, currently numbering approximately four million, have been both a resource and constraint to policy-makers. Without their entrepreneurial skills, business acumen, and access to private finance capital abroad, the growth of the economy during the New Order Era would have been much more modest. A large majority of the 100 billionnaires (in rupiah) identified in an Indonesian press report in 1984 were Chinese (*Indonesia Reports*, 1987, 1988). They were usually the preferred partner to 'bureaucratic capitalists' and foreign investors, although the widespread view that they still dominate the Indonesian economy is difficult to prove. (In 1974 the Indonesian weekly magazine, *Tempo*, reported that Chinese and other non-indigenous Indonesians accounted for 91–94 per cent of the capital invested by Indonesian citizens in association with foreign investors under the foreign investment law. They accounted for 75 per cent of the capital in domestically-owned industries (cited in Weinstein, 1976: 239). However, an analysis by a private research group in 1981 (van der Kroef, 1986: 932) found that in dominantly foreign-owned industries, Chinese Indonesians held less than 10 per cent of the shares, while private Indonesian enterprises held 13 per cent. In domestically-owned industries, the Indonesian government held the major part of the shares, as compared to 27 per cent being held by Chinese Indonesians, and 11 per cent by other Indonesians.)

Policy-makers were constrained by native Indonesian's prejudice against the Chinese, and by racial violence that erupted almost annually. These feelings were based not only on economic factors, but also on the historical memory of GESTAPU to which the Chinese were linked through their assistance to the Indonesian Communist Party. Anti-ethnic Chinese sentiment was a major factor until 1989 preventing normalization of diplomatic relations with China. As van der Kroef points out,

> . . . the most formidable long-term obstacle to Sino-Indonesian diplomatic normalization today is the convergence of *pribumi* suspicion and possibly envy of, and hostility towards ethnic, Chinese Indonesians, with the Indonesian military's fear of China as a long-term strategic threat to Indonesia and Southeast Asia. (1986: 932)

Even direct trade relations with the PRC were not established until 1985, nearly two decades after the New Order crushed the PKI.

Finally, mention should be made of constraints arising from the nature of the New Order regime. The dominant role of Suharto in the foreign policy process was mentioned above. Concern is growing that a succession crisis looms ahead when he passes from the scene. Suharto himself has provided no reassurance. 'Nobody ever knows what Suharto is thinking, or why he does what he does – he has refined to the utmost the Javanese trait of being indirect' (Bonner, 1988, I: 59).

Suharto has used the state to create a regimented society in which independent thought and action are suspect. The closely monitored and self-censored press avoid any direct criticism of New Order policies, and largely limit their treatment of policy alternatives to vague generalities. All political activity on campuses has been strictly prohibited. Authorities say their intent is to create an atmosphere conducive to study, but the cost has been high in loss of the capacity for independent thinking. 'There is growing concern', writes Bonner, 'that the country has lost a generation of potential leaders' (1988, I: 73).

THE EXTERNAL ENVIRONMENT

The most important constraint on the external environment has been economic dependence deriving from Indonesia's integration into the world capitalist system. Due to its absolute size, energy sources, and large informal sector, Indonesia's economy is less dependent on foreign trade than that of any other ASEAN country; the value of total foreign trade amounted to about one-third of the GNP in 1985. However, the pattern of trade leads to a very different conclusion. The role once played by The Netherlands as major trading partner has been taken over by Japan beginning in the early 1970s. Concentration on the large industrial nations has remained high, and diversification has remained consistently low (Weinstein, 1976: appendices).

The situation with respect to investment relations was not much different. In the early years of the New Order, investment was even more concentrated on US sources than had been true for the prewar Dutch dependence. This predominant position of the US was steadily eroded with the inflow of Japanese investment in the mid-1970s. Although there has been a small growth in sources that would balance Japan, the EEC and the NICs, 'Indonesia remains heavily dependent on the large Western industrial nations for investment and is potentially quite vulnerable to Japan' (Crone, 1983: 126).

Since its beginning, the New Order has been heavily dependent on foreign economic assistance. As compared with the Sukarno regime, the amount of aid has increased tremendously and the sources have changed. About three-fifths of Indonesia's accumulated debt of US$ 2.4 billion at the end of 1965 was owed to Communist countries (Weinstein, 1976: Appendix B). In the last several years official assistance from the Inter-Governmental Group on Indonesia (IGGI), the major aid consortium of Western nations, Japan and the international banks, has amounted to between US$ 2.5 and 4 billion per year, which represented about one-third of the New Order's development budget in FY 1986–87. Indonesia currently is one of the largest recipients of Asian Development Bank (ADB) and World Bank loans.

Moreover, the costs of official debt servicing have substantially increased in the last few years, bringing Indonesia's debt service ratio up beyond 40 per cent – higher than what is regarded in the World Bank as the 'critical threshold' of security (33 per cent). External liabilities to both public and private creditors are estimated to be around US$ 42 billion, or about one-third of the country's GNP. 'Decline in new foreign investment since 1983 means that Indonesia has experienced net capital outflow in recent years running in the hundreds of millions or billions of dollars' (Hainsworth, 1987). In an effort to manage these risks, the New Order has maintained high foreign exchange reserves and stand-by lines of credit for emergency use.

Indonesia is now the fifth-largest Third World borrower. It is indeed noteworthy that on the eve of a national legislative election in April 1987 Suharto and his technocrats were willing to make themselves vulnerable to portrayal by nationalists as sacrificing public welfare to appease foreign banks; the government imposed austerity measures, including budget cutting and devaluation, by liberalizing the regulations governing foreign investment and by reassuring foreign creditors that Indonesia would not renege on its debt payments. Besides demonstrating the indispensability of its creditors, these actions reflected the New Order's tight control over domestic sources of opposition (Emmerson, 1986: 379).

During the Sukarno era, there was little correspondence between the trading partners, on the one hand, and the donors/creditors of economic and military assistance on the other. Indonesia traded mainly with Western countries, but most economic and military assistance came from Communist countries, especially China and the Soviet Union, even though the US managed to maintain a small military training program throughout the most hostile years of the Sukarno era. After Suharto took power, military assistance from the US increased sharply, and that from the Communist countries ceased. The sources of military assistance came more into line with the pattern of trade relations, except for Japan, which has given little military assistance. Over the past several years, US military aid – mostly arms sales credits and training – has run between US$ 35 and US$ 50 million per year.

There is debate among scholars about the significance and meaning of these empirical patterns of aid, trade and investment dependency. Analyzing 'the price of aid' during the first decade of the New Order, Weinstein found that 'sometimes [Indonesian leaders] succeeded in deflecting [external pressures], usually by enlisting the support of some of the powers in opposition to the demands of others; on other occasions they had to submit, and in some cases it is hard to say whether they yielded or not' (1976: 234).

Robison argues that, while the 'dependency approach' has some utility in describing the patterns in Indonesia's international economic relations, it is unable to explain the development of Indonesia's economy or the New Order's economic policies. He points out that even though international capital became the 'key element in the conglomerate that is the capitalist class' in Indonesia during the 1970s, economic policy changed to one which placed severe constraints on foreign capital, protecting, subsidizing and financing a nascent domestic capitalist class, despite the continuing dominance of international corporate capital and finance. Thus, the struggle over economic policy in Indonesia has not been a simple reflection of global relations of dependency.

Instead, the development of capitalism in Indonesia has involved a process of accelerated domestic capital accumulation, both private and state. The very development of national capitalist forces has produced a resurgence of economic nationalism. The relationship between national and foreign capital has therefore been a complex one in which various elements of national capital seek selectively to integrate with foreign capital in cases where international capital and corporate resources are required (oil, gas, minerals and more complex industrial processes), or to exclude foreign capital where these resources are no longer so essential (increasingly in light industry). (Robison, 1986: 115)

The sharp downturn in foreign investment beginning about 1975, the decline in the oil market in the early 1980s, and the consequent increased importance of foreign sources of finance, brought the New Order to a 'watershed' in the 1980s, Robison argues. It became less able to resist strong pressures from the International Monetary Fund (IMF), the World Bank and private foreign corporate capital to move away from a state-led national industrialization strategy towards an export oriented strategy of 'allocative efficiency within an international economy'. These rising foreign pressures constitute 'a major challenge to the existing structure of political and economic power in capitalist Indonesia. . . .' (Robison, 1986: 387). But the 'capitulation' has been only partial and heavily symbolic. The IMF's and World Bank's free-market arguments, supported by some economic technocrats, have been counteracted by the protectionists'/nationalists'/engineers' preference for domestic goods and the manufacture of high technology as a long-term development strategy. Other scholars have also pointed out the semi-autonomy of foreign policy in Indonesia. Echoing Weinstein's 'dilemma of dependence', Emmerson writes about the 'apparent contradiction' between the New Order's reliance on Western aid, finance, and investment, on the one hand, and its ostensible desire for autonomy in foreign affairs and fear of enclaves on the other (Emmerson, 1986: 379).

In policy-makers' perceptions of the external environment China has been seen as the major, long-term threat to Indonesian security. Tilman found, 'almost every discussion of the PRC with Indonesian officials includes a quick and certain assertion of Beijing's involvement in GESTAPU followed by an unqualified condemnation of the PRC' (1987: 87). At the same time, many of the élite favored a *rapprochement* primarily in order to eliminate the middle-man profit on Sino-Indonesian trade which, until 1985, had passed through Hongkong or Singapore. The perception of threat overshadowed the perception of economic opportunity until early 1989 when the President, after a meeting with the Chinese Foreign Minister, announced the commencement of a process that will lead to the restoration of diplomatic relations between the two countries. This major change in the foreign policy of the New Order was a response to a clearly changed strategic and external political environment: the apparent end of the Cold war, *rapprochement* among the USSR, China, and Vietnam, and China's relinquishment of its previous vow of assistance to remnants of the PKI.

New Order élites have tended also to associate the USSR with the Indonesian Communist Party, giving rise to generally negative perceptions. Yet these have been tempered by the Sino-Soviet conflict, and the Soviet Union's potential role in containing Chinese expansionism. As a result, New Order policy-makers have not been as alarmed as some of their counterparts in other ASEAN countries over Soviet intentions and actions in Southeast Asia.

Indonesian foreign policy-makers have always felt that Vietnam presented more opportunities than threats. The hostile comments of the Sukarno regime on American military intervention in Vietnam were not rescinded by the New Order government (Weinstein, 1976: 131). Indonesians feel that they have a 'special relationship' with Vietnam due to perceived similarities between the Indonesian Revolution and the Vietnamese struggle for independence. As the two largest countries in Southeast Asia, a leading Indonesian scholar argues, 'Indonesia and Vietnam have common interests to pursue several common strategic choices which can alleviate some of the more intractable problems of superpower and major power intervention in our part of the world' (Sudarsono, 1985: 175).

FOREIGN POLICY OUTPUT

The foregoing discussion has been punctuated with historical perspectives, especially comparisons between the Sukarno and Suharto eras. In order to assist in the identification of change and continuity in Indonesian foreign policy outputs over approximately three decades since independence, the discussion of outputs will commence with a brief historical sketch using a widely accepted periodization.

A.   1945–49: Independence through Negotiation

The overwhelming preoccupation of foreign policy was winning Dutch recognition of Indonesian sovereignty. Independence was sought and attained primarily through a diplomatic process involving third-party mediation, but linked with armed resistance. The leadership of the new Republic was committed to the policy of seeking international recognition by projecting an external stance of peaceful moderation. Nevertheless, two distinctively divergent and competing modes of foreign policy were practised: negotiation (*diplomasi*) and struggle (*perjuangan*).

Once victory for the Republic had been achieved, doubts emerged among the élite that its victory had been at the expense of true

economic and diplomatic independence. The weakness and vulnerability of the Indonesian state was exposed. There was growing
realization of the need for foreign economic aid to support reconstruction and development. But the leaders soon learned that obtaining aid involved them in the quagmire of great power politics. Hence,
the basic tenets of post-independence foreign policy became visible:
a commitment to non-alignment and an attachment to the concept
of an independent foreign policy.

B. 1950–57: Struggling for State Survival under Neo-colonialism

Concerned primarily with domestic rehabilitation, policy-makers
tolerated Western economic interests and a tacit international alignment which were antithetical to the rhetoric of an independent and
active foreign policy. 'The resumption of alien, especially Dutch
and resident Chinese, dominance in the economy and the attendant
colonial pattern of Indonesia's international economic relations was
endured in order to promote national recovery' (Leifer, 1983: 27).
An independent policy was interpreted to mean achieving a balance
between the Great Power blocs. Yet the weight of American influence was evident several times, such as when the Natsir government
succumbed to pressure to prevent the sale of rubber to the People's
Republic of China. The intense competition among political parties
encompassed foreign policy issues, especially the settlement of the
West Irian issue. Foreign policy became interlocked with domestic
economic and political requirements and thus nation building was
one of its main objectives. Yet surprisingly, foreign policy was conducted with a strong sense of continuity and restraint, at least across
four coalition parliamentary governments until mid-1953.

From then on, more emphasis was given to foreign policy. Prime
Minister Ali Sastroamijoyo was attracted by new opportunities for
an international role, which included establishment of diplomatic
relations with the Soviet Union, an attempt to solicit international
support on the West Irian issue by attempting to place it on the
agenda of the UN General Assembly and the hosting of the Asian-
African Conference in 1955. In 1956 Indonesia unilaterally withdrew
from The Netherlands-Indonesia Union, thereby freeing itself from
some of the economic and financial obligations assumed as a condition of the transfer of political sovereignty in 1949. This was a
largely symbolic repudiation of colonial links, however. The Dutch
were allowed to continue holding concessions and operating permits

considered not to be in conflict with Indonesia's interests, and provision for foreign capital was included in the five-year economic plan promulgated in late 1956. Substantial government aid also began to be received, coming largely from the Soviet bloc.

In 1957 the West Irian issue served as a catalyst which transformed the pattern of Indonesian politics. The unsatisfactory way in which Indonesia's claim was treated by the UN General Assembly prompted a decisive challenge to Dutch economic interests in Indonesia. Responding to widespread popular agitation, the Indonesian government expropriated all Dutch-owned enterprises, expelled Dutch nationals, attempted to revise the pattern of its international trade, and issued an archipelagic declaration which extended the breadth of territorial waters over which the Republic claimed exclusive sovereignty. These policies aggravated regional dissent, and Western involvement in regional rebellions made it possible for the issue to be represented in terms of state survival and territorial integrity.

C. 1958–65: Confrontation and Sukarno's Domestic Political Requirements

Foreign policy was given new primacy as it became Sukarno's personal domain and served the goals of nation building and regime survival. The aspirations of Indonesian foreign policy – greater independence and security through balanced foreign relationships, anti-imperialism, and self-reliance – were pursued with great verve and vigor. Foreign policy was increasingly utilized as an instrument to keep political opponents off balance and to promote internal solidarity. Conducted as a continuation of the revolutionary struggle, it took on an expressive and heroic quality and confrontation and coercion were often utilized, such as in settlement of the claim to West Irian and campaign (*konfrontasi*) against Malaysia – the two major foreign policy issues of this period. As the domestic economy deteriorated, Sukarno increasingly attempted to project Indonesia's influence beyond the region in order to restructure the international order. Rhetoric about the dangers of foreign economic involvement escalated. In 1959 the first foreign investment law was repealed, British and Malaysian property was expropriated in connection with the campaign against Malaysia, as was some (non-petroleum related) American property in 1965. There was real improvement in relations with Japan, however, which began to provide significant economic assistance. As Sukarno began increasingly to turn to China for diplomatic support and military aid in the context of the Sino-Soviet split, relations with the Soviets deteriorated after 1959 and aid from the Soviet bloc waned.

D. 1966–88: Pragmatism and Economic Dependence

Regime change brought changes in foreign policy, but these were less in aspirations and goals than in priorities and, above all, in idiom and style. For example, although Suharto has exhibited cautious pragmatism, he largely shares Sukarno's strategic perspective, regional ambitions and maritime, archipelagic doctrine. Confrontation with Malaysia was wound down and priority given to obtaining foreign aid for economic development. New Order policies have attempted to maximize Indonesia's influence over the form and terms of aid and investment. Domestic political conflict has subsided, due to the annihilation or repression of opposition groups and consolidation of power in the military, allowing foreign policy to return to its conventional function of advancing the external interests of the state. With this brief sketch of major developments over four historical periods in mind, the anlaysis of outputs will continue using a topical format.

Goals

The main objective of Indonesian foreign policy, unchanged since independence, has been security in the sense of state survival and territorial integrity.

> The experience of upholding independence in both domestic and international dimensions generated an abiding concern for the integrity of a state beset by social diversity and physical fragmentation. That concern was reinforced by a conviction about the country's attractiveness to external interests because of its bountiful natural resources and important strategic location. A common and consistent theme of Indonesia's foreign policy has been the need to overcome an intrinsic vulnerability. (Leifer, 1983: 173)

In order to protect the integrity of the state and overcome intrinsic vulnerability, successive policy-makers have shown an interest in regional autonomy and an aversion towards foreign enclaves, which might be used as stepping stones for interference by outside powers. Thus, maximizing autonomy in the political and military sense has been a supporting, secondary objective.

Paradoxically, as Leifer again points out, 'the continuous sense of vulnerability has been combined with an equally continuous sense of regional entitlement based on pride in revolutionary achievement, size of population, land and maritime dimensions, natural resources and strategic location' (1983: 173). Similarly, Weinstein found in his interviews with foreign policy élites a feeling of superiority *vis-à-vis* Southeast Asian neighbors which rested not only on the country's size and strategic location, but also on a belief that 'Indonesia's more highly developed sense of national identity made the country more politically advanced, and in effect more genuinely independent, than its neighbors' (1976: 196–7). The sense of entitlement has been reflected in the foreign policies of both regimes; Indonesia under both Sukarno and Suharto aspired to regional leadership and, ultimately, to world leadership of the Non-Aligned Movement. But these aspirations have seldom motivated attempts at territorial aggrandizement.

Analysis of the three occasions when Indonesia has taken action outside its internationally recognized borders does not necessarily lend support to the idea that its policy has been inherently expansionist. Harold Crouch argues that each of the three occasions – the West Irian campaign in the early 1960s, the *konfrontasi* campaign against Malaysia launched in 1963, and the invasion of East Timor in 1975 – were 'more or less rational responses to particular circumstances', had definite immediate objectives, and the means chosen, 'although sometimes proving ineffective in practice, were not obviously inappropriate' (1986: 2). (Note the consistency between this view and Emmerson's, above, on the rationality of Sukarno's policies and the continuity in international outlook and foreign policy between regimes.)

Nevertheless, these three occasions demonstrated that Indonesia was willing to take military action across its borders when it felt its own security was potentially endangered, for instance, fearing the rise of a Communist-led regime in East Timor. More generally, when any of the other principles of Indonesian foreign policy come into conflict with military perceptions of national security vulnerability, actions to achieve security take precedence.

In weighing the likelihood of Indonesian military action outside its borders, several constraints need to be emphasized. The growth of Indonesia's military capacity during the early 1980s has slowed considerably and will most likely not continue at the same rate for the foreseeable future. As noted above, earlier propitious economic circumstances made both the arms-purchasing and the growth in size possible. Second, 63 of the army's 82 infantry battalions (77 per cent) are part of the territorial structure and concerned primarily with internal security and political management. 'These forces would not be easily available for use in a conventional external war . . . most importantly because their territorial functions are vital for the maintenance of internal political stability and the authority of the government' (Crouch, 1986: 7). The invasion of East Timor demonstrated some restraining influence of economic and military dependency; reportedly Suharto's concern over maintaining United States military assistance delayed the invasion until the day after he met with President Gerald Ford and Secretary Henry Kissinger (Bonner, 1988, II: 85). The subsequent attempt to seal off the province from the outside world has revealed policy-makers' sensitivity to maintaining their legitimacy and image in the world community.

Indonesian policy-makers have always contended that the principles guiding their management of foreign affairs are independence or anti-colonialism and anti-imperialism, non-alignment, and everlasting peace. They espoused a 'free and active' foreign policy. 'Active' emphasized that Indonesia would show concern or take a position on international problems, including those involving more powerful nations. Said differently, they would not act in a passive or reactive manner, but rather take initiatives to solve international problems together with other nations. Thus, Sukarno was a founder of the Non-Aligned Movement, and the New Order rejoined the United Nations, joined OPEC, and played a key role in founding ASEAN.

Closely related is the objective of nation-building in the sense of promoting and strengthening national integration and national identity. Sukarno and many 1928 and 1945 generation leaders felt that Indonesia was afflicted by an inferiority complex spawned by the trauma of colonialism. The independent-and-active foreign policy was viewed as a means of regaining self confidence. Sukarno often seemed obsessed with a need to prove that Indonesians were the equal of Westerners. 'When he sat with Kennedy or told the United States to go to hell with its aid', declared one leader, 'it made us feel proud that we were independent enough to tell the United States to go to hell. The Filipinos or Malaysians would never dare to do that' (cited in Weinstein, 1976: 358).

Other objectives have played a role as well. Regime maintenance or survival has been an abiding concern, and both Sukarno and

Suharto equated regime survival with state survival. Under both leaders, foreign scapegoats have been used to explain Indonesia's inability to solve its problems. The anti-Western campaigns of Sukarno constituted 'a way in which a basically conservative élite could provide the illusion of revolutionary progress, without risking its own position in a real internal revolution'. Similarly the Suharto government, by its warnings about international Communist subversion and its heavy reliance on foreign aid, 'has been able both to avoid the kinds of reforms that might endanger its own existence and to compensate for its inability to mobilize domestic resources for development' (Weinstein, 1976: 34). Under both regimes, development aid requested ostensibly for state survival was frequently diverted to much narrower political purposes.

The acquisition of foreign resources for economic development has also been an ongoing objective of Indonesian foreign policy. Among policy élites the belief has persisted that their country can develop economically only with foreign assistance. Aid was necessary for development, and development was a means of giving substance to independence. Sukarno never abandoned the search for foreign aid, even if he did put independence first. Aid has been justified on the ground that it will contribute to the achievement of genuine independence in the long run by providing the means that enable the country to transform its economy and achieve self-sustaining economic growth. During the 1954–65 period when foreign economic involvement came increasingly under attack, Indonesian policy-makers, including Sukarno, were never willing to do without it. Their development strategy emphasized basic and heavy industrialization (dependent on foreign capital and technology), agricultural self-sufficiency, and overcoming inflation through an increase in production, rather than through monetary measures. Then, beginning in 1966, the New Order leaders inaugurated policies which emphasized stringent monetary policy aimed at stabilization, heavy reliance on foreign loans, and an eager welcome to foreign investment (Weinstein, 1976: 206–31).

At the same time, the foreign policy élite have harbored a deep ambivalence about foreign aid since the beginning of the Republic. Suspicion of foreign aid and concern about the dangers of dependence have transcended ideological and political boundaries. The development strategy of the New Order, which has attempted to achieve and maintain economic stability through very strong measures of monetary restraint, has obtained huge foreign credits (debts) and has given a relatively free hand to foreign investors, policy-makers have become increasingly fearful for their independence. This strategy has been widely assailed in Indonesia on the grounds that it has been imposed by Indonesia's creditors and better serves the interests of foreigners and a tiny minority of 'bureaucratic capitalists' than those of the majority of impoverished Indonesians (Weinstein, 1976: 242–87).

Like other ASEAN regimes, the New Order has attempted to maximize its ability to participate in the international economic system and to minimize its dependence. Throughout the 1970s, diversification was mentioned as a goal of trade policy, as a means of controlling the political influence of any one economic partner. But the policy intended to achieve restructuring in trade relations has been relatively ineffective. 'Indonesia is the only country to show changes contrary to diversification: concentration on the single largest partner is higher in 1979 than in 1967, and overall diversification is less in 1979. . . . Japan has remained by far the major trade partner. . . .' (Crone, 1983: 88).

The policy record on investment showed a similar pattern. Overall, the industrialization program has encouraged a continuous flow of foreign investment, so the share of foreign capital was relatively high – estimated at 56 per cent of total private investment in 1979. However, the investment climate has not been positive since 1975, resulting in reduced inflows of investment capital. 'Official estimates of new foreign investment in Indonesia show a decline from US$ 2.9 billion in 1983, to US$ 852 million in 1984, and US$ 699 million in 1985' (Hainsworth, 1987: 174). Because of the need to increase the flow, the policy of diversification of sources was secondary and commitment to it low.

Indonesia's current large and worsening indebtedness has brought pressure 'to reform the various institutional arrangements that inhibit efficient production and trade, and facilitate corruption and the bureaucratic abuse of authority'. Yet, paradoxically, this has also given it 'something of an inside track and a special leverage with these institutions, especially in view of what is seen to be its consistently blue-chip rating in debt servicing and loan repayment' (Hainsworth, 1987: 174, 173).

About 1980 the New Order began to seek a higher profile in world affairs, commensurate with its size and strategic location. It attempted to regain a leadership role in the Non-Aligned Movement and became a leading advocate of a New World Order in politics,

economics and communications. Policy-makers were especially concerned with regional stability, because of the perceived linkage with
national and internal security. The New Order sought to play a
leadership role in ASEAN. Policy-makers have repeatedly supported
ASEAN's concept of a Zone of Peace, Freedom, and Neutrality
(ZOPFAN). It launched a 'dual track' diplomacy on the Cambodian
conflict, holding direct, bilateral talks with Vietnam in addition to
generally supporting ASEAN's positions. The most visible achievement of this approach to date was a series of Jakarta Informal
Meetings beginning in July 1988 when, for the first time, high level
representatives of all conflicting Cambodian factions, ASEAN, Vietnam and Laos met for direct talks. In the third ASEAN summit in
1987, Indonesia's policy-makers stood firm against a proposal of joint
support for American bases in the Philippines. (In light of Soviet
use of bases in Vietnam, however, they regarded the American
bases as strategically acceptable in the short term.) They proposed a
controversial draft treaty for the establishment of a Nuclear Weapon-
Free Zone (NWFZ). On economic matters, Indonesia softened its
restrictions on imports from other members of ASEAN. But this
issue has been a thorny one because it juxtaposes the Foreign Ministry and economic technocrats against the protectionists/national-
ists/engineers.

In its policies towards the Middle East and Africa, the New Order
has been more pragmatic than the Old, due in part to its close
economic relations with Western countries, most of whom were
strong supporters of Israel. In the Arab-Israeli War in 1967, Indonesia avoided taking sides, causing some Muslim countries to accuse it
of being pro-Israel. After failing to attract much Arab economic
assistance or investment capital, nor gaining desired access to Arab
markets, the New Order launched an aggressive diplomatic drive to
improve relations especially with fellow OPEC members. It applied
for and received special status (enjoying all the rights of a regular
member even though the constitution establishes a secular, not
Islamic, state) in the Organization of the Islamic Conference, gave
strong but mainly rhetorical support to the Palestine Liberation
Organization, and initiated the commemoration of the 1955 Bandung
Conference which conceived the Non-Aligned Movement.

Since about 1984 the New Order has sought to improve relations
with Communist countries, primarily in order to diversify its trade
relations. But these efforts had the political purpose of reminding
Western donors that the New Order's generally pro-Western stance

in foreign policy issues should not be taken for granted and partially depended on continuing and increasing amounts of economic assistance.

CONCLUSION

This analysis of foreign policy focusing on the past two decades of Suharto's New Order poses a challenge to any facile or deterministic theorizing. Economic growth through integration with the international capitalist system has been, perhaps, the most critical factor in the maintenance of the regime. Yet the past few years have shown unexpected resilience in surviving an economic slowdown. The patterns of aid, debt, trade and investment suggest economic dependence is worsening, yet without a commensurate decline in policy autonomy, due to such factors as the New Order's good credit rating among donors, its ability to balance one off against another, and its tight control over domestic opposition. 'Where Sukarno struggled for self-reliance without the West, Suharto has tried to achieve it by using the West' (Emmerson, 1987–88: 382). The New Order has proven to be a skillful manager of its external environment. Moreover, aspirations and goals of foreign policy have been relatively constant since Independence.

The regime and its policies may be less impervious to changes from its domestic environment. Communal divisions, the privileged economic position of the Indonesian Chinese, the monopolistic position of first family businesses and a succession crisis are all factors that have potential, in conjunction with behind-the-scenes maneuvers of military officers, for dividing the military. This would likely result in a change of regime and less dependence on the West.

BIBLIOGRAPHY

Bonner, Raymond (1988), 'A Reporter at Large: The New Order', *The New Yorker*, 6 June (Part I), pp. 45–79, and 13 June (Part II), pp. 72–91.

Crouch, Harold (1984), *Domestic Political Structures and Regional Economic Co-operation* (Singapore: ISEAS).

Crouch, Harold (1986), 'Security Concerns Posed by Indonesia's Armed Forces', *Indonesia Issues*, No. 3, November.

Crone, Donald K. (1983), *The ASEAN States: Coping with Dependence* (New York: Praeger).

Emmerson, Donald K. (1986), 'Continuity and Rationality in Indonesian Foreign Policy: A Reappraisal', pp. 88–109 in Karl D. Jackson, *et al.* (eds), *ASEAN in Regional and Global Context* (Berkeley: University of California Institute of East Asian Studies).

Emmerson, Donald K. (1987–88), 'Invisible Indonesia', *Foreign Affairs* (Winter), pp. 368–87.

Hainsworth, Geoffrey B. (1987), 'Indonesia's Economic Downswing and Political Reforms', *Current History*, April, pp. 172–82.

Indonesia Reports (1987), '100 Indonesian Billionaires: What and Who Are They?' Business and Economy Supplement, No. 20 (February), No. 21 (June); 'How They Became Very Rich', No. 23 (October) and No. 24 (November) 1987, and concluding in No. 25 (August) 1988.

King, Dwight Y. (1987), 'Human Rights Practices and the Indonesian Middle Class', *Bulletin of Concerned Asian Scholars* 19, No. 1, pp. 4–13.

Leifer, Michael (1983), *Indonesia's Foreign Policy* (London: Allen & Unwin).

Liddle, R. William (1985), 'Suharto's Indonesia', *Pacific Affairs* 58 (Spring), pp. 68–90.

MacDougall, John A. (1986), 'Military Penetration of the Indonesian Government', *Indonesia Reports* No. 14, March.

Nishihara, Masashi (1976), *The Japanese and Sukarno's Indonesia, Tokyo–Jakarta Relations 1951–1966* (Honolulu: University Press of Hawaii).

Robison, Richard (1986), *Indonesia: The Rise of Capital* (North Sydney: Allen & Unwin).

Sudarsono, Juwono (1985), 'Global Political Trends: An Overview', *Indonesia Quarterly* 13, pp. 169–75.

Thoolen, Hans (ed.) (1987), *Indonesia and the Rule of Law* (London: Frances Pinter).

Tilman, Robert O. (1987), *Southeast Asia and the Enemy Beyond* (Boulder: Westview).

van der Kroef, Justus M. (1986), ' "Normalizing" Relations with China', *Asian Survey* 26, No. 8, pp. 909–34.

Weinstein, Franklin B. (1976), *Indonesian Foreign Policy and the Dilemma of Dependence* (Ithaca: Cornell University).

World Bank (1987), *World Development Report* (New York: Oxford University Press).

7 The Foreign Policy of Malaysia[1]
Richard Stubbs

No country, certainly no Third World country, can stand apart from the changing currents of the international economic and political systems, and Malaysia – with a relatively small population of about 17 million and a predominantly export-oriented economy – is clearly no exception. As a result of this and the idiosyncratic initiatives of individual leaders Chee, 1974; Ott, 1972; Tilman, 1969) the foreign policy of Malaya and Malaysia, as it became known in 1963, has undergone a number of twists and turns. Yet at the same time there has always been an underlying consistency to the country's foreign policy arising out of the need to serve the goals of national integration and national welfare in order to mitigate the problems produced by the fundamental divisions within Malaysian society.

MALAYSIAN SOCIETY AND THE STATE: ORIENTATION AND OBJECTIVES

During the 80 years or so of British colonial rule prior to independence in 1957 Malaya underwent considerable change. Two related aspects of this metamorphosis are significant for this study. First, the British sponsored the development of an export economy based on two commodities: natural rubber and tin. Second, to provide the manpower to fuel the rapid expansion of the rubber and tin industries, the colonial administration encouraged the immigration of Chinese and Indian labor. These policies had major consequences for Malayan society. By the time of independence the Malayan economy was firmly integrated into the international market economy with fully three-quarters of the labor force employed in the export enclave (Pauw and Fei, 1973). The health of the country's economy was, therefore, tied closely to the fluctuating international prices of rubber and tin. Moreover, Malaya had become a racially divided society. The ethnic distribution of the population has changed somewhat over the years with the formation of Malaysia in

1963 – when Sabah, Sarawak and Singapore were added to the Federation of Malaya – and the expulsion of Singapore in 1965; however, by the mid-1980s approximately 55 per cent of the population were Malay, 34 per cent Chinese, 10 per cent Indian and 1 per cent 'other' (Milne and Mauzy, 1986: 66). These were divisions which were manifested in language, religion and culture. This combination of circumstances has meant that the question of the balance of power and the allocation of rights, resources and privileges among the various ethnic communities has remained very much to the fore in Malaysian politics.

These consequences of colonial rule became key factors in the 'bargain' between the Malays and the non-Malays which was struck on the eve of independence and which was designed to accommodate ethnic ambitions, ward off communal conflict and provide the basis for national integration. The explicit aspects of the bargain, which assigned different rights to the Malay and non-Malay communities, were built into the new Constitution (Milne and Mauzy, 1980: 36–43). The implicit aspects of the bargain, which included the recognition that the Malays as the indigenous people of the peninsula and the community with the largest single block of voters would maintain political power while the non-Malays – primarily the Chinese – were to continue to play the leading role in the economy, underpinned routine relations among the ethnic communities. The bargain and its implementation underscored a central feature of Malaysian politics: the reciprocal nature of the relationship between the avoidance of open ethnic violence and national integration on the one hand, and economic development and national welfare on the other. Clearly minimum levels of ethnic harmony and national unity were necessary to achieve economic progress, yet both in turn were dependent upon growth in the Western-capitalist sector of the economy so as to allow the material aspirations of all communities to be met.

This relationship became even more self-evident after communal riots occurred in May 1969 following a divisive election campaign. Ethnic frustrations, especially those of the Malays, threatened to undermine the country's precarious social and political stability. As a result the bargain was reworked in order to reinforce Malay control of the political realm and to allow Malays greater participation in the modern sector of the economy. But, just as importantly, the necessity of expanding the economy so as to create opportunities commensurate with all communities' expectations continued.

National integration and national welfare remained inextricably intertwined.

The responsibility for designing and implementing policies which perpetuated the bargain, in both its original and revised form, fell to the newly emerging Malaysian state. The necessity of mobilizing resources to mount an effective counter-insurgency campaign during the guerrilla war of 1948 to 1960, and the rise of the Alliance Party as a strong central political institution, resulted in the state playing an increasingly key role in Malaysian society. Indeed, the state steadily expanded its scope, capacity and power. In particular the administrative aspects of the state took on a central role in decision-making and in implementing policy. In terms of foreign policy, as traditionally defined, the original influence of the Prime Minister, Tunku Abdul Rahman, and the Foreign Ministry's permanent secretary, Tan Sri Ghazali Shafie, gave way to a greater bureaucratization of the decision-making process (Saravanamuttu, 1983: 16–20). Prime ministers have remained influential (clearly the current Prime Minister, Datuk Sri Dr. Mahathir Mohamad, has had much to say on foreign policy issues); however, as the Foreign Ministry has expanded, officials have played an increasingly important role. As one Malaysian official has noted, foreign policy decision-making in Malaysia is 'tilted in favour of bureaucrats' (Zakaria, 1986: 196). In terms of foreign economic policy, the freedom of the state, and especially the bureaucracy, to act as it wishes has not been so evident. Societal interests have at times been able to exert some influence. This was most evident during the 1970s as the government sought to respond to Malay nationalists' calls for a greater role for Malays in the economy. More recently, however, as the economy has encountered difficulties, the bureaucrats have regained some of their lost autonomy.

The main goals of any state are to maintain order within the country's boundaries, to structure relations among the people and to maneuver within the international system so as to defend the country's territory and population and expand the economy (Skocpol, 1985: 7–8). These goals coincide to a high degree with the implicit aims of the bargain between Malays and non-Malays. Two main sets of objectives have thus emerged for the Malaysian state. The first set of objectives is to maintain national security, and foster national integration by guarding against any external attack and, just as importantly, by guarding against any threat which might induce overt ethnic conflict and the disintegration of society. The second set of objectives is to ensure economic growth and the advancement of national welfare through resource development and export-oriented industrialization. These two sets of interrelated objectives have provided the key imperatives in the making and implementation of Malaysia's foreign policy.

SECURITY AND NATIONAL INTEGRATION: STRATEGIES AND ACTIONS

Within Malaysia threats to the country's external and internal security have been perceived to come from three sources. First, there is the possibility of attacks originating from within East or Southeast Asia, perhaps even sponsored by powers external to the region. Second, there is the possibility of a resurgence of the Malayan Communist Party (MCP) whose support has traditionally come from disgruntled members of the Chinese community. The MCP guerrilla army had posed a major threat during the initial years of the Malayan Emergency, and while it was defeated (Stubbs, 1989), the Communists have generally been perceived to be a latent, and somewhat unpredictable, force threatening the stability of the peninsula. And, third, there is the possibility of frustrations within the Malay community boiling over and precipitating a recurrence of the ethnic violence of May 1969. Gearing the country's foreign policy to limiting such threats has always been a prime preoccupation of the Malaysian state.

In the years directly after independence Malaysia looked to Britain to maintain its security. The strategy of relying on the Anglo-Malayan Defence Agreement signed in 1957 was dictated by necessity. With Britain and other Commonwealth countries having provided the bulk of government troops during the Emergency, Malaysia's own military complement was relatively low. However, reliance on the British was also a policy which fitted into the general pro-Western ethos which pervaded the Malaysian state and the pro-British stance of Prime Minister Tunku Abdul Rahman. The anti-Communist legacy of the Emergency was still a prime determinant of Malaysian foreign policy.

The British connection proved valuable during the period of confrontation with Indonesia from 1963 to 1966, yet it also showed the limitations of such dependence. Initially *konfrontasi* reinforced Malaysian anti-Communist attitudes. Sukarno's regime was seen not only as the sponsor of Communist guerrillas in Sarawak but also as being in league with both the Chinese government, the supporters of the MCP during the Emergency, and the North Vietnamese, the major threat to regional stability. The Malaysian government, therefore, felt comfortable in invoking the Anglo-Malayan Defence Agreement and having British and Commonwealth troops return to defend Malaysian territory. Malaysia also publicly supported the United States' policy on Vietnam, most notably its bombing of North Vietnam. But there was a price to pay. Reliance on the British meant that Malaysian security and stability were left to the whims of British defense policy planners. And Indonesia's diplomatic offensive against Malaysia was more successful than its military offensive; Malaysia was excluded from a number of Third World forums, including the Non-Aligned Movement.

The end of *konfrontasi* in August 1966 and the replacement of Sukarno by the anti-Communist regime of General Suharto, saw the beginnings of a reassessment of Malaysia's foreign policy. Britain's announced intention to reduce its defense commitments east of Suez led to a recognition by some within the Malaysian state that the international environment was changing and that Malaysia's foreign policy would have to change with it so as to safeguard the country's security and allow for national integration. Despite the negotiation during the late 1960s of a five-power defense agreement among Malaysia, Singapore, Britain, Australia and New Zealand, which was designed to replace the Anglo-Malayan Defence Agreement, an increasing number within the state thought it inadvisable to rely too heavily on the new arrangement for any long-term commitment to the defense of Malaysia's territorial integrity. Nor after President Nixon's Guam speech in July 1969, in which he announced the beginning of the US withdrawal from Vietnam, could the US be viewed as a reliable ally. The debate within the state over the future direction of foreign policy reached a milestone when, in 1970, Tunku Abdul Rahman, who had championed the traditional British-oriented approach, resigned as Prime Minister in the wake of the 1969 riots. The new Prime Minister, Tun Razak, was prepared to sanction a new direction for the country's foreign policy.

Out of the search for a new foreign policy approach which would help maintain territorial security and stable ethnic relations two related strategies emerged. The first was tied to an increased interest in using a regional organization to provide a forum to resolve regional problems and to limit the likelihood of external intervention. The second policy arose out of a growing sense within Malaysia that the country needed to diversify its diplomatic relations and to encourage external powers to agree to guarantee the neutralization of Southeast Asia.

Malaysia and ASEAN

The regional organization which eventually developed into the keystone of Malaysia's foreign policy was the Association of Southeast Asian Nations (ASEAN). ASEAN's importance increased with the withdrawal of US combat forces from Vietnam in 1973 and the fall of the Saigon government in 1975. For Malaysia the threat was twofold. First, there was the fear that the Communist victory could be used by the MCP as propaganda to show that communism was on the march. Second, officials in the Malaysian Security Forces expressed unease that Vietnam's huge arsenal of discarded American weapons might be used to aid other Communist movements in the region such as the MCP (Stubbs, 1977). The developments in Indo-China prompted the ASEAN states to convene the first heads of government meeting in Bali in February 1976. The Summit produced a Treaty of Amity and Co-operation and a Declaration of ASEAN Concord which paved the way for greater co-operation among ASEAN members. This interest in co-operation was further reinforced by Vietnam's invasion and occupation of Cambodia in late 1978.

For Malaysia the emergence of ASEAN as an effective regional organization was a major boon. The various regional territorial threats to Malaysia's security and ethnic harmony that flow from Malaysia sharing a border with each of the other ASEAN members have been dealt with through the many official and *ad hoc* arrangements within the Association which have emerged to handle such problems (Zakaria, 1986; Sopiee, 1986). As a result relations with each of the five other members of ASEAN have remained relatively cordial. First, ASEAN has clearly helped to defuse hostility generated between Malaysia and Indonesia during the period of *konfrontasi*. Indeed, Malaysia and Indonesia now enjoy extensive administrative, political and military contacts at all levels. Moreover, because the two countries share a common language, ethnic origin and religion and have similar security concerns, Indonesia has become Malaysia's closest ally.

Second, membership in ASEAN has encouraged Malaysia to collaborate rather than fight with Thailand over the problems that plague their common border – most notably the activities of the Thai-Muslims and the MCP. The Malaysian government succeeded in persuading the Thais that it does not officially support the Malay-Muslims of Southern Thailand despite the pronouncements of the leaders of PAS (the Malay-Arabic acronym for Partai Islam Se-Malaysia, the main Malay opposition party) and the Muslim Students' Union. Traditionally the Malaysian government has feared that any expression of support for the Malay-Muslims would only encourage Thai sympathy for the MCP units based along its southern border (Omar, 1984: 246). Prior to 1976 the Thai army had proved at times to be very unco-operative in the Malaysian government's attempts to deal with the remnants of the MCP; however, since 1977 the armed forces of the two countries have engaged in combined military operations with some success. Indeed, the mass surrenders in recent years suggest that there are now less than 1000 MCP guerrillas operating in the border region. Moreover, the negotiation in 1977 of a revised and more detailed agreement covering the work of the Thai-Malaysian General Border Committee has led to the committee being instrumental in defusing a number of potentially inflammatory border incidents which could have been exploited by the Communists. For example, recently there has been a good deal of friction over Malaysia's implementation of a 200-mile exclusive economic zone and the subsequent arrest of Thai trawlers. That piracy has similarly preoccupied Malaysians while the Thais have been irked by the incursion into Thai territory of a border fence being constructed by the Malaysians for security purposes.

Third, Malaysia has worked through ASEAN to iron out its problems with the Philippines over Sabah. The Philippine claim to Sabah was set aside at the Summit of 1976 when President Marcos took the opportunity to 'eliminate one of the burdens of ASEAN' (Sopiee, 1986: 228). Despite this turn of events the Sabah issue has lingered on in a different form. There remain strong links between the Muslim community in Sabah and the Muslim groups in Mindanao fighting the Philippine government. However, the endeavor by both countries to cultivate ASEAN's co-operative spirit has kept any controversy that has arisen within bounds, despite a resurgence of the Sabah claim in the Philippine Congress since 1986.

Fourth, the secession from Malaysia of Singapore, with its predominantly Chinese population, left a residue of ill feeling which could have occasioned some major squabbles endangering Malaysia's fragile racial equilibrium. Yet the many irritants that have arisen over the years (a recent example being the official visit to Singapore in November 1986 of President Chaim Herzog of Israel which caused indignation in Muslim Malaysia) have generally been dealt with in an amicable rather than an antagonistic fashion. This has been especially noticeable since Malaysia's and Singapore's common membership in ASEAN has become so important to them both. Finally, it seems likely that the incorporation of Brunei into ASEAN will allow for measured discussions of how to deal with the Limbang Valley, Sarawak territory which cuts Brunei in two.

Neutralization

The policy of seeking a neutralized Southeast Asia as a means of increasing Malaysia's security and supporting the country's attempts at creating a sense of national unity and national purpose began to gain currency in the late 1960s. Former Foreign Minister Tun Ismail initiated the discussion in 1968 with his 'Peace Plan' which called for 'the neutralization of Southeast Asia . . . guaranteed by the big-powers' (Saravanamuttu, 1983: 74). Pressure to discard the links with Britain, which Malaysia had depended on quite heavily, had been mounting for some time. There was a growing view within the administration and the Alliance Party that Malaysia should jettison what the current Prime Minister, Dr Mahathir Mohamad, called the 'apron-string complex' (Mahathir, 1971: 33). This argument was buttressed by the fact that, in order to establish its Third-World credentials, Malaysia needed to distance itself from its former colonizers and join with others in staking out a middle ground between the two major power blocs. Hence, starting in 1970, the new Prime Minister, Tun Razak, urged on by Tun Ismail, began searching for ways of bringing about a neutral Southeast Asia (Lau, 1971: 27).

Some initial success was gained in November 1971 when Malaysia was able to persuade the other members of ASEAN to endorse a revised form of the neutralization policy. The Kuala Lumpur Declaration stated that the ASEAN countries would try to 'secure the recognition of, and respect for, Southeast Asia as a Zone of Peace, Freedom and Neutrality free from any form or manner of interference by outside powers' – or ZOPFAN as it became known by its acronym (Saravanamuttu, 1983: 96). Recognizing that it would be difficult to get the support of declared enemies, Tun Razak also opened up contacts with the People's Republic of China. In spite of opposition from the pro-Taiwan members of the Malaysian Chinese Association, the senior Malaysian-Chinese representatives in the coalition government, the relationship developed to such a level that in May 1974 Tun Razak visited China. Diplomatic relations were established and Premier Zhou Enlai stated his support for the idea of a zone of peace and neutrality in Southeast Asia. But the initiative did not produce a formal guarantee from the Chinese nor, despite Malaysia having developed trade relations with the USSR and being on excellent terms with the US government, was one forthcoming from either of the two superpowers. Indeed, notwithstanding the high hopes expressed at the Summit of 1976, the ASEAN governments have faced too many obstacles for ZOPFAN to be implemented as originally envisaged (Saravanamuttu, 1984a).

However, ZOPFAN remains an ideal to which ASEAN members have repeatedly referred in communiqués. An important recent attempt to inject a new impetus into the ZOPFAN approach has been the interest expressed by the Malaysian government in making Southeast Asia a nuclear weapons-free zone. The idea, prompted by the conclusion of the South Pacific Nuclear Free Zone and first raised at the July 1984 meeting of ASEAN Foreign Ministers, has been explored by the Working Group on ZOPFAN and was discussed further at the ASEAN Manila Summit in December 1987 (Muthiah, 1987; FEER, 24 December 1987: 8–9). However, while Indonesia has also advocated such a policy, the other members of ASEAN are known to have reservations, as does the US. It may be, as with ZOPFAN, that the proposal to establish a nuclear weapons-free zone in Southeast Asia will be spoken of favorably as a principle but not acted upon.

Although Malaysia's ZOPFAN initiative has not received the support of the major powers nor been fully implemented, its value should not be underestimated. It provided an important context for Malaysian, and to some extent ASEAN, thinking on the country's and the region's place in international politics. The idea of neutralization, or 'neutralism' (Saravanamuttu, 1983: 99), was extended to embrace the concept of maintaining a policy of 'equidistance' in relations with the major powers. This has proven to be a difficult maneuver. In any case, Malaysia has built on the fact that it was the first ASEAN country to establish diplomatic ties with China. Moreover, despite a number of irritants, including the fact that Chinese leaders, most notably Vice-Premier Deng Xiaoping in 1978, have expressed some support for the MCP (Lee, 1981) and that the

Chinese-sponsored Voice of the Malayan Revolution was broadcast-ing Communist propaganda into the peninsula, Malaysia has main-tained fairly good links – reaffirmed by Mahathir's visit in 1985 – with a country that is still considered within Malaysia as a potential adversary in the long term. Trade and diplomatic relations, first developed in the late 1960s, have also been continued with the USSR and the East European countries. At the same time relations with the US have remained cordial. Indeed, in terms of regional security the two countries have moved closer together during the 1980s as Malaysia has opted to buy more military equipment from the US as well as having Malaysian forces engage in regular exercises with US forces (Muthiah, 1986: 7–10). Closer Malaysia-US ties have offset the decided shift away from Britain which was accelerated during the early 1980s under Prime Minister Dr. Mahathir Mohamad. While better relations were established in 1983, following discussions between Mahathir and British Prime Minister Margaret Thatcher, the old relationship is now long dead.

The policy of neutralization also embraced the idea of maximizing international contacts so as to enable Malaysia to elicit the support of world public opinion should an international or regional crisis threaten to spill over into Malaysian territory. In particular Malaysia has become very active in Islamic organizations. Increased links to the Islamic world were initiated under Tunku Abdul Rahman; continued under Tun Razak, who hosted the Fifth Islamic Foreign Ministers' Conference in Kuala Lumpur in 1974; and given great emphasis by Dr. Mahathir. Mahathir clearly sees such a policy as a means of winning over to the government's side those Malays who are associated with Islamic revivalism and heading off any threat to the solidarity and pivotal position of the United Malays National Organization, the Malay party which dominates the governing coalition. Mahathir has attended Islamic Conference Organization summit meetings and has been careful to maintain good relations with all the Muslim countries of the Middle East including Iran, with whom Malaysia signed a special trade agreement in 1986, and Iraq. Other ways in which Malaysia has emphasized its ties to the wider Islamic community have been through hosting, in May 1983, the UN-sponsored International Conference on Palestine for Asia and the Pacific Region and the establishment of the International Islamic University which will be open to Muslim students from around the world.

Malaysia has also become a major participant in the Non-Aligned

Movement. A Malaysian delegation first attended a Non-Aligned Nations conference in 1970 and since then Malaysia has sought an increased role in the affairs of the Movement. With his elevation to the prime ministership in 1981 Mahathir became especially active in this area. He has acted as a liaison between the Islamic Conference Organization and the Non-Aligned Movement; put forward the argument that Antarctica, like the ocean floor, should be considered part of the international commons; encouraged South-South trade; and gained Third-World support for his anti-drug campaign. His appointment in 1986 as chairman of the steering committee to set up the South Commission, now chaired by the former President of Tanzania, Julius Nyerere, is indicative of the position Malaysia has gained within the Third World.

Mahathir has ranked, in order of their importance to Malaysian foreign policy, first, ASEAN, second, the Islamic Conference Organization, third, the Non-Aligned Movement and, finally, the Commonwealth. His initial distrust of the Commonwealth appears to have been largely because of its perceived dominance by Britain. However, Mahathir attended the Commonwealth Heads of Government Meeting in Vancouver in October 1987 and hosted the 1989 meeting in Kuala Lumpur. Moreover, Malaysia has been a leader in regional Commonwealth meetings and has sought stronger ties with the small Commonwealth countries of the Pacific such as Tonga, Fiji and Western Samoa.

The Cambodian Crisis

Of course, the acid test for Malaysia's two-pronged approach to maintaining territorial security and promoting national integration – regionalism and neutralization – came with Vietnam's 1978 invasion of Cambodia and its immediate aftermath. Malaysia was affected in two ways. First, the movement of Vietnamese troops into Cambodia threatened the political stability of neighboring Thailand and brought Communist forces that much closer to Malaysian soil. Second, the steady trickle of refugees from Vietnam arriving along Malaysia's east coast following the Communist victory in 1975, became a flood in 1979 as these 'boat people' tried to escape the increasingly difficult conditions in their homeland. In the first six months of 1979 alone Malaysia had to deal with nearly 120 000 new arrivals. By mid-1979 Malaysia's main refugee camp on Pulau Bidong, which was originally built to accommodate 12 000 people, housed over 25 000. While

Malaysia has been able to resettle in other countries a large proportion of these refugees, their numbers and the fact that 70 to 80 per cent of them were ethnic Chinese created ethnic tensions, especially along the predominantly Malay east coast, and placed the government in a difficult position (Stubbs, 1980).

Regionalism and the value of ASEAN have clearly been demonstrated since 1979. Any sense of isolation or powerlessness which Malaysia might have felt were dispelled as the ASEAN states cooperated to produce a clearly delineated policy (Sopiee, 1986: 223–4). Malaysia has essentially rallied to Thailand as the member most directly threatened and has concurred in the general call for the withdrawal of Vietnamese troops and the establishment of a free, neutral, independent and democratic Cambodia guaranteed by an international agreement (Mahbubani, 1983/84). Malaysia has played its role in organizing ASEAN's main allies – the US, China, Australia, New Zealand, the EC, Japan and Canada – so as to isolate Vietnam both politically and eocnomically and to provide support for the coalition of Khmer resistance forces. Moreover, Malaysia has responded to the perceived threat posed by the Vietnamese by increased spending on its armed forces. The government's policy of maintaining good relations with a large number of countries has also borne fruit in that it has contributed to Vietnam's inability to gain any significant measure of support either in the United Nations or in the Non-Aligned Movement. Generally the diplomatic actions of Malaysia, in conjunction with the other ASEAN members, have been major factors in shaping world public opinion regarding the Cambodian conflict.

But the Cambodian crisis has also highlighted divisions within ASEAN over which country poses the greatest long-term threat to the region. Malaysia and Indonesia tend to distrust the Chinese as much as, if not more than, they distrust the Vietnamese and their Soviet sponsors. Malaysia is particularly concerned that China looks to Southeast Asia as its sphere of influence; that China will continue to insist on party-to-party support for the MCP; and that China's sheer size, and cultural and economic links to the Chinese ethnic community in Malaysia could have detrimental domestic consequences should tensions rise between Malays and Chinese (Muthiah, 1986: 17; Tilman, 1984: 35). By contrast Malaysia's long-term view of Vietnam tends to be that, although it does present a threat to the stability of the region, a reasonable relationship can be established. Certainly the Malaysian government has expressed a willingness to talk to Vietnam should the Vietnamese wish to open up a dialogue with ASEAN (FBIS, IV, 18 February 1987). Moreover, there is a view in Malaysia that Vietnam will eventually become less dependent on the Soviet Union (Tilman, 1984: 10–11).

The aftermath of Vietnam's invasion of Cambodia also under-scores the dilemmas which have always been evident in Malaysia's neutralization policy. Despite adherence to the ideal of limiting the involvement of the major powers in the region which was contained in the Kuala Lumpur Declaration on ZOPFAN, Malaysia has had to accept that the Chinese have played, and are likely to continue to play, an important role in containing Vietnamese expansionism. Further, given the increased ability of the Soviets to project their military presence in the region through the use of the air base at Da Nang and the naval base at Cam Ranh Bay, a continued role for the US is inevitable, and from the Malaysian point of view probably necessary in order to balance Soviet and Chinese influence. For example, Malaysia looks favorably on a greater role for the US in Thailand as a way of ensuring that the Thai government does not become too dependent on China. In other words, while adhering to its policy of neutrality and equidistance, Malaysia, as it has done in the past, continues to prefer to have closer ties to the Western powers than to the USSR or China.

Malaysia has also had some success in dealing with the refugee problem. The government's world-wide contacts have eased the resettlement of a large number of refugees in over 20 countries around the world. Equally, world public opinion has forced Vietnam to curb the outflow of refugees so that their numbers have gradually diminished. Yet the Malaysian government is still critical of the Vietnamese for not doing more to prevent its citizens from leaving the country. Boat people continue to land on Malaysia's coast and with only Australia, Canada and the US now accepting them in any numbers it appears that the 600 a month being moved to third countries will not be nearly enough to rid Malaysia of all refugees (FBIS, IV, 15 September 1986; FBIS, IV, 25 February 1987). Indeed, the recent increase in the number of Vietnamese refugees reaching Malaysia's shores has meant that the 9000 housed in the country in December 1987 had become 13 000 by August 1988 (Far Eastern Economic Review, *Asia Yearbook 1989*), producing strong Malaysian reactions.

In general, then, it may be said that Malaysia foreign policy has succeeded in safeguarding the country's security and contributing to national integration. The external, regional threat has been contained and sound regional and global networks of political support have been put in place as hedges against any future crises. Moreover, Malaysia has been able to counter internal threats to the country's security by limiting as far as possible any attempts to meddle in Malaysia's affairs and by ensuring that ethnic tensions are not inflamed by external events. For example, by developing links to China possible support within Malaysia's Chinese community for the MCP has been undercut and by being active in the Muslim world the impact of attacks on the government by Muslim revivalists has been minimized. However, the maintenance of good ethnic relations and the process of national integration have traditionally been dependent not just on good external relations but also on a healthy domestic economy. Hence, the extent to which Malaysia's foreign policy has been able to encourage the growth of the domestic economy must now be examined.

ECONOMIC GROWTH AND NATIONAL WELFARE: STRATEGIES AND ACTIONS

The Malaysian economy, despite its boom and bust nature, has generally performed well over the last 30 years. Based on the export of primary commodities – traditionally rubber and tin, to which have been added in recent years palm oil, timber and petroleum – and an expanding manufacturing sector, the GDP has grown by about 6–7 per cent per year and produced a per capita income which in 1987 was US$ 1953 and which, apart from Brunei and Singapore, is the highest in Southeast Asia. The relative health of the economy has been in large measure responsible for the generally stable communal relations within the country. However, the economy has not been without its problems. Indeed, the Malaysian state has felt compelled to step into the international economic arena in order to deal with three key economic issues which have threatened to affect the national welfare and national integration of the country. These issues have concerned the stabilization of commodity prices, the regulation of foreign direct investment, and the wish to maintain economic growth by emulating the economic success of Japan and South Korea.

Commodity Price Stabilization

The main incidents of political instability and communal violence in Malaysia have taken place against a backdrop of low commodity prices. The MCP took advantage of the depressed economy of the late 1940s caused by low rubber and tin prices to gain support for their guerrilla campaign; and in the mid-1970s low prices allowed the Communists to mount a minor resurgence in guerrilla activity (Stubbs, 1989; Stubbs, 1977: 86–90). The steady decline of rubber prices during the preceding decade also proved to be a crucial ingredient in the May 1969 riots. And in 1974 demonstrations in Baling by smallholders and their families over the low price of rubber and the rapidly rising cost of living pitted Malays against the Malay-dominated government for the first time (Stubbs, 1983: 86–90). In an attempt to reduce the effects of fluctuating prices on mine and plantation owners and workers as well as on its own revenues the government has tried to do something about the vicissitudes of the international markets for rubber and tin.

Prompted by the 1974 demonstrations, the Malaysian government set about mobilizing international support for an arrangement which would reduce the volatility of the world price of rubber. In November 1976 it secured a price-stabilization agreement among the Association of Natural Rubber Producing Countries (ANRPC). This was, however, superseded by the International Natural Rubber Agreement (INRA), which brought together producers and consumers. The INRA came into force in November 1980 and became operational in November 1981 in order to counter a prolonged decline in the price of natural rubber (Stubbs, 1984).

Malaysia has benefitted from the INRA. It has prevented the international price of rubber from plummeting to the disastrously low prices of 1974 and therefore helped to avoid any repetition of the demonstrations and political upheavals that they produced. Export earnings have also remained higher than they would otherwise have been. Yet the agreement has not been able to ensure a reasonable return for smallholders and estates. And while the International Monetary Fund's special financing facilities have been available to finance Malaysia's contribution to the agreement, it has nonetheless been a drain on resources. Moreover, the accumulation of nearly 370 000 tonnes of rubber in the buffer stock left producers, and especially Malaysia, in a very weak bargaining position during the recent negotiations to renew the agreement. Malaysia had to agree to less favorable terms than its negotiators had hoped for in order to continue the agreement for a second term, thereby stopping the stockpile from being unloaded onto the market and reducing the price to unacceptably low levels. However, the recent high demand and high price for natural rubber has left the INRA stockpile on a very low level and given a decided boost to the country's rubber industry. Malaysia's participation in the INRA has, thus, met with mixed success.

Malaysia's attempts to manipulate the international tin market in order to save jobs in the domestic tin industry were even less successful. As the world's largest tin exporter Malaysia has been a member of successive international agreements to stabilize tin prices. However, these agreements have had a spotty history of aiding hard pressed tin producers. Thus, faced in 1981 by a refusal on the part of US-led consumer members of the Fifth International Tin Agreement (ITA) to raise the ceiling price, by a sale from the US strategic stockpile of nearly 6000 tonnes, and by perceived pressure from speculators to lower the price still further, the Malaysian government, through a broker, stepped in as the 'mystery buyer' and attempted to corner the market. The price of tin rose and the ITA was forced to raise its floor and ceiling prices. But in February 1982 the London Metal Exchange (LME) suddenly changed its rules, thereby saving traders on the Exchange from major losses and breaking the Malaysian government's grip on the market. The failure to corner the market cost the government about M\$ 660.5 million (*Far Eastern Economic Review*, 20 November 1986: 12). Moreover, the combination of the strain on the Sixth ITA of the drop in prices which followed the 1982 débâcle and the difference in price between Kuala Lumpur and the LME led indirectly to the buffer-stock manager running out of funds. Having exhausted his credit and finding that he was unable to call up more member's contributions, the manager suspended support-price buying in October 1985. The price dropped to well below one-half its level at the height of the government's intervention (Burke, 1986: 13–16). Thus, the government's attempts to assist tin producers may have succeeded in the short term but clearly failed in the long term. By mid-1986 only about 175 of the country's 450 tin mines were operating and the world's major producing countries, including Malaysia, were having to regroup in order to try to limit exports and once again prop up prices (*Far Eastern Economic Review*, 13 November 1986: 110 and 115). Yet along with other commodity prices on the world market, in 1987–88 tin edged its way upwards. But Malaysia has had to deal with considerable suspicion among its fellow tin producers in the aftermath of the 1985 market collapse.

Foreign Investment Regulation

The Malaysian state also has a mixed record in attempting to deal with the issue of foreign investment. The diversification of the Malaysian economy has meant that, although the rubber and tin industries remain important, a number of other areas of the economy, especially the manufacturing and petroleum sectors, have expanded rapidly and contributed significantly to the economy's growth. The success of both these sectors has been fuelled by foreign investment. The benefits and problems associated with having an open economy which relies so heavily on international capital have been the source of much debate within Malaysia.

From independence up to the race riots of 1969 Malaysia courted foreign investors. This policy reflected the dominant mood within the Malaysian state at the time. The Pioneer Industries Act of 1958 put in place a set of incentives which, along with other schemes, was intended to provide loans and technical services to attract as much foreign investment as possible for the development of infant industries. In 1968 the Investment Incentives Act superseded the 1958 Act and extended incentives to cover firms not accorded pioneer status. Since then the Malaysian Industrial Development Authority has offered a range of extensive incentives to foreign investors (Bautista, 1983; Mehmet, 1986: 81).

At the same time as the number of incentives was increasing, measures were being undertaken to bring foreign investment under greater control. The re-evaluation of the role of Malays in the economy, which was prompted by the May 1969 riots, and the wish to ensure that Malay economic frustrations would not create political instability in the future resulted in the New Economic Policy (NEP). Among its objectives were the attainment of an 'ethnic balance' in the various economic sectors and occupations; the creation of more Malay entrepreneurs and managers; and the raising of the share of capital held by Malays (Milne and Mauzy, 1986: 133). But with 60 per cent of corporate assets in foreign hands, some fairly drastic measures had to be undertaken if Malays were to own 30 per cent of corporate assets by 1990, non-Malays 40 per cent and foreigners 30 per cent, as was planned.

Hence, spurred on by the rising tide of economic nationalism – primarily Malay economic nationalism – and the requirements of the NEP, the government moved on a number of fronts. First, in February 1974, the Foreign Investment Committee within the Economic Planning Unit of the Prime Minister's Department was established to formulate guidelines on foreign investment. Second, the Petroleum Development Act, passed in 1974 and amended in 1975, allowed the government's oil company, PETRONAS, to acquire control of joint ventures through mandatory special 'management shares'. And third, the Industrial Co-ordination Act of 1975 required all large manufacturing firms to be licensed by the government and to meet conditions linked to the NEP's 1990 targets for the participation of Malays in the economy. As a result of these policy initiatives foreign investment dropped off markedly. Investors' confidence and trust in the Malaysian government was shaken. As Donald Crone has argued, 'the government had apparently over-stepped the boundary between acceptable control and cutting off the necessary flow of investment' (Crone, 1983b: 107).

By the late 1970s and early 1980s the need for greater amounts of foreign investment to fuel the export-oriented strategy that Malaysia was following became clear. This need was accentuated by the flight of Malaysian-Chinese capital in the face of discriminatory NEP policies. However, it took time for the Malay nationalist elements to lose their influence over the state's economic decision-making and implementing apparatus and for those who argued for a more open economy to regain the ascendency. By following a policy of diversifying the sources of foreign capital Dr. Mahathir, first as Trade and Industry Minister and then as Prime Minister, attempted to 'manage dependency' and to dispel disquiet about the undue influence of foreign investors (Crone, 1983a: 62–6). Gradually, as the state was able to reassert its authority, policies were revised so as once again to attempt to attract foreign investors whose share of Malaysian equity was being reduced to well below the NEP's 30 per cent target set for 1990. The government has repeatedly amended the Industrial Co-ordination Act since 1978 to give more freedom to manufacturers; passed the Promotion of Investment Act, which provides new tax incentives for manufacturing; launched the New Investment Fund to channel money at preferential rates into specified sectors; and revised foreign investment regulations so as to tie the equity stake of foreigners more directly to exports and to make conditions for the employment of expatriate staff less restrictive (Mahathir, 1986).

Overall Malaysia's record of attracting foreign investment and fuelling rapid economic growth has been inconsistent. Nor is it altogether clear that this form of economic growth will ward off open communal violence. While jobs have been created, Malaysians have not always benefitted as much as might have been expected, especially from the Export Processing Zones. Moreover, the relatively poor distribution of wealth in Malaysia, in part at least accentuated by the patterns of foreign investment, may serve to exacerbate ethnic tensions and still leaves open the possibility of future political instability.

'Look East'

Copying the Japanese and South Koreans as a way of giving a boost to the productivity of the Malaysian economy has been a preoccupation of Prime Minister Dr Mahathir since the early 1980s. In part the exhortation to 'Look East' was prompted by a wish to distance Malaysia from the development model represented by the West and particularly Britain. Indeed, a series of incidents involving Britain preceded the announcement in 1982 of the 'Look East' policy. These included: the changes in British universities' fee schedules for foreign students; the rule changes by the LME; the rule change made by the British Securities Council following the 'dawn raid' in which the Malaysian government acquired Guthries, a British company operating in Malaysia; and the 'Buy British Last' campaign which decreed that the Prime Minister's office had to clear all public sector contracts with British firms. The new policy appears to have been the obverse side of this attempt to eradicate the last vestiges of the old colonial ties. And, perhaps not incidently, the policy led to a weakening of the old expatriate- and Chinese-dominated trading companies with their ties to Britain and created opportunities for new, often Malay-dominated, companies to open up new links with Japan.

As the 'Look East' policy took shape emphasis was placed on learning from the Japanese and South Korean models of development, emulating their work ethic and management styles and strengthening Malaysia's economic links with both countries. It was hoped that the many trade and investment deals that were to be struck would provide valuable spin-offs such as training and technical assistance. In part at least the policy has worked. Malaysia appears to have been added to the outer edge of the formation of 'flying geese' or follower countries which have benefitted from Japan's rapid economic growth (Cumings, 1984: 2–3). Yet in many ways Malaysia was already moving into the orbit of the Japanese economy and the 'Look East' policy simply served to accentuate this trend. The result has been that the previous balance which had been sought in Malaysia's economic relations with Japan, the United States and the European Community is threatened. Japan is steadily increasing its share of Malaysia's total trade and investment capital. For example, during the period 1980–85 Japan contributed 20 per cent of the foreign investment in Malaysia's manufacturing sector compared to the 10 per cent contributed by the United Kingdom and 8 per cent by the United States (Mohamad, 1986: 22). There is clearly a danger that eventually Malaysia will become too dependent on its Japanese links. While swapping Japan for Britain may have major short- and medium-term benefits, the economy and, therefore, ultimately the cause of stable ethnic relations, may not always be well served in the long term by decisions made in Tokyo (Saravanamuttu, 1984b; Khong, 1987). The Malaysian government is clearly aware of this problem but doing something about it while maintaining a healthy, growing economy may be difficult.

CONCLUSION

There are, of course, many problems which remain to be faced in the external political and economic realms. The Vietnamese withdrawal from Cambodia may produce potentially divisive and destabilizing issues. The overlapping of territorial claims arising out of the Law of the Sea Agreement, particularly with regard to the Spratley Islands, will have to be negotiated. Among the ASEAN states this might not be too big a problem; however, where Vietnam, Taiwan and China are involved, the possible conflicts could present major difficulties for the region. The issue of how to manage the legitimate interests of the major powers, especially China, will also need Malaysia's attention if the ideal of ZOPFAN is ever to be attained. Finally, the Malaysian state must learn to cope not only with a growing economic dependence on Japan but also with the increased economic power of, and competition from, China. Clearly it is vital to the future of the country that Malaysians continue to keep in check any external political or economic set of events which might threaten

Malaysia's territorial security, kindle open ethnic conflict or inhibit for any length of time Malaysia's economic growth.

NOTE

1. Thanks are due to Dwight King, Linda Lim, Stephen Milne, Martin Rudner, Grace Skogstad and David Wurfel for comments on various drafts of this chapter.

BIBLIOGRAPHY

Bautista, Romeo M. (1983), *Industrial Policy and Development in the ASEAN Countries*. Monograph Series No. 2 (Quezon City: Philippine Institute for Development Studies).
Burke, Gill (1986), *The Tin Crisis* (Kuala Lumpur: Institute of Strategic and International Studies).
Chee, Stephen (1974), 'Malaysia's Changing Foreign Policy', in Yong Mun Cheong (ed.), *Trends in Malaysia II* (Singapore: Singapore University Press).
Crone, Donald K. (1983a), 'Management of International Dependence: The Case of ASEAN', *Contemporary Southeast Asia* 5 (June), 53–70.
Crone, Donald K. (1983b), *The ASEAN States: Coping With Dependence* (New York: Praeger).
Cumings, Bruce (1984), 'The Origins and Development of the Northeast Asian Political Economy: Industrial Sectors, Product Cycles, and Political Consequences', *International Organization* 38 (Winter), 1–40.
Far Eastern Economic Review (FEER), *Asia Yearbook 1989* (Hong Kong: Review Publishing, 1989).
Far Eastern Economic Review (FEER). Various dates.
Foreign Broadcast Information Service (FBIS), Asia Pacific. United States Government. Various dates.
Khong Kim Hoong (1987), 'Malaysia-Japan Relations in the 1980s', *Asian Survey* 27 (October), 1095–1108.
Lau Teik Soon (1971), 'Malaysia and the Neutralisation of Southeast Asia', in Patrick Low (ed.), *Trends in Southeast Asia*, No. 2 (Singapore: Institute of Southeast Asian Studies).
Lee Lai To (1981), 'Deng Xiaoping's ASEAN Tour', *Contemporary Southeast Asia* 3 (June), 58–75.
Mahbubani, Kishore (1983/4), 'The Kampuchean problem: A Southeast Asian Perception', *Foreign Affairs* (Winter), 407–25.
Mahathir Mohamad (1971), 'Trends in Foreign Policy and Regionalism', in

122   *The Foreign Policy of Malaysia*

Patrick Low (ed.), *Trends in Southeast Asia*, No. 2 (Singapore: Institute of Southeast Asian Studies).

Mahathir Mohamad (1986), Speech at the Malaysian Investment Seminar, Waldorf Astoria Hotel. New York. 30 September.

Means, Gordon P. (1976), *Malaysian Politics* (London: Hodder & Stoughton).

Mehmet, Ozay (1986), *Development in Malaysia: Poverty, Wealth and Trusteeship* (London: Croom Helm).

Milne, R. S. and Diane K. Mauzy (1986), *Malaysia: Tradition, Modernity and Islam* (Boulder: Westview).

Milne, R. S. and Diane K. Mauzy (1980), *Politics and Government in Malaysia* (Vancouver: University of British Columbia Press).

Mohamad Yusof Ismail (1986), 'The Development of Heavy Industries in Malaysia: Its Trends, Trade and Investment Potential'. Paper presented at the Canada-Malaysia Conference, Ottawa, Canada.

Muthiah Alagappa (1987), *Towards a Nuclear Free Zone in Southeast Asia* (Kuala Lumpur: Institute of Strategic and International Studies).

Muthiah Alagappa (1986), *US-ASEAN Security Co-operation: Limits and Possibilities* (Kuala Lumpur: Institute of Strategic and International Studies).

Omar Farouk (1984), 'The Historical and Transnational Dimensions of Malay-Muslim Separatism in Southern Thailand', in Lim Joo-Jock and S. Vani (eds), *Armed Separatism in Southeast Asia* (Singapore: Institute of Southeast Asian Studies).

Ott, Marvin C. (1972), 'Foreign Policy Formulation in Malaysia', *Asian Survey* 12 (March), 225–39.

Pauw, Douglas S. and John C. H. Fei (1973),*The Transition in Open Dualistic Economies: Theory and Southeast Asian Experience* (New Haven: Yale University Press).

Saravanamuttu, J. (1983), *The Dilemma of Independence: Two Decades of Malaysia's Foreign Policy 1957–77* (Penang: Penerbit Universiti Sains Malaysia).

Saravanamuttu, J. (1984a), 'ASEAN Security for the 1980s: The Case for a Revitalized ZOPFAN', *Contemporary Southeast Asia* 6 (September), 186–96.

Saravanamuttu, J. (1984b), 'Malaysia's Look East Policy and Its Implications for Self-Sustaining Growth', in *The Malaysian Economy at the Crossroads: Policy Adjustment for Structural Transformation* (Kuala Lumpur: Malaysian Economic Association/Organizational Resources).

Skocpol, Theda (1985), 'Bringing the State Back In: Strategies of Analysis in Current Research', in Peter B. Evans, Dietrich Rueschemyer and Theda Skocpol (eds), *Bringing the State Back In* (Cambridge: Cambridge University Press).

Sopiee, Noordin (1986), 'ASEAN and Regional Security', in Mohammed Ayoob (ed.), *Regional Security in the Third World: Case Studies From Southeast Asia and the Middle East* (Boulder: Westview Press).

Stubbs, Richard (1989), *Hearts and Minds in Guerrilla Warfare: The Malayan Emergency 1948–60* (Singapore: Oxford University Press).

Stubbs, Richard (1984), 'The International Natural Rubber Agreement: Its

Negotiation and Operation', *Journal of World Trade Law* 18 (January/-February), 16–31.

Stubbs, Richard (1983), 'Malaysia's Rubber Smallholding Industry: Crisis and the Search for Stability', *Pacific Affairs* 56 (Spring), 84–105.

Stubbs, Richard (1980), 'Why Can't They Stay in Southeast Asia? The Problems of Vietnam's Neighbours', in Elliot Tepper (ed.), *Southeast Asian Exodus: From Tradition to Resettlement* (Ottawa: Canadian Asian Studies Association).

Stubbs, Richard (1977), 'Peninsular Malaysia: The "New Emergency".' *Pacific Affairs* 50 (Summer), 249–62.

Tilman, Robert O. (1984), *The Enemy Beyond: External Threat Perceptions in the ASEAN Region* (Singapore: Institute of Southeast Asian Studies).

Tilman, Robert O. (1969), 'Malaysian Foreign Policy: Dilemmas of a Committed Neutral', in J. D. Montgomery and A. D. Hirschman (eds), *Public Policy* (Cambridge, Mass.: Harvard University Press).

Zakaria, Haji Ahmad (1986), 'The World of ASEAN Decision-Makers: A Study of Bureaucratic Elite Perceptions in Malaysia, the Philippines and Singapore', *Contemporary Southeast Asia* 8 (Summer), 192–212.

8 The Foreign Policy of Singapore
Linda Y. C. Lim

INTRODUCTION

Singapore became a sovereign nation, reluctantly, in August 1965 when it was ejected from the Federation of Malaysia; it had joined that union in 1963 after 144 years of British colonialism. This historical circumstance, and the country's geographical location, have determined its foreign policy objectives and constraints ever since. As a small island city-state (currently with 2.6 million people situated on 622 square kilometers), Singapore is necessarily dependent for its survival not only on the world market but also on the surrounding Southeast Asian region – even for basic necessities such as food and water (which come mainly from Malaysia). Yet, with its predominantly (75 per cent) Chinese population, and a significant (15 per cent) Malay-Muslim minority, Singapore is ethnically and culturally different from the much larger but poorer neighboring countries of Malaysia and Indonesia, where Muslim Malays are the overwhelming majority.

Within these absolute constraints, national security, nation-building and economic survival are intertwined and dominate the goals of government in general, not only its foreign policy. Maximizing national autonomy has been a secondary goal, but one which involves the management and diversification, rather than the reduction, of external dependence. Regime maintenance, while of utmost importance to the government itself, enters into foreign policy only to the (considerable) extent that the popularity and stability of the ruling party is based on an externally-dependent economic prosperity.

ECONOMY, SOCIETY AND THE REGIME

Since its founding by the British as a free port in 1819, entrepôt trade has been a mainstay of Singapore, and it remains one of the most open national economies in the world, with free trade and

capital flows. Since sovereignty in 1965, export manufacturing, petro-
leum-related activities, financial and business services, tourism, and
transport and communications have developed rapidly, contributing
to a high rate of economic growth and average income levels surpassing those of the poorer European countries. While essentially based
on private enterprise and market forces, the economy is dominated
by the state, with many profit-making state enterprises. Multinationals are also prominent, especially in the manufacturing sector which
they dominate (Lim and Pang, 1986; Lim, Pang and Findlay, 1987;
Lim, 1987a, 1987b).

Economic development has wrought considerable social change.
Educational and skill levels of the multi-ethnic population have risen
rapidly, although ethnic differences remain; birth rates have declined
to below replacement levels; and there is a high rate of female labor
force participation (46 per cent). The government's Housing and
Development Board (HDB) houses 84 per cent of the population in
high-rise apartment blocks. All ethnic groups are now educated in
a single common language – English – with second-language instruc-
tion in their 'mother tongue'; for the Chinese, who belong to many
different dialect-groups, this has become, by official decree and practice, Mandarin. With rising incomes and living standards, education
and travel abroad has become widespread across income groups.

Politically, Singapore has been ruled by the People's Action Party
(PAP) since it was voted into power in 1959, when the city was
granted internal self-government by the British. General elections
are held every four years, and up to 1980 the PAP typically won
between 70 and 77 per cent of all votes cast. In the 1984 and 1988
elections, however, this declined to 65 per cent and 63 per cent
respectively. Between 1968 and 1981, the PAP was the only party
in parliament, and today it occupies 80 of the 81 parliamentary seats,
a dominance based on demonstrated economic success and tight
political controls, which have resulted in small, weak, heterogeneous
and, until 1988, divided opposition parties.

The PAP and the large government bureaucracy which it controls
constitute an 'autonomous state', in the following senses. Selection
into the bureaucracy and into parliament is based largely on academic merit and technocratic performance, a process resulting in a
neo-Confucian 'scholar-bureaucracy'. Top civil servants are frequently indistinguishable from political leaders, since many of the
latter are recruited out of the ranks of the former; both groups
consist mostly of Western-educated intellectuals and professionals.

With some exceptions, members of the goverment are generally not part of the local private business class. They come disproportionately from the working class, from minority Chinese dialect-groups, and from government rather than religious mission schools favored by the middle-class. The government is not subject to external political manipulation. With persistent balance-of-payments and public sector surpluses, and huge foreign exchange reserves, the country has a very small foreign debt to commercial banks, the World Bank or the International Monetary Fund, and does not receive foreign economic or military aid.

As Pang and Chan (1987) have noted, beginning as a social-democratic, anti-colonial party in the 1950s and 1960s, the PAP government's first goal was 'to maximize the people's welfare through an economic and social transformation of Singapore'. Its independence from powerful interest groups enabled it to develop 'an ideology and politics of survival' and to follow policies and programs 'with the twin objectives of improving Singapore's economic prospects and ensuring its survival as a multiracial nation-state'. The strong economic role of the state arose out of these concerns, and a strategy of 'redistribution before growth' was followed. However, pragmatic shifts of ideology and policies have occurred since the 1960s as the country's internal and external circumstances have changed, broadening the party's support base from the Chinese-educated and labor unions to include broad sections of the middle class, especially members of the burgeoning state bureaucracy itself.

Today, the PAP has become more conventionally conservative, with belief in free market ideals being strengthened particularly in the aftermath of the 1985/86 recession which was partly attributed to excessive government intervention in the economy (Ministry of Trade and Industry, 1986). Efforts at deregulation, liberalization and privatization of various government enterprises and functions have begun, and economic growth has reached record levels since the recession. In the process, there has been a definite tilt in government policy towards business (big and small, local and foreign) and away from labor, which in the form of the PAP-controlled National Trades Union Congress (NTUC) has until now been an important actor in Singapore's political economy (Lim and Pang, 1986; Lim, 1987c). This, however, does not necessarily mean that the government has the wholehearted political support of the local private sector, with which it remains competitive in some respects (Lim, Pang and Findlay, 1987; Lim, 1987a, 1987b).

Singapore today is in transition. Politically, there is the transition from the leadership of Prime Minister Lee Kuan Yew to that of a younger generation of leaders, nominally led by First Deputy Prime Minister Goh Chok Tong, but also including Lee's son, Brigadier-General (Reservist) Lee Hsien Loong, the Minister for Trade and Industry. Economically, there is the transition from labor-intensive manufacturing and low-value services to higher-value, higher-skill manufacturing and services which began in 1979. It now includes developing Singapore into a 'total business center' for multinationals, a 'hub city' for the booming Asia-Pacific region, and an 'information technology and services center' for the world, as well as the promotion of locally-owned Singapore-based multinationals and a more active international role for local enterprises. Socially, there is the continuing transition to a modern industrial and even post-industrial society, with lower economic growth and the affluent, well-educated, increasingly middle class, rapidly aging population characteristic of more mature economies, the ranks of which Singapore is now poised to penetrate. The government's goal now is to manage these transitions successfully.

FOREIGN POLICY-MAKERS AND PROCESSES

Government policy decision-making in Singapore is highly centralized:

> The Prime Minister and his close colleagues decide on basic policies, though usually after consultation with relevant groups . . . the decision-making process remains very much top down. (Pang and Chan, 1987)

Foreign policy decision-making is probably more highly-centralized than almost any other area of policy-making, and likely to remain so. For example, foreign policy decisions are rarely discussed in parliament, although various members of the cabinet, and the Prime Minister, are usually involved. This is partly because many foreign policy issues, for example, those concerning security and defense, are considered too 'sensitive' for public discussion or even disclosure; and partly because a high degree of specialization and experience, including the cultivation of personal relationships with foreign politicians and officials, is arguably more important in this than in other policy areas. Foreign policy-makers appear to be somewhat more autonomous in their decision-making than other branches of the government, though consultation may be necessary with other relevant ministries.

Foreign policy is the domain of the Ministry of Foreign Affairs (MFA), an élite and relatively self-contained branch of the civil service. Until 1988 the Minister of Foreign Affairs had always been a member of the minority Indian ethnic group – first S. Rajaratnam, one of Lee Kuan Yew's original inner core of advisers, then S. Dhanabalan, a former technocrat – and Indians are over-represented especially in the upper echelons of the foreign service. This ethnic concentration mainly reflects the meritocratic selection processes of the Singapore civil service, and the greater ability and interest of Indian professionals and technocrats in international relations. It has also been useful in perpetrating Singapore's image, both at home and abroad, as a multi-ethnic nation. At the same time, as members of a small ethnic minority, Indian individuals' chances of becoming prominent on the domestic political front are limited. Many Chinese, on the other hand, consider the foreign service to be a dead-end profession which does not enhance one's political or professional clout at home. Besides Indians, women are also more prominent in the higher echelons of the MFA, including as diplomatic representatives overseas – for example, the current UN representative is a woman – than in other branches of the civil service. Again, this may reflect the fact that their career opportunities are more limited in the central domain of domestic politics.

In the management of external relations, the MFA concentrates mainly on political affairs, where consultation with the Prime Minister's Office (PMO) is obviously crucial. Foreign political relations are not something which greatly concerns Singaporeans, even other branches of government, with the exception of relations with Malaysia, and to a lesser extent, Indonesia. The MFA therefore has a relatively free hand in determining policy in this area, within domestic and external constraints. It is also responsible for smoothing over frictions with foreign parties which arise from the independent actions of other branches of government.

The MFA is also involved in negotiating external trade relations, and here it must work closely with the Ministry of Trade and Industry (MTI); this role has become more important in recent years with the need to counter rising protectionism in the United States and the European Community especially. The MFA has little to do with managing relations with multinationals, since this is the preserve of

the Economic Development Board (EDB, which comes under MTI),
the investment promotion agency which has many more staff at
more locations abroad than the MFA itself. There is also the Trade
Development Board (TDB) under MTI which aids in promoting
Singapore's exports, and to some extent also its foreign purchases.
Singapore policy-makers like to think that 'pragmatism' and
'flexibility' rather than ideology determine the positions they take
on specific policy issues. But the pragmatism is 'tough-minded' and
geared to the 'single-minded pursuit of (national) self-interest' in
foreign policy (Leifer, 1987: 52), judging by the public presentation
of Singapore's foreign policy views by its chief architects. It is – as
Singaporeans pride themselves to be – tough, direct, didactic,
explicit, somewhat abrupt and even arrogant, although Leifer notes
that there is more recently 'greater self-assurance' and 'fewer blatant
expressions of waspishness' (Leifer, 1987: 52). Still, it was said of
former Minister Dhanabalan, who has argued that Singapore's policies must be 'ruthlessly rational':

> He is not beloved by many of his counterparts around the world
> for using diplomatic language that is often too blunt for their
> sensibilities. (Holloway, 1987: 54)

Dhanabalan's successor, Wong Kan Seng, so far operates in much
the same mold. In short, Singapore's 'leadership style' in foreign
policy is very similar to its 'leadership style' in other areas of
government.

DOMESTIC RESOURCES AND CONSTRAINTS

Since becoming a sovereign nation in 1965, Singapore has built up
impressive domestic resources for its foreign policy-makers. The
island's spectacular economic success and rise to prosperity has
caused it to be widely known throughout the world, and it has
become virtually a legend in both economic development and international business. The economic 'model' which Singapore represents
has been admired and held up as an ideal by Western economists
and political leaders, as well as by developing country governments
from Jamaica and Sri Lanka to the Philippines and the People's
Republic of China, who have tried in various ways to emulate it.
Singapore's foreign policy-makers have seized on this high economic profile to promote Singapore in the West as a showcase of

the superiority of market-oriented, private-enterprise capitalism over socialist models of centrally-planned economic development in the Third World. They have explicitly argued that such a showcase must not be allowed to fail, as threatened by growing protectionism in the West, because that would indicate to other developing countries that the 'Western' model of 'democratic' (that is, capitalistic) development was not viable, turning them towards Socialism and Communism instead. The implication is that the West has an interest in ensuring Singapore's continued political survival as a sovereign nation (should that ever be threatened), which itself hinges on its economic viability.

Economic success, including Singapore's hospitality to foreign corporations at home and its large investments abroad, also ensures that the country is able both to negotiate foreign policy outcomes from a position of strength disproportionate to its small size (for example, it has no external debt to Western or Japanese governments, and is a major investor in Malaysia and Indonesia), and to readily fund expenditures related to foreign policy concerns (for example, a large defense budget and sophisticated military equipment, and military aid to the Cambodian resistance and economic assistance to the Philippines). Economic success is the main reason for Singapore's high status and disproportionate influence in international affairs. It also enables Singapore to fob off criticisms of its internal policies on the grounds that the end (stability and prosperity for all) justifies the means (heavy government economic and political control).

In addition to economic strength and political stability, Singapore has built up considerable military strength, with its very well-equipped citizens' army of draftees. The Singapore armed forces are the best equipped, and its air force the largest, in the ASEAN region. Like the rest of the government machinery, the armed forces are run by a scholar-bureaucracy, and are rapidly being transformed into a modern, computerized military whose strength derives from good organization and state-of-the-art military technology (both software and hardware), from strategy rather than manpower, from 'brain' rather than 'brawn' – although it has never yet been tested in combat. Despite the lack of any immediate threat to its security, Singapore constantly emphasizes its military, and a few years ago launched a 'Total Defense' campaign to involve civilians in military preparedness. In the early days of sovereignty, Israel was stressed as the model for the vulnerable young nation's defense. This aggressive posture has since been toned down, but in the government's conception, military strength remains crucial to Singapore's security and political survival as a nation state surrounded by much larger neighbors. Because of its wealth, high savings rate and huge foreign exchange reserves, the country is well able to afford its heavy military expenditures without getting into external debt or constraining economic growth. It receives no military aid from any foreign power, and is a producer, exporter and purchaser of armaments on 'market' terms.

Finally, domestic resources available to Singapore's foreign policy makers include the excellent administrative and diplomatic skills of the foreign service and other sectors of the bureaucracy and easy access to information about the region and the world. These abundant domestic resources together endow Singapore with a capacity for independent action and sometimes even international leadership in foreign policy which is quite unusual for such a small developing country. Within Singapore itself, there is little if any dissension among interest groups on most questions of foreign policy. One occasional exception is the position of Malays on issues of importance to the Islamic world, such as relations with Israel.

At the same time, Singapore's small size and lack of natural resources is a major constraint, rendering the country unable to provide for its own basic needs, and therefore making it heavily and inescapably dependent on its neighbors and on participation in the world market for physical survival. To survive, Singapore needs to import, and therefore it must export. For this it is dependent on foreign capital and foreign labor for augmentation of its own inadequate resources. Small size also means greater concentration of Singapore's manufacturing in relatively few industries (petroleum products, electronics and shipbuilding), resulting in possibly greater vulnerability to external market conditions (compared, for example, to the other Asian NICs).

A second major domestic constraint is the ethnic composition of the population, given Singapore's geographic location. With a population that is 75 per cent Chinese, Singapore is sandwiched between two much larger regional neighbors, Malaysia and Indonesia, whose Malay-Muslim ethnic majorities and their governments sometimes deal harshly with their own significant Chinese ethnic minorities. The fact that Singapore's own entrepôt and investor role in the regional economy to some extent mirrors the middleman functions and business domination of these Chinese minorities in Malaysia and Indonesia only makes relations more awkward. Its very

Chineseness alone makes Singapore potentially unpopular with its nationalistic neighbors, who are also sensitive to the condition of Singapore's own Malay-Muslim ethnic minority. As a mini-state Singapore is in any case constantly preoccupied with political survival and fearful of domination or absorption by these larger neighbors.

THE EXTERNAL ENVIRONMENT: CONSTRAINTS, OPPORTUNITIES AND PERCEPTIONS

The External Economic Environment

Singapore's economic dependence on the world market and on foreign investment is unquestionable. This is an economy built on trade, foreign capital and foreign labor from its very beginnings in the colonial era. Today, Singapore's continued entrepôt role in Southeast Asia makes it one of the most open economies in the world, with total trade amounting to more than three times the island's GDP. Three-fifths of all manufacturing output is directly exported, with much of the rest consisting of inputs sold to these export industries. Financial and business services, transport and communications (for instance, port and airport facilities), commerce (wholesale and retail trade) and tourism are also highly dependent on foreign markets.

When Singapore in the late 1960s embarked on its development strategy of export-oriented manufacturing by multinationals, the external environment was highly favorable. World trade was booming, and multinationals from developed countries, particularly in the electronics industry, were already embarked on a search for low-wage offshore manufacturing sites in developing countries. Today, despite technological change, slower world economic growth, protectionism and reindustrialization in the West, and increased supply-side competition from other developing and newly-industrializing countries, world market prospects for Singapore's changing manufacturing industry remain strong.

Whereas most of Singapore's manufactured exports are destined for world markets, financial and business services, commerce and tourism are dependent mostly on the Southeast Asian market, while transport and communications are dependent on both. This means that Singapore is very vulnerable not only to demand conditions in world markets for its limited range of manufactured exports, but also to economic conditions in neighboring ASEAN countries. In the late 1960s and 1970s, regional conditions were favorable. A boom in petroleum exploration and extraction developed Singapore's petroleum refining and shipbuilding export industries, while accelerated regional economic growth partly financed by external debt and investment led many international banks and financial institutions to establish regional headquarters in Singapore. In the 1980s, however, balance of payments crises, commodity export declines, slow growth and reduced external debt servicing capability in Malaysia and Indonesia reduced their demand for Singapore's port services, financial and business services, commerce and tourism until commodity prices recovered in the late 1980s.

Besides its dependence on external markets, Singapore is also very dependent on foreign investment (Tan, 1984; Chia, 1985; Lim, 1987a; Lim, Pang and Findlay, 1987), with one-third of all firms in the country being wholly or majority foreign-owned, and foreign funds amounting to 40 per cent of all investments in 1981. At the end of 1983, more than S$ 20 billion (about US$ 9 billion) of foreign funds were invested in Singapore, a total which increased in the 1980s by more than US$ 1 billion every year. Nearly half of the foreign funds have flowed into the manufacturing sector, where in 1984 wholly or majority foreign-owned firms accounted for 71 per cent of output, 82 per cent of direct exports and 53 per cent of employment. In 1981 five countries – Britain, United States, Hong Kong, Malaysia and Japan (in that order) accounted for four-fifths of the foreign equity invested in Singapore. Up to 1986 the US dominated new investments every year, followed at a distance by Japan. Since then the strong yen has motivated huge Japanese capital outlays in Singapore, making Japan now the largest source of new foreign investment.

Foreign investment has provided Singapore with many economic opportunities, including the capital, technology, entrepreneurship, managerial and financial expertise required for industrialization, and access to foreign markets for export-oriented industries. Output, employment and productivity growth, industrial diversification and deepening, technological upgrading, incomes and living standards have progressed much more rapidly than would have been the case without foreign investment, which has also contributed substantially to large balance of payments surpluses since the late 1960s.

But there are also constraints, particularly the dependence of this prosperity on the decisions of foreign firms. Reduced investment inflows and lay-offs by multinationals in the 1985 recession, although quickly reversed in 1986, indicate how vulnerable the economy is to a loss of international competitiveness. Dependence on foreign investment also increases the need of the government to control and modify many aspects of social and economic life and behavior in order to ensure a continued favorable climate for investors.

Despite the constraints, the government continues to view foreign investment and exports as crucial to Singapore's economic success and even survival. The report of the Economic Committee set up to investigate the causes of the 1985/86 recession and propose solutions (Ministry of Trade and Industry 1986) affirmed the goal of developing Singapore as an 'international total business center' for multinationals (including home-based multinationals), exporting services as well as manufactures. There was hardly any mention in the report of promoting Singapore's economic role in ASEAN – the region or the regional grouping – perhaps indicating a desire to diversify Singapore's external dependence by shifting it away from the region and more towards the world as a whole. But with rapid growth in the region since 1987, Singapore is now emphasizing its role as a regional services hub as well.

The necessity, and indeed the benefit, of external dependence is recognized and accepted by virtually all major actors in Singapore's domestic political economy, despite some disagreement on the form and extent of such dependence. For example, local capital would like protection from foreign competition in certain sectors, mainly services, and is more inclined towards a regional rather than world market orientation. Labor, on the other hand, favors multinational employment, and so does the state (Lim, 1987a).

What about Singapore's economic role in ASEAN as a regional organization? On the one hand, Singapore is interested in freer trade among the ASEAN member countries because this will improve its access to external resources and markets, as well as benefit its entre-pôt trade and services. Already 40 per cent of present intra-ASEAN trade is accounted for by trade between Singapore and Malaysia, and Singapore and Indonesia. On the other hand, Singapore as a free port with strong links to and heavy trade dependence on the rest of the world will never be part of ASEAN regional import-substituting schemes, whether it be ASEAN industrial projects or a customs union with a common external tariff, since it cannot pay above world market prices for inputs and remain world market competitive in its exports.

In general, Singapore policy-makers are well aware of both the constraints and the opportunities presented by the external economic environment. External dependence is not lamented or resisted, but simply recognized as inevitable, since self-sufficiency is impossible for such a small country, and integration into the world economy has been both necessary and beneficial. As in the case of the smaller developed countries (for example, Norway, Belgium, Sweden), the problems posed by external dependence cannot be solved, only managed, and Singapore has become such a master at the management of its external economic relations that specific cases of 'dependency reversal' have emerged. These include, for example, individual multinationals becoming more dependent on their Singapore production and suppliers than Singapore is on them; Singapore subsidiaries or local partners of multinationals taking over their 'parent' companies abroad'; Singapore companies buying up or establishing high-tech plants in the US and exporting to the world from there (Lim, 1987a); Singapore state and private capital buying up choice real estate in Western countries; and even a 'brain drain' to Singapore of technical expertise from such developed countries as Britain and Australia.

The possibly dark side of this policy is the management and control of the internal environment which the PAP government claims is necessary for the successful management of the country's external environment. Vulnerability to the external environment is used by the government as justification for its internal policies such as restrictive press laws, continual efforts to shape the values and attitudes of the population, and harsh treatment of all groups with slightly different views. Despite the government's claims, many Singaporeans increasingly believe that these internal controls are not essential for external management, but rather are domestic political tools designed to maintain the PAP in power. External economic dependence, then, rather than dictating internal political controls, is in fact being manipulated for domestic partisan political ends. For example, in the 1984 general elections the PAP claimed that election of opposition candidates would discourage multinationals from investing in Singapore. In fact, the opposition declared its support for continued multinational involvement, and multinational representatives publicly welcomed the election of opposition MPs as a sign of 'political maturity'. Foreign investment has since increased.

The External Political Environment

Singapore's geographical location in the center of Southeast Asia causes it to be affected by political conditions in the region as a whole. The prime concern of policy-makers since 1965 has been Communism in Indo-China, especially Vietnamese expansionism. This threatens Singapore in several ways. First, there is the possibility that Vietnam might provide moral or military support to left-wing insurgent movements which exist in the other ASEAN countries, particularly Thailand and the Philippines, thereby undermining these countries' political stability and economic prosperity which would adversely affect Singapore, given its dependence on the regional economy, and the necessity of regional political stability for the attraction of foreign investment to Singapore. Second, the Vietnamese invasion and occupation of Cambodia presents an intolerable precedent which threatens Singapore in its position as a small nation similarly vulnerable to and ever fearful of attack or take-over by larger neighbors. Third, the close relationship between Vietnam and the Soviet Union makes anti-Communist Singapore nervous about its possible effect on the regional balance of power between the great powers in Southeast Asia.

Besides and because of Vietnam, politically ASEAN is perceived as extremely important to Singapore. Membership of ASEAN makes Singapore part of a larger unit in countering potential Vietnamese aggression or subversion; it also ensures that neighboring countries accept Singapore's sovereignty with its membership of the regional organization (Leifer, 1987).

Beyond ASEAN as an organization, Singapore policy-makers see as important the political stability of the other member nations. In the mid- to late-1980s the Philippines under Marcos (and to some extent also under Aquino) was a concern. But Singapore's major concern within this group of countries has always been its relationship with Malaysia, its closest neighbor and one of its three top trading partners, in which it is a major foreign investor. Singapore's links with the large Chinese ethnic minority in Malaysia, its own significant Malay minority, the ethnic sensitivities of the predominantly Malay government in Malaysia, and close economic ties involving both competition and complementarity, all combine to make this special relationship a complicated and delicate one.

Within ASEAN, Singapore is also constrained by the sensitivities of the other member nations with respect to its external relations.

For example, being predominantly Chinese and therefore ethnically different from the other countries has constrained Singapore's formal diplomatic relationship with the People's Republic of China, which was until recently viewed with some suspicion by Malaysia and Indonesia especially.

Finally, Singapore like its ASEAN neighbors is concerned with the role of major world powers in the region, and does not want to see them come into contest or conflict here. It has excellent ties with the West and is apprehensive about the Soviet Union's growing regional role and intentions, though a similar apprehension about China waned in the 1980s. Unlike its Southeast Asian neighbors, the Singapore government does not appear to perceive a threat in Japan's proposed remilitarization.

FOREIGN POLICY OUTPUTS

Singapore's formal foreign policy orientation is non-alignment in international affairs. It considers itself to be a member of the Third-World bloc at the United Nations, is a member of the non-aligned group of nations, and the UNCTAD Group of 77, and is anxious to preserve this Third-World status for the economic benefits, such as GSP tariff preferences, which it enjoys as a Third-World country. However, like the other ASEAN nations, Singapore is fundamentally pro-Western and anti-Communist in its orientation, and some government leaders have recently been critical of the principle of non-alignment and of the Non-Aligned Movement, which is seen as pro-Communist.

The main objectives of Singapore's foreign policy are to secure its political survival as a sovereign nation state, and to ensure its continued economic prosperity – each of which depends on the other, and both of which are subject to the constraints of small size and dependence on the regional and world environments. The objective of military security has led to massive internally-financed defense expenditures and the development of modern armed forces. Within the region, the Singapore government supports a strong US military presence (currently in the Philippines) – though not on its own territory – opposes a Soviet military presence (in Vietnam), and contributes to the support of the anti-Vietnamese Cambodian resistance movement on the Thai border.

To ensure its own political survival, Singapore's political and diplomatic objectives have focused, on the one hand, on developing strong positive relationships with governments of neighboring countries. Active membership in ASEAN is an important component of this strategy. On the other hand, Singapore takes a tough stand internationally on any violation of the territorial integrity of sovereign states, especially small ones, on any grounds whatsoever. It is probably best known for its leadership of the ASEAN group in opposing UN recognition for the Vietnamese-backed regime of Heng Samrin in Cambodia, on the grounds that

> to make the world safer for other small states we must prove that no state, not even Vietnam, can be allowed to violate these fundamental principles. If Vietnam succeeds, other aggressors might be encouraged and make the world a more dangerous place for small states. (Singapore's Minister of State for Foreign Affairs, speaking at the UN General Assembly in October 1986. Quoted in Leifer, 1987: 52.)

In addition,

> ASEAN's commitment to the principle of national sovereignty over the Cambodia issue reinforces indirectly the respect of ASEAN's partners for Singapore's independence. (Leifer, 1987: 52.)

In addition to opposing the Vietnamese occupation of Cambodia, the Singapore government has publicly opposed other similar international incursions, such as the US invasion of Grenada in 1983 (despite its own ideological opposition to Marxism and general support for US foreign policy), and for a long time objected to the Indonesian occupation of East Timor (despite its ideological opposition to the left-wing Timorese liberation movement, and at the risk of antagonizing a large and powerful near neighbor). For Singapore, the principle of the sovereignty of small states must never be violated. In this it shares a common interest with Brunei, with whom there is a close relationship.

Singapore's autonomy has also been an issue in occasional policy moves which have annoyed 'big brother' Malaysia. One recent example was Singapore's arrest, trial and incarceration for fraudulent business practices of Tan Koon Swan when he was leader of the Malaysian Chinese Association, second most important political party in the ruling government coalition. This action antagonized Chinese Malaysians, but was seen by the Singapore government as necessary for salvaging the integrity of its stock market and financial sector, which had been undermined by Tan's malpractices.

Another very contentious incident involved the 1987 state visit to Singapore of Israel's President Chaim Herzog, which upset both the Malay-Muslim minority in Singapore and Muslims in Malaysia, who protested the Singapore government's insensitivity to their feelings. Prime Minister Lee Kuan Yew's dubious claim that he was not informed in advance of Herzog's visit and would have disallowed it if he had known, was a rare admission that this decision might have been a mistake. A few weeks later, however, Lee's son Brigadier-General Lee Hsien Loong said in a public speech that Singapore Malays were not inducted into the airforce because the government did not want them to face a conflict between duty to their country and duty to their religion, should Singapore's enemy in a time of a war be a Muslim nation. This statement affronted both Singapore Malays, who felt their loyalty questioned (as it had already been over their reaction to the Herzog visit), and Malaysia, which felt it was being unfairly targeted as the likely enemy.

In these and other incidents, Singapore has put its sovereign rights first, above diplomatic considerations, and although this has annoyed its neighbors, it has not yet caused Singapore to bear any adverse consequences. Even Singapore Malays assert their country's right to sovereign decision-making, and resent the intervention of others (for example, Malaysians) supposedly 'on their behalf'. For its part, the Singapore government has never commented on its neighbors' policies which discriminate against their ethnic Chinese citizens, being at pains to assert its identity as a Singaporean rather than Chinese nation, and being sensitive also to the feelings of its own Malay-Muslim minority. It has demonstrated its lack of favoritism towards ethnic Chinese by its ruthless rejection of Vietnamese 'boat-people' refugees who were ethnic Chinese. And in recognition of its neighbors' ethnic sensibilities, Singapore will not establish full diplomatic relations with the People's Republic of China until at least Indonesia joins the Philippines in doing so. This diplomatic move is expected by 1990 without jeopardizing Singapore's close economic relations with Taiwan.

Relations between Singapore and Malaysia improved considerably in 1988 and 1989, with reciprocal visits of Prime Ministers and senior cabinet officials, the signing of water and natural gas agreements, plans for developing a second Causeway or other surface transportation link between the two countries, and increased inflows of Singapore investments into Malaysia, especially in the neighboring state of Johore. Yet some irritations remain, such as Singapore's ever-tightening restrictions on foreign workers, most of whom are Malaysians.

Among the other ASEAN countries, relations with Brunei have always been close, and Singapore has begun disbursing in-kind economic assistance to the Philippines. Official contacts with Indonesia have become more frequent and relations generally closer, with Singapore troops even being allowed to train on Indonesian soil. Friction with Thailand over Singapore's forced repatriation of over 10 000 illegal Thai foreign workers in 1989 has apparently been smoothly resolved.

Singapore's established practice of putting its sovereign rights and autonomy first extends beyond the region to its relations with the superpowers as well. A notable case was the so-called 'Hendrickson affair' of 1988, when Singapore expelled an American diplomat whom it accused of interfering in its domestic politics by consorting with opponents of the government. The US retaliated by expelling a Singapore diplomat in the US, and anti-US protests and even rare public demonstrations were mounted in otherwise tightly-controlled Singapore (obviously with the government's approval if not its organization). This event came on top of persistent US objections to human rights and press freedom violations in Singapore, including restrictions on US-owned publications. But Singapore was clearly not constrained in this foreign policy action by its heavy economic dependence on US trade and investment; on the contrary, it is likely that this heavy mutual dependence actually enabled Singapore to act with impunity against its close friend, which it knew would not and could not retaliate in any serious way. The incident was probably motivated by domestic politics, since the government used it to discredit potential popular opposition candidates who had had contact with Hendrickson as disloyal agents of a foreign power, and to justify their political detention. But within a few months, good relations were restored between the two countries. Singapore had once again walked away unscathed from a skirmish it had instigated with a major foreign power, suggesting that some degree of 'dependency reversal' has occurred in the political as well as the economic realm of its external relations.

Economically, Singapore as a small nation dependent on world trade and open access to foreign markets strongly believes in free trade, is a practitioner of what it preaches, and a forceful advocate for free trade internationally. It typically joins with other developing countries in denouncing the escalating protectionism of developed countries, but has also broken ranks with the developing countries where their policies have opposed free trade. It has even refused to participate in ASEAN regional co-operation schemes involving trade restrictions, such as the ASEAN Industrial Projects.

For Singapore, economic self-interest always overrides ideological and political beliefs and even stated policy. Thus, to the displeasure of its ASEAN neighbors and the US, private traders in Singapore trade increasingly with Vietnam despite the government's official support and even promulgation of an economic boycott of that nation. Other trade-related issues which have made Singapore unpopular with its friends include its role in the international traffic in some endangered wildlife species, and official tolerance until recently of widespread violation of intellectual property rights, especially in the audio and video industries. This last issue has been settled, however, as it began to threaten the free foreign market access for Singapore's other manufactured exports, as well as Singapore's own budding development of proprietary technology. In other such conflicts Singapore's insistence on the principle of government non-interference in free trade usually serves its economic self-interest.

As noted above, Singapore's foreign policy does not include policies to reduce its external economic dependence, which is regarded as both inevitable and, on balance, beneficial to the economy as well as to political survival. But diversification of external dependence has been a policy goal alongside maximizing trade and foreign investment; as a result Singapore's trade and foreign investment flows are less concentrated by partner and investor country than is the case for many other developing countries. In 1986, its three largest trading partners were the US, Japan and Malaysia, accounting for 18.9 per cent, 14.5 per cent and 14 per cent of total trade respectively. Between 1980 and 1986, US firms accounted for 47 per cent of all new non-oil manufacturing investment, European Community firms for 22.5 per cent, and Japanese firms for 18 per cent; the Japanese share rose to 41 per cent, and the US share dropped to 37 per cent, in 1986 (Ministry of Trade and Industry, 1987). In 1985 US firms accounted for 21 per cent of total sales in the manufacturing sector, while Japanese firms accounted for 12 per cent, compared with 38 per cent for Singapore firms (Department of Statistics, 1987). Recently, as a consequence of the 1985/86 recession, more efforts have been made to cultivate economic relations with a broader range of countries, and with some success. Already Singapore's external trade and investment relations are increasing with other Asian Pacific countries, and decreasing, in relative terms, with the West.

Singapore does not believe in regulating multinational corporations in the sense of restricting their activities relative to those of local corporations. Multinationals are subject to the same government controls and regulations which apply to local firms, and these have not been inconsiderable. During the 1985/86 recession many multinational as well as local companies complained of excessive bureaucratic intervention in their businesses, and some deregulation has begun following the report of the Economic Committee. There do, however, remain sectors of the economy where foreign, and even local private, participation is not permitted – usually sectors monopolized by the government or state agencies, for example, in utilities and communications, though this too may change. The restrictions or regulations which remain often seem to reflect a state-vs-private-sector rather than foreign-vs-local distinction. But the privatization of state assets and functions has begun, and foreign firms have been allowed limited participation in the equity of privatized enterprises. At the same time the government is actively encouraging large local private and state-owned enterprises to 'go multinational'.

Government regulation of the financial sector remains more onerous than international financial firms favor, and is a deterrent to Singapore's continued growth as an international financial center. And despite fairly successful attempts to develop Singapore into an information services center with a lively printing and publishing industry, the government has been persistently heavy-handed in its treatment of the foreign press, where it has perceived that press to be interfering in Singapore's domestic politics, or undermining its economy. In 1986 and 1987 alone there were conflicts and restrictions involving *Time*, the *Asian Wall Street Journal*, the *Far Eastern Economic Review*, and the *Economist*.

In general, the government's position is that though it favors free enterprise in principle, where free enterprise conflicts with the national interest, the government must intervene to protect the national interest even at some cost to the economy. External economic dependence in and of itself is not seen as necessarily jeopardizing the national interest, and so government intervention is not often motivated by a desire to reduce such dependence. Despite this economic dependence, however, the Singapore government is resolutely independent in its foreign policy, determined to frequently – and often defensively – assert its sovereign rights, and to resist what it too readily perceives as foreign 'interference', even from close friends like the US and Malaysia. It nevertheless remains ever ready and willing to criticize foreigners and foreign countries and governments for their policy shortcomings, reflecting a curious blend of insecurity and arrogance in government policy-makers. For example, after making a fetish of foreigners not being entitled to comment on Singapore's domestic politics, Prime Minister Lee Kuan Yew was himself forced to apologize to the Australian Prime Minister for criticizing his immigration policy while on a state visit to Australia in 1988.

Finally, in both the economic and the political realms of its external relations, Singapore appears to be making a fairly graceful transition to its assumed status of a developed nation in the 1990s. It accepted and has adjusted to its 'graduation' from developing-country eligibility for US GSP, and has embarked on a modest development aid programme for the Philippines, as well as increased its investments in neighboring countries. As a responsible citizen of the world community of nations, Singapore has even sent 21 policemen to join the UN peace-keeping force in Namibia.

Judging by Singapore's continued peaceful, unthreatened and unquestioned sovereign existence, its economic prosperity, its extensive trading relations, and its friendly political relations with nearly all countries of the world, including the West, the Soviet bloc, China, Japan, the ASEAN countries and the rest of the Third World, foreign policy-makers have been highly successful in realizing their objectives. Where conflicts and contradictions arise between different foreign policy objectives, political sovereignty and economic viability always dominate over ideology and state-to-state relations. As Leifer has put it,

> Those in charge of the destiny of Singapore never take its future existence for granted. They are moved by the apprehension articulated by Lee Hsien Loong that 'overnight, an oasis may become a desert', and by the conviction that 'goodwill is no substitute for self-interest'. (Leifer, 1987: 53)

Nevertheless,

> In order to survive and prosper, Singapore is obliged to learn to live with its neighbours . . . [Since priority in foreign policy was

indicated by Lee Hsien Loong, who pointed out that] 'a wise nation will make sure that its survival and well-being are in the interests of other states'. (Leifer, 1987: 55)

CONCLUSION

The objectives of Singapore's foreign policy, necessitated by its small size, geographical location and ethnic character, are to ensure the country's economic prosperity and political survival, both of which are closely intertwined, and to preserve the regime. Economic prosperity has been achieved by active participation in the world market in alliance with multinational capital, giving the rest of the world – including its regional neighbors – both a direct economic interest in Singapore's survival, and a symbolic interest in its continuation as a model of successful, outward-oriented Western-style capitalist development. Economic prosperity has made possible a strong self-funded military capability to deter potential external enemies, thereby preserving national security, which is further enhanced by membership in ASEAN and an absence of superpower alliances. Overall, Singapore's foreign policy is characterized by a pragmatic self-interest which prevails over ideology in matters related to national sovereignty and economic prosperity. External dependence is viewed as an inevitability, not a problem, and has been successfully managed, even used to advantage. Despite occasional problems and mistakes, the government has generally been successful in meeting its foreign policy objectives, and has met little domestic opposition to its foreign policies, a situation which is unlikely to change in the foreseeable future.

BIBLIOGRAPHY

Chia Siow Yue (1985), 'The Role of Foreign Trade and Investment in the Development of Singapore', in Walter Galenson (ed.), *Foreign Trade and Investment, Economic Growth in the Newly Industrializing Asian Countries* (Madison, Wisconsin: The University of Wisconsin Press), 259–97.

Department of Statistics, Singapore (1987), *Report on the Census of Industrial Production 1985*. Singapore, January.

Holloway, Nigel (1987), 'Blunt graduate from a tough school of leaders, an interview with S. Dhanabalan', *Far Eastern Economic Review* 8 January, 54–8.

Leifer, Michael (1987), 'Overnight, an oasis may become a desert', *Far Eastern Economic Review* 8 January, 52–5.

Lim, Linda (1985), 'Singapore's Elections: Snatching Defeat from the Jaws of Victory', *Southeast Asia Business* No. 4 (Winter), 20–5.

Lim, Linda Y. C. (1987a), 'Capital, Labor and the State in the Internationalization of High-Tech Industry: The Case of Singapore', in Mike Douglass and John Friedmann (eds), *Transnational Capital and Urbanization on the Pacific Rim, Proceedings of a Conference*, Center for Pacific Rim Studies, UCLA, Summer.

Lim, Linda Y. C. (1987b), 'The State and Private Capital in Singapore's Economic Development', in *Political Economy: Studies in the Surplus Approach*, Vol. 3, No. 2, 201–22.

Lim, Linda Y. C. (1987c), 'Export-Led Industrialisation, Labour Welfare and International Labour Standards in Singapore', in Lionel Demery and Tony Addison (eds), *Wages and Labour Conditions in the Newly Industrialising Countries of Asia* (London: Overseas Development Institute).

Lim, Linda and Pang Eng Fong (1986), *Trade, Employment and Industrialisation in Singapore* (Geneva: International Labour Organization).

Lim, Linda, Pang Eng Fong and Ronald Findlay (1987), 'The Political Economy of Poverty, Equity and Growth: Singapore 1959–1987', paper presented for the World Bank Workshop on the Political Economy of Poverty, Equity and Growth, in Fez, Morocco, 25 April–4 May 1987. (To be published by the World Bank.)

Ministry of Trade and Industry, Singapore (1986), *The Singapore Economy: New Directions*. Report of the Economic Committee, February.

Ministry of Trade and Industry, Singapore (1987), *Economic Survey of Singapore, 1986*.

Pang, Eng Fong and Chan Heng Chee (1987), 'The Political Economy of Development in Singapore 1959–1986', in Pang Eng Fong and Chan Heng Chee (eds), *The Political Economy of Development in ASEAN* (Singapore: Institute of Southeast Asian Studies).

Tan, Augustine (1984), 'Changing Patterns of Singapore's Foreign Trade and Investment since 1960', in You Poh Seng and Lim Chong Yah (eds), *Singapore: Twenty-Five Years of Development* (Singapore: Nan Yang Xing Xhou Lianhe Zaobao) 38–77.

Wilairat, Kawin (1975), *Singapore's Foreign Policy: The First Decade* (Singapore: Institute of Southeast Asian Studies).

9 Philippine Foreign Policy
David Wurfel

In comparison with other countries in the region the Philippines and its policies have four major distinguishing characteristics. First, the Philippines has been more dependent for trade, investment, credit, and military assistance on one power over a longer period than any other Southeast Asian state. Despite the growing intrusion of Japan into the region, the Philippines remains most tightly linked with the US. It is, of course, the only ex-colony of the US in the region, with a cultural as well as structural legacy. Second, as a consequence of the first point and despite the abrupt changes of regime type in 1972 and 1986, there has not been a full foreign policy restructuring. Helping to sustain a unique relationship and fostering special perceptions of the external environment is the Philippine's geographical separation from other Asian countries. The fourth distinguishing characteristic is that, with the possible exception of Burma or, for a time, Cambodia, the Philippines has the weakest state structure in the region, measured in terms of ability to maintain order, implement decisions, and extract resources, with only the early martial law years being at variance from that pattern. This is manifest in foreign policy by the weakness of the bureaucracy, the child of patronage politics. As a result the policy process has been easily affected by the pressures of intra-élite rivalries, organized interests – both foreign and domestic – and the intrusions of elected politicians, their business friends, and their wives. Together these four characteristics give Philippine foreign policy its distinctive flavor.

SOCIETY, ECONOMY AND POLITY

Philippine society is loosely structured, dominated by a complex pattern of patron-client relations which arose from the ancient bilateral kinship system overlayed by increasing economic inequality. Human relations beyond the nuclear family tend to be calculated for mutual benefit. Traditionally the weak seek protection not so much in group cohesion as in finding a strong patron. Patrons who do not fulfill the obligations traditionally incumbent upon their superior wealth and power are abandoned. However, crisis assistance from relatives or friends creates an undying debt of gratitude. Such cultural values seem to have had an impact on Filipino thinking about international relations (Wurfel, 1966: 152ff). Philippine society more recently, because of the nature of economic policies followed, has been rent by increasing class conflict. A substantial number of peasants and workers, led by some intellectuals, have thus adopted Marxist analysis which glorifies class struggle.

Though the Philippines is home to over 85 distinct languages and dialects, among the approximately 90 per cent of Christian Filipinos cultural cohesion is greater than it is in most other Southeast Asian societies. However, the two most significant ethnic minorities, the Chinese and the Moros, do have an impact on foreign policy. The Chinese, who now number only a few hundred thousand, are important because of their disproportionate economic influence and because their ancestral homeland is a nearby great power. The Moros, or Filipino Muslims, numbering perhaps three million, and concentrated in Mindanao and the Sulu archipelago, were never assimilated to the Filipino nation. A combination of social change, international currents, and perverse government policies, particularly in the matter of land rights, led to an intensified Muslim consciousness in the late 1960s, and to rising armed conflict, which turned Manila's attention toward the Muslim world (Wurfel, 1985: 222–7).

In 1972 the Philippines stood third in ASEAN in terms of per capita GNP – a 'middle ranking developing country' by worldwide standards. But by the mid-1980s it had become ASEAN's poorest, and is now struggling to regain the 1981 per capita GNP in the 1990s. The economy was dominated by a largely indigenous entrepreneurial élite (the distinctly Chinese role declined from the 1950s as assimilation progressed) with legitimate and influential access to the policy process (see Agpalo, 1962 and Stauffer, 1966). This weakened state autonomy. Despite past state interventions, for example attempts at land reform and minimum wage laws, wealth and income are more inequitably distributed than elsewhere in Southeast Asia. In fact, the concentration of wealth has grown in the last generation, which has contributed to growing unrest. Besides being highly inequitable, the Philippine economy is heavily dependent on US trade, investment and credit, a legacy of the colonial era.

The Philippine polity, though profoundly affected by socio-economic structures and indigenous cultural values, has borrowed major institutions from the US, by way of the colonial experience. Formal independence in 1946 was preceded by 30 years of almost complete internal self-government, with free elections. The bureaucracy was immersed in patronage politics by the 1920s. Democratic institutions operated primarily for the benefit of the élite; only in the late 1960s did populist tendencies assert themselves, interrupted by the imposition of martial law in 1972. Since the departure of Marcos and the end of the authoritarian period in February 1986, populist democratic tendencies have re-emerged; but the socio-economic élite, which has not significantly changed in composition, appears to be reasserting its dominance through patronage politics. Though mass participation is greater than in the 1960s, the political role of the military has also grown. This holds the possibility of future confrontation. In all periods political parties, important for electoral victory, have had almost no impact on policy.

Despite the rapid expansion of middle class political participation in 1985–86, before that the trend had been towards polarization between ideological extremes. In fact, the Philippines has the strongest Communist-led insurgency in Southeast Asia. It began, like the Viet Minh, as an anti-Japanese guerrilla force during the Second World War, growing to be a threatening revolutionary army – the Huks – at the gates of Manila in 1950, after which it was crushed with US military aid, charismatic leadership and a taste of reform. It rose again in the late 1960s under new leadership, but was apparently put down after the declaration of martial law. In fact, however, martial law created the political conditions for its revival; the New People's Army and the National Democratic Front were vehicles for the greatest Communist strength ever by the early 1980s, achieved without significant foreign aid. The doctrinaire anti-Communism which serves the interests of the military institution re-emerged with new vigor after 1986.

POLICY-MAKERS

Although the degree of involvement of particular individuals varied from issue to issue, foreign policy-makers are essentially the top political élite, since the role of the bureaucracy has seldom been very important. Before martial law these numbered 30–40 persons, primarily elected officials (the President, and leading members of Congress), prominent cabinet members, as well as influential Church leaders, journalists, and businessmen. The élite were almost all male and highly educated (87 per cent were college graduates and two-thirds had a second university degree – though less than 15 per cent had any education abroad) (Makil, 1970; Simbulan, 1965; Wurfel, 1979).

The top élite after 1972 took on a somewhat different shape. Power was, of course, more tightly concentrated in the President and his family. Elected legislators were gone, as were journalists. A few generals entered the top élite as did a few businessmen financially linked to the President and his wife (the 'cronies'), replacing families of old wealth. The cabinet became relatively more important. The change in business representation in the top élite had a broader significance: those with old wealth, engaged in commerce, agriculture and manufacturing with relatively minor links to foreign capital (roughly eqivalent to the Marxist category of 'national bourgeoisie') were out, while the 'compradors', new wealth that was heavily dependent on foreign credit, capital and technology, were in. This was not, however, a simple shift in economic structure, but an over-night transformation of political access and influence determined by Ferdinand Marcos. The 'relative autonomy' of the neo-patrimonial Philippine state from the old élite had been sharply increased. By 1980, however, the economic interests of the cronies had become so wide and so distinct from the priorities of technocrats, that crony political influence was directed against that bureaucratic élite, at one point nearly dislodging the Prime Minister. Pressures from the new economic élite thus had again reduced state autonomy, a distinction between the Philippines and the East Asian NICs which may help explain the former's relatively poor economic performance (Johnson, 1985).

The values and attitudes of the top élite produced images of the Philippines that had consequences for both national power and foreign policy. The shifting self-image had at least two salient dimensions, Asian identity and world importance, in some way linked. Soon after independence, explicitly under Quirino and implicitly under Magsaysay, the Filipino élite saw itself as apart from Asia, but able to form a 'bridge' between Asia and the West (Lopez, 1966: 29–31). This would have meant a uniquely important world role. But during the 1950s, as Filipino leaders came into closer contact with their Asian neighbors, they became aware of the low regard in which they were held, precisely because they were not seen as 'Asian', and of their consequent incapacity to play any role as bridge. A new spate of realism spawned the sense of being a small, weak country. This low posture was functional for gaining greater acceptance in the Asian community, while the pre-Western cultural heritage was resurrected in art, dance and historical research.

By the 1970s, under Ferdinand and Imelda Marcos, self-deprecation was abandoned for unprecedented world ambition, culminating in an unsuccessful bid to host the UN General Assembly meetings. The greatest boost to the national ego, however, was the highly favorable world press treatment of the non-violent 'revolution' of February 1986. But the quick turn in the world press to sharp criticism, the seriousness of internal problems, plus the empowerment of a genuinely modest president in Mrs Aquino, revived the 'small, weak' self-image.

THE POLICY PROCESS

general

A well institutionalized foreign policy process is one which relies heavily on a specialized bureaucracy and which usually conforms to procedural norms. By these standards 1972 was a turning point, in different directions. Before martial law constitutional guidelines were taken much more seriously, with the Supreme Court often being asked to adjudicate constitutional disputes. As a result the Supreme Court sometimes made decisions with important foreign policy consequences, for instance, on the criminal jurisdiction of the US under the bases agreement (Dodd, 1968) or on the rights of US businessmen under the Parity Amendment to the 1935 Constitution. Congress also had an important role.

After 1972 President Marcos assumed for himself all power, and the new constitution and the courts were used, often capriciously, to justify his acts. He exercised all executive and legislative powers without a National Assembly until 1978, and even after that he could override the legislature with his own decrees at will. The exercise of his unlimited power to make decrees became increasingly irregular, with secret decrees as well as public ones. Decisions lost legitimacy and became more difficult to implement, Not just foreign policy, but the entire decision-making process was poorly institutionalized.

In the constitutionalist era a confidante of the President had noted that the Philippines did not have a 'truly professional' foreign service (Corpuz, 1966: 64). He also pointed out that diplomats did not owe their primary loyalty to the foreign service, or even to the President,

patron, client

but to their Congressional patrons who secured the job. More than a decade later the President himself noted the need to 'further professionalize the service' (Marcos, 1980: 213).

However, there had been a shift in 1972 towards a greater role for the Department of Foreign Affairs, and for other bureaucratic agencies involved in the making of foreign economic policy, for instance, the Department of Finance, the Central Bank, the National Economic Development Authority or the Board of Investments. This was a consequence of both the emphasis on an increased role for 'technocrats' (top bureaucrats with high academic qualifications and no political backers besides the President) and of the absence of a legislature sharing in policy or patronage. Career diplomats felt that their influence had been enhanced in the first few years of martial law; even the First Couple usually accepted their advice on foreign affairs. But by the late 1970s power and wealth had so corrupted the top leaders that decisions were increasingly made on personal whims without rational analysis. The fact that the First Lady more often substituted for Mr Marcos as his illness worsened also helped explain the situation. The policy process lacked institutionalization in both essential respects.

Thus it is fair to say that the 'rational choice' model of foreign policy decision-making, requiring a solid institutional base, was by itself seldom the most useful approach to understanding Philippine decisions. Intra-élite politics and the leader's imperative were, on the other hand, important in explaining Philippine foreign policy throughout, and were dominant on many occasions. Before 1972 intra-élite politics was structured in large part by the struggle between legislative and executive branches inherent in a system of checks and balances, though, of course, there were also factions within cabinet, and personal rivalries within the Department of Foreign Affairs. The nationally elected Senate usually had several members with presidential ambitions, intent on making life difficult for the incumbent chief executive. The most celebrated conflict over foreign policy was that between the pro-American President Ramon Magsaysay and the nationalist Senator Claro Recto in the mid-1950s. This was complicated by the fact that the under-secretary of foreign affairs was a protegé of Senator Recto, while the secretary spoke for the President. Thus intra-bureaucratic rivalries were linked to those between Recto, with some Senate backing, and the President (Romani, 1956: ch 6; Abueva, 1971: ch 19). Perhaps the greatest impact of this controversy was the scuttling of the Garcia-Ohno

Agreement on Japanese reparations. Political rivalries intervened to delay an important foreign policy decision again in the 1960s. President Macapagal, acceding to an American request, asked Congress for funds to send a contingent of Filipino troops to Vietnam. Senate President Marcos, who was soon to be Macapagal's opponent in the 1965 elections, took a nationalist stance against it. But after he was elected, Marcos himself pushed through Congress essentially the same proposal (Buss, 1977: 42–3, 46–7). The legislative role in policymaking re-emerged strongly after an elected Congress reconvened in July 1987.

DOMESTIC RESOURCES AND CONSTRAINTS

With a population of over 50 million and a per capita GNP of several hundred dollars, rising steadily, plus a wealth of natural and human resources, the Philippines by the late 1970s should have been able to qualify as a 'middle power', at least in the Third World. With nearly a quarter of a million men under arms, in regular and militia forces, neither was Philippine military strength insignificant. The level of output of the institutions of higher education provided the Philippines with a pool of skills that was used both at home and around the world. The United Nations and its agencies had given prominent positions to several Filipinos, most particularly to Rafael Salas, Marcos' former executive secretary, who was under-secretary general and director of the UN Population Programme. The financial resources and sophistication of the Philippine corporate world were also sufficient to be making an impact abroad.

But whatever the potentials – which could be realized only in the context of a confident self-image – Philippine constraints far exceeded resources, not uncommon in the Third World. One constraint that had been painfully obvious even in the 1970s was that created by a divided political culture, with many Muslims rejecting Filipino identity, then rising in rebellion. Coming as it did in conjunction with a world oil crisis, with Muslim states the major suppliers, this jeopardized Philippine petroleum supplies.

In some ways the very nature of the political system was a constraint. A ruling élite with a neo-colonial mentality quickly turns to the dominant power when resources are needed. And a neo-patrimonial system – in which support is recruited by distributing material benefits, from both private and public sources, controlled by the patron – with an expanding population and increasing political mobilization is always seeking new resources to reinforce and extend clientage. Since the bureaucracy in such a system is weak, and thus also extractive capabilities, it will have an even greater tendency to turn to the international patron for help, as happened especially under Roxas, and Quirino, and again under Marcos. Philippine bargaining power on the world scene, already constricted by pressures from the world capitalist system, was limited by these domestic tendencies.

The most serious constraint until 1986 was regime legitimacy at home and abroad; already low in the mid-1970s, it declined further as the 1980s progressed. After the assassination of Ninoy Aquino, the world was more aware of how Mr. Marcos dealt with opponents and how the Filipino people felt about his government. Armed opposition spread to more and more provinces. His need for American support grew.

The growing political instability which declining legitimacy produced also affected economic decisions. Billions in investments left the country in the months after the assassination of Aquino. By the end of 1986 the Philippines had become the first country in the region to register negative economic growth for three years straight. The GNP declined by nearly 10 per cent with the Philippines' increasingly referred to as 'the sick man of Asia'. The expanding debate in the US Congress on military assistance highlighted corruption in the Philippine armed forces. The utilization of existing diplomatic skills and the training of younger foreign service officers also deteriorated. Many of the factors which allow a nation to mobilize its resources and then apply them to foreign policy were in decline

Even when governmental legitimacy rebounded after February 1986 and national pride swelled at the unique, non-violent method used to banish a dictator, the extent of economic devastation and military incompetence only became more obvious; national power itself did not rebound, for capabilities were not rebuilt. Nevertheless the promise of more rational and honest economic management did initially improve Philippine bargaining power with the IMF and private banks. By 1987, however, political stirrings in the military revived Filipino self-doubt about stability as well as international misgivings. A patronage binge by Vice-President and Foreign Minister Salvador Laurel had further weakened the Department of Foreign Affairs. Laurel's successor, Raul Manglapus, found the restoration of at least minimal professionalism a difficult task in 1988, especially since he was himself subject to patronage pressures.

THE EXTERNAL ENVIRONMENT: CONSTRAINTS AND PERCEPTIONS

While international constraints may have appeared to some to be more severe than those emerging from the domestic political economy, they were often intertwined with domestic initiatives or failures. Dependence on the US in several respects was not simply an imposition of the world system on the Philippines – though in part it *was* that, dating back to 1898 when Dewey sailed, uninvited, into Manila Bay – but was also a reflection of the attitudes, actions and inactions of Filipino leaders, which helped transform assymetrical interdependence into 'dependency'. It was fair to say, as some did (Pomeroy, 1977), that that leadership was itself the creature of American colonialism. But after more than 40 years of possession of the apparatus of legal sovereignty, with the bargaining potential which that involves, the colonial heritage does not seem to be a fully adequate explanation of all that has happened. Even the declaration of martial law, which was so convenient for American military and economic interests, and was stamped with US approval, was to a considerable degree a product of raw Filipino ambitions within the framework of intra-élite competition. Even as one recognizes the impositions of the world system, it is not possible to ignore the Philippine political process.

Classical *dependencia* would deny any autonomy to either leadership formation or foreign policy in the Third World. But here it is necessary to assert the semi-autonomy of both, as would appear to be the view even of some writers in the dependency mode (for instance, Sunkel, 1969). Nevertheless, we must reiterate that the scope of autonomy in the Philippines over time has been less than for most other Southeast Asian states. Dependence has both economic and military dimensions. Economic dependence can be quantified in the areas of trade, investment, aid, and debt, moving from the oldest form of world-wide economic relationships to the form most recently of major interest.

Trade

Philippine trade was skewed toward the metropolitan power more strongly than that of any other Southeast Asian colony. Just before independence 80 per cent of Philippine trade was with the US, and in 1946 the Bell Trade Act of the US Congress legislated an extension of free trade until 1974. Reliance on US markets, and high US prices, helped to determine the costs of Philippine production in sugar, once the major export, thus making later efforts at diversification very painful. Reliance on American suppliers, on the other hand, made Filipino consumers keenly aware of and loyal to American brands, thus inhibiting production and sales by Filipino entrepreneurs in the same product line. Nevertheless, Philippine trade with the US did drop from nearly 75 per cent in 1950 to about 33 per cent in 1973, a lessening of trade dependence. Yet in the 1980s the US, though rivaled by Japan, was still the major trading partner, the only case in Southeast Asia where that position had hardly changed in 50 years.

Investment

American investment built up over the colonial period until it was $ 173 million by the late 1930s. This investment – according to US sources – grew to nearly $ 450 million by 1961, but at a declining rate as 1974 approached, the date on which special status for Americans, that is, parity with Filipino citizens, was to come to an end (Villegas, 1983: 181).

While American investment in the Philippines by some standards may have seemed modest – Golay claimed that direct US investment in 1977 was only about 4 per cent of the assets of all non-governmental enterprises (Golay, 1983: 159) – by other standards it was extensive. A Philippine government study just before martial law found US-controlled firms had holdings of over $ 2 billion, amounting to 80 per cent of all foreign investment. Furthermore, 43 per cent of the sales of the top 50 Philippine corporations were made by firms with more than 50 per cent US equity, while in certain industries American dominance was even greater (Poblador, 1971). Nor was command of economic resources limited to investment capital: through interlocking directorates foreign-owned banks sometimes exercised control without much equity. And for every dollar foreign investors brought into the Philippines they borrowed $ 25 locally (Villegas, 1983: 11; Doherty, 1979).

This last phenomenon was so upsetting to Filipino entrepreneurs, who had to compete for scarce credit, that in 1977 – reviving a similar, unsuccessful, move in 1971 – a government committee was established to screen credit applications by foreign corporations, and then moved towards a policy to restrict approval. The US Ambassador came to the defense of American business interests on this one, however, and Philippine restrictions crumbled. Here was a clear negative link between the extent of American economic interests and Philippine government autonomy.

Aid

Government to government grants and loans may also constrain the recipient's autonomy. In the 1940s the threat of withholding of 'aid', in the form of war damage payments, was used to force the adoption of the 'parity amendment' to the Philippine constitution. In the early 1950s, when the US was still the only significant source of intergovernmental assistance, the offer of $ 250 million over a five-year period was made conditional on the signing of an agreement requiring the Philippine government to undertake certain reforms, upon recommendation of US advisers (Wurfel, 1959). While the US still calibrates its grants and loans to signal political favor or disfavor to recipients – AID releases to the Philippines in the four years prior to martial law were $ 56.2 million, compared to $240.5 million in the next four year period (Bello and Rivera, 1977: 50) – American leverage by the 1970s had been reduced by the fact that Japanese official development aid had become greater than that from the US. Yet in many situations the Japanese acted in concert with US policy anyway.

Debt

Foreign debt did not become a major constraint in the Philippines until the 1970s. This was, in part, an imposition of the external environment and, ironically, a consequence of Philippine policy designed to avoid the constraints of foreign investment. (It was noted, quite correctly, by officials in 1972 that foreign equity might flee on threat of political instability, whereas borrowing put capital under Filipino control.) The timing in the great spurt in foreign indebtedness – from $2.2 billion in 1972 to $ 9 billion by 1979, and then a threefold jump by 1985 – was at first linked to the world oil crisis of the early 1970s which produced hundreds of billions of 'petrodollars' which needed to be recycled. Bankers avidly peddled loans, seducing many a hapless Third-World leader. As the debt grew larger – World Bank loans to the Philippines, 1973–76, grew 1060 per cent, faster than to any other recipient – and interest rates climbed, the creditors' concern about repayment also escalated and thus their tendency to impose more conditions (Bello, 1982). But not until 1984 did non-performance on IMF conditions slow down lending.

Military
Military bases themselves have an ambivalent implication for dependency. The imposition of the bases agreement practically as a condition for legal sovereignty certainly demonstrated a neo-colonial status in 1946. Furthermore, the hundreds of millions of dollars of US expenditures each year to maintain and operate the bases flows into the Philippine economy and creates another type of economic dependence; this is an amount that the Philippines has come to count on. The presence of US forces also serves as an ultimate fallback, a potential source of assistance to a government facing a serious insurgency. The US began to play such a role in 1973–74, but then phased it out; calculations of political cost both in the Philippines and in the US cautioned against it.

However, just like a major investment of foreign capital after it is made, the bases once established can become a kind of hostage. They give bargaining power to the Philippines as long as the US wants to continue operating them without hindrance. This may have played a role in the secret funding of the Philippine contingent in Vietnam. But it was not until the negotiations began in 1975 on the bases agreement revision that the Philippine government appeared to recognize the full potential of its leverage. American withdrawal from Vietnam had actually increased the bases' strategic value, further enhanced by the US desire to project a presence in the Middle East.

In any case, US military assistance provided the overwhelming majority of supplies needed by the Philippine armed forces. In FY 1975 the Marcos budget revealed that ₱ 81 million was allocated to 'logistical services' and ₱ 45 million to a 'self-reliant defense posture', meaning investment in a Philippine-based small arms industry. In the same year US military assistance (grants and sales), mostly arms/ and equipment, totalled $ 54.8 million, or more than ₱ 363 million (US DoD, 1978; RP; 1975, 459, 465). Military supplies still come primarily from the US. It was this kind of logistical dependence that gave the Joint US Military Advisory Group (JUSMAG) advice such weight (see below). The slowing down of US military aid deliveries in the last years of the Marcos-Ver regime because the Armed Forces of the Philippines (AFP) would not follow the advice being given was thus 'self-reliance' purchased at considerable cost. What must be noted, however, is that the cost *was* shouldered because the line of advice was seen as threatening to the power of regime incumbents. This was, in fact, a pattern: deviance from the role of dependent élite was most often initiated only when top decision-makers felt their short-term power in jeopardy. Quirino in early 1950 was another case in point. Even in 1986 one could see this phenomenon, with Mrs. Aquino being most sharply critical of the US just at the point she felt she was not being supported by the White House.

The evidence of dependence on the US along several dimensions is quite impressive. But to argue 'dependency', or loss of autonomy, one must go further to show common interest between dominant and dependent élites and, I would insist, shared values and attitudes as well – what is frequently referred to as the 'neo-colonial' mentality. Shared élite values and interests are certainly both present in the Philippine case. But the introduction of import substituting industrialization in the late 1940s created new frictions, both between Americans and Filipinos and within the Filipino élite. A rupture was avoided by the Laurel-Langley Agreement of 1955 which provided for a compromise in which Filipinos could impose tariffs on US imports until 1974 more rapidly than the US could tax Philippine imports, while 'parity rights' for US businesses in the Philippines were greatly expanded. Filipino exporters, Filipino manufacturers and American investors in the Philippines all got something. Nevertheless, the rise of economic nationalism in the late 1950s indicated that the expanding group of Filipino manufacturers still felt disadvantaged.

The imposition of martial law and the ascendency of Marcos neo-patrimonialism from 1972 restored an earlier level of commonality between Filipino and American élite interests. Marcos, challenged politically by nationalist manufacturers and their friends, sought either to crush them or control them with martial rule. The single incident which most dramatically revealed the new pattern of shared interest was the Westinghouse contract to build (with outmoded technology) a nuclear power plant. Though the *New York Times* reported that a Marcos crony pocketed $ 30–40 million as middleman for the deal, subsequent indications are that persons closer to the centers of political power in both Washington and Manila received even more substantial benefit. The challenge of the revolutionary movement by 1979 further expanded areas of common political interest between the Marcos and US élites.

PERCEPTIONS

The Americanization of Filipino élite values and attitudes, the psychological dimension of neo-colonialism, brings us to the sharing of American perceptions of the external environment. In the late 1960s the *Far Eastern Economic Review* had noted that some viewed 'the Philippine political establishment as so closely tied to the US that it fails to conceive the possibility of separate national interests' (*FEER*, 28 December 1967). President Diosdado Macapagal, speaking for the Liberal Party, reminded his audience that 'Our party believes that if our Republic is to endure . . . our people must remain committed to . . . the free world led by the United States in the ceaseless struggle between democracy and communism' (Macapagal, 1961: 96–7). As leading members of Congress debated the sending of Filipino troops to Vietnam in 1965, they relied primarily on *Time* and *Newsweek* as sources of information, without questioning the journalistic biases; there were almost no independent Filipino sources on Vietnam. In fact, Vietnam was not even considered a 'crucial issue' by most members of the élite (Makil, 1970, Table II); it was before Congress only as a result of an American request.

When Ferdinand Marcos defeated Macapagal in 1965 he enthroned a new level of rhetorical autonomy, declaring that the 'first principle' underlying Philippine foreign policy was 'the conscious exercise of national independence and sovereignty on each and every issue', then led the Philippines into closer dependency on the US. Shared perceptions with the US of the world economy became relatively more important in the 1970s as technocrats trained at Wharton and Harvard took over management of foreign economic policy.

Marcos' ambivalence was perhaps more blatant, but not fundamentally different from that which underlay the policies of some of his predecessors. Even those Filipino leaders capable of flights of cold war rhetoric harbored a deep-seated love/hate relationship to the US which colored, unevenly, their world image. Macapagal out of power became quite critical of the US in the 1980s. A world image consistently inconsistent with that of the US also became the dominant one in intellectual circles by the early 1970s. Already in the 1950s Senator Claro Recto, the most renowned nationalist, had declared 'Asia for the Asians' and opposed a whole range of US policies with lengthy arguments that challenged standard American perceptions (Constantino, 1965).

But only three significant aspects of the external environment were seen differently by the Philippine and American ruling élites: Japan, the Borneo situation, and the world-wide colonial question. In no case, however, was the difference great enough to put a severe strain on Philippine-American relations and by the 1980s these differences had faded. The view of Japan in the 1950s was based, of course, on the fact that Filipinos, unlike Americans, had suffered an invasion and brutal occupation (Wurfel, 1986). But it was also linked to the Filipino image of Philippine-American relations. The absolute amount of postwar American aid to Japan, the enemy, was greater than that to the Philippines, the loyal ally (or client), for which Filipinos are still deeply resentful. Thus the Japanese obligation to pay reparations was much larger in Filipino than in American eyes, which produced policy conflict.

Differences over Sabah were less open, on a less salient issue, but still led to friction. While the US viewed the creation of Malaysia as an orderly transfer of power by a colonial ruler, which would lead to a stable pro-Western regime, most Philippine leaders, including the fiercely anti-Communist Macapagal, were not only sympathetic to Sukarno's charge of 'neo-colonialism', but were even concerned that there was a national security threat because left-wing Chinese from Singapore would have easy access to the Borneo territories (Fernandez, 1962). These images were, of course, useful, since they served to justify the Philippine opposition to Malaysia which was more firmly based on an entirely different ground, the territorial and proprietory claim to Sabah.

The third and final difference was derived not only from contrasting experiences between the Philippines and the US but from the awareness in Manila by the 1950s that the Philippines' international image needed bolstering. Thus the Philippines came to view colonial issues in the United Nations not as cold war questions, as the US often did, but as situations demanding a show of solidarity between colonial and ex-colonial peoples. This was the issue area in which there was greatest divergence between the US and the Philippines in the General Assembly.

Finally élite perceptions of foreign threats should be noted. Perhaps because of geographical isolation, Filipino leaders had less of a sense of threat from any direction than those in other Southeast Asian countries. Interviews in the early 1970s produced the conclusion that even senior military staff 'appear relatively unconcerned about foreign threats' (Maynard, 1976: 466). In the early postwar years the recollection of a real Japanese threat was strong, and is still latent. While the fear of China was reinforced by Cold War rhetoric in the 1950s and 1960s, it quickly dissipated as the US shifted its stance and Beijing avoided aiding the New People's Army (NPA). The 'threat of Vietnam' was sustained by Filipino participation in the war, even as non-combatants. But when the Americans withdrew, fears of and interest in Vietnam subsided, despite the invasion of Cambodia. Occasional reports of Soviet submarines from Camh Ranh Bay disgorging supplies on the Philippines coast seem to be without basis and are believed only on the far right. The unconcern about foreign threats may, in part, have been a side effect of most Filipinos' exaggerated notion of the efficacy of American power which was not really shaken even in 1975, since American strength *in* the Philippines was not affected. Certainly the highest salience reserved by the élite for US words, actions and capabilities cannot be doubted. Only a distinct minority define those words and deeds as seriously threatening.

FOREIGN POLICY OUTPUT

In talking about attitudes and images and about the changing structure of economic relations we have already suggested some possible patterns in the shifts of Philippine foreign policy since independence. It is now appropriate to group those patterns in four periods, though the differences between periods are not great. Philippine foreign policy has experienced a slow evolution, with no fundamental change in basic orientation because there have been no fundamental changes in the character of élites or élite images or in the nature of constraints.

Postwar Reconstruction: Pure Neo-Colonialism – 1946–57

Given the magnitude of wartime destruction and the granting of independence to a nation in ruins, the degree of economic and military dependence on the US was probably inevitable. The urgency of economic recovery displaced concerns for autonomy.

After more than three years of Japanese military oppression American colonialism looked very good by comparison. The Philippines was the only country in the colonial world that referred to the return of the Western colonial power at the end of the Second World War as 'liberation'. The US imposition of a constitutional amendment to favor American business, endorsed by President Manuel Roxas but faced with opposition in the Congress of the Philippines, was still supported in a referendum. The retention of 23 American bases with free rent for 99 years had been a prerequisite of the granting of independence. A Joint US Military Advisory Group was set up in March 1947 to train the new Philippine armed forces.

Elpidio Quirino, the second president, was faced with a growing Communist-led peasant rebellion in Luzon, and within a year witnessed the victory of Mao Zedong in China. He was not well regarded by Washington, because of corruption and mismanagement, and his call for an Asian NATO and more economic aid had been dismissed (Welch, 1984: 300–1). So that in early 1950 he briefly explored the question of neutralism (Buss, 1979: 29) apparently to attract the American attention that he had failed to get in a more suppliant mode. But with the invasion of South Korea in June, the Chinese threat became real and thus also the felt need for US protection. In 1951 he signed a rather weakly worded Mutual Security Treaty with the US. Both security and economic welfare goals took precedence over autonomy in Philippine policy priorities.

But the further growth of the Communist-led Huks nearby Manila was Quirino's main concern, as it was that of the US. American military aid increased and Ramon Magsaysay was appointed secretary of defense to reorganize and revitalize the armed forces. But in order to get substantial new economic assistance, Quirino had to sign an agreement that committed the Philippine government to tax, labor and agrarian reform and gave American advisers considerable opportunity to shape the policies in question. The Quirino-Foster Agreement was, in effect, institutionalized neo-colonialism, giving a peculiar legitimacy to American penetration of the Philippine political process, despite objections from some Filipino Congressmen. American penetration continued at a covert level with CIA guidance and support for Magsaysay's successful presidential campaign in 1953.

Magsaysay's pro-American sentiments were not hidden; during the campaign he said, 'I was not so sure . . . after we were given our independence that American-Philippine unity would last undiminished. These doubts are gone. We belong together and know it' (Abueva, 1971: 214n). It is not surprising that Magsaysay hosted the conference that created the US-dominated SEATO. He endorsed US policy in Vietnam after the Geneva Conference and some of his friends and supporters worked with the CIA to establish a Filipino civilian presence there. In fact, it may be said that Magsaysay's pro-Americanism stimulated the growth of the Filipino nationalist movement.

The Nationalist Interlude: 1957–72

Vice-President Carlos Garcia, who succeeded to the presidency when Magsaysay died in a plane crash in 1957, was much more sympathetic to the new nationalism than had been his predecessor. For a time it appeared that autonomy goals might be given highest priority. Senator Recto and his slogan 'Asia for the Asians' became so influential under Garcia that many Americans were frightened. But Recto's recommendation that the Philippines recognize Communist China was not followed. In fact, despite the rising tide of nationalism in the Congress and the press, Garcia felt the need to make the traditional pilgrimage to Washington to ask for aid. The Philippines continued to be a mainstay of SEATO. Nevertheless, Vice-President Macapagal, with a more pro-American image and reputedly some American financial backing, defeated Garcia's bid for re-election in 1961, primarily because charges of widespread corruption seemed justified to the voters.

For all of his pro-American rhetoric, however, Macapagal's foreign policy initiatives gave the US some discomfort. He had a long-time personal interest in the claim of the Sultanate of Sulu in the southern Philippines to North Borneo. In June 1962 Manila presented such a claim to the British, complicating plans for the formation of Malaysia. In the meantime Macapagal also became enthused about an old Philippine dream of a pan-Malayan federation, to be a counter to Chinese influence in Southeast Asia. After preparatory talks Macapagal and Sukarno, together with a somewhat reluctant Tunku Abdul Rahman of Malaysia, held a summit meeting in Manila in July 1963 where there was agreement in principle on the formation of a tripartite MAPHILINDO. But the dispute over

North Borneo caused the Philippines to withhold recognition of Malaysia later in the year, so that attempts to implement the MAPHILINDO idea failed. At the same time Sukarno's increasingly aggressive stance caused Macapagal to back away from that entente under pressure from his own intelligence advisers as well as the US. The US quietly scuttled Philippine efforts to get serious negotiations on their territorial claims. Macapagal's frustrations led him to change Philippine independence day from the US-determined 4 July and to end American diplomatic representation of Filipinos abroad in the absence of Philippine missions (Sussman, 1983: 210–28).

Yet in economic terms Macapagal's policies were quite congruent with US interests. He devalued the peso and removed foreign exchange controls, as well as undertaking other recommendations made by the IMF and favored by exporters. Before the end of his term he had requested Congress to authorize the sending of Philippine forces to South Vietnam. But the US regarded him as unreliable. The traditional Philippine ambivalence about the US had produced too much policy variance. US war damage funds which could have been released before Macapagal's re-election bid in 1965 were not; for this and other reasons he lost to Ferdinand Marcos. Marcos more skillfully wove the nationalist strain into a foreign policy that gained wide support without upsetting the Americans. In fact, he became quite successful at inducing expanded American aid and putting it to his own political benefit, as in the construction of school houses before the 1969 elections. And it was Marcos who received secret American funds to support Filipino troops in Vietnam.

Foreign Policy for Regime Survival: 1972–86

Even though the declaration of martial law in 1972 marked a severe restructuring in domestic politics, the break with the Philippine tradition of foreign policy was much more modest. It is true, however, that with the disbanding of the elected legislature the President was more completely in charge than ever before. For instance, the Taiwan Lobby in Congress which could have blocked relations with Beijing, was rendered nearly impotent. Furthermore, a regime which relied heavily on a greatly expanded military was much more concerned about its arming and supply. An authoritarian regime also had the capability to reduce the penetration of the system by friend and foe alike. Access to government officials by foreigners was, for the first time, restricted. Foreign support for labor unions and other NGOs was regulated. Military intelligence became both more pervasive and more effective.

Changes in the policy process were closely related to the declaration of martial law. But coincidentally there was also a change in the international environment in the 1970s which helped give a new cast to foreign policy. Strategic threats and challenges receded. There was no Korean invasion, no descending Chinese horde, nor even a new Malaysia on the border. The final Communist conquest of South Vietnam and Cambodia in 1975 had been a foregone conclusion for some time. Even top military officers were not concerned about foreign threats. Thus President Marcos had unchallenged control of the policy process and was not diverted by strategic fears. He could devote his attention to domestic priorities, as he did. He bolstered the regime by neutralizing its enemies and building support among key groups within society. For the first time regime survival became the dominant theme of Philippine foreign policy. It was designed to deny support to Muslim rebels and the New People's Army, and to win over intellectuals, the economic élite, and the middle class while solidifying support among the military. Marcos' policies were 'developmentalist' (in the sense used by Weinstein, 1976) since he saw rapid economic growth as the most likely source of legitimacy.

One nationalist critique had been of the ridiculous extremes to which anti-Communism had been carried – exclusion of the Yugoslav basketball team from a Manila tournament by President Macapagal is often cited as the zenith of this tendency. The Philippines had diplomatic relations with no Communist-ruled state until President Marcos' second elected term, when, prodded by nationalist industrialists, he exchanged ambassadors with Yugoslavia and Rumania. The big break came when an embassy was opened in Beijing in June 1975, following a visit by the First Couple. Nationalist intellectuals, including some senior foreign service officers, were assuaged. The Americans, of course, had already shown the way and the Civil Liberties Union of the Philippines claimed that 'The truth is that the "bold" and "innovative" moves taken by the Department of Foreign Affairs, which it passes off for "independence", are the latest variation of its traditional subservience to America's global interests' (CLUP statement, 15 October 1975). This was probably an exaggeration, but the American shift did permit the Philippine initiative to take place without disturbing the Washington-Manila axis (Quisumbing, 1983: 26–8). Thus the Marcos moves did not warrant being called a full restructuring.

Establishing relations with China served another purpose. The President gained Chinese assurances that they would provide no aid to the Philippine Communist movement – the Chinese were also eager for diplomatic relations. Undoubtedly, this proved a persuasive argument for Marcos' reluctant military brass. Furthermore, the Chinese promised small but steady shipments of oil to the Philippines at a time when Arabs were showing their displeasure with Marcos' military action against the Moros.

Diplomatic exchange with the Soviet Union was not accomplished until 1977. Since the Soviet's allies within the Philippines, the old Communist Party, had already been co-opted by Marcos, Moscow had a lower priority – but Moscow itself also showed less interest in the Philippines than did Beijing. In the same year the Philippines recognized the three Indochina states, and Vietnam pledged to refrain from the use of force or subversion.

The increasing prominence that Philippine foreign policy gave to ASEAN was also a response to the nationalist desire for a stronger Asian orientation. The membership of Indonesia, both a Moslem country and a major oil exporter, gave ASEAN added importance. Marcos was able to gain Jakarta's understanding of and sympathy on the Moro problem, plus expanded oil supplies. Good relations with Malaysia, made easier by Marcos' announcement in 1976 that he intended to drop the Philippines' Sabah claim, was facilitated within the ASEAN framework, helping to cut off the MNLF's foreign supply line. Furthermore, President Marcos described ASEAN in 1980 as an organization in which 'there are exchanges which indicate a common and mutual interest in security . . .', apparently referring to the anti-Communist intelligence network (*Manila Journal*, 18 February 1980).

Aside from ASEAN, Third-World affinity was shown by an (unsuccessful) effort to gain observer status at the Non-Aligned Conference in Colombo in 1976, an ostentatious appearance by the First Couple at the UNCTAD conference in Nairobi in the same year, and the hosting of UNCTAD in Manila in 1979, when Marcos helped draft the statement issued by the Group of 77 developing countries. Though designed to mollify Filipino nationalists, these events also provided an ego-satisfying role for the First Couple. (One has to recognize the existence of more than one level of motivation.)

Expanding ties with the Muslim world to help interdict support for the Moro forces included Imelda's visits to Cairo and Riyadh, and a Manila invitation to King Hussein, as well as a stronger pro-Arab stance on the Palestinian question. But the most dramatic and successful move was the opening to Colonel Muamar Khaddafi, who both supplied and influenced Nur Misuari, the MNLF leader, then living in Tripoli. The First Lady went to Libya as the President's emissary in December 1976 and, following personal talks in which she apparently persuaded Khaddafi to cut military aid to the Moro forces, a Philippine government team hammered out an agreement with Misuari for a cease-fire and Muslim 'autonomy' in parts of Mindanao and Sulu (*Manila Journal*, 9 January 1977). The Tripoli Agreement was never fully implemented, however.

While the effort to project the Philippine image as a successful, developing, non-aligned country may have been fun for the leadership, the effort to satisfy the military required some long, hard bargaining with the US. For Marcos it was most important to provide up-to-date arms and equipment for an armed force which was his strongest political supporter. But by 1974 the 'human rights bloc' in both the US House and Senate had growing influence, just as detailed reports of arbitrary arrests and torture of Philippine political dissidents began to reach Washington. Given the mood of Congress, Marcos had to find a new means to get the US to equip his forces. Familiar with US base rental arrangements in Spain, Portugal, Turkey and Greece, he perceived 'rentals' as politically more certain than 'aid', and laid the ground carefully. After a meeting of his National Security Council in April 1975 the President complained, echoing Recto, that 'The bases, like magnets, only invite attack by any nation hostile to the US' and suggested that the Philippines might take them over, then negotiate new terms with the US for their use. Anti-American stories began to appear more often in the controlled press. In Washington consternation prevailed; not all officials understood the Marcos strategy, nor the limits to his bargaining power (Wideman in *Philippine Times*, 16–31 May 1976).

In April 1976 formal talks began in Washington on revision of the bases agreement. But Marcos, overplaying his hand, asked for too much, was rebuffed and decided to wait for Carter (Romualdez, 1980: 52ff). In the Carter administration serious thought was given to moving the bases to Guam, should they become too costly. But after the Iranian revolution and the Soviet invasion of Afghanistan, Clark Field and Subic Bay suddenly became essential way stations to a new cradle of conflict, and were revalued upward by the Pentagon.

Philippine demands for broader jurisdiction over criminal acts by US servicemen, and continued insistence on generous base rentals delayed agreement, however, until January 1979. The US did not give on the jurisdiction question, and the designation of a 'Philippine Base Commander', with the Philippine flag flying alongside the American, was a cosmetic change that did not satisfy the nationalists. The Philippines received $ 500 million in military grants and credits over a five-year period, in addition to 'economic aid'. This amounted to a doubling of the level of US military assistance. And with Reagan in office the next five-yearly review of the bases agreement was completed early, in June 1983, with military aid raised to $ 900 million for the period, including a higher grant component and lower interest rates. Congress tried to delay delivery as Marcos' abuses became more obvious, but the Bases Agreement did reduce his vulnerability.

Despite the extreme importance of the military dimension, probably the most urgent task for foreign policy under Marcos was to mobilize international resources for economic growth. The economic élite were the prime beneficiaries of the President's efforts, but he realized that without a general sense of economic progress he would lose legitimacy in the eyes of the Filipino people as a whole. His policies sought to attract more foreign capital, with numerous new concessions – from new areas for 100 per cent foreign investment to maintenance of low wages – and to expand foreign borrowing, influenced by successful export-oriented industrialization elsewhere. New foreign investment entered at a sharply accelerated rate from 1973, but expectations were not sustained; the 1973 inflow in constant dollars was never again equalled.

With the increased emphasis on credit by 1978 commercial loans from private international banks were greater than all government sources, bilateral or multilateral. But private banks acted on assurances of viability by the WB/IMF and its Philippine Consultative Group. The World Bank, in order to back up its assurances, exercised increasing influence over essential elements of Philippine government economic policy – as was admitted in a leaked memorandum from the Bank itself (Bello and Rivera, 1977: 97, citing draft by Gould). In 1976 the Marcos government formally agreed to three years of 'close economic supervision' by the IMF, renewed in subsequent agreements. World Bank officers gained some legitimacy within the Philippine policy process, at least as great as that of American advisers in the 1950s.

The events of the early 1980s indicate, however, that World Bank/ IMF supervision was no more effective than the influence of the technocrats – who shared World Bank/IMF views – over the cronies in the Marcos regime. Marcos and his cronies were powerful enough to divert foreign resources, which came in at higher and higher interest rates, to their own purposes, rescuing failed enterprises and salting away dollars abroad. It was such escapades that pushed the Philippine foreign debt up to $ 26 billion by 1983 while productivity declined. World economic conditions were certainly not favorable – a point which Marcos frequently reiterated – but no other country in Southeast Asia combined rising debt and falling GNP to the degree that the Philippines did. It was a curious combination of circumstances: World Bank/IMF control over the economy increased, but it was not sufficient to head off disaster instigated by the even greater power of the bureaucratic capitalists around Marcos over the distribution of credit from government institutions. Thus Philippine economic decline – which started as a great push for development – had to be blamed as much on autonomous patri- monialism as on dependency. Marcos' foreign economic policy, largely viewed as a success in the mid–1970s, by the end of his term had put the country in an unprecedented tailspin.

Aquino Foreign Policy

Mrs. Aquino came to power in a manner unique in Philippine his- tory. Not only were military intervention and unprecedented mass demonstrations necessary to implement her electoral victory, but she emerged without the prior blessings of the White House, loyal to Marcos almost to the end – though this is not to say that the CIA or the State Department were unsympathetic. Her unprecedented popularity gave her the potential of a new autonomy in both national and international realms. That popularity was reconfirmed in the constitutional plebiscite of February 1987 and the legislative elections of May. But she did not utilize her charismatic power as she might have. Charisma was merely used to reinvigorate neo-patrimonialism, substituting for the economic resources that were no longer available. Foreign policy at first had relatively low salience under Aquino, perhaps because of her confidence of legitimacy achieved through charisma and electoral processes. She thus felt no compulsion to use foreign policy for regime survival as had Marcos.

Furthermore, a much more open regime, over which the President has ineffective control, is more penetrable by foreign interests. Thus Pentagon pressure exercised through the Philippine military helped to scuttle a more prolonged cease-fire, and the CIA moved in rapidly to promote armed anti-Communist vigilantes, working through cabinet-level contacts. The apparent use of delayed aid delivery by the Pentagon to press for greater military reform even goaded President Aquino herself into sharp criticism of Washington in May 1987 – shades of Marcos.

The most important foreign policy issue of the decade, the fate of US military bases, was deliberately downplayed by Mrs. Aquino. At the beginning of the election campaign in late 1985 she had favored the removal of the bases, but by January 1986 had become comfortable with a different formula: respect the present agreement until it expires in 1991, and then 'keep my options open' (Agence France Press, 2 January 1986). This position was carefully crafted to hold together the disparate wings of her coalition, though her opponents on the Left believed that she would decide to renew in 1991. She stuck with this position after assuming office, for it avoided distracting attention from more urgent political and economic issues. Though it worried Pentagon officials, the State Department recognized the constraints on her and was hopeful about the President's ultimate choice.

The new element in the situation was the constitution ratified in February 1987. Though proposed clauses outlawing foreign military bases had been defeated in the Constitutional Commission, two crucial provisions were adopted – small steps towards dependency reversal. One provided that if the bases agreement were to be extended in 1991, it would have to be elevated from an executive agreement to a treaty and would thus require concurrence by a two-thirds vote of the Senate. Furthermore, the constitution's 'declaration of principles' stated that 'the Philippines, consistent with the national interest, adopts and pursues a policy of freedom from nuclear weapons in its territory'.

Even though the US refuses to confirm officially the presence of nuclear devices at Clark Field or Subic Bay, the belief that they are there is almost universal in well-informed circles. Thus the utility of the bases for the US, *if* this provision were fully implemented, would be severely restricted. In August 1987, without consulting the President, ten members of the President's party out of the 24 newly elected senators sponsored a bill that would outlaw 'possession, storage, or transport' of nuclear weapons on Philippine territory

(*Washington Post*, 21 August 1987). In June 1988 it passed the Senate overwhelmingly. Thus it appeared that diplomatic nuances preferred in the executive branch might not determine Philippine policy. But the bill was stalled in the House and the Secretary of Justice ruled that regulation of nuclear weapons was the President's prerogative. When a new base compensation package was signed by the US and the Philippines on 17 October 1988, providing a record $ 960 million over two years, there was an exemption of 'transit, overflights or visits by US aircraft or ships' from any requirement of Philippine government approval for 'storage or installation of nuclear weapons'.

Finding 16 Senate votes to endorse renewal of the bases agreement in 1991 might be difficult. But the outcome is still very uncertain. Some senators, despite nationalist rhetoric, when face to face with the economic costs to the Philippines of US base withdrawal, might acquiesce. Yet, if Mrs Aquino, having lost her current popularity, should endorse an extension while the US presses its demands clumsily, nationalist rhetoric could carry the day. In any case, if the Senate should fail to ratify a new bases agreement, the danger of a successful military coup – if not already transpired – should not be discounted. For the impending loss of a large portion of US military aid could be the most effective unifier of a factionalized armed force. But by the end of 1988 there was increasing talk in both Washington and Manila of phased withdrawal of the bases. A speech by Secretary Manglapus in January 1989 suggested that the bases, for various reasons, might become 'obsolete'. He concluded, 'Whatever the developments, we are preparing for eventual conversion of US facilities to civilian use' (*Philippines Free Press*, 28 January 1989).

Whatever the strains in US-Philippine relations, however, relations with the other superpower were initially much worse. An endorsement of the Marcos 're-election' in February 1986 by the Soviet ambassador – almost unique in the Manila diplomatic community, naturally soured the incoming Aquino administration towards the USSR. But by 1988 the Gorbachev aura had warmed relations, though some officials had a hard time burying the Cold War. The first ever visit by a Soviet foreign minister on 22 December produced an invitation for Mrs Aquino to go to Moscow, which was accepted. Shevardnadze won favor by assuring Filipinos that the Soviet Union had never supported and had no intention of supporting the Communist Party of the Philippines/NPA insurgency (*FBIS*, 22 December 1988, p. 45). His hint that the Soviets might dismantle their bases in Vietnam even before Washington made any decision to withdraw from Clark Field or Subic Bay was also well received.

A state visit to Japan, on the other hand, was earlier on President Aquino's agenda than for any of her predecessors, indicating Japan's rising economic importance to the Philippines. Cory was also attracted by the great outpouring of sympathy for Ninoy shown by the Japanese public after his assassination, a sympathy transferred to her in 1986.

Economic constraints frustrated expressions of autonomy by some in Aquino's government, for example, the statement by Solita Monsod, head of the National Economic Development Authority, in 1986 favoring 'selective repudiation' of the foreign debt, especially loans purloined by Marcos and his cronies. IMF/World Bank pressures have since helped to subordinate that view to the 'full repayment' stance of the Secretary of Finance and the Central Bank. Some of the same IMF/World Bank conditions, pushing 'liberalization', as had been imposed on Marcos have again been accepted. Debt to equity schemes will expand the role of foreign capital. But now economic nationalists have the benefit of a free press and representation in Congress. The debt rescheduling agreement initialed in 1987 – less favorable than Argentina's – was not approved by cabinet and had to be renegotiated. Bills have been introduced in Congress to reduce the debt service payment to 25 per cent or less of exports, compared to the 1987 rate of 42 per cent. A bill creating a powerful, congressionally dominated foreign debt commission was passed, but was vetoed by the President. Thus the desire for greater economic autonomy is pushing against the constraints, but the trend in decision-making up to 1988 has favored the IMF/World Bank. In December the government promised the IMF to reduce budget deficits and scale down growth targets.

Initial indications are that Congress will indeed have an impact on relations with ASEAN. Some leading legal minds appear to be interested in reviving the Philippine claim to Sabah, blinded by juridicial and nationalistic argument to the adverse political consequences such a revival would have for regional consensus. In fact, the Aquino administration eagerly sought ASEAN support in May 1987 on the question of Mindanao autonomy. Negotiations with Nur Misuari of the MNLF broke down, despite a rather generous offer by Ambassador Emmanuel Pelaez, and the Philippines needed the understanding of Islamic nations to prevent Misuari from mobilizing them against Manila. Thus initiatives by Congress on Sabah and by the Department of Foreign Affairs on Muslim autonomy may collide, the consequence of constitutional separation of powers without strong executive leadership.

In fact, many observers fear that the Philippine government in the next two or three years will suffer severe immobilism, given the President's unwillingness at times to exercise the power she has available. Immobilism will jeopardize economic growth, inhibit foreign policy initiatives, and broaden opportunities for foreign penetration. It could eventually trigger a military takeover.

CONCLUSION

The degree of Philippine dependency that we have noted, perhaps unique in Southeast Asia, is certainly the consequence of the international environment. The Philippines is the only ex-colony of a superpower in the region, which left it with the legacy of US military bases.

Even the structure of the domestic political economy is a legacy of Spanish and American colonialism – large landholdings, weak industry, and an electoral system which fosters neo-patrimonialism and undermines bureaucratic effectiveness. But in the last 40 years that structure has become thoroughly integrated with Filipino culture. A process which is the result of interaction between structure and culture has a dynamism of its own, not simply determined by the external environment. The domestic political economy, through military corruption, incompetence and the failure of social reform, has created an insurgency which has seemed to survive its own crisis and is not likely to fade away. The horrendous foreign debt, unparalleled in the region, is also in large part a result of the domestic system – the unrestrained greed of neo-patrimonialism in an authoritarian setting. Thus, the future of Philippine dependency, or its reversal, will rely as much or more on internal dynamics as on developments in the world capitalist system.

BIBLIOGRAPHY

Abueva, Jose (1971), *Ramon Magsaysay, A Political Biography* (Manila: Solidaridad).

Agpalo, Remigio (1962), *The Political Process and the Nationalization of the Retail Trade in the Philippines* (Diliman, Quezon City: University of the Philippines, Office of the Coordinator of Research).

Bello, Walden and Severina Rivera (1977), *Logistics of Repression and Other Essays* (Washington, DC: Friends of the Filipino People).

Bello, Walden *et al.* (1982), *Development Débâcle: The World Bank in the Philippines* (San Francisco: Institute for Food and Development Policy).

Bonner, Raymond (1987), *Waltzing with a Dictator: The Marcoses and the Making of American Policy* (New York: Random House).

Broad, Robin (1988), *Unequal Alliance: The World Bank, the IMF and the Philippines* (Berkeley: University of California Press).

Buss, Claude (1977), *The United States and the Philippines* (Washington, DC: American Enterprise Institute).

Constantino, Renato (ed.) (1965), *The Recto Reader* (Manila: Recto Memorial Foundation).

Constantino, Renato (1984), *The Nationalist Alternative*, revised edn (Quezon City: Foundation for Nationalist Studies).

Corpuz, O. D. (1966), 'The Realities of Philippine Foreign Policy', in Frank Golay (ed.), *The United States and the Philippines* (Englewood Cliffs, NJ: Prentice-Hall).

Dingman, Roger (1986), 'The Diplomacy of Dependency: The Philippines and Peacemaking with Japan. 1945–52', *Journal of Southeast Asian Studies*, 17:2, 307–21.

Dodd, Joseph W. (1968), *Criminal Jurisdiction under the United States Philippine Bases Agreement, A Study in Cojurisdictional Law* (The Hague, Netherlands: Nijhoff).

Doherty, John F. (1979). *A Preliminary Study of Interlocking Directorates* (Quezon City).

Espiritu, Augusto C. *et al.* (1978), *Philippine Perspectives on Multinational Corporations* (Quezon City: UP Law Center).

Fernandez, Alejandro (1962), 'Threat from Malaysia?' *Philippines Free Press*, 24 February.

George, T. J. S. (1980), *Revolt in Mindanao* (Kuala Lumpur: Oxford University Press).

Johnson, Chalmers (1985), 'Political Institutions and Economic Performance, The Government-Business Relationship in Japan, South Korea, and Taiwan', in Robert Scalapino, S. Sato and J. Wanandi (eds), *Asian Economic Development – Present and Future* (Berkeley: Institute of East Asian Studies, University of California).

Jose, Vivencio R. (ed.) (1984), *Mortgaging the Future: The World Bank and IMF in the Philippines* (Quezon City: Foundation for Nationalist Studies).

Lichauco, Alejandro (1973), *The Lichauco Paper: Imperialism in the Philippines* (New York: Monthly Review Press).

Lim, Robyn (1978), 'The Philippines and the "Dependency Debate": A Preliminary Case Study', *Journal of Contemporary Asia*, 8, 2, 197–209.

Lindsey, Charles (1985), 'The Philippine State and Transnational Investment', in Robert B. Stauffer (ed.), *States and TNCs in the Capitalist World Economy: Case Studies on Relationships* (Sydney: Transnational Corporations Research Project, University of Sydney).

Lopez, Salvador (1978), 'Trends in Philippine Foreign Policy', in M. Rajaretnam, *Trends in the Philippines* (Singapore: Institute of Southeast Asia Studies).

Lopez, Salvador (1966), 'The Colonial Relationship', in Frank Golay (ed), *The United States and the Philippines* (Englewood Cliffs, NJ: Prentice-Hall).

Macapagal, Diosdado (1961), *'The Common Man' and other speeches*, compiled by Vicente Martinez (Manila).

Makil, Perla Q. (1970), *PAASCU/IPC Study of Schools and Influentials, 1969–70* (Quezon City: Ateneo de Manila, Institute of Philippine Culture).

Marcos, Ferdinand (1980), 'The Canons of Our Foreign Policy', 23 June 1978, in *Presidential Speeches*, Vol. VIII.

Maynard, Harold (1976), 'Military Elite Perceptions in Indonesia and the Philippines' (Ph.D. dissertation, American University).

Ohno, Takushi (1986), *War Reparations and Peace Settlement: Philippines-Japan Relations, 1945–1956* (Manila: Solidaridad).

Paez, Patricia Ann (1985), *The Bases Factor: Realpolitik of RP-US Relations* (Manila: Center for Strategic and International Studies of the Philippines).

Pomeroy, William J. (1977), *An American Made Tragedy: Neo-colonialism and Dictatorship in the Philippines* (New York: International Publishers).

Quisumbing, Purificacion (1983), *Beijing-Manila Détente, Major Issues: A Study in China-ASEAN Relations* (Quezon City: UP Law Center).

Republic of the Philippines (1975), *Presidential Budget*.

Romani, John (1956), *The Philippine Presidency* (Manila: Institute of Public Administration, University of the Philippines).

Schirmer, Daniel B. and Stephen R. Shalom (eds), (1987), *The Philippines Reader, A History of Colonialism, Neocolonialism, Dictatorship and Resistance* (Boston: South End Press).

Shalom, Stephen (1981), *The United States and the Philippines: A Study of Neocolonialism* (Philadelphia: ISHI).

Simbulan, Dante (1965), 'A Study of the Socio-Economic Elite in Philippine Politics and Government, 1946–1963' (Ph.D. Dissertation, Australian National University).

Stauffer, Robert (1966), *The Development of an Interest Group, The Philippine Medical Association* (Quezon City: University of the Philippines Press).

Sunkel, Osvaldo (1969), 'National Development Policy and External Dependency in Latin America', *Journal of Development Studies*, I:1.

Sussman, Gerald (1983), 'Macapagal, the Sabah Claim and Maphilindo: The Politics of Penetration', *Journal of Contemporary Asia*, 13:2, 210–28.

Taylor, George (1964), *The Philippines and the United States: Problems of Partnership* (New York: Praeger).

Tsuda, Mamoru (1978), *A Preliminary Study of Japanese-Filipino Joint Ventures* (Quezon City: Foundation for Nationalist Studies).

Villegas, Edberto M. (1983), *Studies in Philippine Political Economy* (Manila: Silangan).

Welch, Richard E. (1984), 'America's Philippine Policy in the Quirino Years (1948–1953): A Study in Patron-Client Diplomacy', in Peter W. Stanley, *Reappraising an Empire* (Cambridge, Mass.: Harvard University Press).

Wurfel, David (1959), 'Foreign Aid and Social Reform in Political Development: A Philippine Case Study', *American Political Science Review*, LIII:2, 456–82.

Wurfel, David (1966), 'Problems of Decolonialization', in Frank Golay (ed.), *The United States and the Philippines* (Englewood Cliffs, NJ: Prentice-Hall).

Wurfel, David (1979), 'Elites of Wealth and Elites of Power, The Changing Dynamic: A Philippine Case Study', *Southeast Asian Affairs, 1979* (Singapore: ISEAS).

Wurfel, David (1985), 'Government Responses to Armed Communism and Secessionist Rebellion in the Philippines', in Chandran Jeshurun (ed.), *Governments and Rebellions in Southeast Asia* (Singapore: Institute of Southeast Asian Studies).

Wurfel, David (1986), 'Philippine-Japanese Relations: The Economic and Cultural Determinants of Mutual Images in an Unequal Cooperative Dyad', *Journal of Northeast Asian Studies*, V:2.

10 The Foreign Policy of Thailand

Clark D. Neher

Central to an understanding of Thai foreign policy are a number of historical factors which stem from the Kingdom's role within the larger international political-economic system as well as from internal forces unique to Thailand. As the only nation of Southeast Asia never to be formally colonized, Thailand has not shared the xenophobic traditions of its neighbors. This first historical factor helps explain the remarkable assimilative character of the Thais. The lack of colonial experience allowed the Thais to adapt and adopt those aspects of Westernization which they deemed appropriate to their traditional culture. Thus Thailand's evolution from a traditional to a modern society has been relatively smooth.

From the first factor flows the second, Thailand's pragmatic orientation to relations with other nations. The nation's leaders have shown a willingness to 'bend with the wind' even when this flexibility meant the loss of territory and violation of principles. Thailand made accommodations with the European colonialist powers by ceding territory and joined Japan in declaring war against the allies in the Second World War, thereby allowing the nation to emerge from the war with only minor dislocation.

A third important factor influencing Thai foreign policy is that there has never been a social revolution which fundamentally changed Thai politico-economic structures. The 1932 'revolution' was in reality a *coup d'état* staged by Western-educated bureaucrats and military officers. Power shifted from the royal princes to new élites, but the masses remained little affected by the change in leadership, and both political institutions and social processes have since changed rather slowly.

Finally, despite the Kingdom's formally independent status, Thailand has been historically vulnerable to outside forces including its neighbors and European colonialism. Thai foreign policy has been influenced by the economic penetration of the industrialized West and, more recently, Japan. However, Thai society never became fully dependent on the major capitalist powers.

THAI SOCIETY

The high capacity of Thailand's leaders to use the symbols of tradition to achieve modern ends, on the one hand, and modern means to sustain traditional prerogatives, on the other, is a major theme of Thai society. It was during the Ayuthayan period (1350–1767) that the Thais adapted the concept of the *deva raja* (god-king) from the Indianized Khmers. The perception of the kings as god-like remains, even today, an important element of the veneration shown the monarch by his subjects. During the same period a *sakdi na* (power over fields) system was introduced that provided structure and hierarchy to the social and political relationships of the Thais. Although the *sakdi na* system ended in 1932, the informal hierarchical character of the society remains.

Decisions tend to flow from the top down, from patron to client. The result is a highly integrated society, held together by a web of relationships based on reciprocity. Patron-client ties are informal, two-person relations in which a patron of higher socio-economic status uses his or her resources and influence to provide benefits for a client of lower socio-economic status. Clients reciprocate by offering their patron such benefits as deference, votes, labor, or other services.

Thailand's few interest groups, weak political party structure, and ineffective legislative bodies have made relatively more important the pervasive patron-client ties that often perform the same functions as the more formal Western-style institutions. These informal ties help communicate information from the kingdom's leadership to the masses and, less effectively, from the masses to the leadership.

At the national level among the political élites, patron-client networks also form. Who rules in Thailand depends on the capacity of various clientage groups to control the key positions of government. In recent Thai history, the configuration of groups within the military has usually been most important. There is a constant shifting of clients from one military patron to another. Stability lasts only so long as the prevailing faction is able to meet the demands of its clients and to undermine competing factions.

Nevertheless, Thailand is now undergoing rapid societal changes. New values are emerging in conflict or inconsistent with traditional values. For example, patron-client ties often no longer meet modern expectations and new demands for a greater role in political processes. The traditional values of 'knowing one's place' in the status hierarchy and respect for authority are being eroded.

ECONOMY

The traditional Thai economy was based on wet rice cultivation and the production of sugar, tin, teak, pepper and forest products. Domestic trade and export of Thai products were monopolized by the monarchs. Increased economic contacts with the West transformed the Thai subsistence economy into a capitalist one. Money was introduced as the medium of exchange and traditional corvée labor was replaced by wage labor (Termsak, 1986: 165–233). Thailand was integrated into the world capitalist economy with European control over rice exporting, rice milling, banking, shipping, and major industries such as teak and tin (Suehiro, 1985: 714). The growth of the post-Second World War economy was based on development capital from the state, the ethnic Chinese business entrepreneurs, and foreign or multinational corporations and aid agencies.

In the past three decades, because of the assimilation of the Chinese into Thai society, most Chinese capital has been considered indigenous rather than foreign. Earlier governments had pursued discriminatory policies against the Chinese. However, because Chinese business acumen was found necessary for economic growth, bureaucrats gradually formed alliances with them. Political, bureaucratic, and military rulers so allied advanced into economic activities eventually controlling banking, insurance, shipping, rice milling and exporting, and profitable manufacturing (Suehiro, 1985: 717). The postwar government also formed state enterprises in order to 'Thaiize' the economy, but local Chinese took over the most influential positions with military leaders as board members. The Chinese gained security for their economic activities while the government élites reaped pecuniary gain. The regime of Marshal Sarit Dhanarat (1957–63) began the era of rapid economic development with emphasis on infrastructure, import substitution industrialization, and an open door to foreign investment. Major manufacturing industries were created by multinational corporations, and local Chinese groups, in co-operation with military-political-bureaucratic rulers.

Thailand's consistent economic growth in the past decades has fundamentally changed the character of the citizenry. An educated middle class has emerged in Bangkok, as well as in the provincial capitals and small towns of the kingdom. The nation's major agencies for economic development now include highly trained and educated technocrats, mostly graduates of the rapidly expanding university system, with more public-regarding values. With per capita income growing for two decades at an average annual rate of over 6 per cent, to just under $1000 (compared to $150 20 years ago), and with literacy becoming universal among the younger generation, Thailand has joined the ranks of the Newly Industrializing Countries (NICs). Rice, rubber, tin, and teak made up 80 to 90 per cent of all exports in the 1950s, but declined to just 40 per cent in the 1980s, with manufactured goods filling the gap. Despite the diversification, however, 70 per cent of the populace continued to be involved in agriculture.

Dramatic change even in the lives of rural Thais stems in part from communication networks that pervade the nation. Infrastructure, such as roads, railroads, electricity, and transportation, is now in place. Moreover, Thai farmers, compared with most Third-World agriculturalists, have been spared the crisis of severe rural inequality (Girling, 1986: 190). Nevertheless, rural Thais are no longer the passive peasantry read about in textbooks. The most vivid evidence of the politicization of the Thai peasantry was during the 1973–76 democratic period, when farmers began to organize to express their grievances. As with many Third-World nations, the Thai economy has also been characterized by a pattern of development in which the urban citizenry benefit disproportionately. The average per capita income in Bangkok is at least twice that of the most prosperous rural region in the Central Plains.

THE REGIME

The semi-democratic government of Thailand is dominated by the military, the monarchy, top level bureaucrats, and key members of parliament. The Prime Minister is chosen by a coalition of parties (with the informal approval of the military), and major ministries are given to retired military figures, famous politicians, or high-level bureaucrats.

There is some difficulty in categorizing the regime as 'military' or 'civilian,' because the Thai army has militarized the political system and, in turn, has been 'civilianized' by it. Until July 1988, the nation was led by General Prem Tinsulanond, who retired from the army

in 1981 and became a 'civilian' Prime Minister. Prem's military connections were as important as his bureaucratic and political alliances
for keeping him in the top government position, which he held
longer than any elected prime minister in Thai history. His successor,
former General Chatichai Choonhaven, was named Prime Minister
following the July 1988 elections when the political party he led
received the plurality of votes. Like Prem, he had combined a military career with politics.

Modern Thai history has been noted for the absence of institutionalized norms of succession, with the *coup d'état* the more or less
standard means by which Thai governments changed. The political
system was highly centralized and corrupt. Personalism, concentrated on building patron-client factions rather than on innovative
programs, characterized almost all regimes.

Thai regimes have changed in important ways, however, since the
'democratic period' of 1973–76 when the military were ousted by a
student-led revolt and replaced by civilian leaders and a constitutional system of government. Thai politics have become more
institutionalized and open, with civilian technocrats and politicians
ensconced in power and the public's attitudes inimical to army intervention. No successful coup has taken place since 1977. Two coup
attempts fizzled out when the King, leading politicians and bureaucrats, the intelligentsia, as well as some powerful generals, overwhelmingly opposed them. The King's opposition was particularly
crucial because he is venerated throughout the kingdom.

A number of institutions have arisen in recent decades with functions that are displacing the personalistic rule of the past. These
new institutions, which include interest groups, business associations,
political parties, non-governmental associations, and decentralized
ministerial units, have a high degree of legitimacy. Political parties
are more coherent in structure and better able to represent citizens'
demands. The parliament has become a legitimate institution for the
expression of opposition to the government and to the military.

Western scholars have for years referred to the Thai regime as a
'bureaucratic polity', but many are now suggesting that new extrabureaucratic groups are increasingly influencing domestic and foreign
policies. Business and middle class interests, for example, are now
represented in the elected parliament in larger numbers than ever
before. This trend has transformed the Thai polity from one based
narrowly on the interests and demands of bureaucrats and military
officers to one with broader political participation (Suchit Bunbong-

korn and Sukhumbhand Paribatra, in Jackson, Sukhumbhand, and Soedjati, 1986: 52).

THE POLICY-MAKERS AND POLICY PROCESS

The persons who wield the most influence on foreign policy-making in Thailand are the ranking generals, leading bureaucrats in the Ministry of Foreign Affairs (MFA), cabinet ministers, including the Prime Minister and his advisors, political party coalition leaders, and leading doyens of the aristocracy. When the policy concerns national security, for instance perceived threats from Thailand's Communist neighbors, the military leaders monopolize decision-making. For two decades up to the end of the Vietnam War, the Thai military negotiated directly with the American Embassy, often bypassing the Ministry of Foreign Affairs. The parliament played virtually no role in formulating foreign policy on questions of national security. In fact, because national security was defined broadly, the military dominated almost all facets of Thai foreign policy up to 1975. The military monopolized policies regarding border disputes, the purchase of weapon systems, the defense budget, and American military aid to Thailand. Even refugee issues have been handled by the military-dominated National Security Council.

But on issues that do not affect Thai national security, the Ministry of Foreign Affairs has long been the key player. The conduct of routine diplomacy and trade relations, for example, is carried out by ministry officials. The MFA is considered to be 'élitist' because of the large number of aristocratic families which have played a dominant role for generations (Funston, 1987: 232–5). About two-thirds of the MFA officials come from Bangkok with a plurality attending the prestige secondary schools of the capital. The Ministry of Foreign Affairs has had a reputation as conservative and anti-Communist. MFA policies toward Indo-China, for example, are often criticized by Thai academics as excessively rigid. Since a large number of senior ministry officials studied in Europe and the United States, the ministry's world view is heavily Westernized. But in the past decade, this reputation for conservative élitism has been mitigated by the advancement of qualified technocrats to top positions (Funston, 1987: 234).

Until the appointment of Prime Minister Chatichai, the major government spokesman on international relations has been the Minister of Foreign Affairs, Air Chief Marshal Siddhi Savetsila. His close ties to military officers and his leadership of the Social Action Party, a major participant in the coalition, assured a degree of autonomy to the MFA. The highly respected Siddhi reflected the interests of the military and cabinet members in the Prem government. Despite the close ties between Minister Siddhi and Prime Minister Chatichai, the views of the Ministry of Foreign Affairs in the late 1980s have not always prevailed, especially on international trade matters and relations with Vietnam. Chatichai and his personal academic advisors have become the major spokesmen for foreign policy matters.

Post-Second World War foreign policy in Thailand has been characterized by continuity of means and goals. That is not to say that Thai foreign policy has been stagnant or incapable of adaptation and change. Indeed, the strength and success of contemporary Thai foreign policies stem from the capacity of the policy-makers to 'bend like the bamboo with the wind'. Yet despite numerous changes of leadership, because the Thai bureaucracy, the traditional bedrock of governmental stability, has changed only incrementally, there have been few unexpected lurches in policy-making. In fact, Thai foreign policy has exhibited both continuity and success, contributing to a high degree of institutionalization. 'A policy which is successful tends to become institutionalized, and if bureaucrats take credit for this success, such institutionalization tends to perpetuate or reinforce the role of the bureaucracy as well as the policy' (Suchit Bungbongkorn and Sukhumbhand Paribatra, in Jackson *et al.*, 1986: 74).

DOMESTIC RESOURCES AND CONSTRAINTS

The major domestic advantage of Thailand is the fact that the Thai political system 'works'; that is, the political system has been able to cope with societal demands by meeting them and defusing unrest.

Because Thai society is ethnically more homogeneous than that of its neighbors, the Kingdom has not faced serious problems in that regard. Ninety per cent of the 55 million Thais are Buddhist and Thai speaking, all living in a contiguous geographic area. The contrast between Thai homogeneity and the ethnic and linguistic heterogeneity of Indonesia and the Philippines is striking. One result of this homogeneity is the high degree of legitimacy enjoyed by successive regimes.

Regime legitimacy is high also because of the unique role of Thailand's King Bhumipol Adunyadej. The pomp and ceremony surrounding the king's 60th birthday in 1987 were spectacular, befitting the nation's universal veneration for a monarch who has reigned 41 years. The King's many accomplishments, his steadfastness, exemplary life, and his role as symbol of all that is great in Thailand have made it difficult to imagine a successor. For the present, the King is one of the nation's most important assets.

Striking evidence of this homogeneity, and high degree of regime legitimacy, is the stunning change, since 1979, in the fortunes of the Communist-led guerrilla insurgency that threatened Thai security for two decades. By the mid-1980s the movement's United Front had collapsed, most of the cadres and leaders had defected, and the guerrilla military bases had been wiped out. The loss of support for the Communist Party of Thailand (CPT), while rural-based revolutionary movements have thrived in other parts of the world, stems from internal, as well as external, conditions. Domestically the improvement in the living conditions of many rural Thais, and the gradual democratization of the polity have undercut support for the party. Moreover, since the 1960s the successive regimes in power have initiated a workable amnesty program and a number of rural development projects, particularly in areas where insurgency had been greatest. Today, the Thai government does not face an internal threat by forces seeking to overthrow the established order, an important resource affecting Thailand's role in the world system.

Regime legitimacy is also strengthened by economic success. Thailand has sustained an overall 6 per cent annual growth rate in the 1970s and 1980s, far higher than most Third-World nations, and enjoys an abundance of natural resources (except for oil). The 1987 decline in world oil prices reduced the trade deficit by about US$ 1 billion, a 40 per cent drop, and economic growth for that year reached 7 per cent (with only 2 per cent inflation), the same growth rate as in South Korea and Taiwan. In 1987 applications for foreign investment tripled compared to the previous year, while exports increased 20 per cent. The Sixth Five-Year Plan emphasized the decline of the public sector and the expanded role of the private sector as the 'locomotive' of Thailand's economic development.

A primary resource for contemporary Thailand is the new highly educated and technologically trained middle class. Thailand's universities are graduating ten times more graduates than two decades ago. This new class of industrialists, bankers, and service oriented personnel have little patience with the inefficiencies that have characterized military dominated bureaucratic regimes. They desire the stability of a moderate government that encourages technocrats to run the ministries, holds the lid on corruption, and insists on a meaningful role for political parties and parliament. Thailand's economic growth has brought about a significant new class concerned with effectiveness and stability, and supportive of the overall political system.

Notwithstanding these significant resources, there still exist constraints on the system which potentially could jeopardize the nation's present strength and confidence. A major constraint has been undistinguished leadership. Because the military has dominated the office of prime minister since 1932 and has exercised veto power over other high-level positions, many highly competent persons have chosen not to become involved in politics. Politics is considered 'dirty' and lacking in prestige for most Thais. Personalism has resulted in corruption which pervades politics from the top levels of government to the village headmen. Furthermore, the centralized nature of the bureaucracy requires that all decisions, no matter how minor, must be considered by each bureaucratic level. This lack of delegation of authority places an untenable administrative burden on the central bureaucracy, so that delay and frustration are the result. In addition, the bureaucracy suffers from inter- and intraministerial factionalism.

Related to, and exacerbated by these bureaucratic problems, is a series of economic problems that have not yet been resolved. As discussed above, the Thai economy is one of the strongest of the Third World. On the other hand, fully one-third of rural Thais live below the poverty line with large numbers of farmers facing severe problems of indebtedness and landlessness. Thailand's fifth and sixth Five-Year Plans purport to give more attention to the rural economy and to a more equitable distribution of income, although urban areas have traditionally received the greater share of the government's public funds for development. Still Bangkok, with a population over six million, cannot provide the services necessary for its influx of migrants from the countryside. This is linked to a further constraint on Thai policy-making, the depletion of natural resources. Land is now scarce and is increasingly in the hands of wealthier landowners. The resulting flow to Bangkok exacerbates the already overwhelming problems of too few jobs for too many migrants. Reduction in Thailand's forests – which once covered 60 per cent of the country, but now cover 30 per cent – worsens the land problem by causing drought, flooding, aridity, and soil erosion. Deforestation threatens a major export. Although still comparatively rich in other resources, the Kingdom depends on oil for energy but produces almost none. Thailand pays the bulk of its export earnings for energy and the government is reluctant to raise energy prices for fear of massive protests.

These constraints could worsen and interact on each other, so as to severely strain the capabilities of the political system, but, as yet, Thailand is better off than most Southeast Asian countries.

EXTERNAL ENVIRONMENT

Scholars who have adapted a Marxist political economy framework for analyzing Thai society argue that the external environment has influenced Thai foreign policy more than internal political and economic considerations. These scholars insist that Thailand exists in a dependency relationship *vis-à-vis* the major capitalist nations, that domestic political behavior is a form of neo-colonialism, and that only by a fundamental structural change in Thai society can the nation break out of its dependency.

Peter Bell has argued that the influence of the United States is the most significant single element in modern Thai history and that Thailand's relationship to the world economy shaped the class forces and the nature of the Thai state. He suggests that American influence ensured that Thai politics would be dominated by the military with a stable economic and political climate for capitalist development and regional anti-Communism (Bell, 1987). Bell writes that although it would not be fair to imply that the Thais gave over complete control of their society and institutions to an external force, the US clearly was the stronger partner of a dominant/subordinate relationship during most of the post-1932 period. In the 1970s and 1980s 'export promotion' policies brought the country into the area of international competition, with concomitant domestic economic problems. Those economic problems came to dominate foreign policy, according to Bell, and widened Thailand's relations with other great and regional powers. Because foreign capital thoroughly interpenetrated Thai capital, Bell argues that the state ended up in the hands of a dependent bourgeoisie.

Many other scholars, however, write that while Thailand has been highly dependent on the Western world, the Kingdom has retained the capacity to set its own policies. The view of these scholars and this essay is that the term 'interdependent' is more appropriate than 'dependent' for describing the context of Thailand's foreign and domestic policies.

Thailand was indeed forced open by capitalist countries in the nineteenth century when unequal treaties were thrust upon the Kingdom. The most famous, the Bowring Treaty of 1855, allowed the British to buy land, to trade freely, and to enjoy extraterritorial rights. By 1928 Thai exports to British colonies accounted for 77 per cent of the total Thai export earnings (Termsak, 1986: 221). These treaties allowed capitalism to penetrate Thailand rapidly, transforming the Thai economy from pre-capitalist self-sufficiency into capitalist interdependency with the Western powers. This penetration undermined the monopolies of royalty and led to immigration of Chinese laborers and craftsmen who eventually came to dominate much of the capitalist mode of production.

Thailand's involvement in the world system had an inevitable impact on Thai politics and foreign policies. The traditional aristocracy eventually lost their monopoly of power as entrepreneurs (mostly Chinese) and Western-educated bureaucrats moved into dominant positions. The economy was transformed to one characterized by diversity replacing the single-crop traditional rice economy. These economic changes helped transform the feudal society under an absolute monarchy to a capitalist society under the power of a bureaucratic-military polity, and eventually a pluralist bourgeois polity, whose economic leaders shared interests with capitalist great powers.

At present, Thailand's economy is inextricably a part of the world economy, influenced by international trade, capital flows and price cycles. Since the 1960s Thailand has changed from import substituting industry to an export-oriented economy. Seventy per cent of the applications to the Board of Investment are from foreigners, almost half of these from Japan. One-fourth of all imports to Thailand come from Japan. But Thai exports are more diversified than ever with 18 and 14 per cent going to the United States and Japan respectively.

Notwithstanding the economic impact of the world system, the operative criterion for deciding foreign policies has remained rational calculation of national interest based on the judgements of the particular leadership at the time. To be sure interests of that leadership have come to hold much in common with the world capitalist system.

But that does not necessarily constitute domination of the former by the latter.

Thai foreign policy has also been influenced by political-strategic dimensions of the external environment. Specifically, post-Second World War Thai foreign policy has had to respond to the changing impact of the United States, China, Vietnam, and Japan.

For almost three decades after the war, Thai foreign policy was almost exclusively intertwined with that of the United States, the degree of attachment varying according to the assessment of the Communist threat to Thailand. The purpose of American aid in the 1950s, 1960s and early 1970s was 'to increase Thailand's capability to defend its independence against Communist subversion and insurgency and to assist Thai efforts to alleviate the economic and social conditions which impair the nation's internal security' (Steinberg, 1986: 98). The highest point in this relationship came in 1962 with the Rusk-Thanat Communiqué which affirmed that American obligations to Thailand were not dependent on any other treaties or nations. The obligations were 'individual as well as collective' with the United States asserting its willingness to counter any Communist threat. In the mid-1960s the United States established air bases where some 50 000 US troops were stationed. These bases became crucial to US tactics in the Vietnam War.

The close ties began to change in the early 1970s when it became clear that the United States planned to extricate itself from Vietnam. Perhaps the most important event precipitating the change was the Nixon Doctrine, announced in July 1969. This new approach stressed the need for Asian self-reliance in internal security and military defense matters and provided a rationale for US withdrawal. By the time that the Communists prevailed in Indo-China, the US had begun the process of withdrawing all of its troops from Thailand.

China's impact on Thailand in the postwar period befit the traditional fear Thailand has had toward its huge neighbor to the north. Relations were particularly hostile as long as the Chinese supported the illegal Communist Party of Thailand, an organization led by Sino-Thais. However, the rise of a more pragmatic leadership in China and increasing conflict between Vietnam and China in the mid-1970s heralded a dramatic change in Thai-Chinese relations. For example, China ended its support for the CPT after diplomatic ties were re-established between the two countries in 1979. China has now replaced the United States as a principal guarantor of Thai sovereignty against a potential threat from Vietnam. The continuation of the crisis in Cambodia has assured the survival of Thai-Chinese alliance since both nations share the goal of reducing the Vietnamese presence. Once that crisis is solved, and once Thai-Vietnamese relations are normalized, the Chinese connection will decline in importance.

Vietnam has also played a major role in determining Thai foreign policy. The Vietnamese invasion of Cambodia in December 1978 shocked the Thai people and government. The occupation of Cambodia with Vietnamese troops was deemed a direct threat to the security of the Kingdom because there was no longer a buffer between the traditionally hostile nations. The continual border disputes, including armed Vietnamese incursions into Thai territory threatened to escalate and the famine and fighting in Cambodia brought thousands of refugees to Thailand. But as the Vietnamese began to withdraw troops from Cambodia in 1988, and signal a desire for normalization of relations with the ASEAN states, a new context was created.

In sum, Thailand's interdependence with the world economic system and with the great as well as regional powers are significant constraints on and determinants of Thai foreign policy.

FOREIGN POLICY OUTPUTS

Since the Second World War Thai foreign policy can be chronologically categorized as follows: 1945 to early 1970s – the era of Pax Americana when Thailand chose an exclusive and all-encompassing relationship with the United States; from the early 1970s to the present – a period first called 'equidistance' among the great world and regional powers, as Thailand sought a way to respond to the Communist victory in Vietnam and the decrease in American interest in the region and later termed 'omnidirectionality', a more independent foreign policy. Within these two periods there are variations and inconsistencies (the aberrant and strident anti-Communist regime of the reactionary Thanin, 1976–7, for example); however, the patterns are clear.

Regime Maintenance

Throughout the Kingdom's history, Thai leaders have placed regime maintenance as their first priority in determining foreign policy. The objective has been to retain the essence of Thai society: Buddhism, King, and nation, intertwined with efforts to preserve the power of particular governments. In achieving this objective, Thai leaders have been willing to accommodate great powers by judicious diplomacy and to sacrifice territory and principles for the long run gain of regime linked to societal survival and integrity. The means to this end have been pragmatic and flexible. The success of this policy is shown by Thailand's ability to stay free from the colonialism which was thrust upon every other Southeast Asian nation and to limit the effects of Japanese occupation in the Second World War.

The decision of Marshal Phibun to side with the Japanese, following Japan's sea-landing in December 1941, was a calculated and ultimately successful attempt to reduce the physical destruction of the country and to maintain the regime. Thailand emerged from the war considerably more stable and secure than any other nation of Southeast Asia. The people suffered few real economic hardships and Phibun largely maintained control over the country's administration. Domestic Thai politics were also intertwined with the signing of the SEATO Treaty. Marshal Phibun needed military and economic assistance as well as legitimacy from the Western world to shore up his regime against threats from rival factions. The American commitment and aid provided that support and helped keep Phibun in power until 1957.

Until 1975, as mentioned, the predominant foreign policy of Thailand was alliance with the United States. The authoritarian governments of Phibun Songkhram (1948–57), Sarit Dhanarat (1957–63), and Thanom Kittikachorn (1963–73) allowed no dissent about this alliance except for peripheral issues. (See Morrison and Suhrke, 1978: 108–41). Each of these leaders used the alliance with the United States as a means of legitimizing their regimes by claiming the support of the world's leading democratic power. They received American aid for building up the military and for economic development. This support from the United States helped them undermine and/or suppress domestic opposition to the military regimes. Thailand's close ties with the United States also reflected a patron-client relationship between the Americans and the Thai domestic hierarchy. The United States acted as the patron, while leading Thai generals and officials were clients. These clients then distributed the new resources to their own patronage networks in order to perpetuate their power base (Girling, 1981: 92).

In 1975 when the Communists prevailed in Indochina, Thai policy-makers sought a policy of 'equidistance' by developing alliances with new friends and former enemies. Part of the reason Thai foreign policy moved toward a more even-handed policy was that domestic politics had changed decisively, albeit temporarily, in 1973. A student-led revolt had succeeded in ousting the military rule of Thanom and had brought a civilian government into power. 'Equidistance' better satisfied the demands on the regime.

After the military returned to power in 1976, Thai foreign policy continued to pursue a balance between the American alliance and the desire to improve ties with China and ASEAN. The new military regime under Kriangsak Chomanond understood that its own maintenance was conditioned on the support of extra-bureaucratic groups including the increasingly important educated middle class, intellectuals, and economic interest groups. A heightened sense of nationalism among these groups was the context for their support of a policy that no longer was exclusively pro-American.

Security

For the past three decades, the perceived security interests of foreign policy-makers in the United States and Thailand have been for the most part congruent. The leadership of both countries have set forth generally conservative policies opposing revolution. The victory of the Chinese in 1949 and the North Korean invasion of South Korea led to mutual interest being expressed in the Southeast Asia Treaty Organization (SEATO) collective defense treaty of 1954. The treaty made concrete a series of declarations by the leaders of both countries regarding the imminent Communist threat to Southeast Asia. The SEATO Treaty was tested by the crisis in Laos in 1960–62 stemming from the potential inclusion of leftist and neutralist forces in the Lao government coalition. In this case, Thailand, under Marshal Sarit, believed that a clear threat to Thai security existed, while the United States perceived only peripheral danger. The United States eventually accepted the Thai view (a case of the tail wagging the dog) and began to provide military and covert support to the right-wing forces in Laos.

Thailand's decision to ally with the United States was a security response to a perceived threat. The 'special relationship' forged during this period had as its goal the survival of Thai society against revolutionary forces. To strengthen the alliance, in 1962 Minister of Foreign Affairs Thanat Khoman persuaded Secretary of State Dean

Rusk to sign a communiqué which affirmed that the United States regarded the preservation of the independence and integrity of Thailand as vital to the national interest of the United States. The obligation of the United States to protect Thailand no longer depended on the prior agreement of SEATO Treaty members. The Rusk-Thanat Communiqué became the cornerstone of Thai-US relations and a base for mutual support during the Vietnam War.

As the United States escalated its military involvement in Vietnam, Thailand became a somewhat reluctant partner in war. Although Thai foreign policy-makers perceived a united Communist Vietnam as a potential threat, Thai officials were wary of a full commitment to the war effort against their neighbor. On the one hand, most Thais supported the hawkish goals of the United States to confront 'Communist aggression'. On the other hand, many wanted to keep their options open in case the Americans did not prevail.

President Lyndon Johnson's decision to halt bombing in 1968 and seek a negotiated settlement undercut the Thai government's confidence that the Americans would easily win. Even more strikingly, when President Nixon's 'Guam Doctrine' was enunciated in 1969, there arose a sense among government leaders, that, as with the Laotian crisis, the United States commitment was not unconditional. Thailand was also sensitive to the world's criticism of the country as an American lackey. However, Thai military leaders, especially from late 1971 to October 1973, when they ruled under martial law, continued to support American policy.

The Thai Foreign Minister during the era of Vietnam was Thanat Khoman, a pragmatist, who began in 1969 to attempt to open relations with China. His attempts were deemed premature by the military and Thanat was dismissed from his post following the November 1971 coup. The return to an exclusive alliance with the United States remained the cornerstone of Thai foreign policy until the military was overthrown in the student-led revolt of October 1973.

The opening up of Thai society, with new freedom of the press and eventually an elected national assembly, resulted in vigorous debate about the effectiveness of the American alliance for Thai national security interests. The rising nationalism provided the rationale and impetus for Thai demands for the United States to close its bases. Critics argued that the US forces had come to Thailand not to defend that country but to use it as a launching pad to fight the

Vietnam War. The timing of the request coincided with the view of the Nixon administration that withdrawal from the bases would not jeopardize American interests. The planned withdrawals were negotiated and carried out by 1976, after the Communists had gained victory in Indochina.

A confluence of forces, then, occurring in the mid-1970s, brought about a partial restructuring of Thai foreign policy. The American disengagement from Indo-China occurred simultaneously with the rise of a truly civilian elected regime. Also coincident was the Mayaguez incident in 1975 when the United States used Thai soil without first requesting permission. The incident marked the lowest point in Thai-US relations since the Second World War. Most crucial was the rise of Vietnam as the major power in Southeast Asia and China as its chief antagonist. These factors led Thai foreign policy-makers to see that the dominant-subordinate relationship between the United States and Thailand was an anachronism no longer appropriate for the new configuration of power in the area. The Vietnamese invasion of Cambodia in December 1978 precipitated further change in Thai foreign policy. Vietnam remained the principal enemy, but Thailand no longer relied exclusively on the United States for its security. In a significant turnabout, China became allied with Thailand and shared many parallel views about relations in Southeast Asia – a shift made easier by the earlier emergence of a *de facto* Sino-US alliance.

The US and Thailand nevertheless continued a security relationship which was annually shored up by the joint military exercise, Cobra Gold, which combined air, land, and sea operations. In addition the two countries agreed to set up a joint war reserve stockpile in Thailand which was to be operational in 1991. The stockpile consists of non-nuclear weaponry designed to deter Vietnamese aggression. The United States sold Thailand 12 F-16 fighter bombers to counter Vietnamese border incursions and the presence of Soviet-piloted MIG-23s in Vietnam.

The Thais have moved toward omnidirectionality (the term is that of Foreign Minister Siddhi) as security concerns have changed. In 1985 Siddhi wrote that security issues could no longer be seen autonomously and in relation to one patron-protector (the United States). Instead, he argued that the best guarantee of Thai security was a flexible policy based on active, open diplomacy with friends and foes. The top priorities became ASEAN relations, a recognition of China's important patron role in the region, and settlement of the Cambodian situation (see Chu Cheow, 1986). Thailand's new omnidirectionality has reflected changes in leadership in China, the Soviet Union, and Vietnam, where more pragmatic regimes appeared to be less threatening. Moreover, omnidirectionality means a more active role in international affairs rather than just as a client of the United States. For example, Thailand became a non-permanent Security Council member in 1985. Omnidirectionality also is viewed as a means to improve the economic well-being of the Kingdom by establishing economic ties with more countries willing to aid and trade with Thailand. Yet, omnidirectionality did not preclude a 'special relationship' with the United States for security support, especially during the presidency of Ronald Reagan. This policy of omnidirectionality has been popular with virtually all segments of Thailand's educated and articulate populace.

Thailand's most recent attempt to assure its security stems from the Vietnamese occupation of Cambodia. Support for China's provision of weaponry through Thailand to the anti-Vietnamese forces, the mobilization of the ASEAN powers against Vietnam, and the attempts to isolate Vietnam in the world community, are examples of Thai policy designed to weaken their prime adversary. Thailand's close ties with the United States and China, and these great powers' promises of support to Thailand in case of an invasion were part of the anti-Vietnamese strategy. In a 1985 study of élites in Bangkok, 97 per cent of the respondents cited Vietnam as a threat, 74 per cent identified the form of Vietnam's threat as direct military aggression, and only 1.1 per cent indicated a willingness to accommodate Vietnamese domination of Cambodia as a way to deal with the issue (cited by William Turley, in Grintner, 1987: 160). To offset the clear military advantage of Vietnam (with 1.2 million armed soldiers versus 240 000 total armed Thai forces), the Thai government increased defense spending, including the purchase of some 12 F-16 fighter jets from the United States.

The Thai-Chinese alliance is an example of an 180 degree turn in policy from the previous decades when China was viewed by Thai leaders as the primary threat to Thai security. The relationship is ambivalent because many older Thais, who were socialized to view China with alarm, continue the earlier perception. However, the use of China as a countervailing force against Vietnam has become the more significant factor in Thai foreign policy. Because both nations have a common interest in deterring Vietnam, the relationship is more one of security co-operation than security dependence (Theera Nuchpiam, in Jackson and Wiwat, 1986: 271).

The Thai government has assisted both China and the United States in channelling supplies to the Khmer Rouge and KPNLF forces on the border with Cambodia. Moreover, China has provided Thai military forces with weaponry including artillery, tanks, and armoured personnel carriers. Thailand's alliance with China has caused tension between Thailand and those ASEAN countries that continue to see China as the major threat to Southeast Asia. Indonesia, in particular, has argued against the Thai policy, claiming that a more conciliatory policy toward Vietnam is the best means to resolve the Indo-Chinese conflict.

Most analysts of international relations in Southeast Asia agree that Vietnam does not seriously threaten Thai territory with an invasion. The desperate economic conditions within Vietnam itself, the attempts of the Soviet Union to improve relations with ASEAN, and the beginning of Vietnamese withdrawal of troops from Cambodia indicate that an invasion threat is negligible. Prime Minister Chatichai responded to these conditions in 1988 by calling for the transformation of Vietnamese battlefields into marketplaces to expand Thai trade with and investment in Vietnam. This policy change was opposed by officials in the Ministry of Foreign Affairs who believed that Chatichai was unduly persuaded by his academic advisors to take an unprecedentedly conciliatory stand toward Vietnam.

Thai assistance to the tri-partite resistance forces in Cambodia has been part of the Kingdom's strategy to undermine Vietnamese strength in Indo-China. The Thais, who prefer to 'fight the war outside their own territory', until recently found the stalemate in Cambodia preferable to a stable, economically vital Vietnam and a Vietnamese-dominated neighbor. Nevertheless, in 1989 Prime Minister Chatichai, in a move which caused consternation among ASEAN allies, invited the Vietnamese-supported Prime Minister of Kampuchea, Hun Sen, to Bangkok for talks on how to resolve the Cambodian impasse. This change in policy direction was described as the essence of omnidirectionality.

After the end of the Vietnam War, the Thais redirected their foreign policy toward an alliance with China, support for the Cambodian rebel groups at the Thai border, and a leadership position in ASEAN, while retaining a 'special relationship' with the United States, all designed to contain Vietnam's position in Southeast Asia.

But since 1988 Prime Minister Chatichai has determined that there are also prospects of increased Thai influence in Indo-China by economic means.

Though the United States was engaged in a policy of improving relations with the Soviet Union, the Thai continued into the mid-1980s to be apprehensive about a parallel improvement in their own ties with Moscow. Until the Soviet Union ceased to be the principal support for the Vietnamese occupation of Cambodia, spokesmen indicated, Thailand would continue to view the Soviet's role as pernicious. But in the spirit of omnidirectionality, Prime Minister Prem's 1987 trip to Moscow was designed to improve relations and to initiate and expand trade ties.

Thailand's relations with its ASEAN allies have been strong, for the most part, although periodic disputes with Malaysia regarding insurgencies in both countries, and disagreements with ASEAN countries on trade and the specifics of the Indo-China conflict have caused tensions within the association. But thus far, ASEAN has been willing to give Thailand, as the front-line state, the major say in ASEAN's security policies toward Vietnam (Zakaria Haji Ahmad, in Jackson, *et al.*, 1986, p. 351).

Autonomy and Development

While regime maintenance and security now rank as the most important determinants of Thai foreign policy, Thai leaders have also been vitally concerned with maximizing the autonomy of the state and reducing dependency on more powerful nations. As a 'peripheral' Third-World society, Thailand has been buffeted by the world economy in ways that have reduced Thai independence. However, the dominant-subordinate US-Thai relationship has evolved into more equitable ties now that the Thai understand that the Kingdom is no longer a centerpiece of American foreign policy.

In 1986 Foreign Minister Siddhi noted that Thai foreign policy would concentrate more on economic matters, focusing on markets, investments, exports, tourism, and protectionism. As a means to achieve the goal of development and a higher level of living for Thais, the government has instituted an economic policy more open to the investment of foreign firms. An American Chamber of Commerce poll in 1987 indicated that 96 per cent of American business executives in Bangkok expressed optimism about Thailand's investment climate. This optimism stems from successive Thai government policies forbidding labor strikes, guaranteeing foreign firms against nationalization, moderating corporate tax obligations, decreasing dependence on foreign oil by developing natural gas alternatives, and promoting private sector growth as the 'locomotive' of Thai development. These policies have been designed to strengthen a flourishing economy, 'improve the welfare of the citizenry', and maintain a business-oriented regime in power.

Because Thailand is no longer imminently threatened from any outside nation, the relationship between the United States and Thailand has changed from one centering on security concerns to one often concerned more with economic and refugee issues. The most contentious issues are trade relations and intellectual property rights. Rising trade deficits caused the United States to take protectionist measures on sugar, rice, and textiles, all of which were thought to affect Thai exports negatively. The United States Congress, reacting to domestic political considerations, has subsidized American rice farmers and restricted the amount of Thai goods allowed to enter the country. In January 1989 the United States Trade Representative applied trade sanctions in response to Thailand's refusal to meet US demands on intellectual property rights.

In Thailand today the Japanese increasingly dominate trade and foreign investment. In 1987 Japan accounted for 45 per cent of the value of applications for investment, a figure three times the value of the next biggest foreign investor, Taiwan, whereas in the decade previous Japanese and American shares of long-term investment had been roughly equal. Japan's important economic role reflects a Thai analysis that Japan can best provide the technology and capital needed for Thailand to become a newly industrialized country.

At the same time, the Thai government has become more sensitive to Japanese domination of trade and investment relations. In the 1970s Thailand depended on Japan for 25.5 per cent of its exports and 31.2 per cent of imports (Girling, 1981: 98). The Thai government has attempted to diversify economic relations and establish Thai-owned trading firms to assure self-reliance. However, the government has for the most part left trade policy to the private sector, initiating policies when the government deemed there to be a national security concern, or when foreign relations change, as with China. It has not imposed nationalist restrictions on Japanese imports or investment.

In carrying out foreign policy, Thai leaders have posited a linkage between economic development and the enhancement of external and internal security. For example, the military, under the leadership of Army Commander-in-Chief Chavalit Yongchaiyut, introduced a strategy of 'Politics over Military' whereby the military played a major role in developing rural areas considered threatened by insurgency. Under this strategy, 'national security' was broadly defined in terms of the nation's stability, achieved through political, military, economic, and social actions to improve the lives of Thai citizens. Thailand's counterinsurgency campaign in the 1960s and 1970s, based primarily on military measures, was unsuccessful in quelling the rebel forces. Once political measures were launched under Prime Ministers Kriangsak and Prem – and the international context changed – the Communist Party of Thailand halted its armed insurgency. Army Commander-in-Chief Chavalit accepted the view that Communist insurgency is directly related to conditions of poverty, corruption, and abuses of power.

To protect the country from international financial crises, in the early 1980s the Thai government initiated a series of structural readjustments designed to diversify and make more efficient the domestic economy, and to broaden foreign investment incentives. These policies improved the debt-service ratio, reduced the percentage of the budget deficit, reduced inflation dramatically, and ended the balance of payments problems by devaluing the baht. The Sixth National Economic and Social Development Plan (1986–90) was specifically designed to enhance the national welfare by emphasizing the private sector and exports. Foreign investments in 1988 increased substantially over all previous years and merchandise exports increased in value terms by 28 per cent over 1987.

In contrast to the isolationist policies chosen by its neighbor Burma, Thai economic policy in the area of trade, debt maintenance, and investment reflected a belief in the inevitability of international interdependence. These policies were formulated to assure an inflow of foreign capital as an impetus to development. The success of the policy has been demonstrated by the high economic growth rates and by the capacity of successive governments to perpetuate their power and retain a high degree of legitimacy from the citizenry. The new economic diversity and the consequent lack of dependence on any one export market reduces Thailand's dependence on the ups and downs of particular foreign economies. As Thailand's trade relations increasingly are with its Asian neighbors, and these trade partners are themselves economically robust, the Thai economy will be further cushioned against economic downturn outside the region.

Consequences of foreign economic policy affect all of Thailand's other foreign policy goals. The vigorous state of the economy heightens the degree of legitimacy the government receives from the citizenry, undermines insurgent propaganda, contributes to the national welfare, and assures greater autonomy from foreign forces.

Nation-Building

In contrast to its neighbors in Southeast Asia, Thailand is essentially homogeneous with a single religion and language predominating throughout the Kingdom. That fact has meant that the crisis of nation-building has been less severe than that of its neighbors. The most important of the ethnic groups are the Chinese and the Thai Muslims. The Chinese, who comprise an estimated 10 per cent of the population and who live mostly in urban areas, have been largely assimilated into all aspects of Thai life. The traditional Chinese domination of the Thai economy has been buttressed by their new role in politics where an increasing number of ethnic Chinese-Thai are participating in parliamentary elections and holding high-level positions in the bureaucracy. It is increasingly difficult to know who is Chinese-Thai because of intermarriage and the adoption of Thai ways among Chinese families.

During the rule of Marshal Phibun, Thai nationalism was defined largely in anti-Chinese terms, against both the Chinese in Thailand and China. The anti-Chinese policies of Phibun included discrimination in myriad aspects of Thai economic and political life. When China supported the insurgent activities of the Communist Party of Thailand in the 1960s and 1970s, distrust of the Chinese-Thai and their links with China was again reinforced. During the present era, however, when the two nations have formed an alliance, discrimination has lessened and nationalism has taken a different form.

A more serious problem of nation-building results from the concentration of Thai Muslims in the four border provinces adjacent to Malaysia. These provinces, with over 70 per cent of the population Muslim, have at various times been Thai vassal states, independent kingdoms, and putative Malay states. Thai Muslims have inhabited the area in the south for centuries. Because the Thai authorities discriminate against them, sometimes producing sharp reactions, and because their traditions and religion make it difficult to become assimilated into Thai society, they have been treated as a potential threat to the unity of the Thai nation.

Both the majority Thai and the Thai Muslims view each other with distrust and fear. The threat of insurgency and separatist movements have increased their mutual antipathy. (To alleviate the tension, the Thai government has made attempts to improve socio-economic conditions in the four southern provinces and to be more sensitive to Muslim teachings. The government initiated economic development programs in the 1960s including the building of roads throughout the south, rubber replantation programs, and the promotion of education.) These programs have had mixed success: large numbers of Thai Muslims continue to fail to identify themselves with the Thai state. Their antagonism continues to jeopardize the stability of the nation, especially since Thailand is an oil importer and desires positive relations with Islamic Middle Eastern nations. In addition, border problems with Malaysia, related to the activities of both the Malayan Communist Party and the Thai Muslim separatist movements, have created tensions. However, the institution of ASEAN has helped both nations to negotiate their differences. For example, the Thai and Malay militaries have co-operated in countering the terrorist activities of the Malayan Communist Party, which have periodically spilled over the border into Thailand, and in defeating the Thai Communist Party in the south. A co-operative policy toward Malaysia thus has payoffs for nation-building.

The attempt to promote a sense of identity with the nation is also important in gaining the support of ethnic minorities and securing the borders in north and northeast provinces. Communist insurgency has been controlled in the areas bordering Burma and Laos. However, the Thais have had border skirmishes with Laotians and with the Vietnamese-backed Cambodians, especially in the areas where some 250 000 refugees are languishing. Because the mountainous northern region is populated by minority hill tribe peoples, and northeasterners are ethnically Lao (and in some areas, Cambodian), the importance of nationalism in these volatile areas is significant.

CONCLUSION

Thai foreign policy, then, is reactive as well as proactive to both internal and external forces as well as responsive to a multiplicity of goals. Although the means change as befits the particular circumstances, the over-arching goal is to secure nation, King, and Buddhism from threats. In the attempt to achieve this objective, Thai foreign policy-makers seek to maximize the Kingdom's security and autonomy, maintain the regime in power, promote national welfare objectives, in particular economic development, and build the nation's unity. In 1985 Foreign Minister Siddhi articulated the major dimensions of multifaceted 'omnidirectionality': strengthening both the country's external and internal security and economic status.

Whereas Thai foreign policy, in the past, was crisis and security oriented, the new foreign policy has been an instrument to enhance the national well-being as well. Thailand's interdependence requires flexible responses to particular circumstances. In the main, Thailand has opted for a diversified economy open to investments from foreign firms, and favorable to freer trade. Multinational corporations have been welcomed within the context of self-interest as determined by the leaders in power.

The pragmatic and interdependent foreign policy of the Thai government has been remarkably successful in securing at least one goal, the sovereignty of the Kingdom. No other Southeast Asian nation has been independent from formal colonization. Thai political institutions are congruent with the Kingdom's traditional culture and the authorities have been accepted as legitimate by most sectors of the society. The rulers' conservative economic policies, for the most part, have also been successful, without the unrestrained greed, oppressive bureaucracy, and dependency that have marred the economic performance of so many Third-World countries. Thailand's continuing capacity to cope with changing demands and to assert its own destiny, protected from menacing internal and external forces, remains intact.

BIBLIOGRAPHY

Bell, Peter F. (1987), 'Foreign Policy of Thailand: A Political Economy Analysis', unpublished paper presented to the conference on Managing the External Environment: The Political Economy of Foreign Policy in Southeast Asia, Windsor, Ontario, May 1987.

Bradley, William, *et al.* (1978), *Thailand, Domino by Default? The 1976 Coup and Implications for US Policy* (Athens: Ohio University Press).

Caldwell, Alexander (1974), *American Economic Aid to Thailand* (Lexington: Lexington Books).

Chai-Anan Amudavanija and Sukhumbhand Paribatra (1987), 'In Search of Balance: Prospects for Stability in Thailand during the Post-CPT Era', unpublished manuscript.

Cheow, Eric Teo Chu (1986), 'New Omnidirectional Overtures in Thai Foreign Policy', *Asian Survey*, Vol. XXVI, No. 7 (July).

Darling, Frank (1965), *Thailand and the United States* (Washington, DC: Public Affairs Press).

Funston, John (1987), 'The Role of the Ministry of Foreign Affairs in Thailand: Some Preliminary Observations', *Contemporary Southeast Asia*, Vol. 9, No. 3 (December).

Girling, John (1986), 'Is Small-Holder Cultivation Viable? A Question of Political Economy With Reference to Thailand', *Pacific Affairs*, Vol. 59, No. 2 (Summer).

Girling, John (1981), *Thailand: Society and Politics* (Ithaca: Cornell University Press).

Grinter, Lawrence E. and Young Whan Kihl (1987), *East Asian Conflict Zones: Prospects for Regional Stability and Deescalation* (New York: St Martin's Press).

Ingram, James C. (1971), *Economic Change in Thailand, 1850–1970* (Stanford: Stanford University Press).

Jackson, Karl D., Sukhumbhand Paribatra and J. Soedjati Djiwandono (1986), *ASEAN in Regional and Global Context* (Berkeley: Institute of East Asian Studies, University of California).

Jackson, Karl D. and Wiwat Mungkandi (1986), *United States-Thailand Relations* (Berkeley: Institute of East Asian Studies, University of California).

Likhit Dhiravegin (1985), *Thai Politics: Selected Aspects of Development and Change* (Bangkok, Tri-Sciences Publishing House).

Morell, David and Chai-Anan Samudavanija (1981), *Political Conflict in Thailand; Reform, Reaction, Revolution* (Cambridge: Oelgesclager, Gunn Hain).

Morrison, Charles E. and Astri Suhrke (1978), *Strategies of Survival: The Foreign Policy Dilemmas of Smaller Asian States* (New York: St Martin's Press).

Muscat, Robert J. (1966), *Development Strategy in Thailand: A Study of Economic Growth* (New York: Praeger).

Neher, Clark D. (1987), *Politics in Southeast Asia* (Cambridge: Schenkman Publishing Co.).

Neher, Clark D. (1987), 'Thailand in 1986: Prem, Parliament, and Political Pragmatism', *Asian Survey*, Vol. XXVII, No. 2 (February).

Neher, Clark D. (1988), 'Thailand in 1987: Semi-Successful Semi-Democracy', *Asian Survey*, Vol. XXVIII, No. 2 (February).

Permtanjit, Grit (1981), *Political Economy of Dependent Capitalist Developpment: Study on the Limits of the Capacity of the State to Rationalize in Thailand*, unpublished Ph.D. dissertation, University of Pennsylvania.

Randolph, R. Sean (1986), *The United States and Thailand* (Berkeley: Institute of East Asian Studies, University of California).

Suehiro, Akira (1985), *Capital Accummulation and Industrial Development in Thailand* (Bangkok: Chulalongkorn University Social Research Institute).

Silcock, Thomas Henry (ed.) (1967), *Thailand, Social and Economic Studies in Development* (Canberra: Australian National University Press).

Termsak Chalermpanalanupap (1986), 'A Historical Analysis of Underdevelopment, Dependency, and the Impact of Indochinese Refugees,' unpublished Ph.D. dissertation, University of New Orleans.

Tilman, Robert O. (1987), *Southeast Asia and The Enemy Beyond, ASEAN Perceptions of External Threats* (Boulder: Westview Press).

Wilson, David (1962), *Politics in Thailand* (Ithaca: Cornell University Press).

11 The Foreign Policy of Burma

John Badgley

Burma's leaders have followed a singular path in foreign affairs. While their neighbors have been drawn into pacts, alliances, and various treaty commitments, the Burmese have chosen to enter no arrangement of a political or economic nature that would suggest alignment between East or West, North or South. Only the Non-Aligned Movement attracted their attention as founding members, and that attraction waned as Soviet-oriented governments gained control of the organization. Isolation from world and even regional affairs became Burma's hallmark, until after the 1988 coup, when a new regime opened the country to joint ventures and oil exploration.

For purposes of comparative analysis we have settled on five key concepts as descriptors of foreign policy goals held in common by all governments: security, autonomy, regime-maintenance, welfare, and nation-building. While Burma's foreign policy has varied to meet demands primarily from domestic sources, as well as changing world views of key leaders, it has hewn to several principles. The paramount goal, until recently, has been autonomy in world politics, to keep imperialism at bay and to assert central governmental control over contending internal forces. In the name of social and economic justice, all leaders adhered to some version of socialism until 1988. Such ideology helped rationalize the strengthening of the state in its modern role as nation-builder and welfare provider; however, in practice the highest priorities have been given to policies designed to maintain the power of a new class of officialdom.

THE HISTORICAL CONTEXT OF FOREIGN POLICY

So what accounts for Burma's policies, especially over the past quarter century? Why such vehement anti-capitalist sentiment? Why should a country blessed with substantial natural resources, a literate population, a reasonably well-trained business and managerial sector equal to their counterparts in Malaysia and Thailand, have turned away from ideas of progress well accepted in the remainder of non-Communist Southeast Asia and embraced isolation? Why, four decades after independence, do officials still look inward for their identity and their enemies? Why, indeed, does rebellion persist with its heavy consequences for foreign policy formulation? This chapter is too brief to give any definitive answer to these questions; however, an explanation is needed to grasp the antecedents for behavior that otherwise seems irrational and bizarre.

Several decades hence historians may observe that Burma's uniqueness is insignificant compared with what it shares in global trends among agrarian peoples. However, unique policies just noted suggest significant institutional and cultural differences between Burma and its neighbors. Burma's last monarch was seized and by the British dispatched to India, where he lived in ignominy until his death, long before revolution swept Indo-Chinese monarchs from their thrones. This act decapitated a Theravada Buddhist polity that had endured for eight centuries in various locales and dynastic reincarnations along the Irrawaddy River ever since the Pagan dynasty was founded. Yet the language and sentiment of the diverse Burmese peoples shaped into a single sovereign empire persisted. While no monarchical pretender has appeared in Burma since independence, both U Nu and Ne Win have practised and encouraged behavior and language associated with the traditional court. Common use of astrologers and cosmological symbols, appeals to the Buddhist *sangha* for support, suppression of minorities by Burmans, the ethnic majority, re-assertion of their language as the only acceptable medium of education in a multilingual society (until 1986 when English was re-introduced) – such policies from the top suggest traditionalization of government. This is congruent with the search for security through isolation from outside influences, a recurrent practice by Burmese kings during periods of regime consolidation. Indeed, the very aggressiveness of Burmese military leaders in suppressing minority autonomy movements shadows the behavior of monarchs in early Pagan, Toungoo, and Konbaung dynasties who successfully pulled the same peoples away from alternative suzerains in present day Thailand, Yunnan (China), Manipur (India), and Laos (Lieberman: 241–4; Hagesteijn: 104–5).

Such political contours reflect the image of the nation held in the mind of key leaders, and Burma has shared with only one other agrarian Southeast Asian country, Vietnam, a persistent vision by one leader which dominates all others. Ne Win has been Burma's

Ho Chi Minh. Ne Win was one among a group of student leaders in the mid-1930s who harbored a powerful revulsion against British rule. Calling themselves Thakins, the Burmese word for 'master' (which was used for British officials), the students successfully satirized their colonial rulers while claiming legitimacy for themselves as successors. However, it was not Ne Win, whose economic circumstances had forced him out of school, who led the Thakins. The student association president, Aung San, was chosen and his views prevailed for a decade through the period of collaboration with the Japanese, during the secret negotiations with the British to turn against the Japanese, and after the war when the Labour government came to power in the United Kingdom and promised Burma its independence, which was declared on 4 January 1948. Tragically, Aung San was assassinated only months before realizing his dream, and the moderate U Nu was chosen as his successor. Throughout this period Ne Win had been a military commander, seeking no political role within the Anti-Fascist People's Freedom League (AFPFL) which was the congerie of political groups led by the youthful Thakins through the first decade of independence. Aung San, and U Nu after him, saw Burma as a union of diverse political communities which was designed at the crucial Panglong Conference in 1947 as a grouping of five states which could reconsider the nature of their union a decade after independence (Aung San, 1946: 21–93).

Most Thakins rejected Marxism-Leninism as their ideology, but accepted Marx's vision of capitalism's pending collapse. Their first foreign policy decision was not to join the Commonwealth, the only ex-British colony that failed to do so; and their second significant choice was to join the United Nations. They established relations with India, and then the People's Republic of China, the first state to do so, marking out their principle of amicability with the major Asian powers, neutrality in the bi-polar world shaped by the Cold War, and determination to avoid involvement in the alliances pressed on their neighbors. As the Korean War ended and the Indo-China war expanded, U Nu had widespread support within the AFPFL to seek a global stage for his vision of non-alignment. With Nehru, Sukarno, and Tito he established a movement which pulled Burma even further into world politics (Johnstone, 1963: 125–210).

U Nu and the AFPFL leaders held open elections, but had recurrent struggles with insurgents who, in 1949–50, threatened the government's existence. But for Ne Win's ability as commander of an army decimated by Karen and Burma Communist Party (BCP) defections to insurgent forces, the AFPFL government would have collapsed. That debt was not forgotten by either party. Insurgencies in north central Burma and the delta were eventually extinguished through persuasion and occasional fighting; however, the possibility of Karen, Shan, Kachin, and BCP coalition into a major opposition army remained alive and ever more threatening as the 1958 deadline approached for revision of the Union. Meanwhile, the AFPFL opened Burma to substantial foreign influence by accepting aid from many foreign powers, thereby inviting criticism from those who viewed strict autonomy as a higher goal than the welfare improvements sought through foreign aid and investment.

Convinced that splits within the AFPFL were causing his regime to collapse, U Nu invited Ne Win to govern between 1958–60 while he sought to heal breaches in his party; those critical of this move feel Ne Win left the Prime Minister no choice by threatening a coup 'to prevent collapse of the Union itself'. As military commander, General Ne Win administered the government with some skill, cleaning up Rangoon and removing allegedly corrupt officials (Trager, 1966: ch. 6; Badgley, 1962: 24–8). He returned power to U Nu in 1960, then claimed that foreign powers were manipulating ethnic insurgencies in 1962 and again displaced U Nu's party from power.

When Ne Win seized power in 1962 he sloughed off the former AFPFL leadership as a spent force, although many observers gave U Nu's regimes high marks for social justice and economic growth (Walinsky, 1962: 565–83; Mya Maung, 1971: 90–113). Retiring from the army, Ne Win took the title of Chairman, Burma Socialist Program Party (BSPP or *Lanzin*), and has retained this paramount political post for a quarter century, while creating a syncretic socialist regime. During its formative decade the BSPP consolidated remnants of several political parties as well as ex-insurgent leaders while Ne Win governed by decree. Then, in 1974 a much criticized constitution was adopted by the new parliament, the *Pyithu Hlutdaw*, with its membership elected from the single slate created by *Lanzin*. Although nominally under civilian control, this regime has been dominated by ex-colonels and senior officers from Ne Win's old Burma Independence Army. Within that group various factions have competed for Ne Win's favor as he chose fluctuating paths in foreign and domestic policy.

FOREIGN POLICY-MAKERS AND FOREIGN POLICY PROCESS

Thus far Burma's foreign policy has been seen as an instrument of statecraft by two men, U Nu and Ne Win. One might be skeptical of this view as over-simplified. Yet a dozen foreign ministers have served in the 40 years since independence, and one is hard-pressed to associate any particular departure with any one of them. Without exception, each has served at the will of U Nu or Ne Win, and policy is notable for its adherence to the wishes of whoever held the topmost position. Under both men there has been a steel hand on the tiller of Burma's foreign policy, a hand guided by astrologers and personal whim as well as foreign and domestic constraints. Independence was established on a propitious date determined by U Nu's astrologer, and 40 years later Ne Win demonitized most of his currency because of an astrologer's advice about the need for multiples of 15 in all currency if his regime was to survive. In the intervening decades many key moves seem to have been tied to such notions.

Buddhism is, of course, Burma's dominant religion and the *sangha*, or organization of monks, has been a significant element throughout Burma's history. In the first years after his coup, Ne Win set about purging the monks whom leaders of the major sects viewed as heretical. The missionary zeal of Burma's two elderly Thakins, U Nu in opposition and Ne Win in government, fueled the fire of heresy trials, and spurred competing fund-raising for monasteries and meditation centers favored by each man and his followers. Only on rare occasions in the past has Buddhism been in such ferment in Burma. And through its arcane interpretations by monks who have Ne Win's confidence, it retains a prominent role in foreign policy decisions.

Deference to 'the old man' is still omnipresent, even after *Lanzin's* collapse in 1988. Policy changes were discussed in the supreme council of the *Pyithu Hlutdaw*, with recommendations then made to Ne Win for decision. Personnel decisions at the ministerial level were made in secret dialogue between Ne Win and his councillors, and a move by any minister that failed to agree with Ne Win's sense of propriety was sufficient cause for dismissal and public humiliation. These removals never triggered rejection of Ne Win's policies or actions by other ministers within *Lanzin* or the military, suggesting that he retained a high sensitivity to the groupings and interactions among his followers. The retirement benefits and overseas opportunities of high officials were in constant jeopardy. He has had a remarkable ability to allow each potential successor enough latitude to move beyond a policy acceptable to most other ministers, then to fire the culprit dramatically and pull the ship of state back in a direction that preserved his own base of power. Foreign policy has been an instrument which has helped Ne Win retain power, despite the collapse of Burma's economy in recent years (Silverstein, 1977, *passim*; Steinberg, 1986: *passim*).

Burma's *Lanzin* party was the chief instrument for political consolidation of the Ne Win regime between 1962 and 1988. It was critical to regime survival, but was also a cause of the increasing erosion of the economy. While it claimed over two million members and candidates, and could marshall thousands of marchers and flag wavers on public occasions, *Lanzin* was a top-down organization dominated by the changeable beliefs of its Chairman. *The Correlation of Man and His Environment*, the official ideological basis for all *Lanzin* policies, was sanctioned by Ne Win in his first post-coup years and remained the philosophic foundation for policy-making. As a syncretic compound of Buddhism and socialism, it offers sanction for nearly any interpretation, or desire, on the Chairman's part.

Parallel to *Lanzin* in structure is a pyramid of village, township, and divisional councils. Generally chaired by co-opted military officers, they still function as administrators of all civil and security tasks. *Lanzin* councils inter-related with these bureaucratic councils which culminated in the elected parliament, the *Pyithu Hlutdaw*.

The higher ranks of both government and political organizations are clearly dominated by the military. No institution equals the Burmese army in cohesion or power in contemporary Burma. It numbers 170 000 and has been seasoned through four decades of continuous struggle to defeat a dozen guerrilla groups. Ne Win has given extraordinary rewards to victorious commanders, and rapid punishment for officers viewed as disloyal or incompetent. Indeed, he sought confrontation with any rising star who might challenge his paramountcy (Wiant, 1981: 69–71).

The army has successfully transformed tens of thousands of young villagers into soldiers and college graduates into officers, the core of whom are drawn from the military college in Maymyo. While many units have suffered high casualties in battle, their willingness to return with even greater ferocity can only be explained by a high morale and a supply of equipment equal or superior to that of their enemies. Furthermore, most of these men are Burmans while most of their enemies are Karens, Kachins, Shans, or Mons, in league with the BCP in recent years.

Amenities offered the military have distinguished them as Burma's new class, and more senior officers have learned to expect substantial rewards in civilian jobs through early retirement. The charisma and fear of Ne Win prevailed for four decades and contributed to the caution evident among those who might oppose his policies. Only one abortive coup, in 1977, has been reported, although some 200 captains and majors were dismissed in 1987, ostensibly for inefficiency. The 18 September 1988 coup elevated General Saw Maung into the premiership, and destroyed both *Lanzin* and constitutional government; however, Ne Win continues to review and sanction, or veto, policy decisions by the cabinet dominated by senior military officers.

DOMESTIC CONSTRAINTS AND CAPABILITIES

The heart of *Lanzin* philosophy during its early years in power was designed to strengthen the state, ostensibly to sustain the welfare of peasants and workers. To gain this end Ne Win's ministers transformed larger private enterprises into national corporations, while they sought to develop a powerful co-operative movement at the town and village level – all aimed at relieving economic injustice left from the previous U Nu administration and British imperialism (Wiant, 1981: 66–71). However, the inexperience and corruption of the new class of managers led the economy into a startling reversal of the growth trends established in the first 15 years of independence. Productivity and exports declined, the balance of payments position deteriorated, and urban riots in 1968 permitted Ne Win to call in a new group of leaders. Again he turned to his army colleagues and drew Brigadier San Yu into the key chief-of-cabinet post, replacing Brigadier Tin Pe. Dozens of senior officers were retired and the new leadership again turned outward for help. Missions to the Asian Development Bank, the World Bank and the International Monetary Fund invited return visits by experts who suggested major changes. The Green Revolution was introduced, low level technicians from Japan and Germany re-entered after a ten-year hiatus to assist in modernizing production and marketing cereal and forestry products. Rice and teak exports rose rapidly by the late 1970s, and oil exploration held the promise of Burmese self-sufficiency in petroleum products (Hill, 1986: 22).

Burma's economy had historically been its strongest feature but by the late 1960s – and again in the late 1980s – had become the major cause of weakness. In the 1930s Burma was the largest rice exporter in the world, so by regaining control over their economy the young Thakins promised widespread prosperity as they envisioned profits being returned to the producers. The promise was not fulfilled. While paddy production finally reached postwar levels in the late 1970s, the value of rice exports has never equalled that of prewar years. Burma's share of the world market has declined from over half to less than 5 per cent. Large gains in agricultural productivity during 1975–80 came from new rice strains and miracle hybrids of other crops plus widespread irrigation and marketing improvements. But productivity plateaued as the farmers were locked into a price system that gave them no incentives for greater risks in developing fallow land or new crops. Four-fifths of all farm land remains in private hands, the vast majority owned by small producers.

While by 1980 Burma had become respected in the Third World because of its parsimonious national debt, that favorable situation was possible only because of the temporarily high value of its primary products on the world market. By 1984 the rosy glow of Burma's decent 5–6 per cent growth rate faded as a combination of grim trends coalesced to cause an acute depression. Rising OPEC prices had coincided with declining domestic oil production. Other exports – rice, tungsten, teak, lentils – dropped in value due to a decline in world prices as well as declining totals of available product. Government corporations also were tied to a price system that gave them no incentive. The once favorable trade balance shifted and ate into the half billion dollar reserve fund. Social expenditures had tripled between 1962 and 1982 as urban areas grew and required more government services. Burma's total exports declined nearly 60 per cent in value between 1980 and 1987, until over half the earnings were being used for debt repayment. For this reason the government sought 'least developed' status from international lending agencies, which would permit some loans to be changed to grants and others to be refinanced with 50-year extended payments (Carver, 1987: 75). Foreign reserves declined to US$ 30 million in 1986 and the Burma aid consortium has since 1984 provided loans and grants rising to a half-billion dollars annually by 1987, from a pre-1980 level below

US$ 100 million. The dismal state of Burma's economy is precipitating policy changes to avoid total financial collapse that would have been entirely unacceptable to Ne Win and his *Lanzin* party in the past.

A key domestic constraint for Burma is the proportion and placement of indigenous minorities, unable or unwilling to assimilate to the majority, and their external ties. Approximately 27 million Burmans in the central plains are surrounded by some ten million peoples of different ancestry, customs, and languages mainly occupying the mountainous frontier region. The combination of geography and cultural diversity are powerful forces shaping traditional and current Burmese foreign policy.

Control over their territory has always been a potent issue for Arakanese and Chin to the west, for Nagas and Kachins in the north; for Palaungs, Lisu, and Wa in the northeast Shan hills, for Shan, Karens, and Mons to the east along the Thai border. Native to the broken terrain they inhabit, often using dialects unintelligible to one another, these minorities have always complicated the lives of Burman rulers. These people must be won to the government's side if most of Burma's minerals and forest products are to be developed, and national boundaries are to be secured.

Christian proselytizing commenced even before the first Anglo-Burmese War in 1825, and missionary activity by Protestants and Catholics alike was encouraged by the British. Entire clans and villages converted and evangelical efforts continue to flourish, though external support was banned after 1963. Religious differences reinforced ethnic boundaries. In sum, these ethnic minorities constitute a significant problem for the government as long as they lack loyalty to the Rangoon regime. Some measure of that cost is in illegal foreign exchange earnings alone, which exceed total official earnings. Metals and precious stones, major exports in the past, now return only a fraction of their previous revenue to the government for they are largely sold on the black market. Opium production and export is largely controlled by hill tribes, and their Chinese trading partners.

THE EXTERNAL ENVIRONMENT

Geopolitical facts certainly help shape Burma's foreign relations. To the east and west the country is sandwiched between the two most populous nations in the world, each with bordering provinces larger than Burma. Tibet's experience with the PRC and India's rapid interventions in Goa and Sri Lanka, as well as its influence over Nepal and Bangladesh suggest imperial acts by great powers concerned that their borders be secure. So Burmese can be expected to act defensively towards their giant neighbors. Security has been a crucial issue among Burmese thereby permiting Ne Win to use fear of these colossal neighbors, of great powers, and of Thailand as a rationale for maintaining a relatively powerful military, not designed to repel massive invasions, but effective in repressing potential indigenous allies of any foreign power.

Covert Chinese support – first from Taiwan for the KMT irregulars left from the Second World War, then for the BCP – has been an irritant and has aroused vigorous charges of interference from time to time, reaching a peak during the Cultural Revolution. However, the long and difficult boundary settlement process has been resolved, trade is expanding, both legal and illicit, and only the Kachin Independence Army is still reportedly assisted from outside (Lintner, 1987).

With India, Burma has had no specific problem and signed a territorial waters treaty in 1987, the most recent measure of their amity. The Naga and Pakistan conflicts once touched on Burma's borders but have receded into history while visits between high officials have resolved lesser issues. Bangladesh is a neighbor nearer in size, and Burma has settled their boundary problem, as well as assisted in crises precipitated by Bangladesh's tragic floods. Smuggling and insurgent movements across the Arakan border mirror problems with Thailand, the nation most salient in contemporary foreign policy concerns. In the years when Thailand was allied solely with the United States, relations remained cool; however, as Thai policy has shifted in the 1980s to an active military and political alliance with China, Burma has welcomed Thai officials as kindred spirits. Numerous joint ventures are under way with Thai businesses, especially in fisheries and timber products, and major hydro and transport projects are being explored.

While Burma never joined any of the Southeast Asian regional organizations, there has been recurrent interest in the region's future. Burma did participate in the Southeast Asia Games and expects to host them in the near future. Universities (before their closure in 1988) were establishing courses in Southeast Asian studies which anticipated intensified relations in the future.

The domestic constraints outlined earlier helped to form a foreign policy that perceived the world as more dangerous than benevolent. The huge build-up of American forces during the Indochina conflict, seen as threatening, doubtless influenced the xenophobic steps taken by Ne Win's *Lanzin* cabinets during the height of that war; however, hostility to US policy would not account for the cultural chauvinism that characterized that era in Burma's policies. Shifts in policy priorities in the 1980s have taken place as the external environment appears increasingly peaceful, congruent with the original hopes of U Nu.

FOREIGN POLICY OUTPUTS

For a year after the 1962 coup Ne Win favored a group whose spokesman was Brigadier Aung Gyi. While accepting removal of foreign advisers as vital to autonomy, they still saw the need for aid, especially from Japan. With massive plans for industrialization, they tilted towards Japanese support as compared to the carefully balanced aid packages U Nu had tailored. Their schemes vanished overnight when Aung Gyi was unceremoniously fired by Ne Win in 1963, the first of many whose power apparently threatened the Chairman.

For five years thereafter the chief-of-cabinet function was awarded to Brigadier Tin Pe who supervised the application of *Lanzin's* ideology, which steered Burma's citizens away from all foreign contact. Private enterprise was nationalized, forcing hundreds of thousands of Chinese and Indians out of Burma under exclusionary decrees. Cultural chauvinism led Burma to retire from leadership in international bodies, while domestically promoting Burmanization of all minority cultures. The policy was oppressive for those accustomed to the freedom of U Nu's governments, and many educated citizens fled, others took up arms and revitalized the notion of a federated insurgent force, which eventually formed under the banner of the National Democratic Front (NDF).

In a similar vein, officials working on programs dealing with health, children, the elderly, nutrition, family planning, and tropical diseases were frustrated by ministers who feared the Chairman's wrath if he perceived any foreign involvement as excessive. Even Burmese serving as senior executives in UN agencies were generally ignored by their own government. The continuing drain of experienced managers, professionals and intellectuals accentuated the international isolation. Thousands of Burmese trapped by the system fled to nearby countries to wait out the trauma that will likely accompany transition after Ne Win passes from the scene.

Though foreign investment or even joint ventures remained taboo until recently, since the early 1970s Ne Win has gradually increased Burma's use of foreign aid for development purposes. The evolving shift back from autonomy in world affairs to greater acceptance of a dependence on donor nations and international agencies offers some hope for improvement of welfare and nation-building. These two goals, while always stressed in the annual speeches of ministers and party officials, long took a back seat to the prime objective of regime maintenance. Autonomy appears to have been of greater importance to Ne Win than U Nu, but both men promoted the notion of non-alignment more than any of their regional counter-parts. Sacrifice of critically important foreign aid in the name of self-sufficiency during most of the 1960s can only be explained in this way.

Burma's trade policy failed completely in controlling the black market, which played a pre-eminent role in all aspects of economic life until 1988, when a free market was legalized. Were these earnings properly taxed and the profits retained in Burma rather than siphoned off by traders in Thailand, India, China, Malaysia, and Singapore, the government would enjoy a far more favorable balance of payments situation. Perhaps no single factor has so helped the insurgents' causes as their ability to control such a large portion of Burma's exports. The two-tiered economy would be inexplicable but for the historical division between Burmans and the minorities.

The first significant decision to break up the two-tier system was taken in August 1987 when Ne Win called an extra-ordinary session of the parliament to legitimize his decision to return rice trade to the private sector. Given the importance of rice to the economy, it seemed likely that other commodities would follow. But that result did not come in time to save the regime. Other efforts to attack the hemorrhage in illicit trade have been ineffectual or worse, as with the demonetization scheme. Three times Ne Win has withdrawn certain denominations of currency believed to be used primarily by illicit traders, then re-issued different denominations. In September 1987 both 75 and 25 *kyat* notes were demonetized, replaced by 90, 45 and 15 *kyat* notes, numbers recommended to Ne Win by an astrologer. The citizenry was simply bilked of large amounts of savings, which many had withdrawn from banks out of fear their accounts might be sequestered. A policy aimed at foreign black marketeers and their local counterparts caused widespread misery domestically.

While Ne Win's objective, regime-maintenance, and the corollary, securing the state against insurgent armies, have both been minimally achieved, the cost in terms of welfare, economic development and, most recently, autonomy from demands by international lending agencies, has been very high. To extract itself from the current collapse, the government must accept Asian Development Bank, IMF, and IBRD requirements for loans and grants. Japan is particularly influential within these agencies and on a bilateral basis, as well, for it has long since become Burma's major economic aid donor, giving in excess of US$ 1.2 billion since the mid-1950s (Steinberg, 1986: 128–30). The European Community, West Germany, the PRC, and the United States lag well behind in total aid and influence.

In a similar fashion, the long-term internal security problem is not easily resolved, despite some success in repression of NDF armies in 1986–87. Private armies still run arms and goods into the country, while smuggling valuable teak, gems, rice and, of course, opium, out through Thailand, India, and Bangladesh. By maintaining good relations with all its neighbors, Burma has gained some co-operation in attacking the opium problem, which in recent years has reportedly been reduced by a third in volume (Lintner, 1987). Joint narcotics control teams have increasingly interdicted opium shipments. An outpouring of enthusiasm welcomed the Thai princess's visit in 1986, while Ne Win's personal visitation and gift of a jade Buddha to the King on his 60th birthday symbolized an unprecedented warmth and respect between the two countries' leaders. But the complex movement of Lisu, Akha, Palaung, Kachins, Karens, and Mons across the porous borders is impossible to control, and some groups of minorities will continue to seek external support in their struggle with the majority Burmans until they perceive their interests to be represented in Rangoon – by a different regime.

The effort to fend off First- and Second-World influences, as well as possible Chinese and Indian threats, has succeeded at considerable cost. Burma's drop from a reasonably prosperous Third-World status in the early 1960s to a least developed status by 1989 is a consequence of the goals to achieve autonomy, keep Ne Win in power, and integrate the minorities into one national Burmese culture. The consequent disaffection of intellectuals, most ethnic leaders, and much of the population as critical shortages mounted is a result of foreign phobias held by Ne Win especially. For him, enemies far outnumbered friends as the years passed and his power became more absolute. On occasion he referred to his job as *okkatha*, chief of the Burmese, as like holding a tiger's tail. Given his perception of the job, one needs little imagination to feel the pressures that accompany his position. A half-century has passed since he joined Aung San, U Nu, and the Thakins in their revolutionary movement against the British. Burma has ventured down a singular path since, much of it designed by Ne Win himself through military officers acting in his name. While failing economically in recent years, they have achieved a traditionalization of society. Most Burmese take pride in their heritage while they see the traditions of their neighbors eroding amidst rapid modernization. Industrialization has a price which many Burmese have not wanted to pay, and Ne Win has catered to that sentiment.

Foreign policy has been a reflection of domestic constraints in Burma, far more than a reaction to foreign pressures. Had any of the major world powers seriously pressed Burma to alter its course, the nation might have taken a different turn. Until a kind of commonwealth can be devised to accommodate internal demands on the state, and as long as the external environment continues to tolerate the isolation sought by the government, many regard it as unlikely that policy will change fundamentally. However, morale and economic conditions are sufficiently depressed by recent domestic policy errors to require major changes, whether in a succession crisis or by the Chairman's order. Burma remains a complex society, searching for a benevolent political system. As leaders maneuver to gain power, the priorities of foreign policy will shift. As Burmese Buddhists are fond of saying, the only certainty is change itself.

BIBLIOGRAPHY

Anderson, Benedict (1983), *Imagined Communities: Reflections on the Origin and Spread of Nationalism* (London: Verso).

Aung San (1946), *Burma's Challenge* (Rangoon: Defence Services Historical Institute).

Badgley, John (1962), 'Burma's Military Government: A Political Analysis', *Asian Survey*, II: 6, August.

Badgley, John (1965), 'Burma and China: Policy of a Small Neighbor', in *Policies Towards China*, A. M. Halpern (ed.) (New York: Council on Foreign Relations, McGraw-Hill).

Badgley, John (1970), *Politics Among Burmans* (Athens: Ohio University Press).

Badgley, John (1974), 'Burmese Communist Schisms', in *Peasant Rebellion and Communist Revolution in Asia*, John Wilson Lewis (ed.) (Stanford: Stanford University Press).

Carver, Liz (1987), *Far Eastern Economic Review*, 16 April.

Economist Intelligence Unit (1986–87) EIU *Country Profile: Thailand and Burma* (London: Economist Publications).

Hagesteijn, Renée (1985), *Circles of Kings: Political Dynamics in Early Continental Southeast Asia* (Leiden: unpublished PhD dissertation).

Hill, Hal and Sisira Jayasuriya (1986), *An Inward-Looking Economy in Transition, Economic Development in Burma Since the 1960s* (Singapore: Institute of Southeast Asia Studies), Occasional Paper No. 80.

Holsti, K. J. 'From Diversification to Isolation: Burma, 1963–7', in Holsti, *et al.*, *Why Nations Realign: Foreign Policy Restructuring in the Postwar World* (London: Allen & Unwin, 1982).

Johnstone, William C. (1963), *Burma's Foreign Policy – A Study in Neutralism* (Cambridge, Mass.: Harvard University Press).

Leach, Edmund R. (1954), *Political Systems of Highland Burma* (London: London School of Economics and Political Science).

LeBar, Frank, M., Gerald C. Hickey and John K. Musgrave (1964), *Ethnic Groups of Mainland Southeast Asia* (New Haven: Human Relations Area Files Press).

Lieberman, Victor (1984), *Burmese Administrative Cycles* (Princeton: Princeton University Press).

Lintner, Bertil (1987), *FEER*, 28 May.

MacDougall, Hugh and John A. Wiant (1985), 'Burma in 1984', *Asian Survey*, XXVL, 2, February.

Maung, Mya (1971), *Burma and Pakistan: A Comparative Study of Development* (New York: Praeger).

Silverstein, Josef (1977), *Burma: Military Rule and the Politics of Stagnation* (Ithaca: Cornell University Press).

Steinberg, David I. (1981), *Burma's Road Toward Development, Growth and Ideology Under Military Rule* (Boulder: Westview Press).

Steinberg, David I. (1986), 'Burma: Unasked Questions, Unanswered Issues', in *Southeast Asian Affairs 1985* (Singapore: Institute of Southeast Asian Studies).

Tasker, Rodney (1987), *Far Eastern Economic Review*, 16 April.

Trager, Frank (1966), *From Nation to Republic* (New York: Praeger).

Walinsky, Louis J. (1962), *Economic Development in Burma 1951–60* (New York: Twentieth Century Fund).

Wiant, Jon A. (1981), 'Tradition in the Service of Revolution', in *Military Rule in Burma Since 1962*, F. Lehman (ed.) (Singapore: Maruzen).

12 The Foreign Policy of Vietnam

Gareth Porter

Vietnamese foreign policy has been the product of the interaction between a strongly nationalist, self-confident Marxist-Leninist state and a largely hostile external environment. As the first such state in Southeast Asia Vietnam has been occupied, attacked, pressured and isolated by external powers ever since its founding in September 1945. In response to those external pressures the Vietnamese state generated domestic capabilities for the pursuit of security and autonomy that were unusually large, given the poverty of Vietnamese society. In combination with large-scale external assistance, those capabilities were sufficient to defeat larger external powers in two long wars fought in all three countries of Indo-China.

During the three decades that encompassed those two wars, foreign policy served the functions of security, specifically as defense of national independence and territorial integrity, and the maintenance of the revolutionary state led by the Communist Party. Maximizing autonomy, defined by the Vietnamese as avoidance of economic dependence that could compromise its freedom of political action or its ability to industrialize, was also an important function of foreign policy. The domestic welfare function of foreign policy first became important only when Vietnam was recovering from its long resistance war against the French and under pressure to forego further armed struggle for reunification.

Since the reunification of the two zones of Vietnam in 1975, Vietnam has been engaged in a 'third Indo-China conflict' (1978–89) with China over the future of Cambodia. Hanoi initially interpreted this conflict as posing another challenge to Vietnamese security requiring the subordination of domestic welfare goals. But the state's failure to solve Vietnam's socio-economic crisis and the effects of economic isolation from the global capitalist system are bringing about a fundamental redefinition of both security and autonomy that puts greater emphasis on economic growth through participation in the global economic division of labor.

THE SOCIO-POLITICAL CONTEXT

The Vietnamese economy is predominantly agricultural, with about 60 per cent of the labor force engaged in agriculture, of which 63 per cent are involved in grain production (*Tap Chi Cong San*, 1986: 75). In the North, where cultivable land per capita is extremely limited, almost all farmers work in agricultural co-operatives in which the land is collectively owned. In the South, 70 to 80 per cent of the rural population are 'middle peasants', most of whom can survive economically on family farms (Cao Van Luong, 1983: 12–23). There farmers continue to own their own land, although most of them belong to 'production collectives', in which tools and labor are shared. The state dominates industrial production with nearly 3000 state-owned or joint state-private enterprises, but it controls less than 50 per cent of retail goods on the market (SRV Statistics General Department, 1985: 58; Le Can, 1987: 19).

The Socialist Republic of Vietnam (SRV), like its predecessor, the Democratic Republic of Vietnam (DRV), is a one-party state in which political power is concentrated in the hands of the leadership bodies of the Vietnamese Communist Party (VCP). Membership on the Party leadership bodies is determined by the Central Committee's Politburo itself through a complex process of co-optation, in addition to consultation with lower echelons. Political participation is widespread, in the sense that all citizens are encouraged to be politically active through officially-sponsored mass institutions, such as labor unions, the peasants' union, or the women's union. But popular participation is generally confined to criticizing policy implementation and personal abuses by state and party personnel. Since 1986, newspapers and the National Assembly, which previously served merely as propaganda organs for the party, have begun to criticize the state's execution of policies and expose official corruption and abuse, giving the political system some rudimentary characteristics of a pluralistic system. Decision-making power, however, remains concentrated in the hands of the party leadership.

Although in theory the ruling Communist Party represents the interests of the proletariat and working masses, the state/party bureaucracy has been separated from those basic social strata by their power and privileges. For nearly three decades that bureaucracy has controlled the distribution of economic and social benefits to the rest of society, and has had preferred access to housing, consumer goods, education, medical care and travel, among other things

(Nguyen Trung Thuc, 1987: 106; Haubold, 1987: 102). A new class of relatively prosperous state cadres was created, however, by the state's provision of subsidized goods to state-operated production units, joint state-private corporations, the state trade sector and local government units. The disparity between official prices for goods and market prices has given cadres the opportunity to profit at the expense of the population and the state itself by selling the goods to merchants or distributing them among themselves at heavily subsidized prices. Since the early 1980s, the party leadership has been edging towards the complete dismantling of this system of subsidized distribution, which has contributed to budget deficits and runaway inflation, but it has been prevented from doing so by conservative opposition and the fear of making inflation even worse (Nguyen Van Linh, 1987: 36–45).

The SRV, which has declared the bourgeoisie a class enemy, has also unwittingly nurtured a parasitic relationship between the party/state bureaucracy and a class of wealthy businessmen existing at the margins of society. These businessmen could not prosper without a system of state subsidies that provides the impetus for diversion of goods into the private sector. State cadres profit from the existence of a class of businessmen ready to buy goods in bulk for resale on the free market. This alliance between bureaucrats and businessmen, unlike other such alliances in Southeast Asian political systems, does not benefit the members of the top level of party leadership, though some Central Committee members and the next several layers of bureaucrats who are responsible for policy implementation are compromised by it.

The victims of the structures and policies of the Vietnamese Communist regime have been the workers and peasants, whose living standards have continued to decline during the 1970s and 1980s. Grain production has hovered between sufficiency and starvation levels since the end of the Vietnam War, with the average consumption of grain at 290–295 kilograms per capita per year (enough to supply only about 1800 calories per person per day) (*Tap Chi Cong San*, 1986: 71). By 1985, basic salaries provided only 20 to 30 per cent of the income of the average worker's family (Van Giang, 1986: 104), forcing long hours at extra jobs.

THE FOREIGN POLICY-MAKING ELITE

Major Vietnamese foreign policy decisions are made by the Political Bureau of the VCP Central Committee, a body which now has 14 full members and one alternate. The leadership of the VCP was extraordinarily stable throughout the three decades between the August Revolution and the end of the Vietnam War in 1975. The 1980s, however, have been a period of leadership succession. A new generation of leaders in their 50s and 60s which entered the party in the 1940s replaced a founding generation of party leaders then in their 70s in two waves at the 1982 and 1986 party congresses.

The goals and belief system of the current party leadership began to depart significantly from those of the first generation of party leaders by the end of the 1980s. While both generations held the goal of a socialist society under the leadership of the Vietnamese Communist Party (VCP) and have been guided by Marxist-Leninist methods of analysis, the second generation has undergone a fundamental shift in its view of the world.

The first generation viewed the Vietnamese revolution as part of a global struggle against imperialism and capitalism in which 'one side disappears and the other survives' (*mot mat, mot con*). It viewed the US as the leader of imperialist nations and the long-term enemy of the world revolution and, from 1978 onward, a pro-Western China as the immediate enemy of Vietnam. It viewed the integration of the Vietnamese economy into either the Soviet bloc or global capitalist economic division of labor as endangering Vietnamese independence and development. And it defined Vietnamese security primarily in terms of keeping its enemy's influence and military presence out of Laos and Cambodia. In sum, the traditional worldview divided the world into two camps engaged in a struggle for global dominance.

But between 1984 and 1988, as the new generation consolidated its grip on power, it carried out a far-reaching revision of this traditional VCP worldview: the party leadership now views the 1980s as representing a 'new stage of development' in the world that has brought about 'infrastructural changes in international relations' and is 'changing men's way of thinking'. The primary changes revolutionizing the Vietnamese worldview are the development of the technological revolution and the internationalization of production, which have created a single world market and mutual interdependence between socialist and capitalist systems. The new level of interaction is in turn 'gradually breaking down the barriers' of Cold War blocs.

〈In this new 'interdependence' worldview, Vietnam's security lies not so much in the military defense of Laos and Cambodia as in achieving an 'optimal position in the international division of labor' in order to achieve rapid economic development (Porter, 1989).〉

The unambiguously bipolar model of the world held by the first generation of leaders during its two wars of resistance has given way to a more complex view of the Third World. Hanoi once regarded Third World states with extensive political and economic links with the West as tools of imperialism. The current leadership, however, emphasizes the common problems shared by Vietnam and capitalist states of the Third World, such as obtaining export markets and fair prices for their primary goods and creating jobs, far more than the differences that divide them. Indeed this generation concedes that Vietnam has much to learn from developing capitalist states about economic development (Porter, 1985: 9; Nguyen Le Minh, 1986: 115–17; Vo Thanh Cong, 1987: 73–8).

THE FOREIGN POLICY PROCESS

〈Only the Politburo of the VCP Central Committee can make important foreign policy decisions requiring urgent action. It has the authority of the full 116-member Central Committee when the latter is not in session, and it meets at least weekly – and, when necessary, daily – to review developments, compare assessments and make decisions. A foreign policy decision that represents a fundamental departure from a line previously established by a National Congress of Party delegates, however, must be approved by a Plenum of the Central Committee.〉

As a policy-making institution the Politburo is distinctive for its tradition of collective leadership going back to the 1950s, when an ageing Ho Chi Minh was training the younger members of the leadership to carry on after his death. That generation of leaders, including Premier Pham Van Dong, Defense Minister Vo Nguyen Giap, as well as Truong Chinh and Le Duan, both of whom served as First Secretary of the Party, accepted the idea that the Political Bureau should continue to be a body of equals in which no single figure dominated policy-making (Le Duc Tho, 1960: 36). The present party leadership continues to be a collegial body, in which General Secretary Nguyen Van Linh may be the single most influential figure but does not dominate it. The members of the Politburo have always tried to reach decisions by consensus. Thus the leadership avoids issuing definitive statements on issues on which there are sharp differences of view. Under those circumstances, contrasting views may show up in official organs. Prior to negotiations with the US on normalization of relations in 1978, for example, an article in the party theoretical journal expressed hope for a constructive US policy toward Vietnam, while the military journal expressed pessimism on that score.

In recent years, a new policy struggle has emerged within the party leadership between those who are determined to dismantle rapidly the system of government distribution of subsidized goods and of detailed economic planning and controls, on one hand, and those who wish to move cautiously and gradually towards that goal on the other. Like the struggle over Gorbachev's program of reform in the Soviet Union, the new political fault line in Vietnamese politics has implications for all policy issues, including foreign economic relations and even national security policy. More conservative leaders, for example, may also resist institutional changes pushed by reformers to attract foreign investment; there could also be distinct differences over how much risk to Vietnamese security in Cambodia should be accepted in moving to end Vietnam's economic isolation. The balance of power within the leadership between reformers and conservatives, therefore, is a factor in the foreign policy-making process.

The intertwining of party and state leadership in the SRV ensures that foreign policy-making by the Politburo is highly institutionalized. The major state institutions and party committees are represented in that body, and the data and analysis that are produced in each are brought to bear. In 1987, for example, the Politburo included the Minister of National Defense, the Minister of Foreign Affairs, the Minister of the Interior, the Chairman of the State Planning Commission, the Prime Minister, a Vice-Chairman of the Council of Ministers and the President of the State Council. Also included were the Chairmen of the Party Commission on Party Organization and of other key party commissions.

Foreign policy-making is also institutionalized in the way in which the leadership arrives at its 'definition of the situation'. Marxist-Leninist ideology has provided the categories and assumptions on which such a definition is based. For Vietnamese party leaders the first step in defining the situation at each new juncture has been to assess the 'correlation of forces' (*so sanh luc luong*) between revolutionary and counter-revolutionary forces on the global, regional and local levels. When the Politburo met intensively for nine days in September-October 1974 to decide on the military offensive that ended the war in South Vietnam, it considered the problem first in the context of the 'correlation of forces' both within Vietnam and on the world stage (Hoang Nguyen, 1986: 79).

This assessment is not simply a matter of comparing relative military or economic strengths; it is an exercise that uses the 'power of abstract thought' (namely, Marxist dialectics) to integrate less tangible socio-political factors into the equation. Hanoi's leaders have viewed major historical changes in world politics as the working out of four 'fundamental contradictions' on the global plane: between the socialist and imperialist camps; between the working class and the capitalist class in the capitalist states; between the oppressed nations and the imperialist states; and among imperialists and monopoly capitalists. Longer-term changes in global politics – the strengthening of the system of socialist states, the progress of the national liberation movement and of workers and other progressive movements in capitalist countries – all contribute, in this view, to the weakening of imperialism and capitalism and the transition from capitalism to socialism in the world. In this Vietnamese calculus, the material superiority of their enemies – the US and other advanced capitalist states – has long been de-emphasized, though not ignored, in arriving at a net assessment of this global 'correlation of forces' (Porter, 1984: 12–15: Hoang Nguyen, 1986: 73).

Although the Vietnamese leadership has tried to guard against over-optimism in its assessments by preparing to deal with the 'worst possible situations' (Hoang Nguyen, 1986: 79), Hanoi's dialectical reasoning has sometimes led to misperception and miscalculations. Ideologically-based assumptions about a waning capitalism, weak and unstable bourgeois governments in Southeast Asia, the central importance of the Vietnam War in global politics and the irreversibility of socialist revolution in China skewed perceptions of the external situation and contributed to Hanoi's isolation from the capitalist world in the 1980s.

DOMESTIC RESOURCES AND CONSTRAINTS

Vietnam's ability to advance its foreign policy objectives has been facilitated by several characteristics of the Vietnamese revolutionary state. The continuity of leadership in the VCP over several decades as well as the long-term vision and dialectical analysis of Marxism-Leninism has given the Communist regime the strategic clarity and self-confidence necessary to persevere in protracted conflicts. The Communist state has also been able to draw on the strength of Vietnamese national identity, which developed in response to two thousand years of Chinese attempts to dominate Vietnam and 80 years of French colonialism.

Compared with other post-colonial Southeast Asia countries, Vietnam developed a strong state structure during the 1945–54 period that had wide and active popular support. The DRV built a formidable apparatus of social and political control which virtually eliminated any possibility for organized opposition. During the resistance to the French (1946–54), regional Administrative Committees were given very wide authority to send individuals to detention camps for actions detrimental to the national security (Nguyen Van Huong, 1972: 43; Fall, 1956: 35). The state was also able to extract a high level of resources from the population in relation to its extremely low level of economic development.

The political strength of the state has been translated into an extraordinarily high level of military capabilities for the country's size and level of economic development. The DRV was able to build an army of some 300 000 men by 1953 and mount a major counter-offensive against the French expeditionary corps; only a few years later, it gave the go-ahead for armed struggle in South Vietnam even when its socialist allies were opposed to it and went on to sustain a successful war effort even against the US. Even more impressive, in the face of the Chinese military threat the SRV was able to increase its armed forces from 615 000 after the war to more than a million men – the fourth largest in the world – by the end of 1980 (Thayer, 1983: 316). The Vietnamese military has shown that it is capable of operating simultaneously on multiple fronts by coping with a major Chinese invasion in February 1979 even without committing its regular forces, while also carrying out economic, pacification and military operations in both Cambodia and Laos. Despite the economic disaster of the 1980s, the SRV has been able to provide as much as US$ 30 million in economic assistance to Cambodia annually (Turley, 1986: 199).

Communist Vietnam's primary domestic weaknesses have long been a backward, capital-starved agricultural economy and an economic management system that inhibits economic growth. The Red River Delta in northern Vietnam and the central coast, with a dense population on a relatively small agricultural land base that is vulnerable to flood and drought, have always been food deficit areas. Since reunification, southern agriculture has not been able to make up for this basic disadvantage. Thus the SRV has continued to have a food deficit: from 1976 to 1980 it had to import a total of 5.6 million tons of grain, while during the following five years imports totalled about 1 million tons of grain (Le Can, 1986: 17). In 1988 the SRV had another major food deficit of 1.5 million tons after a crop failure in 1987 because of drought, typhoons and insect infestation and policies which provided little incentive for increased production (Wain, 1988).

The party leadership's mistakes have contributed to internal weakness. The government has promoted state industries which had no incentive to produce efficiently, since their losses were subsidized by the state, and which were bound by centrally determined plans that were inevitably unrealistic. Total industrial production remained virtually stationery from 1976 to 1980, and the production of state-owned enterprises and state-private joint enterprises actually declined by 6.5 per cent during that period (Vo Nhan Tri, 1985b: 20, 46). The quality and efficiency of the state-operated economy continued to decline in the 1980s (Le Can, 1986: 19).

Subsidies to state enterprises as well as heavily subsidized distribution of goods to workers, cadres and civil servants (the latter accounting for an estimated 7 per cent of GDP by the early 1980s) contributed to growing budget deficits which helped to destroy the value of the Vietnamese *dong* (International Monetary Fund, 1982: 19). Shortages of all consumer goods and agricultural inputs, the systematic diversion of state property into the black market, competition among state agencies for the purchase of limited goods and the withholding of goods from the market by both state and private commercial sectors pushed consumer prices up faster and faster during the 1980s (Vo Nhan Tri, 1985a; Nguyen Dan Khanh, 1987: 63). Malnutrition has emerged as a serious socio-economic problem for the first time since the mid-1950s (Vo Nhan Tri, 1985a: 21). The chronic food deficit and consumer good shortages make the SRV far more dependent than it would otherwise be on assistance from the Soviet bloc and weaken the Vietnamese ability to gain room for maneuver *vis-à-vis* its main ally. The political consequence of this economic decline and rising social inequity has been a general loss of confidence in the party and general cynicism towards the regime (Ha Huu Son, 1986: 99–100). Domestic dissatisfaction extends to

Vietnam's involvement in Cambodia, putting pressure on the SRV to terminate its military occupation there (Chauncey, 1988: 71).

Another domestic factor limiting Vietnamese capabilities, at least until the late 1980s, was the necessity to integrate into a reunified Communist Vietnam several million South Vietnamese small traders, service personnel, technicians and others who had experienced historically unprecedented economic opportunities and social mobility during the war and were essentially unassimilable in the much more static society of the SRV. Their dissatisfaction provided the 'push' factor underlying the escape by millions of Vietnamese by boat after 1975, which helped to harden public attitudes in the West against the regime.

Vietnam's ethnic Chinese, or *Hoa*, population of 1.2 million, most of whom have continued to identify themselves as Chinese despite efforts to get them to accept Vietnamese citizenship, have also been a net disadvantage to Vietnamese foreign policy. Some were actively involved in Mao's Cultural Revolution in the mid-1960s, in direct defiance of the political line of the SRV, demonstrating their potential as an instrument of Chinese intervention in Vietnamese society (Benoit, 1981: 144; Porter, 1980: 55; Chang, 1982: 9–19). Others were successful traders whose assets were taken over by the state in early 1978. The *Hoa* resistance to Vietnamese policies and massive exodus from Vietnam in a situation of rising Sino-Vietnamese tensions, invited PRC political intervention and contributed to the breakdown of relations with Beijing.

THE EXTERNAL ENVIRONMENT

Vietnam's geography has consciously or unconsciously shaped its concept of security. Located at the edge of the Asian landmass, Vietnam's two river deltas which hold most of its population are linked by a thin sliver of coastal land in Central Vietnam which could be cut with relative ease. As a consequence, the Vietnamese have looked to the mountainous interiors which are shared with both Cambodia and Laos as secure rear areas in the event of attack from the outside (Turley, 1986: 180; Lim Joo-Jock, 1979: 13).

Vietnam's border with China is another source of vulnerability. The mountains separating Vietnam from China have presented no barrier to Chinese penetration of Vietnam, since there is easy passage through three passes, and Vietnam's coastline is merely an extension of China's. The absence of similar Chinese access to Burma or Thailand made Vietnam the logical target of Chinese expansion over the centuries. Vietnamese concern with autonomy from China, therefore, has been a common feature of all Vietnamese regimes down to the present.

Similarly, the location of Laos and Cambodia, both weaker states and less economically developed societies, on Vietnam's western borders has given Vietnam opportunities for military and political influence and reason for concern about influence from outside powers, including, at various times, Thailand, France, the US and China. Imperial Vietnam was deeply involved in both Laos and Cambodia in the nineteenth century in a geopolitical rivalry with Thailand. The traditional lack of control over tribal minorities in mountainous eastern Laos by royal goverments based in the western lowlands has also facilitated Vietnamese intervention, both political and military.

Given the close geographical relationship between Vietnam and its two Indo-Chinese neighbors, Indo-China was a 'single strategic unit' during Vietnam's two wars against outside powers. During the war with the US this strategic unity was reflected in Hanoi's need to move supplies and troops through the 'Ho Chi Minh trail' in the panhandle of Laos and eastern Cambodia and for sanctuaries from US air and ground operations on the Cambodian side of the border.

The international political and economic system has imposed severe constraints on Vietnamese foreign policy. The refusal of the US and other capitalist states to support Vietnamese independence against the French in early postwar years and US financial and military assistance to the French side from 1950 to 1954 eliminated the option of a 'Titoist' Vietnam – Marxist-Leninist but independent of the Soviet camp politically and militarily. The triumph of the Chinese revolution in 1949 and the consequent physical link between the DRV and the Soviet Union through China became critical to the DRV's survival.

The power balance between the US and the socialist camp from the 1950s to the 1970s, however, was a constraint on Hanoi's pursuit of its security. By mid-1950s the US had achieved a hegemonial position in Southeast Asia which the Soviet Union and China were not prepared to challenge. When the US threatened direct intervention in the war in 1954, Moscow and Beijing put pressure on Hanoi to accept the division of the country and to eschew armed struggle in South Vietnam for an indefinite period. The US intervened directly in Vietnam and Laos, building up anti-Communist regimes aimed at destroying Communist movements without provoking a strong political-military response from Moscow or Beijing. The US also had the diplomatic clout to orchestrate the diplomatic and economic isolation of Vietnam from Western capitalist states as well as from most of the Third World until the early 1970s.

The increasingly bitter Sino-Soviet polemics of the 1960s, which Hanoi sought to limit, were far more a burden for the DRV than a benefit. They encouraged US moves towards direct military intervention in Indo-China. Washington was able to play Moscow off against Beijing (as it did at the 1962 Geneva Conference on Laos and at the time of Tonkin Gulf crisis of 1964). Mao refused to cooperate with the Soviet Union in supporting the DRV in 1965 and was unwilling to deter a US military assault on the DRV by threatening either retaliation or direct combat involvement (SRV Foreign Ministry, 1979: 46–7).

Although Soviet and Chinese aid was crucial to the Vietnamese war effort, the DRV had great difficulty maintaining the political-diplomatic support of its allies for its war strategy. Until 1969 the PRC pressed Hanoi to keep the US bogged down and to reject negotiations (Nguyen Van Vinh 1968; SRV Foreign Ministry, 1979: 51–4). And in 1971–72 both Moscow and Beijing gave higher priority to détente with the US than to diplomatic support for the DRV's strategy, weakening Hanoi's bargaining position *vis-à-vis* the US during the critical period of the peace negotiations.

Postwar Chinese policy restricted Hanoi's choices by pressing for a commitment to oppose 'hegemony' (a code word for Soviet policy), assuming the traditional Chinese role of protector of the interests of the *Hoa* in Vietnam and supporting Pol Pot's aggressive posture toward Vietnam. This Chinese role, combined with Vietnamese dependence on external assistance available only from the Soviets, made it impossible for the SRV to continue to maintain a delicate balance between Beijing and Moscow as it had during the war. Soviet military and economic aid estimated at more than US$ 2 billion annually during 1979–85 made it possible for Vietnam to carry out its occupation of Cambodia. But the Soviet Union has also demanded a *quid pro quo* for its support, in the form of membership in COMECON, a Treaty of Friendship and Co-operation and access to Vietnamese military facilities at Cam Ranh Bay and Danang Airbase.

The US role in postwar regional politics has also constituted a major constraint on Vietnamese policy. After it retreated militarily from the Southeast Asian mainland, the US further constricted Vietnam's room for diplomatic maneuver in 1978 by 'playing the China card', aligning with the PRC not only against the Soviets but against Vietnam as well. That US policy was reinforced after the Vietnamese occupation of Cambodia began in 1979.

The political situation in Cambodia has presented both constraints on and opportunities for Vietnamese policy. Prince Norodom Sihanouk's popularity and his neutralist policies permitted Hanoi to pursue a non-interventionist policy until 1965 and then to use Khmer territory as a sanctuary. Lon Nol's reversal of Sihanouk's policy in 1970 impinged on Vietnamese security in the border region and forced Vietnam into alliance with the Khmer Rouge. Pol Pot's later military initiatives against the Vietnamese border constrained Vietnam's ability to maintain normal relations with Democratic Kampuchea, while Cambodia's internal turmoil facilitated Vietnamese military occupation in 1979.

Unlike the Communist Party of Kampuchea, whose internal conflicts produced a leadership hostile to the Vietnamese party, the Lao Communist leadership has always been willing to follow Hanoi's lead, giving the Vietnamese greater flexibility in strategy and tactics there. The weakness and vulnerability of any Lao central government, however, given Laotian geography, economic underdevelopment and ethnic diversity, have constrained Vietnamese efforts to consolidate the Vietnamese-supported government there.

The broader socio-economic and political situation in Southeast Asia beyond Indo-China has been another constraint on Hanoi's policy. After the fall of the civilian government in Thailand in 1947, no regional state supported the DRV diplomatically against the French, and after Sukarno's overthrow in Indonesia, none gave active support against US intervention. The failure of either Maoist insurgencies or urban political forces to bring any changes in the general anti-Communist, pro-Western orientation of regional states frustrated postwar Vietnamese efforts to exploit the US retreat in Indo-China and replace ASEAN with a new regional security organization.

In the 1980s regional and global political and economic systems operated to maximize the pressure on Vietnam to withdraw from Cambodia. ASEAN failed to splinter along lines of divergent strategic perceptions and interests and officially supported Thailand's hardline policy toward Cambodia. The integration of the ASEAN states and China into the Pacific Basin system of economic co-operation centered on Japan meant that resources flowed into China and Thailand, as well as to the other ASEAN states, while Vietnam was systematically denied resources. This denial of capital and technology exacerbated the SRV's socio-economic crisis.

At the same time, the system of trade, finance and investment in the Pacific, which has been closed to Vietnam in the past, now presents opportunities for Vietnam to arrest its economic decline and attempt to catch up with its neighbors. The relatively rapid economic growth of the ASEAN states in the 1970s and 1980s because of expanded trade and foreign investments provides an alternative model for Vietnam. The fact that many Japanese firms are prepared to invest in Vietnam once the West ends its isolation policy gives credibility to the option of integration into the dynamic Pacific Basin system of economic co-operation.

Economic relations with the Soviet bloc, a vital source of support for its foreign policy objectives, have become a constraint on Vietnam as well. In the 1950s and early 1960s the DRV had embraced the notion of self-reliant development, in which it would build a heavy industrial sector that would obviate reliance on the Soviet Union for defense and consumer goods. During the war, however, the DRV had to depend heavily on Soviet shipments of consumer goods as well as agricultural inputs. After Moscow converted the bulk of its assistance to repayable loans, Hanoi had to supply much of its tin, tea, coffee, fruit and other industrial crops to the Soviet Union in return for spare parts, machinery, oil and fertilizer. In order to ensure that Vietnam maximized its exports to the Soviet Union, the SRV also had to co-ordinate state plans with Moscow (*Tap Chi Cong San*, 1985: 82; Thayer, 1978: 217). After joing COMECON in June 1978, the SRV integrated its own five-year plans with those of the other COMECON members and devoted even more of its mineral, marine and tropical food production, as well as its handicrafts to export to the Soviet Union (Duy Hoang, 1979: 6).

Vietnam's growing trade imbalance with the Soviet Union and weak exports to hard currency economies has led to the accumulation of very heavy foreign debt. In the first half of the 1980s the SRV had annual trade deficits with the USSR averaging about US$ 900 million (Pike, 1987: 135). By mid–1987 the SRV had incurred a debt to the Soviet Union of nearly US$ 6.5 billion. In addition, Vietnam owed US$ 1.67 billion to convertible currency creditors, for a total debt of US$ 8.1 billion, compared with a total national income estimated at around US$ 11 billion (Butler, 1987: 19).

Vietnam's need to increase exports to the Soviet Union not only limits opportunity for expanded trade with capitalist states but creates new imbalances within the Vietnamese economy. Labor and capital which were once going to increase food production for Vietnamese consumption are now used to produce goods for export. An example is the shift by a co-operative near Hanoi from pig production to the production of embroidered silk and carpets for export. The shift meant a loss of both pork and manure for rice production (Werner, 1984: 51).

The SRV's present dependent economic status gives the Soviets some leverage on economic issues as well as political-military relations, including the continued Soviet use of naval and air bases in Vietnam. In 1980 and 1981, for example, Moscow refused to give firm pledges of aid to Vietnam's third five-year plan until, it got Vietnamese commitments on unspecified conditions (Rosenberger, 1983: 216).

FOREIGN POLICY OUTPUTS

The development of Vietnamese foreign policy may be divided into eight distinct stages, punctuated by a series of major external developments. The salience of different *functions* of foreign policy has also shifted from one period to another as output has fluctuated between conflict-oriented strategies and relatively more accommodative strategies, and between different levels of concern for security and territorial integrity. The most significant linkages between internal and external inputs and foreign policy outputs are noted in the following schematic overview of the stages of development of Vietnamese policy output.

1945–50: During the anti-French resistance war, DRV foreign policy was a means by which the state could both advance the struggle for independence from French imperialism and also maintain the DRV regime in power. Welfare goals, meanwhile, had to be sacrificed. In the initial months after the August Revolution of 1945, the DRV confronted a Chinese Kuomintang occupation force north of the seventeenth parallel which was protecting anti-Communist parties (the Vietnam Nationalist Party and the *Dai Viets*) which sought to overthrow the regime. The DRV agreement with France in March 1946 allowing a limited number of French troops to remain in Vietnam for a period of five years was aimed at facilitating the withdrawal of the Chinese troops, which presented an immediate threat to the regime's existence, and at consolidating the new regime politically, economically and militarily. In reoccupying the country, however, the French also tried to replace the DRV with a dependent Vietnamese regime, first in the South and then in the entire country. ⟨Thus the security and regime maintenance aims of the DRV were tightly linked during its first few years.⟩

The dominant strategic orientation during the period of national resistance war was towards military intervention in Laos and Cambodia to weaken the French expeditionary corps, co-operation with any government or political element that would oppose the French, and ⟨disinterest⟩in supporting Communist revolution in neighboring countries – a 'united front from above' in Marxist-Leninist terms. The Vietnamese armed, trained and fought alongside non-communist nationalists in Cambodia and co-operated with the anti-French civilian government in Thailand until it was overthrown in late 1947 (Porter, 1983: 64–6). Identification with the socialist camp in the world was publicly muted as Ho Chi Minh tried unsuccessfully to enlist Washington's support for Vietnamese independence. The general strategic orientation can best be explained by both constraints (the absence of any physical link with the Soviet Union or Chinese Communists; the weakness of indigenous Communist movements in Laos and Cambodia) and opportunities (the availability of non-Communist allies in Cambodia and Thailand), and the DRV's subjective analysis of contradictions within the capitalist camp.

1950–54: Independence, territorial integrity and regime maintenance continued to be the goals of DRV foreign policy as the DRV endeavored to move toward the final, counter-offensive stage of the resistance war. When the Chinese Communist revolution made it possible to link Vietnam physically with the socialist camp, the DRV adopted a strategy of clear-cut alliance with the Soviet Union and China against the 'imperialist camp', declaring itself the 'focal point' of conflict with imperialism. Simultaneously, it shifted its focus in Laos and Cambodia to organizing and supporting forces under the control of newly-created Communist parties. Despite its new link with the Soviet bloc, the Vietnamese adopted independent stances on the question of peace negotiations with the French, defying the Soviet suggestion that a Korean-style truce was in order (Porter, 1980: 232–3). The shift to a more 'left' line can be explained by the new opportunities presented by the Chinese Communist victory and the disappearance of moderate allies of the DRV in Thailand and Cambodia (Porter, 1983: 66).

1954–59: The end of the resistance war and the temporary division of Vietnam at Geneva marked a new stage in the DRV's foreign policy. Security as a function of foreign policy was subordinated to domestic welfare goals, and regime maintenance became less important, given the swift consolidation of power by the DRV over North Vietnam as French troops departed. The strategic orientation of DRV foreign policy shifted towards accommodation with non-Communist neighbors and support for relaxation of East-West tensions.

A major DRV foreign policy concern was to obtain assistance from the Soviet Union and China for economic rehabilitation in anticipation of its first five-year plan (1961–65). The DRV supported a Soviet global strategy for the world Communist movement that was defensive rather than offensive. Hanoi called for negotiations on East-West conflicts, peaceful co-existence with non-Communist regimes and gradual strengthening of the socialist camp (Porter, 1980: 237–40).

In Laos and Cambodia the Vietnamese pursued a policy of minimizing conflict by supporting domestically conservative, anti-Communist but neutralist princes in both countries and downgrading relations with the Cambodian Communists. Hanoi did not respond when the Lao government threatened the DRV's leftist allies, the Pathet Lao, and the US set up a military training mission in Laos in 1958 (Halpern and Friedman, 1969: 38–48). Hanoi refrained from attacking the pro-US, right-wing military dictatorship in Thailand and from supporting the Malayan Communist Party's denunciation of Malayan independence as a fraud.

In effect, the DRV went along with a Soviet international line which many Vietnamese considered dangerously weak, giving up the high level of autonomy in foreign policy they had maintained in the previous period. The tighter constraints imposed by an unfavorable balance of power, as reflected in the pressures of its allies for a peaceful struggle for reunification, and the need for internal consolidation after long years of heavy economic sacrifices explain this phase of Vietnamese policy.

1959–73: DRV policy during this period re-emphasized security and reunification goals. It also served closely-related ideological and autonomy functions, while welfare goals were consciously sacrificed and regime maintenance was no longer a major concern. The primary strategic orientation of Vietnamese policy was towards autonomous decision-making, the use of military force throughout Indo-China and support for Communist movements against pro-Western regimes. Reversing its line on armed struggle in Indo-China, the DRV sent troops to Laos and began supporting armed struggle against the US-supported regimes in Laos and South Vietnam in 1959. In the early 1960s Hanoi began to criticize the Soviet peaceful co-existence line, ultimately branding it as 'revisionist' and adopted a more militant line embraced by the Chinese of support for armed struggle against imperialism wherever possible throughout the Third World (Donnell and Gurtov, 1969: 166–72; Porter, 1980: 247–51). Meanwhile, Hanoi deliberately reduced its dependence on Soviet assistance for its five-year plan, relying instead on more internal accumulation to build its heavy industry in order to assure autonomy in defense and foreign policy (Le Duan, 1965: 318–19).

Despite the opposition of both socialist allies, Hanoi was prepared in December 1963 to risk military confrontation with the US over the armed struggle in the South, and decided in mid-1964 to prepare for direct participation in the war by infiltrating regiments into the South. After the US openly intervened with combat troops, the DRV committed much of its army to the war in the South. When Soviet policy became more supportive of the DRV following Khrushchev's ouster in November 1964, Hanoi de-emphasized 'anti-revisionism' and economic self-reliance for the duration of the war (Donnell and Gurtov, 1969: 173–97).

During this period Hanoi also gave political support to the Malayan Communist Party's armed struggle and retaliated against Thai collaboration with the US war effort in Indo-China by providing military training to Thai Communist cadres and then provided material and political support to a Communist armed insurgency in northeast Thailand (Girling, 1968: 396; Gurtov, 1975: 12–27). These policies were specifically aimed at weakening the US political-military posture in the region. Excepted from this trend was Cambodia, where Hanoi continued to support Prince Norodom Sihanouk and opposed the armed struggle of the Communist Party of Kampuchea (Porter, 1983: 74–84).

The turn to a more militant revolutionary posture in this period can be explained primarily by constraints – the US-supported efforts by the South Vietnamese and Lao governments to destroy what was left of the Lao and South Vietnamese Communist movements, thus raising the cost of accommodation too high. At the same time the DRV's optimistic worldview and its capacity to generate resources for state security made possible the pursuit of ambitious foreign policy objectives despite an unfavorable regional and global balance of power.

1973–78: The signing of the Paris peace agreement ending the Vietnam War marked another shift in Vietnamese policy in which welfare and security objectives were more compatible, and autonomy became more important, albeit in a redefined form. The strategic orientation was limited diplomatic accommodation with the US as well as with non-Communist regimes in the region, abandonment of support for revolutionary movements, and withdrawal from active military involvement in Cambodia.

Hanoi pursued the goal of autonomy by trying to have balanced economic relations with both the socialist states and the West, and to maintain a political balance between Moscow and Beijing. The key to Hanoi's strategy for economic growth and autonomy was the US$ 3.25 billion in reconstruction aid promised in connection with the peace agreement by President Richard Nixon. While it was losing some of its autonomy by agreeing to co-ordinate state plans with the Soviet Union in 1976, Hanoi hoped to regain it by obtaining loans and grants from the West. In negotiating with the Carter administration on normalization of relations in 1977, Hanoi rejected the US offer of unconditional establishment of diplomatic relations, demanding at least some of the US reconstruction aid as part of the agreement. This policy decision was based in part on the belief that the US would be forced by its weakened military position in the region and the desire of US oil companies to get their former concessions back to agree to the Vietnamese condition for normal relations (Chanda, 1986: 149–60; Thayer, 1978: 226–7).

Hanoi avoided siding openly with Moscow against Beijing. But it made no concession to Beijing to head off the growing tensions with China over territorial issues, political orientation and the *Hoa*. The Vietnamese believed that Maoist policy towards Indo-China was chauvinistic, reflecting the traditional Chinese desire to keep Vietnam weak, divided and pliant and that they had to stand up to Chinese pressures, waiting for more orthodox Marxist leaders to ultimately emerge and restore a more friendly policy towards Vietnam (Porter, 1981a: 81). The SRV thus failed to appreciate that anti-Maoist leaders also interpreted Vietnamese actions as arrogant and anti-Chinese.

Hanoi gradually disengaged from its relations with the Thai and Malayan Communist parties, pursuing normalization of state-to-state relations with the ASEAN states. But it refused to accept the legitimacy of ASEAN, which it attacked as an instrument of US imperialism. Instead the Vietnamese demanded that the ASEAN states signal a new independence of the US by abandoning ASEAN and negotiating a new regional security arrangement with Vietnam (Thayer, 1978: 219–22; Porter, 1985: 2–4).

Hanoi's hardline ASEAN diplomacy reflected its massive misperception of both the degree of dependence on the US and the class character of the existing ASEAN governments. Hanoi viewed the dominant faction of the ruling classes in the ASEAN states as the representatives of the 'big landowners and comprador bourgeoisie'. It believed that the defeat of the US in Vietnam would have a great ripple effect through the region, encouraging populist and anti-imperialist forces in Thailand, Malaysia, Indonesia and the Philippines to oppose these reactionary forces (Porter, 1985: 2–3).

The combination of limited accommodation and new diplomatic demands reflected both objective changes in opportunities and constraints and Vietnamese misperceptions. Vietnam's devastated economy and the inadequacy of aid from the socialist camp was a constraint that took on new salience. There were also new opportunities for Vietnam to increase its influence through diplomacy: on the one hand, the US had withdrawn its forces from the mainland of Southeast Asia, immediate threats to Vietnamese security and territorial integrity had eased, and the ASEAN states were shifting from dependence on US military power to their own diplomacy in dealing with Vietnam. But on the other hand uncompromising positions in relations with the US, China, and the ASEAN states were based on over-optimistic assumptions.

1978–84: During this period, security re-emerged as the primary function of Vietnamese foreign policy at the expense of domestic welfare and autonomy. The strategic orientation was towards alliance with the Soviet Union, direct military engagement in Cambodia and efforts to maximize global diplomatic support and minimize opposition to SRV policy in the protracted conflict with China.

Vietnam's identification of China as the main and immediate threat to the Vietnamese revolution was the key shift in strategic orientation in Vietnamese policy. That led the SRV to forge a *de facto* alliance with the Soviet Union to bolster its power position *vis-à-vis* China. Hanoi joined COMECON in June 1978, signed a new Treaty of

Friendship and Co-operation with Moscow, and permitted Soviet use of naval and air bases at Cam Ranh Bay and Danang in return for Soviet material support for Vietnam's occupation of Cambodia and a security commitment in the event of a Chinese invasion of Vietnam.

Hanoi's diplomacy towards ASEAN and the US was geared towards positioning itself for protracted conflict with China. In the latter half of 1978 the SRV withdrew its objection to ASEAN, renounced ties with Communist parties in the region and proposed negotiations with ASEAN on making the entire region a neutral zone. It also tried to normalize relations with Washington by dropping the demand for postwar reconstruction assistance, in order to divide the US from China.

The Vietnam People's Army, however, was the key instrument of policy during this period. Hanoi reverted in 1978 to direct military intervention in Cambodia to oust the hated Pol Pot regime, to exclude Chinese influence from Indo-China and to ensure against any future anti-Vietnamese regime arising in Phnom Penh. Meanwhile, the SRV was nearly doubling its regular military forces to cope with the military threat from China, which exploded in a full-scale invasion of the northern border in January 1979.

Vietnam was overly optimistic about the 'correlation of forces' when it decided on the military occupation of Cambodia. It overestimated the degree of contradiction between Chinese and American interests, and underestimated the unity and determination which the ASEAN states would show in pressing for the withdrawal of Vietnamese troops from Cambodia. Finally the Vietnamese failed to realize in 1978 how severe Vietnam's internal economic problems were or how much increased militarization and economic isolation would worsen them.

Vietnam's turn towards military intervention and alliance with the USSR can be viewed as an output triggered by new external constraints (Chinese and Pol Pot pressures on the SRV) and opportunities (the internal disunity of the Pol Pot regime and popular disaffection with it), and made possible by Vietnamese capabilities and advantageous external conditions (sufficient Vietnamese military power and the availability of a willing major power ally.) The constraints and enabling conditions were in turn filtered through critical subjective factors: Hanoi's own security doctrine of Indo-China as a single strategic arena and its optimistic assessment of the relationship of forces.

1984–88: In this period, domestic welfare once again became a central objective of foreign policy, even though it had to be balanced against the claim of conventional security. The strategic orientation combined continued military operations in Cambodia, plans for military withdrawal and peace negotiations, and new efforts to link the Vietnamese economy with the capitalist world.

The underlying cause of this shift in strategic orientation was Vietnam's failure to meet the basic needs of the population. The direct cause, however, was the SRV's chronic trade imbalance and its ability to pay back its hard-currency debts as well as its debt to the Soviet Union. SRV leaders concluded in mid-1984 that the country's neglect to build up its exports was a 'strategic problem', and that it had to remove the embargo imposed on Vietnam by the capitalist countries to achieve a breakthrough in exports (Luu Van Dat, 1986: 65). Based on that strategic decision, the SRV undertook a series of interrelated initiatives in economic relations, military policy and diplomacy.

First, Hanoi prevailed on its reluctant client in Phnom Penh, the People's Republic of Kampuchea (PRK), to agree to meet with former Chief of State Norodom Sihanouk (a meeting that Sihanouk initially rejected), and to join in proposing a peace plan for Cambodia aimed at reconciliation with the non-Communist resistance. The plan provided for Vietnamese military withdrawal, the elimination of the Pol Pot forces, the negotiation of a political accord excluding the 'Pol Pot clique' and national elections in the presence of 'international observers' (Institute of International Relations, 1986: 131–2).

While positioning itself for possible negotiations the SRV took steps to avoid being bogged down in a long-term military occupation of Cambodia. It negotiated with the PRK government in late 1984 and early 1985 an agreement that all Vietnamese troops would definitely be withdrawn unilaterally by 1990 (Porter, 1988: 125–6). Although few were withdrawn in 1985 and 1986, the Vietnamese did withdraw 20 000 troops in late 1987 and pledged to withdraw 50 000 more in 1988, suggesting that they were serious about meeting their 1990 – later changed to September 1989 – deadline.

Meanwhile the SRV was drafting a new, far more liberal investment code aimed at making Vietnam competitive with other Southeast Asian states, which was finally promulgated in late 1987 (Vietnam News Agency, 1988). The new Cambodia strategy and the new posture on international trade and investment were prompted by the understanding of the Party leadership that Western capital would be necessary to break out of economic stagnation, and that Vietnam had to make concessions both in foreign policy and in the domestic economy to achieve that end (Pomonti, 1987: 1, 8). Without abandoning its national security objectives, Hanoi was in the process of rebalancing those objectives and the achievement of economic growth.

CONCLUSION: THE POLITICAL ECONOMY OF VIETNAMESE FOREIGN POLICY

⟨The central dynamic in the political economy of Vietnamese foreign policy has been the interaction between the international system, state structure, ideological orientation and the domestic economy.⟩ For Vietnam, foreign policy has been primarily a means of ensuring national independence, territorial integrity and security, and Vietnam has had uniquely strong domestic capabilities for these purposes: a centralized state with strong extractive capabilities, an ideology that provided the leadership with a sense of control over historical forces, and a fiercely nationalistic people.

But the capabilities of the Vietnamese state to cope with external pressures have also exacted a high price. The direct costs to Vietnamese society, in the form of economic resources diverted to or destroyed in political-military conflict, have been great. But perhaps even more important have been the indirect costs, in the form of political, administrative and economic deformities resulting from the concentration of state power needed to mobilize resources and to maintain national discipline in two resistance wars.

Vietnam's Marxist-Leninist worldview, so vital to its success in two resistance wars, has proven costly since 1975. The problem is not that ideology has prompted Hanoi to sacrifice Vietnamese strategic or security interests for the sake of global revolution against capitalism and imperialism; the SRV's continued identification of the US as the long-term enemy of the world revolution did not stand in the way of pragmatic diplomatic policies towards Washington. What it has done is to distort Vietnamese perceptions and analysis, causing Hanoi to be overconfident of its understanding of the external environment. The net result has been Vietnam's isolation from the world capitalist system even into the 1980s, which exacerbated its internal socio-economic crisis.⟩

One of the strengths of the Vietnamese state, which made it

possible to pursue its security goals against much larger powers, turned out to be a major source of weakness in the 1980s. The bureaucratic structure that exercised centralized control over food supplies in order to support resistance forces in the 1950s and to maximize its autonomy from the Soviets in the early 1960s had not only stifled all economic initiative but appropriated a disproportionate share of society's goods for itself. The downward spiral of the economy, the growing popular hostility towards the bureaucratic strata, and the bitter criticism of the SRV's policies, both foreign and domestic, are seriously undermining the foundations of Vietnam's foreign policy capabilities.

Vietnam's economic and political crisis has undoubtedly been the primary stimulus to change in Vietnamese domestic economic policy as well as foreign policy. The imperative of breaking out of economic stagnation has given impetus to the shift in VCP worldview from 'two camps' to 'interdependence' theses. The result is that in late 1980s Vietnam was in the very early stage of restructuring its foreign policy to put primary emphasis on economic interaction with the capitalist world while de-emphasizing its ideological and security ties with the Soviet bloc. The first manifestations of that restructuring was the Vietnamese decision on withdrawal of its troops from Cambodia unilaterally ahead of its original 1990 deadline. That restructuring may be slowed or accelerated by external opportunities or obstacles, but its fundamental direction is already clear.

BIBLIOGRAPHY

Benoit, Charles (1981), 'Vietnam's "Boat People"', in David W. P. Elliott (ed.), *The Third Indochina Conflict* (Boulder, Col.: Westview Press).

Butler, Steven (1987), 'Scramble for Business with Hanoi', *Bangkok Post*, 6 May.

Chanda, Nayan (1986), *Brother Enemy* (San Diego: Harcourt Brace Jovanovich).

Chang, Pao-min (1981), *Beijing, Hanoi and the Overseas Chinese*

(Berkeley: Institute of East Asian Studies, China Research Monograph, No. 24).

Chauncey, Helen (1988), 'Vietnam and the United States', The Wilson Center, Smithsonian Institution, Vietnam Today, Occasional Paper No. 34, August.

Donnell, John C. and Melvin Gurtov (1969), 'North Vietnam: Left of Moscow, Right of Peking', in Robert A. Scalapino (ed.), The Communist Revolution in Asia (Englewood Cliffs, NJ: Prentice-Hall).

Duy Hoang (1979), 'COMECON and Vietnam', Vietnam Courier, No. 6, June.

Fall, Bernard B. (1956), The Viet Minh Regime: Government and Administration of the Democratic Republic of Viet-Nam (New York: Institute of Pacific Relations).

Girling, John L. S. (1968), 'Northwest Thailand: Tomorrow's Viet Nam?' Foreign Affairs, Vol. XLVI, No. 2, January.

Gurtov, Melvin (1975), China and Southeast Asia – The Politics of Survival (Baltimore, Md.: The Johns Hopkins University Press).

Ha Huu Son (1987), 'Contributing Ideas to the Party Congress: The Farmers Feeling toward the Party', Saigon Giai Phong, 27 October 1986, JPRS.

Halpern, A. M. and H. B. Friedman (1960), Communist Strategy in Laos (Santa Barbara, Calif.: The Rand Corporation).

Hanoi Domestic Service (1988), 'Excerpts' of article by Nhan Dan special correspondent, 14 June, Foreign Broadcast Information Service, FBIS-EAST-88-118, 20 June 1988, 55–8.

Haubold, Erhard (1987), 'Let Us Count Your Dollars', Frankfurter Allgemeine, 9 January 1987, 7–8, JPRS-SEA-87-026, 24 Feburary, 102–6.

Hoang Chi (1987), 'The World Situation and the Foreign Policy of Our Party and State', Tap Chi Cong San, No. 8, August 1986, JPRS-SEA-86-208, 1 December.

Hoang Nguyen (1986), 'Looking Back on the Diplomatic Front over the Past 40 Years', Tap Chi Cong San, No. 11, November 1985, JPRS-SEA-86-034, 24 February.

Hoang Van Thai (1983), Lien Minh Doan Ket Chien Dau Viet Nam-Lao-Cam-Pu-Chia [The Vietnamese-Lao-Kampuchean Alliance for United Struggle] (Hanoi: Su That).

Hoang Tung (1978), The Tien Cong cua Ba Dong Thac Cach Mang [The Offensive Posture of the Three Revolutionary Currents] (Hanoi: Su That).

Institute of International Relations (1986), The Vietnamese People's Struggle in the International Context (Hanoi: Foreign Languages Publishing House).

International Monetary Fund (1982), 'Socialist Republic of Vietnam: Recent Economic Developments', 14 May.

Kissinger, Henry A. (1979), The White House Years (Boston: Little, Brown).

Le Can (1987), 'Our Situation and Tasks', Tap Chi Cong San, No. 8, August 1986, JPRS-SEA-86-208, 1 December.

Le Duan (1965), Giai Cap Vo San voi Van De Nona Dan Trong Cach Mang

Viet Nam [The Proletariat and the Peasant Problem in the Vietnamese Revolution] (Hanoi: Su That).

Le Duan (1981), *May Van De ve Dang Cam Quyen* [Some Problems of the Party in Power] (Hanoi: Su That).

Le Duan (1984), Speech to Sixth Plenum of CPV Central Committee, 3 July 1984, FBIS, 20 August.

Le Duc Tho (1960), 'Report on Amending the Party Statute', *Van Kien Dai Hoi* [Congress Documents], Vol. II (Hanoi: Central Committee of the Vietnam Workers' Party).

Le Ngoc (1986), 'Agriculture, The Main Front: Perceptions and Reality', *Thong Ke*, December 1986, JPRS.

Lim Joo-Jock (1979), *Geo-Strategy and the South China Sea Basin* (Singapore: Singapore University Press).

Luu Van Dat (1986), 'Canvassing Foreign Trade Strategy in the First Stage of the Transitional Period of Our Country', *Ngoai Thuong* [Foreign Trade].

Nguyen Dang Khanh (1987), 'Why Are Rapid Price Changes Occurring on the Market and at State Stores?' *Quoan Doi Nhan Dan*, 13 January 1987, JPRS-SEA-87-060, 27 April.

Nguyen Huu Dao (1986), '40 Years of Developing the Ownership Role of Workers and Farmers', *Tap Chi Cong San*, No. 11, November, JPRS-SEA-86-034, 24 February.

Nguyen Le Minh (1986), 'Providing Jobs in the Cities', *Nhan Dan*, 23 August 1986, JPRS-SEA–86–198, 7 November.

Nguyen Trung Thuc (1987), 'Ideological Life: Words and Actions', *Tap Chi Cong San*, No. 4, April 1987, 81–4, JPRS-ACT-97-003, 3 September.

Nguyen Van Huong (1972), 'Su Nghiep Bao Ve Doc Lap, To Do, Bao Ve Thanh Qua cua Cach Mang va Hinh Luat cua Nuoc, VNDCCH' [The Task of Defending Independence, Freedom, and the Fruits of Revolution and the DRV Criminal Code], in Vietnam Social Sciences Committee, Law Institute, *Mot So Van De ve Nhat Nuoc va Phap Luat Viet Nam* [Some Problems of the Vietnamese State and Law] (Hanoi: Khoa Hoc Xa Hoi).

Nguyen Van Linh (1987), Speech to Third Central Committee Plenum, 31 August 1987, Hanoi Domestic Service, 31 August 1987, FBIS, 2 September.

Nguyen Van Vinh (1968), Talk before the Fourth Conference of the Central Office for South Vietnam, in US Department of State, *Working Paper Reviewing Evidence of North Vietnamese Involvement in Military Operations in South Vietnam* (Washington, DC).

Pike, Douglas (1987), *Vietnam and the Soviet Union: Anatomy of an Alliance* (Boulder, Col.: Westview Press).

Pomonti, Jean-Claude (1987), Interview with CPV General Secretary Nguyen Van Linh, *Le Monde*, 8 December.

Porter, Gareth (1980a), 'Vietnam's Ethnic Chinese and the Sino-Vietnamese Conflict', *Bulletin of Concerned Asian Scholars*, Vol. 12, No. 4, October-December.

Porter, Gareth (1980b), 'Vietnam and the Socialist Camp: Center or Periphery?' in William S. Turley (ed.), *Vietnamese Communism in Comparative Perspective* (Boulder, Col.: Westview).

Porter, Gareth (1981), 'Vietnamese Policy and the Indochina Crisis', David W. P. Elliott (ed.), *The Third Indochina Conflict* (Boulder: Westview).

Porter, Gareth (1983), 'Vietnamese Communist Policy toward Kampuchea: 1930–1970', in David P. Chandler and Ben Kiernan (eds), *Revolution and its Aftermath in Kampuchea: Eight Essays*, Yale University Southeast Asia Studies Monograph Series, No. 25.

Porter, Gareth (1984), 'Hanoi's Strategic Perspective and the Sino-Vietnamese Conflict', *Pacific Affairs*, Vol. 57, No. 1, Spring.

Porter, Gareth (1985), 'Vietnam-ASEAN Relations: A Decade of Evolution', *Indochina Report* (Singapore), No. 2, April-June.

Porter, Gareth (1988), 'Toward a Kampuchean Peace Settlement: History and Dynamics of Sihanouk's Negotiations', *Southeast Asian Affairs 1988* (Singapore: ISEAS).

Porter, Gareth (1989), 'The Transformation of Vietnam's Worldview: From Two Camps to Interdependence', paper, annual meeting of the Association for Asian Studies, Washington, DC, March.

Rosenberger, Leif (1983), 'The Soviet-Vietnamese Alliance and Kampuchea', *Survey*, Vol. 227, No. 118/119, Autumn-Winter.

Socialist Republic of Vietnam, Statistics General Department (1985), *So Lieu Thong Ke 1930–1984* [Statistical Data 1930–1984] (Hanoi: Statistics Publishing House).

Socialist Republic of Vietnam (1979), *Su That ve Quan He Vietnam-Trung Quoc* [The Truth about Vietnamese-Chinese Relations] (Hanoi: Su That).

'Some Facts and Figures on Vietnam-Soviet Union Economic and Cultural Co-operation' (1986), *Tap Chi Cong San*, No. 11, November 1985, JPRS-SEA-86-034, 24 February.

Thayer, Carlyle A. (1978), 'Vietnam's External Relations: An Overview', *Asia Pacific Community*, Vol. 9, No. 2, January.

Thayer, Carlyle A. (1983), 'Vietnam's Two Strategic Tasks: Building Socialism and Defending the Fatherland', *Southeast Asian Affairs, 1983*.

Turley, William (1986), 'Vietnam/Indochina: Hanoi's Challenge to Southeast Asian Regional Order', in Young Whan Kihl and Lawrence E. Grinter (eds), *Asian Pacific Security: Emerging Challenges and Responses* (Boulder, Col.: Westview).

Van Giang (1986), 'Salaries and Wages, A Hot Issue', *Lao Dong*, 9 January 1966, JPRS-SEA-86-082, 12 May.

Vietnam News Agency (1988), Law on Foreign Investment in Vietnam, 11 January 1988, FBIS-EAS–88–007, 12 January.

Vo Nhan Tri (1985a), 'The Third Five-Year Plan 1981–85: Performance and Limits', *Indochina Report*, October, December.

Vo Nhan Tri (1985b), 'Socialist Vietnam's Economic Development 1975–85: Policies and Performance', paper for Conference on Vietnam, University of Sussex, October 1985.

Vo Thanh Cong (1987), 'Overall and Rigorous Saving of Technical Material and Labor is a State Policy', *Nhan Dan*, 8 January 1987, JPRS-87-047, 2 April.

Wain, Barry (1988), 'Vietnam Seeks Aid as its Harvests Falter', *The Wall Street Journal*, 11 May.

Werner, Jayne (1984), 'Socialist Development: The Political Economy of Agrarian Reform in Vietnam', *Bulletin of Concerned Asian Scholars*, Vol. 16, No. 2, April-June.

13 Cambodia's Foreign Policy
Gareth Porter

For Cambodia* the stakes in foreign policy have been far greater than for most Third-World states. Cambodia's relatively small size, its weaker social and governmental structures compared with those of Vietnam, and the regional conflicts of the 1960s and 1970s centering on its powerful eastern neighbor have all made it highly vulnerable to external penetration and, ultimately, the loss of its independence.

All four of Cambodia's regimes since 1954 have been concerned about its survival as a nation. But only the Royal Government of Prince Norodom Sihanouk was able to translate that concern into an effective policy for maintaining national independence. Since Sihanouk's overthrow in 1970, each successive regime has restructured foreign policy in line with its own 'definition of the situation' and the perceived interests of the ruling élite, but none has been successful in achieving its main foreign policy aim. The Khmer Republic (1970–75) relied primarily on the support of the US to expel the Vietnamese Communist presence in Cambodia and crush the domestic Communist insurgency. The Democratic Kampuchea regime of Pol Pot (1975–79) pursued political-military confrontation with Vietnam on the illusory assumption of virtually equal national strength. The current regime, the Vietnamese-sponsored People's Republic of Kampuchea (PRK) – the name until 1989, accepted as its main premise the inability of Cambodia to maintain a viable state and society without Vietnamese intervention, at least for a time.

For each of the first three regimes, foreign policy served the dual functions of maintaining Cambodia's independence and of regime consolidation or survival. Under both the Khmer Republic and Democratic Kampuchea, in fact, regime maintenance appears to have become, in effect, the primary, though unspoken, purpose of

* This was the name of the country until 1970, and was again adopted by the Phnom Penh government in 1989. It will be used throughout except when the proper name of an organization or a particular regime requires otherwise.

foreign policy. The foreign policy of the PRK, like that of its predecessor regimes, is aimed at regime survival but has implicitly subordinated the aim of independence to the aim of building a state structure
that can once more succeed in imposing peace and order on the
country in the aftermath of the Pol Pot débâcle.

This devolution of Cambodian foreign policy from the function of
maintaining national independence to that of state building is obviously a direct consequence of Vietnam's occupation since 1979. In
a longer-term perspective, however, it can only be understood as a
result of the progressive destruction of Cambodia's capabilities for
maintaining national independence and of unrealistic foreign policy
decisions by Cambodian governments during the 1970s. This chapter
will show how these two key factors have contributed to the present
combination of internal and external constraints on Cambodian
autonomy.

SIHANOUK AND THE ROYAL GOVERNMENT: 1955–70

Cambodia after independence could be considered as a pre-capitalist
or 'bureaucratic-royal' regime, resting on a ruling coalition of royalty
and high-level government functionaries (Vickery, 1984: 267). The
Khmer élite had never acquired large landholdings and therefore
had no capital to invest in industry or commerce. Instead it was
oriented toward the state bureaucracy and content to gain its wealth
by venality and arrangements with Chinese merchants who controlled rice trading, the import-export trade and most domestic commerce, as well as small industry. The few larger industrial enter-
prizes, such as soft drinks and rubber production, were owned by
foreign companies (Willmot, 1967: 52–60, 87, 99).

After 1954 the Cambodian government and politics was dominated
by Samdech (Prince) Norodom Sihanouk, who abdicated as king
in 1955 to enter partisan politics. Sihanouk eliminated the non-
Communist leftist opposition Democratic Party as a significant influence in politics, and replaced the parliamentary system with a 'guided
democracy' in which the biannual National Congress of the *Sangkum
Reaster Nium* (People's Socialist Community Party) was the central
political institution (Sihanouk, 1973: 164). He curbed criticism of the
Sangkum regime by arbitrary arrest and tight control of the press
(Vickery, 1986: 15; Osborne, 1973: 73).

As a regime of the pre-capitalist, traditional right, the Sangkum unified those political figures and groups who had been both pro-monarchist and anti-Communist (Vickery, 1982: 97–9, 101, 105; Kiernan, 1985: 181). During the 1960s, however, differences over economic policy and resentment of Sihanouk's personal style of ruling brought about anti-monarchical and economic liberalizing trends within the Sangkum, while Sihanouk remained hostile to both foreign and domestic capital. What united Sihanouk and the pro-capitalist right was their common determination to suppress the underground Communist Party of Kampuchea (CPK).

In 1963 Sihanouk nationalized the import-export trade as well as foreign banking, setting up mixed state-private companies aimed at diverting profits from Chinese and French businessmen to the state and later converting them to state agencies. The Royal Government was never a 'state capitalist' regime, however, since state bureaucrats did not undertake the function of capital accumulation for economic development. Instead, the new state-controlled companies were sources of patronage and corruption for officials, including at least one closely identified with Sihanouk's wife Monique (Roy, 1970: 35; Kirk, 1971: 85–6). After even Sihanouk recognized that state control over trade had failed, these state monopolies were terminated.

Political factions within the Sangkum regime corresponded with several networks of corruption and finance which linked various parts of the administration with groups of private businessmen (Pomonti and Thion, 1971: 90–1). Sihanouk's own political interests centered on maintaining his unchallenged hegemony in the political system, maintaining the loyalty of the dominant conservative group in the Sangkum and at the same time maintaining his popularity with the rural masses. The other major political-financial networks, such as those led by Sirik Matak and Army General Lon Nol, wished to emerge from Sihanouk's shadow politically and to enhance their own financial positions.

Foreign policy decision-making during the Sihanouk period was highly personal, depending primarily on his own definition of the national and external situation and his operational code as a states-man. Sihanouk, who prided himself on his political realism, was a pessimist about Cambodia's future, because of the country's weakness *vis-à-vis* Vietnam and his belief that Communism had funda-mental long-term advantages both globally and, more particularly, in Asia. He accepted the likelihood that, at some point, Cambodia would succumb to Communism, and that his task was to delay that development as long as possible (Armstrong, 1964: 120–1, 127; Gordon, 1966: 54–5).

Sihanouk believed that the critical factor in preserving Cambodia's independence would be whether it could maintain national unity. That assumption, in turn, dovetailed with his view that the monarchy remained the single greatest unifying influence within Cambodia (Sihanouk, 1973: 166). Sihanouk's foreign policy was aimed at consolidating national unity under his leadership by weakening the left (including the non-Communist Democratic Party and the Communist Party of Kampuchea). The adoption of a neutralist foreign policy in 1955 helped Sihanouk to reduce the domestic appeal of the Democratic Party, which had previously criticized the 1955 military assistance agreement with the US (Smith, 1965: 84–5). His neutralist posture also reduced the risk of being attacked by Beijing or Hanoi when he repressed the CPK (Devillers, 1963: 159).

Sihanouk's decision to terminate US military and economic aid was also a response to domestic political concerns. The US commercial import program had spawned a privileged élite of importers who quick amassed fortunes. Sihanouk feared that US assistance had made sectors of the Khmer élite dependent on US largesse and thus potentially responsive to US manipulation (Sihanouk, 1973: 135, 140).

The external environment during the Sihanouk period brought steadily increasing pressures on Cambodia for involvement in the Indo-China conflict. In the late 1950s the US sought to move Cambodia from neutralism to a more pro-Western posture. Washington supported groups and individuals who oppposed Sihanouk's relations with Communist bloc states (National Security Council, 1956: 9). It also welcomed, if it did not inspire, Thai and South Vietnamese government support for the Khmer Serei movement of Son Ngoc Thanh in its aim of overthrowing Sihanouk (Osborne, 1973: 62–3).

After the US began its direct military intervention in South Vietnam, however, the Vietnamese Communist forces fighting the South established rest, training and logistics bases on the Cambodian side of the border. The Democratic Republic of Vietnam (DRV) in North Vietnam also pressed Sihanouk for other forms of co-operation, including the transshipment of weapons for Communist forces through the port of Sihanoukville. Viet Cong use of these sanctuaries brought increased US pressure on Cambodia in the form of air and artillery attacks of Cambodian territory and demands from the US military for a massive invasion to clean out the sanctuaries. The pressure for such an invasion grew especially intense after the US embarked on the policy of 'Vietnamization.' Under the Nixon administration, the US carried out secret B-52 raids on suspected sanctuary areas inside Cambodia.

As a Khmer nationalist, Sihanouk viewed the Vietnamese as an historical aggressor against Cambodia, and believed that the DRV had the same ambition as pre-colonial Vietnamese emperors: to colonize Cambodia, using the Khmer Communists as their agents (Armstrong, 1964: 105–6, 120). With regard to China, which Sihanouk believed would eventually become the dominant regional power, he was more hopeful, calculating that China would prefer to maintain Cambodia's neutralist position to demonstrate its peaceful intentions toward small neighboring states. Sihanouk also detected significant divergences between the interests of Beijing and those of Hanoi with regard to Cambodia which would give the PRC another reason for serving as the chief guarantor of Cambodian neutrality (Smith, 1965: 116–17; Gordon, 1966: 56, 59).

Sihanouk viewed the US as ignorant of political realities in Southeast Asia and bumbling in its policies (Armstrong, 1964: 136–9). He was certain that Washington, in search of 'pawns' to use against the Communists, conspired with the Bangkok and Saigon regimes and his exiled foe Son Ngoc Thanh to weaken and ultimately overthrow his government (Smith, 1965: 129–39). When armed struggle resumed in Indo-China, Sihanouk was convinced that a Communist victory and a reunified Vietnam were inevitable. He doubted that the US would then be able to do much to guarantee Cambodia's independence and neutrality (Leifer, 1967: 132, 153, 173). After observing the ill-concealed US role in the overthrow of the Diem regime in South Vietnam, in fact, Sihanouk was convinced that he would be next on the American 'hit list' (Shaplen, 1986: 83; Leifer, 1967: 144).

As the Viet Cong forces fled from US military pressures into sanctuaries in Cambodia, Sihanouk saw Vietnamese dependence on his government's co-operation as giving him some leverage on the Vietnamese regarding future relations (Porter, 1983, 78, 94, fn. 85). He also blamed Hanoi for the Khmer Rouge armed struggle against his government that began in 1968 (Smith, 1968: 75; Taylor, 1976: 146–7).

Sihanouk's foreign policy orientation was non-alignment combined with accommodation to the Asian Communist states if necessary. In dealing with China and North Vietnam, he tried to maximize the incentives for those states to co-exist peacefully or even co-operate with his regime. By opposing US intervention in Indo-China, he hoped to create obligations on the part of the PRC and DRV to maintain 'correct' behavior toward Cambodia. At the same time he kept open the option of alignment with the US as an inducement for the Communist states to maintain friendly relations with Cambodia (Leifer, 1976: 176; Armstrong, 1964: 125–6).

While Sihanouk's primary aim was always to prevent any effort by the Vietnamese Communist movement to interfere in Cambodia's internal affairs, developments in Indo-China repeatedly forced him to shift the emphasis in his policy. In the first phase, from the Geneva Accords of 1954 until 1956, Sihanouk obtained both a unilateral offer of protection by the US under the Manila Pact of 1954 and US military aid without any Cambodian obligation to the Western bloc. In 1956, however, he began a new phase, rejecting American pressures to join SEATO. He began to accept aid from the PRC and in 1958 entered into formal diplomatic relations with Beijing, while agreeing only to trade relations with the DRV.

Alarmed at the prospect of civil war with external power involvement breaking out in Laos, Sihanouk pressed in 1960 for the establishment of a neutral zone in Indo-China including both Laos and Cambodia. After the resumption of armed struggle in South Vietnam in 1960 he moved further away from the US, breaking diplomatic relations with Thailand in 1961 and South Vietnam in 1963, and terminating US economic and military assistance in late 1963. Finally, after denouncing US intervention in Indo-China at a conference of anti-US Indo-Chinese forces, he broke diplomatic relations with the US in 1965.

In 1964–65 he also began to prepare for the eventual defeat of the US and the anti-Communist side in the war by seeking international guarantees of Cambodian neutrality and territorial integrity through an international conference. When that failed, because of US refusal to support such a conference, he tried to get the Vietnamese Communists to sign guarantees of his borders and neutrality before they had defeated the Saigon regime. In order to obtain such guarantees, Sihanouk had to forfeit, in effect, his neutral posture *vis-à-vis* the struggle for Indo-China. For Sihanouk, neutralism was not the objective of his policy but a means to the objective of the survival of the existing regime, if possible, and the independence of Cambodia in any case.

From 1965 through 1969 he negotiated a series of understandings and agreements under which his government not only tolerated the enlargement of Vietnamese bases in Cambodia but assisted them by transshipment of weapons. Sihanouk sought to exploit the increasing Vietnamese Communist dependence on Cambodia by negotiating a favorable border settlement as well as a formal commitment to withdrawal of Vietnamese forces after the war. In return for according diplomatic status to the DRV and the National Liberation Front in 1967, Sihanouk did get the written agreement of both to recognize and respect the existing borders (Porter, 1983: 77–8).

In the final two years of his regime, Sihanouk attempted to manipulate the Vietnamese both on the Khmer Rouge insurgency and on the increasingly intrusive Vietnamese presence. In 1968 the Royal Government threatened to withdraw its co-operation with Viet Cong sanctuaries and move closer to the US unless the Vietnamese forced the Khmer Communists to end their armed struggle (Heder, 1979b: 14). He also tried unsuccessfully to get Hanoi to restrict Communist use of Cambodian sanctuaries by tolerating US B-52 attacks on base areas, authorizing minor harrassment of the sanctuaries by government troops, re-establishing a US embassy in Phnom Penh, and putting public pressure on the Vietnamese (Kirk, 1971: 108–10; Shawcross, 1979: 113–14; Heder, 1979b: 14–15). Finally, Sihanouk did get a written promise from the Communist 'Provisional Revolutionary Government' that all Vietnamese forces would be withdrawn as soon as peace was restored in Vietnam (Heder, 1979b: 24).

In summary, Sihanouk's diplomacy evolved through four distinct stages, beginning with pro-Western neutralism from 1955 to 1958, then shifting to a balanced neutralism from 1958 to 1961, to a neutralism that clearly leaned toward Beijing in the 1961–65 period, and finally, from 1965 to 1970 to an active involvement on the Vietnamese Communist side of the war while looking to Beijing and, to a lesser extent, Washington, to restrain the Vietnamese Communists.

The main internal constraints on Sihanouk's foreign policy were factors that raised the political costs to Sihanouk of reducing US influence in Cambodia and accommodating the Vietnamese, thus indirectly contributing to his downfall. These constraints included a backward, stagnant economy, weak socio-political linkages between the peasantry and the urban-based élite, social and economic dependence on foreign aid, a prebendary state apparatus, and widespread resentment on the part of various factions in the Sihanouk regime of Sihanouk's political dominance and policies.

The Cambodian economy, dependent on rice and rubber exports for 85 to 90 per cent of its hard currency earnings did not generate sufficient foreign exchange to finance the level of imports demanded by the urban élite and middle class (Kirk, 1971: 82; Prud'homme, 1969: 273). The US commercial import program filled the trade gap, thus allowing the Royal Government to maintain the acquiescence, though not the enthusiastic support, of the middle and upper urban strata.

Sihanouk's attempt to insulate his society from US political influence (and probably to symbolize a move towards accommodation with the Hanoi regime) by ending US economic and military assistance in 1963 provoked a political reaction among those who had directly benefitted. The urban élite reacted to the aid cut-off, nationalization measures and economic austerity by turning increasingly anti-Sihanouk (Osborne, 1973: 87–90; Roy, 1970: 351). Another key socio-political element whose personal and institutional interests were obviously served by US assistance was the military leadership. Commercial aid provided US$ 111.7 million between 1955 and 1962 in military salaries alone – one-third of the total spent on salaries for that period – and also provided US$ 104 million in military matériel (Forcier, 1975; Smith, 1965: 125). Sihanouk's termination of the program caused the Khmer armed forces' inventory of weapons to erode rapidly because of a lack of spare parts. The deep dissatisfaction in the military leadership, led by Sihanouk's old ally, General Lon Nol, ultimately contributed to the plot to overthrow the prince.

The combination of economic dependence and the venality of the bureaucratic élite also limited Sihanouk's ability to isolate the society and economy from the Viet Cong troop presence. Prior to the French protectorate, the monarchy had rewarded its officials not with salaries but with a percentage of the taxes they collected, and members of the royal family were given control over provinces as *apanage*. After independence, officials had to pay for their government positions and viewed them as a financial investment to be used to maximize personal profit (Vickery, 1982: 101; Osborne, 1973: 84; Pomonti and Thion, 1971). The massive smuggling of rice by Chinese merchants to Viet Cong troops had the complicity of high-ranking officials of the government, who were paid a part of the profits (Osborne, 1973: 104–5; Kirk, 1971: 85–6). Of the estimated 300 000 tons of rice that was 'exported' by Cambodia in 1966, about 40 per cent was sold to the Viet Cong forces at premium prices, and therefore represented a loss of hard currency and tax revenues to the state (Prud'homme, 1969: 255, Table 12).

In 1964 the government had tried to compensate for the loss of US commercial aid by compulsory purchases of rice at below-market prices for export (Prud'homme, 1969: 76–7). In 1967 it was driven by the loss of rice exports to use military units to attempt to collect paddy from the farmers at prices one-third below those paid by the Vietnamese. In the context of peasant resentment towards a government bureaucracy identified with the interests to whom most peasants were indebted, that effort triggered the first significant Communist uprising in Cambodia, as rebels attacked military units collecting paddy in Battambang (Kiernan, 1982: 169). The financial crisis caused by the diversion of rice to the Viet Cong and the new threat of domestic Communist insurgency, which was generally viewed as linked with Hanoi, further weakened urban middle-class support for Sihanouk's policy.

Finally, the sharp rift between Sihanouk and a large part of the political élite was a serious constraint on his ability to maneuver successfully in a highly threatening external environment. In part this disunity was a result of Sihanouk's highly personal regime, which left no room for leading members of the bureaucratic élite to share political power. There were also conflicts between Sihanouk's desire to reduce external economic dependence and his commitment to 'Khmer Socialism', on the one hand, and most of the élite's preference for close relations with Washington and liberalization of the economy, on the other. The growing intrusiveness of the Vietnamese troop presence and its impact on the urban economy added to Sihanouk's unpopularity with the urban middle and upper classes. In 1969–70 a group of high-ranking bureaucrats and aristocrats, led by Sihanouk's old rival Sisowath Sirik Matak and the Prince's former close ally General Lon Nol, saw their opportunity to raise the Viet Cong troop issue against Sihanouk. In March 1970 their carefully laid plans culminated in the overthrow of the Prince while he was abroad, after a series of violent demonstrations against Hanoi and the Viet Cong.

Sihanouk's flexible diplomacy of neutralism, accommodation and balance of power was well chosen to maximize Cambodia's chances for avoiding foreign intervention and its loss of independence. Sihanouk managed to keep Cambodia out of the regional conflict and to keep the backing of Beijing and Hanoi against his own domestic Communist movement. But the Vietnam conflict inevitably spilled

across the border, creating a dilemma for Sihanouk: his accommodation with the Vietnamese came at the cost of increased internal
political instability. What had been a successful foreign policy in
terms of Sihanouk's strategic aims hastened the end of the Royal
Government.

THE KHMER REPUBLIC: 1970–75

The new regime abandoned Sihanouk's intricate diplomacy of incentives and instead pursued a confrontation with the Vietnamese Communists with American backing. This restructuring of foreign policy
soon turned into a self-destructive débâcle. What was to become the
Khmer Republic represented the same social and political forces that
had governed during the Sihanouk period but without Sihanouk and
the monarchy. Although it established a republican parliamentary
government in October 1970, Lon Nol eliminated the old national
assembly in 1972, was elected President in a rigged election and
established a new national assembly in which every seat belonged to
the political party controlled by Lon Nol's younger brother (Kiernan,
1985: 347–8).

The coup group's demand in March 1970 that Vietnamese forces
be evacuated from Cambodia immediately, combined with its overthrow of Sihanouk, triggered the most important changes in Cambodia's external environment since the country's independence.
Those moves signalled to Hanoi that the new regime was co-operating with the US in attempting to destroy the sanctuaries and possibly
to capture the nerve center of the war effort (Truong, 1985: 177).
The Vietnamese responded by forming a new alliance with Sihanouk
and the Khmer Communist leadership of Pol Pot, then began moving
beyond their sanctuaries to arm the Khmer Rouge and help them
organize the population.

The Vietnamese moves quickly changed the face of the countryside
in Eastern Cambodia, and direct, open US military intervention in
the form of tactical airstrikes soon followed. The impingement of
the two main protagonists in the Vietnam war on Cambodia constituted the main features of the external environment for the Khmer
Republic for the next five years.

The new regime's 'definition of the situation' when it decided on
confrontation with the Vietnamese was based more on emotion than
on careful calculation. Lon Nol and Sirik Matak viewed themselves

as leading a war of salvation against Vietnamese invaders. They counted on primordial anti-Vietnamese nationalism to unite the population behind the regime's policy. That assumption appeared at first to be borne out by the rush of urban students and youth to volunteer to fight the Vietnamese, which quickly swelled the army from 35 000 to 120 000 men.

The orders for the army to carry out systematic massacres of Vietnamese civilians residing in Eastern Cambodia in April 1970 underlined the essential character of the war for the Khmer Republic. Lon Nol himself was motivated by a mystical, racist doctrine of 'Neo-Khmerism', which aimed at a union of Khmers, Chams, hill-tribes and even the Mons of Thailand and Burma against the Vietnamese and reconquest of the Khmer Krom areas of South Vietnam (Kiernan, 1985: 148).

It seems doubtful, however, that the coup group would have launched an anti-Vietnamese policy without external backing. There is some evidence that Lon Nol and Sirik Matak had official US assurance of support for ousting Sihanouk and expelling the Vietnamese (Hersh, 1983: 178–81). In any case, the anti-Sihanouk plotters certainly assumed that the US would provide both political and material support for a confrontational policy towards the Vietnamese.

In late 1972 the character of the war began to change dramatically, as the Vietnamese retreated from the battlefield and turned over the fighting to the Khmer Rouge. Thus what had been a war for national salvation for the Khmer Republic regime turned into a struggle against an internal revolutionary movement led by a former king who was still revered by Khmer peasants. While the overt function of foreign policy remained the defense of national independence, the latent function of the regime's foreign policy was increasingly regime maintenance.

The efforts of Lon Nol to stay in power was severely constrained by several internal factors. Cambodia's society, economy and governmental structure disintegrated under the weight of modern warfare, which could only be financed by ruinous inflation. Total exports plummeted to one-fiftieth of what they had been before the war and the government had to import 280 000 tons of rice by 1974 (Kiljunen, 1984: 6–7). Dependent on the US for money, weapons, and food as well as for tactical airstrikes, the regime was unable to take care of the main victims of the war – the refugees and the urban poor, products of the war's socio-economic dislocation. Incompetence and corruption resulted in widespread starvation, and the general collapse of urban morale (Hildebrand and Porter, 1976: 22–9, 50–3; Shawcross, 1979: 224–6). The Khmer Republic's war effort was also constrained by its lack of legitimacy outside urban areas because of peasant alienation from urban-based élites and the Communist insurgents' identification with Sihanouk. Indiscriminate US bombing of the most heavily populated areas of Cambodia, which killed tens of thousands of civilians, created an enormous pool of recruits for the insurgents (Chandler, Kiernan and Lim, 1979: 2–3; Shawcross, 1979: 174–5, 202–4, 213–19; Kiernan, 1985: 307–8, 350–5).

When the civil war began in April 1970, the Khmer Communist movement had between 2400 and 4000 active insurgents, relatively few of whom were armed with modern weapons (Kiernan, 1985: 284; Heder, 1979b: 13–14). By the end of 1972 the Khmer Rouge army had 50 000 men organized in regiments, and was strong enough, with logistical support from the Vietnamese, to do battle with the Republican Army. The army of the Khmer Republic – riddled with corruption, payrolls padded with the names of non-existent soldiers, and made up of troops who were seldom paid on time, if at all – was no match for it. By early 1975, desertion and defection had reduced it to only 60 000 actual combat troops, in contrast to its paper stength of 230 000 (Shawcross, 1979: 261, 355). When the Khmer Rouge captured the southern end of the Mekong River in late March, it paved the way for the successful assault on Phnom Penh the following month.

DEMOCRATIC KAMPUCHEA: 1975–79

The Democratic Kampuchea (DK) regime was an experiment in Third-World totalitarianism: a highly centralized, totally collectivized and planned socio-economic system directed by the clandestine CPK under a tiny core of ruthless and insecure leaders. The regime, usually identified with its Prime Minister, Pol Pot, abolished private property, money, markets and most of the socio-economic functions of the family in its bid to build the most revolutionary society in the world. It regarded the poor peasantry as its political base, while scorning the role of the urban population in general and the educated élite in particular. The former urban population, dispersed to the countryside to become laborers, were discriminated against in food distribution, and suffered mass starvation and arbitrary execution.

The group led by Pol Pot combined a voluntarism more extreme than that of Maoism with a millenarianism typical of past Southeast Asian peasant rebellions. They sought to build a powerful agrarian-based Khmer state by constructing water control projects and using natural fertilizer, like the ancient kingdom of Angkor, which had used forced labor to build impressive irrigation works in the thirteenth and fourteenth centuries.

When the Pol Pot group came to power, they had neither firm control over the entire party and state apparatus nor full support for their internal and foreign policies. Pol Pot attempted to eliminate all those who were not considered loyal to the leadership group. Leading figures in the party central committee were killed during the first year for having opposed Pol Pot's socio-economic line. Cadres who had been linked with the Vietnamese during the war were regarded by the Pol Pot group as Vietnamese agents and were arrested and executed beginning in 1976. Cadres in the Eastern zone who argued against the military confrontation with Vietnam as needlessly provocative were targetted for purge in 1978 (Heder, 1980a: 28; Kiernan, 1983: 170–2; Vickery, 1985: 191–2).

Foreign policy, like all policy decisions, was made by a small group of four people in the CPK leadership, consisting of Pol Pot, Foreign Minister Ieng Sary and their wives. Their 'definition of the situation' combined the assumption that the Vietnamese would ultimately try to annex Cambodia with the delusion that Cambodia was even stronger than Vietnam. For years, the Pol Pot group had viewed the Vietnamese as the 'hereditary enemy' of Cambodia and held that there was no possibility for a peaceful settlement of differences. Now they believed Vietnam was in a weakened condition after the war, while the DK had shown its strength by defeating the US without external help. Therefore, the time was ripe for Cambodia to take the offensive against Vietnam (Chanda, 1986: 96–101; Kiernan, 1985: 329–61).

The international context after the Vietnam War offered both advantageous conditions and potential dangers for the regime. China was actively opposing any expansion of Vietnamese influence in Southeast Asia and was ready to provide military assistance to build up the Khmer Rouge army. Hanoi was preoccupied with economic reconstruction and still concerned about maintaining correct relations with Beijing. Under these conditions the Vietnamese refrained from demanding extensive co-operation from the DK or from actively plotting its overthrow. On the other hand, rising Sino-Vietnamese tensions after mid-1977 prompted Hanoi to view Pol

Pot's overtly hostile actions as part of a Chinese strategy (Chanda, 1986: 84–90; Porter, 1981b: 5–6).

The Pol Pot group's perception of the external environment was both overoptimistic and exaggerated external threats. Convinced that Hanoi had been trying for years to gain control of the Khmer party, and eager to demonstrate its new power, the Pol Pot group ignored the evidence of Vietnamese willingness to co-exist. The Vietnamese treaty with Laos in mid-1977, which provided the basis for close political-military co-operation, was viewed by the Khmer Rouge leadership as evidence of Vietnam's intention to impose a hierarchical relationship on Cambodia (Chanda, 1986: 95). Pol Pot created a grand conspiracy theory that the CIA, the KGB and Vietnamese intelligence services were all working together to subvert the DK regime (Porter, 1981a, 95–7; Democratic Kampuchea, 1978).

Although Pol Pot's ideological allies in the ultra-left 'gang of four' in China were ousted in late 1976, he counted on Beijing's animosity towards the Vietnamese as the basis for a strategic alliance against Hanoi. The DK leadership viewed the PRC as a kind of insurance policy against miscalculation *vis-à-vis* Vietnam – a source not only of arms and diplomatic support, but deterrence against an all-out Vietnamese military assault through a threat of military intervention. In the 1978 showdown with Hanoi the Pol Pot group found that they had overestimated the Chinese stake in maintaining it in power when the PRC failed to deliver effective deterrent threats.

The DK foreign policy orientation was to reject all forms of co-operation with Vietnam while maintaining a state of military tension on the Vietnamese border. Pol Pot refused to negotiate on the territorial issue once Vietnam had rejected unilateral demands for changes in the border line by Phnom Penh. The DK then asserted its claims through military force, launching artillery attacks and raids on Vietnamese villages in April 1977. There was even talk of reconquering the Khmer Krom territories of South Vietnam (Heder, 1979: 165; Vickery, 1985: 193). After Vietnam retaliated in late 1977 by striking deep into Eastern Cambodia and making contact with anti-Pol Pot dissidents, DK leaders were determined to continue the military confrontation with Vietnam. In 1978 the DK rejected a Vietnamese proposal for a cease-fire and an international presence on the border and stepped up its offensive deep into Vietnamese territory.

Meanwhile the DK essentially closed its doors to the rest of the world, including international organizations. The Pol Pot obsession with autarchy was so extreme that even a grant of US$ 20 million from the PRC for commodity aid was not used (Chanda, 1985: 79). When malaria was recognized as a serious problem for the labor force in 1976, the DK refused offers of international health and medical assistance, except for limited shipments of medicine from China.

Given internal socio-economic and political constraints Pol Pot's ultra-leftist internal policies and chauvinistic aggressiveness toward Vietnam were extremely risky. The socio-economic policies weakened the DK's ability to maintain its autonomy from Vietnam by driving an otherwise loyal segment of the party into the arms of the Vietnamese. The effort to leap over stages of development while cutting Cambodia off from all foreign sources of assistance except China also resulted in a sharp decline in agricultural production compared with the prewar level and a sick and exhausted population (Heder, 1980c: 47; Charny and Spragens, 1984: 82; Summers, 1981, 10–11; Ito, 1978). Even more damaging politically, however, was the fact that so much of the food was taken away from the producers for storage, either to trade to the Chinese for weapons or to prepare stocks for the support of troops in a war with the Vietnamese (Kiernan, 1984: 2; Ito, 1978; Vickery, 1984: 140–2). The massive killings by Pol Pot of the CPK's own cadres eventually drove what had been loyal party leaders in the Eastern Zone into rebellion and alliance with the Vietnamese (Heder, 1981: 25; Kiernan, 1983: 178–98). It also alienated not only the former urbanites but poor peasant supporters, who began to fear the unpredictability of Pol Pot's bloody purges (Heder, 1980: 29). As a consequence, there was little resistance to the Vietnamese invasion in December 1978. On the contrary, the population – as even DK Deputy Premier Ieng Sary admitted – actually rallied to the Vietnamese occupying forces and the new government after the ouster of the DK regime (Paringaux, 1979).

THE PEOPLE'S REPUBLIC OF KAMPUCHEA: 1979–89

In yet another restructuring of Cambodia's foreign policy, the leadership of the People's Republic of Kampuchea (PRK) abandoned the virulent anti-Vietnamese orientation of previous regimes and made Cambodia a client state of Vietnam. The PRK was dependent on Vietnamese troops for protection against the Khmer Rouge army, and followed the Vietnamese lead in all major policy matters. Its establishment with the help of Vietnamese forces in January 1979 reflected the agreement by opponents of Pol Pot both inside and outside Cambodia that they had no choice but to co-operate with a Vietnamese military intervention to eliminate the Pol Pot group from power.

The leadership of the PRK has consisted of three distinct elements: first, those who were part of a contingent of Khmer Communists who spent the period from 1954 to 1970 in Vietnam receiving political and military training; second, those who had held responsible positions in the DK; third, those who had not been either officials in the DK or members of the earlier Vietnamese-dominated Indochinese Communist Party, including both party members who broke with Pol Pot between 1970 and 1975 and those who had never been in the party before 1979.

In the first phases of the new Khmer People's Revolutionary Party (KPRP) from 1981 to 1984, the Hanoi-trained cadres clearly dominated leading party organs, both in numbers and in control of key positions. Pen Sovan, the leading figure in that group, was named the first Party Secretary, Minister of Defense and Chairman of the State Council. But in 1984–85, the balance shifted dramatically in favor of the ex-DK officials and figures who had not been party members before 1981. In the 1985 Central Committee the Vietnamese-trained leaders were the smallest of the three groups. The ex-DK group dominated the Politburo, and the party secretary was President Heng Samrin of the DK Eastern Zone group (Vickery, 1986a: 73–83).

The divergent backgrounds of the Hanoi-trained and ex-DK party leaders had undoubtedly made for some degree of tension between them. But these cannot be translated automatically into differences of view on relations with Vietnam, because both groups are interested, ultimately, in Cambodian autonomy from Vietnam. Both Pen Sovan of the 'outside' group and Heng Samrin of the former DK group reportedly opposed the return of former Vietnamese inhabitants to Cambodia, and the latter reportedly expressed his intention to expel them eventually. Sovan, who had been considered the most trusted by Hanoi of all PRK leaders, was relieved of all his positions in December 1981 and disappeared from the Cambodian political scene altogether (Kiernan, 1981: 2).

Both groups chose to depend on the Vietnamese with great reluctance. President Heng Samrin is said to have ruled out reliance on

Vietnamese forces until mid-1978 because of fears that the Vietnamese wanted to take over Cambodia and to have agreed only when the situation of anti-Pol Pot resistance forces became desperate (Heder, 1981b). He and other Eastern Zone cadres concluded that the Pol Pot regime had become a greater threat to Cambodia's survival as a nation than their traditional enemies. In effect, the PRK leadership set aside the aim of maintaining independence from Vietnam temporarily in order to establish an orthodox Marxist-Leninist state. PRK foreign policy thus has served primarily state-building and regime maintenance functions, at present, with the recovery of autonomy a longer-term aim.

Because of the PRK's dependence on Vietnamese military forces to stay in power, Vietnamese officials in Cambodia have had extraordinary power over PRK policies through the Vietnamese advisory mission. Foreign policy, like all other aspects of PRK policy-making, was formulated and implemented under the overall guidance of a special organ ('B-68') headquartered in Ho Chi Minh City. Deputy directors of that committee in Phnom Penh oversaw key policy areas: foreign affairs, economic policy, party affairs, military affairs and security. These committee members dealt directly with cabinet ministers and top party leaders, providing political and policy guidance (Quinn-Judge, 1985; *Bangkok Post*, 8 October 1982).

The Vietnamese ambassador to Cambodia from 1979 to 1985, Ngo Dien, who also served as B-68 deputy for foreign affairs, met daily with PRK Foreign Minister Hun Sen and passed on the latest messages from Hanoi, along with recommendations on specific policy problems. In addition to Dien and his deputy, there were 15 more Vietnamese advisers working with the heads of departments in the Foreign Ministry (Quinn-Judge, 1985; *Bangkok Post*, 8 October 1982). Prior to 1982, these Vietnamese specialists were called 'experts' and were actually authorized by Hanoi to make decisions on policy. During 1981, according to a Vietnamese source, they were ordered to use the term 'advisers' and to begin a transition to offering only opinions to PRK officials starting in 1982. The Vietnamese also began reducing the number of experts/advisors, both in the provinces and in the ministries (Kiernan, 1982: 194), but their influence remained a major factor in PRK policies. By the end of the decade, however, the Vietnamese advisers had departed and the PRK regime was making its own policy decisions.

The orientation of the PRK's foreign policy has been toward dependent alliance, reflecting the weakness of the regime and its aims of state-building and regime maintenance. The PRK's main foreign policy aim has been to get as much help as possible from Vietnam and the Soviet bloc to build a military-political-administrative apparatus that did not previously exist – to transform itself from a puppet regime into an administration ultimately capable of surviving without Vietnamese military occupation. This orientation has meant accepting tight integration into Vietnamese strategy for the entire Indo-Chinese peninsula. The PRK's embrace of the Vietnamese strategic principle of Indo-Chinese solidarity has gone so far as the adoption of Vietnamese holidays such as the anniversary of the 1954 Viet Minh victory over the French garrison at Dienbienphu (Chandler, 1985: 183).

More importantly, in February 1979, the PRK signed a Treaty of Friendship and Co-operation with Vietnam to last 25 years, which led in turn to a series of other treaties in military, economic, political and commercial fields. Beginning in 1984, the PRK began discussing with Vietnam and Laos an economic division of labor among the three countries. Vietnam and Cambodia agreed that Vietnam would provide technical expertise in agriculture and manufactured goods in return for Cambodian fish, rice, timber and forestry products. Such exchanges were already taking place by then through twinning arrangements between Vietnamese and Cambodian provinces (Hiebert, 1984). While these arrangements were probably equitable within the narrow confines of Vietnamese-Cambodian relations, they further tied Cambodia's fate to that of Vietnam.

Perhaps the most politically sensitive form of co-operation between the two states has been on the issue of Vietnamese immigration into Cambodia. The PRK agreed in 1982 to allow not only former Vietnamese residents but others who had entered the country after liberation from Pol Pot to settle in Cambodia. While the PRK ordered a tightening up on illegal immigration, it further approved the principle that 'trusted friends or close relatives' of Vietnamese residents could also come to visit or live, thus seeming to leave open the possibility of significantly greater Vietnamese immigration (PRK, 1982). (By 1986, however, Vietnamese residents nationwide were estimated at only about 260 000 – half the prewar level of Vietnamese population in Cambodia.) (Vickery, 1986b: 3; Hiebert, 1984).

Even in its early years, on the issues of Vietnamese troop withdrawal and a political settlement of the Cambodia conflict, which most directly affected regime survival, the PRK did assert its own interests which diverged somewhat from those of Hanoi. Because of its very weakness and instability, the PRK was able to resist Vietnamese suggestions in 1982–83 that it agree to the principle of Vietnamese troop withdrawal by a date certain (Chia Sim, 1988: 39). In negotiations in 1983–84 on a schedule for withdrawal of Vietnamese troops, the PRK would only agree to a ten-year timetable for withdrawal. Only in 1985 did the PRK regime agree to the complete withdrawal of Vietnamese troops by 1990. Similarly, Phnom Penh resisted Vietnamese suggestions for a dialogue between the PRK and Prince Norodom Sihanouk in 1982 and 1983 (Porter, 1988b: 125; Hun Sen, 1988: 28).

As a consequence of nearly a decade of war, political violence and dislocation, the PRK has faced formidable internal constraints on its efforts to build an orthodox Marxist-Leninist state through dependence on Vietnam. The most obvious constraint is the existence of a fully-armed, well-trained Khmer Rouge army, which is supplied by China from across the border in Thailand. The Khmer Rouge, with a troop strength estimated between 25 000 and 35 000 men, cannot control any large territory or population as long as the Vietnamese troop presence remains, but it has an unknown capacity to disrupt security and intimidate the population once the Vietnamese have left. While Norodom Sihanouk's *Moulinaka* has about 15 000 troops, of which about half operate in the interior of Cambodia, Sihanouk's forces retain mass popular support nearly two decades after his fall from power in 1970, and he commands international support as well (Porter, 1988a: 812–14).

Major internal constraints on PRK success are the political-psychological obstacles to the development of the PRK armed forces. By 1986 those armed forces were still troubled by difficulties in recruiting manpower, poor motivation and combat performance, draft-dodging and desertion (AFP dispatch, 21 June 1986; FBIS, 21 July 1986). These problems are related to the shaky legitimacy of the PRK. The hegemonial role of the Vietnamese discouraged most Khmer from making a political commitment in support of the PRK, given the suspicions of Vietnam left by collective memories of nineteenth century Vietnamese occupation. The residual popular fear of a return by Pol Pot's Khmer Rouge, on the other hand, has encouraged acquiescence in the *status quo*, so it helps PRK to remain in power. Since the PRK is the only administration that could conceivably block the re-emergence of Khmer Rouge rule, there is little predisposition to want it to be dissolved.

An economy that has never fully recovered its prewar production levels and fears of popular reactions to government interference in the economy make the PRK an extraordinarily weak state. In late 1982 an FAO mission called the PRK 'a system in which there are no taxes, no central bank, no backing for currency and not even levy of fees for supply of services like electricity, transport and water' (FAO, 1982: 14). By 1983 the amount of land planted to rice during the monsoon season had stagnated at 1.3 million hectares compared to 2.4 million hectares in 1968–69, the last year of peace. The 1.7 million ton 1983 rice crop was 30 per cent smaller than the 1968–69 crop, but it had to feed a population that was probably about the same as the 1969 population – around seven million people (Kohlschuetter, 1984; Charny and Spragens, 1984: 92, 98; Vickery, 1986: xvi; Migozzi, 1973: 208).

By 1988 the PRK had still not yet been able to reach its prewar level of agricultural output, and several years earlier PRK officials had predicted that it would be 1994 before it could so so (Tep Henn, 1988; Kohlschuetter, 1984). The failure to restore prewar food production levels reflects the destruction of the rural infrastructure, shortages of cattle and buffalo and a dearth of trained technical specialists, most of whom either died during the DK period or fled from Cambodia (Shaplen, 1986: 74; FAO, 1982: 6; Spragens, 1984). But the most critical constraint on agricultural recovery is the labor force, reduced by the massive deaths of the Pol Pot period to about the size it had been in the mid-1950s, when it had to feed about 4.7 million people (Charny and Spragens, 1984: 98; Spragens, 1984). Adult males are also physically weak from poor nutrition, and over half of the children suffer from moderate to severe malnutrition (FAO, 1982: 54–7).

There were no agricultural taxes or required sales to the state from 1979 to 1983, because the PRK was reluctant to take any rice away from hard-pressed peasants. The PRK was thus totally dependent on foreign food assistance – from both the Soviet Union and international organizations – to feed its civil servants and military personnel (Vickery, 1986b: 4–5; Vickery, 1986a: 130). Agricultural taxes have been collected since 1984, but only on production above the average level for the country. Moreover, the government has relied on exhortation rather than coercion in getting farmers to sell their crops to the state (Vickery, 1986a: 145; Hiebert, 1984: 4–5). The PRK apparently was able to purchase less than a third of the 300 000 tons it hoped to obtain from the 1985 harvest, mainly because it cannot pay sufficiently high prices (Hiebert, 1986: 5).

The dominant factor in the PRK's external environment thus far has been Vietnam's willingness to make the sacrifices necessary to build up a new state apparatus virtually from scratch and its commitment to complete withdrawal by late 1989, which forced Phnom Penh to plan for the eventual assumption of main responsibility for its own survival. During 1979–80, the PRK administrative structure was only barely functioning. After nearly a decade of Vietnamese occupation, however, the PRK administration had stability and even some self-confidence. Initially the Kampuchean People's Revolutionary Armed Forces (KPRAF) consisted of the remnants of the East Zone opponents of Pol Pot. Two years later, under Vietnamese guidance, it had four brigades on their way to becoming two divisions. By 1988, as the Vietnamese withdrawal began to pick up speed, there were between 45 000 and 60 000 regular army troops and another 100 000 militiamen. Thousands of officers have returned from training in Vietnam and other Soviet bloc countries (McBeth, 1984: 26; Eiland, 1985: 108–9; *Asahi Shimbun*, 1988: 7).

The Soviet Union provided an estimated US$ 90 million in economic assistance to the PRK during its first five years of existence, supplying all of the country's petroleum, machinery, equipment and trucks, as well as consumer goods and raw materials, in return for Cambodia's rubber production (*The Nations Review*, 19 March 1984; Dyuzhilov, 1985). But this aid was insufficient to permit the agricultural economy to return to its prewar level of production.

Foes of the PRK and its Vietnamese sponsors, led by China, the US and ASEAN, on the other hand, have ensured that the resistance forces will remain in the field, while effectively preventing aid from the capitalist world to the PRK for economic recovery and development (Charny and Spragens, 1984: 1–16). ASEAN succeeded in getting the rump DK regime seated in the United Nations General Assembly from 1979 through 1981, and the same body has seated the CGDK repeatedly since its formation in 1982. While the PRK regime is recognized by the Soviet Union and other Soviet-bloc states, outside that sphere only India offers recognition.

On the other hand, external supporters of the resistance forces fighting against the PRK, including the PRC, are constrained in some ways by the fact that the Khmer Rouge forces are almost universally regarded with moral revulsion. As Vietnam moved toward complete withdrawal of its troops by late 1989, external policies that might have increased the prospect of a Khmer Rouge takeover became increasingly unacceptable. The major capitalist states in particular found themselves moving inexorably toward the acceptance of the PRK as the main barrier to Pol Pot's forces.

CONCLUSION

The foreign policy of Cambodia exhibits a striking decline from the relatively successful maneuvering of Norodom Sihanouk in pursuit of independence through the disasters of the Khmer Republic and DK to the dependent foreign policy of the PRK. This chapter has shown how that decline has reflected progressive destruction of the country's capabilities for maintaining independence, and finally even its ability to build a state that can maintain order without foreign intervention. The US military intervention in Vietnam, which caused the Vietnam War to spill over into Cambodia, introduced the single most important constraint on Sihanouk's ability to maneuver successfully. The weaknesses of the economy and government institutions, however, also limited the capabilities of the Royal Government and contributed to its downfall.

The American encouragement of the Lon Nol group to believe it could solve Cambodia's problems by waging war against the Vietnamese, and the subsequent US destruction of much of Cambodian rural society further undermined those capabilities. The ultra-leftist internal policies of the Khmer Rouge leadership completed that process of weakening the economic, political and military bases of Cambodian independence. Without this string of disastrous developments, which left the population ready in 1979 to accept Vietnamese troops, Cambodian foreign policy could have succeeded in maintaining its autonomy from Vietnam.

This analysis also highlights the critical importance of realistic appraisals of internal and external circumstances. While the definition of the situation of three of the four regimes began with a fear of Vietnamese aggressive designs on Cambodia, only Sihanouk analyzed the situation in all its complexity, recognizing both opportunities for maneuver and the perils of confrontation with the country's more powerful neighbor.

050

BIBLIOGRAPHY

Armstrong, John P. (1964), *Sihanouk Speaks* (New York: Walker and Company).

Barnett, Anthony (1980), 'A Time for Pragmatic Marriage', *New Statesman*, 14 March, 388–9.

Barnett, Anthony, Ben Kiernan and Chanthou Boua (1980), 'Bureaucracy of Death', *New Statesman*, 2 May, 669–76.

Carney, Timothy (1982a), 'Kampuchea in 1981: Fragile Stalemate', *Asian Survey*, January, 78–87.

Carney, Timothy (1982b) 'Heng Samrin's Armed Forces and a Military Balance in Cambodia', paper for Princeton Conference on Kampuchea, 12–14 November.

Chanda, Nayan (1981), 'The Survivors' Party', *Far Eastern Economic Review*, 12 June, 22.

Chanda, Nayan (1986), *Brother Enemy* (San Diego: Harcourt Brace Jovanovich).

Chandler, David, with Ben Kiernan and Muy Hong Lim, *The Early Phases of Liberation in Northwestern Cambodia: Conversations with Peang Sophi* (Melbourne: Centre of Southeast Asian Studies, Monash University).

Chandler, David (1986), 'Cambodia in 1984: Historical Patterns Reasserted?' *Southeast Asian Affairs, 1985* (London: Heinemann Educational).

Charny, Joel and John Spragens, Jr. (1984), *Obstacles to Recovery in Vietnam and Kampuchea* (Boston: Oxfam America).

Chia Sim (1988), Speech in Prey Veng Province, Phnom Penh Domestic Service, 30 October 1988, FBIS, 16 November.

Democratic Kampuchea (1978), *Livre Noir: Faits et Preuves des Actes d'Agression et d'Annexion du Vietnam Contre le Kampuchea* (Phnom Penh: Ministry of Foreign Affairs).

Devillers, Philippe (1963), 'Dynamics of Power in Cambodia', in Saul Rose (ed.), *Politics in Southern Asia* (New York: St Martins Press).

Dyuzhilov, Ivan (1985), 'Trade with USSR Surveyed', *Foreign Trade*, 4, 25–6, trans. in JPRS-SEA-85-107, 6 July 1985, 114–17.

Eiland, Michael (1985), 'Kampuchea in 1984'. *Asian Survey*, January, 106–11.

Food and Agricultural Organization, Office for Special Relief Operations (1982), *Kampuchea: Report of the Food and Agriculture Assessment Mission, October-November 1982*.

Forcier, Pierre (1975), 'La Rupture des Accords de Coopération Entre Le Cambodge et Les USA: Quelque Conséquences' (Ottawa: Institute for International Co-operation, University of Ottawa).

Foreign Broadcast Information Service (1978), 'Chinese Delegation Supports Pol Pot's Treaty offer to Hanoi', *Trends*, 15 November.

Gordon, Bernard (1966), *The Dimensions of Conflict in Southeast Asia* (Englewood Cliffs, NJ: Prentice-Hall).

Gurtov, Melvin (1975), *China and Southeast Asia: The Politics of Survival* (Baltimore: The Johns Hopkins University Press).

Heder, Stephen R. (1979a) 'Kampuchean-Vietnamese Conflict'. *Southeast Asian Affairs 1979* (London: Heineman/Educational).

Heder, Stephen R. (1979b), 'Kampuchea's Armed Struggle: The Origins of an Independent Revolution', *Bulletin of Concerned Asian Scholars* 11, No. 1, 22–5.

Heder, Stephen R. (1980a), 'Revolution and Counter-Revolution in Kampuchea', *AMPO: Japan-Asia*, 12, No. 3, 24–33.

Heder, Stephen R. (1980b), 'From Pol Pot to Pen Sovan to the Villages', in Khien Theeravit and MacAlister Brown (eds), *Indochina and Problems of Security and Stability in Southeast Asia* (Bangkok: Chulalongkorn University Press).

Heder, Stephen R. (1980c), *Kampuchea October 1979–August 1980*, mimeographed.

Heder, Stephen R. (1980d), *Kampuchean Occupation and Resistance* (Bangkok: Institute of Asian Studies, Chulalongkorn University) Asian Studies Monographs No. 27.

Heder, Stephen R. (1981a), 'The Kampuchean-Vietnamese Conflict', in David W. P. Elliott (ed.), *The Third Indochina Conflict* (Boulder, Col.: Westview Press).

Heder, Stephen R. (1981b), interview with Hem Samin, original transcript. 8 July.

Hersh, Seymour M. (1983), *The Preview of Power: Kissinger in the Nixon White House* (New York: Summit).

Hiebert, Murray (1984), 'Cambodia and Vietnam: Costs of the Alliance', *Indochina Issues*, 69, September.

Hildebrand, George C. and Gareth Porter (1976), *Cambodia: Starvation and Revolution* (New York: Monthly Review Press).

Hun Sen (1988), Interview with *Tap Chi Quoc Phong Toan Dan*, Hanoi Domestic Service, 18 June 1988, FBIS, 21 June.

Ito, Tadashi (1978), 'Cambodia: Run by the Jungle-Green Comrades', *The Japan Times*, 20 October.

Kiernan, Ben (1979), 'Vietnam and the Governments and People of Kampuchea', *Bulletin of Concerned Asian Scholars* 11, No. 4, 19–25.

Kiernan, Ben (1980), 'New Light on the Origins of the Vietnam-Kampuchea Conflict', *Bulletin of Concerned Asian Scholars*, 12, No. 4, 61–5.

Kiernan, Ben (1981), 'The New Political Structure in Kampuchea', *Dyason House Papers*, 81, No. 2, 1–8.

Kiernan, Ben and Chanthou Boua (1982). *Peasants and Politics in Kampuchea: 1942–198* (London: Zed Press, 1982).

Kiernan, Ben (1983b), 'Wild Chickens, Farm Chickens and Cormorants: Kampuchea's Eastern Zone under Pol Pot', in David P. Chandler and Ben Kiernan (eds), *Revolution and its Aftermath in Kampuchea: Eight Essays* (New Haven: Yale University) Southeast Asia Studies Monograph Series No. 25.

Kiernan, Ben (1984), 'Why Pol Pot? Roots of the Cambodian Tragedy', *Indochina Issues* 52.

Kiernan, Ben (1985), *How Pol Pot Came to Power* (London: Verso).

Kiljunen, Kimo (ed.) (1984), *Kampuchea: Decade of Genocide* (London: Zed Press).

Kirk, Donald (1971), *Wider War* (New York: Praeger).

Kohlschuetter, Andreas (1984), 'Karl Marx Must Wait', *Die Zeit*, 27 April, 9–10.

Leifer, Michael (1967), *Cambodia: The Search for Security* (New York: Praeger).

McBeth, John (1984), 'Fear of Khmerization', *Far Eastern Economic Review*, 2 August, 26–7.

Migozzi, Jacques (1973), *Faits et Problèmes de Population* (Paris: Edition de Centre National de la Recherche Scientifique).

Osborne, Milton (1973), *Politics and Power in Cambodia* (Camberwell, Australia: Longman).

Osborne, Milton (1979), *Before Kampuchea: Preludes to Tragedy* (North Sydney: Allen & Unwin).

Paringaux, R. P. (1979), 'Had It Not Been for the Vietnamese Attack We Would Have Given Our People Affluence by 1980', *Le Monde*, 2 June.

People's Republic of Kampuchea, Council of Ministers (1982), Circular No. 38 'Concerning Organization and Administration of those Vietnamese People Making Their Livelihood, Staying and Dwelling in Kampuchea', 9 October.

People's Republic of Kampuchea, Phnom Penh Domestic Service (1986). Documentary Article on PRK-USSR Co-operation Agreements from 7 January 1979 Liberation to 1985, 1 November.

Pomonti, Jean-Claude and Serge Thion (1971), *Des Courtisans aux Partisans* (Paris: Gallimard).

Porter, Gareth (1981a), 'Vietnamese Policy and the Indochina Crisis', in David W. P. Elliot (ed.), *The Third Indochina Conflict* (Boulder, Col.: Westview Press).

Porter, Gareth (1981b), 'Vietnam in Kampuchea: Aims and Options', *Indochina Issues* 16, May.

Porter, Gareth (1983), 'Vietnamese Communist Policy towards Kampuchea: 1930–1970', in David P. Chandler and Ben Kiernan, (eds), *Revolution and its Aftermath in Kampuchea: Eight Essays* (New Haven: Yale University) Southeast Asia Studies Monograph Series, No. 25.

Porter, Gareth (1988a), 'Cambodia: Sihanouk's Initiative', *Foreign Affairs*, Vol. 66, No. 4, Spring.

Porter, Gareth (1988b), 'Toward a Kampuchean Peace Settlement: History and Dynamics of Sihanouk's Negotiations,' *Southeast Asian Affairs 1988* (Singapore: ISEAS).

Prud'homme, Rémy (1969), *L'Economie du Cambodge* (Paris: Presses Universitaires de France).

Quinn-Judge, Paul (1985), 'Cambodia: Keystone of Hanoi's Plan for Indochina', *Christian Science Monitor*, 22 October.

Roy, Daniel (1970), 'The Coup in Phnom Penh', in Marvin and Susan Gettleman, Lawrence and Carol Kaplan (eds), *Conflict in Indochina* (New York: Vintage).

Shaplen, Robert (1966), *The Lost Revolution* (New York: Harper and Row).

Shaplen, Robert (1986), 'The Captivity of Cambodia', *New Yorker*, 5 May.

Shawcross, William (1979), *Sideshow: Kissinger, Nixon and the Destruction of Cambodia* (New York: Simon and Schuster).

Sihanouk, Norodom with Wilfred Burchett (1973), *My War With the CIA* (New York: Pantheon).

Sihanouk, Norodom (1980), *War and Hope: The Case for Cambodia* (New York: Pantheon).

Smith, Roger (1964), 'Cambodia', in George McT. Kahin (ed.), *Governments and Politics of Southeast Asia* (Ithaca, NY: Cornell University Press).

Smith, Roger (1965), *Cambodia's Foreign Policy* (Ithaca, NY: Cornell University Press).

Spragens, Jr., John (1984), 'Hunger in Cambodia: Getting Beyond Relief', *Indochina Issues* 43, February.

Summers, Laura (1981), 'Co-operatives in Democratic Kampuchea', unpublished paper prepared for SSRC Conference on Kampuchea, Chiang Mai, Thailand, 11–13 August 1981.

Taylor, Jay (1976), *China and Southeast Asia* (New York: Praeger Publishers).

Tep Henn (1988), Statement for Vietnamese radio and television, 7 January 1988, FBIS, 19 January.

Thion, Serge (1982), 'The Pattern of Cambodian Politics', paper for Princeton University Conference on Kampuchea.

Thion, Serge and Michael Vickery (1981), *Cambodia: Background and Issues*. (Phnom Penh: Church World Service Kampuchea Program).

Truong Nhu Tang, with David Chanoff and Doan Van Toai (1985), *A Viet Cong Memoir* (New York: Vintage).

United States House of Representatives, Committee on Government Operations (1972), *US Economic Assistance for the Khmer Republic (Cambodia) Thirteenth Report*. 16 June.

United States National Security Council (1958), NSC 5809, 'US Policy in Mainland Southeast Asia', 2 April. Declassified document.

Vickery, Michael (1984), *Cambodia, 1975–1982* (Boston: South End Press).

Vickery, Michael (1986a), *Kampuchea: Politics, Economics and Society* (Boulder, Col.: Lynne Reinner).

Vickery, Michael (1986b), 'Cambodia's Tenuous Progress', *Indochina Issues*, 63, January.

Willmott, William E. (1967), *The Chinese in Cambodia* (Vancouver: University of British Columbia Publications Center).

14 Lao Foreign Policy
Martin Stuart-Fox

As the smallest and weakest of the three states of Indo-China, and the only one without access to the sea, Laos faces severe constraints in the formulation and pursuit of foreign policy. The Lao People's Democratic Republic (LPDR) is economically underdeveloped, socially fragmented and its military weakness is reflected in the presence for most of its existence of substantial foreign forces on Lao territory. Yet even given such limitations, opportunities do exist for the pursuit of specifically Lao national interests – notably preservation of the Lao state, development of a Lao national identity, and maximization of internationally provided resources for economic development.

The abolition of the 600-year-old Lao monarchy and proclamation of the Lao People's Democratic Republic (LPDR) on 2 December 1975 marked an abrupt restructuring of Lao foreign policy (Holsti, 1982). Despite the formation of three nominally neutral coalition governments (in 1957, 1962 and 1974) the foreign policy of the Royal Lao government (RLG) had, since Lao independence was achieved in 1953, been predominantly pro-Western. Throughout what the present government terms the '30-year struggle' from 1945 to 1975, the RLG was a major recipient of American aid, advice, and political pressure. Its foreign policy was tailored accordingly. In 1975, however, the LPDR became a member of the Communist bloc, with a stated foreign policy of close alignment with Vietnam and the Soviet Union.

This radical re-direction of Lao foreign policy initially has left the country even more economically dependent and less autonomous than it had been previously. As the government of a nominally neutral state, the RLG had at various times drawn upon aid from both the Soviet bloc and the West. After 1975 American and other Western aid all but dried up, and the new regime found itself heavily dependent on the Soviet bloc for aid and advice. There were, however, compensations. The former *de facto* division of the country into spheres of influence – Chinese in the north, Vietnamese in the east, and Thai and American in the population centres along the Mekong River – gave way to a unitary Lao state in which for the first time since independence the entire population shared in a single

administration and officially a single political culture. The opportunity was thus provided for the ruling Lao People's Revolutionary
Party (LPRP) to build an integrated and unified Lao nation out
of a disparate and divided population. In addition, both regime
maintenance and military security were assured. These were benefits
for which a high degree of dependence on the Socialist Republic of
Vietnam (SRV) was not, in the view of the Lao government, too
high a price to pay (cf. Stuart-Fox, 1981a).

HISTORICAL CONSTRAINTS: GEOGRAPHY AND ETHNOGRAPHY

As a landlocked state Laos is necessarily dependent on the goodwill
of neighboring countries for transshipment of both imports and
exports. In practical terms, this necessitates maintaining good
relations with either Thailand or Vietnam, and preferably both.
Access to the south through Cambodia is a long-term possibility, but
not presently practicable. In the meantime Laos is dependent on
road access via Vietnam or on road or rail via Thailand.

The geographical frontiers of the present Lao state are in part an
historical legacy of French colonialism. Only the arrival of the French
in Indo-China prevented what remained of the Lao principalities
from being incorporated permanently into a greater Thai state. As
it was, most of the populous west bank territories remained part of
Thailand – all the northeastern Isan region with its predominantly
Lao population. What remained, the sparsely populated east bank
areas of Champassak and Vientiane, together with the northern
principality of Luang Prabang, was eventually incorporated by the
French into their protectorate of Laos. In effect, therefore, demarcation of the western border of Laos left the majority of ethnic Lao
within the state of Thailand. Less than 20 per cent of ethnic Lao
remain in Laos. The Mekong river, which traditionally had served
as a means of communication between Lao territories, became for
much of its length an artificial barrier between Lao and Lao.

The northern, eastern and southern borders of Laos make somewhat better sense, at least geographically. But even these frontiers
divide ethnic groups – the Lu and some Sino-Tibetan hill tribes in
the north, the hill Tai in the northeast, some Austronesian tribal
groups in the south. The resultant racial mix in Laos leaves the
ethnic Lao with a bare majority of the total 3.6 million population.

Some 60 ethnic groups, few of which have much in common either with each other or with the Lao, make up the remainder. As all the principal ethnic groups spill over the frontiers of Laos into neighboring states, a supra-ethnic Lao national identity has been slow to develop. Not surprisingly, creation of such an identity remains a priority goal for the present regime, and a major consideration in the formulation of foreign policy.

Geography and ethnography have been the primary factors shaping the historical relationship between Laos and its neighbors. China was traditionally remote and benevolent: nominal tributary relations did not weigh heavily upon the Lao. Only after 1949 did the People's Republic of China take a closer interest in Lao affairs. The presence of American military personnel in Laos led the Chinese to carve out a sphere of interest in the north of the country through construction of a road network running south from the Chinese-Lao border. To this day, access to northern Laos is easier from Yunnan than it is from the Lao capital, Vientiane, and the present Lao regime is acutely aware of the potential the Chinese possess for interference in the region.

The role of Laos' next two most powerful neighbors, Thailand and Vietnam, has historically been of more pressing concern. Over the centuries both states extended their territories south at the expense of the Khmer empire. But then so too did the Lao, and Cambodia has been the sole neighboring state the Lao have never had cause to fear. However, whereas the Vietnamese concentrated their forces first against Champa and then against the Khmer, Thai expansion in the nineteenth and twentieth centuries occurred at the expense of both Khmer and Lao. Historically, therefore, Vietnam has presented less of a threat to Lao sovereignty than have the Thai. The very cultural similarity between Thai and Lao has constituted a threat of national extinction for the Lao, for if 80 per cent of all ethnic Lao can be absorbed within the Thai state, why not the remainder?

By contrast, Vietnam has been seen in a rather different light, as a potential counterweight to the Thai rather than a major threat to Lao sovereignty. For the Pathet Lao, the eventual victors in the 30-year struggle, close and friendly relations with the Vietnamese Communist movement was the *sine qua non* for gaining political power. Over the years, the revolutionary Lao-Vietnamese relationship was broadened and strengthened, based as it was on a common ideology and shared experience. Close personal ties also developed between the revolutionary élites of Vietnam and Laos, both of which traced their origins to the same Indochinese Communist Party (Langer and Zasloff, 1970).

Since the declaration of the LPDR at the end of 1975, this historical relationship has continued to exert a major influence on Lao foreign policy – not through sentiment, nor from a sense of gratitude, but through reinforcement of institutional ties which were already in place.

THE LAO COMMUNIST REGIME AND THE FOREIGN POLICY PROCESS

Laos is a People's Republic, modelled along classical Communist lines. Despite the enlargement of the LPRP Central Committee at both the Third and Fourth Party congresses, the governing élite remains remarkably small. There is a notable overlap, especially at the upper levels of power, between personnel in the Party, the government, the army and mass organizations (Stuart-Fox, 1986a: 81–4). Political power is thus highly concentrated: decision-making tends to take place primarily at the highest level of the party; that is, by the Politburo and the party secretariat. This is the case particularly where foreign policy is concerned, for a number of reasons. The first is that almost all foreign policy decisions are political; few are of a technical nature that could be safely left to Ministry officials. A second reason is that the Ministry of Foreign Affairs is the only Lao government department which by mutual agreement and respect for Lao sensitivities has had no Vietnamese advisors attached to it. In theory, Vietnamese influence on Lao foreign policy is exercised by the same means as those open to other nations, through official representation from the Vietnamese ambassador and his staff, or from visiting Vietnamese delegations. In practice, however, such influence is rarely exerted because the Vietnamese enjoy much more effective access to the upper echelons of the LPRP. The Lao Ministry of Foreign Affairs thus tends to be by-passed since all major decisions, even down to provisions of visas for visiting scholars, are routinely referred to the party secretariat.

The figure primarily responsible for foreign affairs in the LPDR is Phoune Sipaseuth, sixth ranking member of the LPRP Politburo, member of the party secretariat, member of the Inner Cabinet of the Council of Government, and Minister of Foreign Affairs. Below him in the Ministry stand five vice-ministers, the first of whom,

Thongsavath Khaykhamphithoune, often stands in for the frequently ailing Phoune. Thongsavath is a member of the Party Central Committee, so also is Inpong Khaignavong, who serves as vice-president of the Committee's Foreign Affairs Commission. None of the other three vice-ministers are Central Committee members. The five vice-ministers are each nominally responsible for one of the five departments into which the Ministry is divided.

Foreign policy decision-making in the LPDR takes place within the context of a clearly defined ideological framework. All members of the LPRP Politburo are committed Communists, all veterans of the 30-year struggle. During that struggle they learned the importance of receiving assistance from the Communist Bloc – from the Soviet Union, from China, but most of all from Vietnam. Proletarian internationalism is more to Lao leaders than high sounding rhetoric: it is the only guarantee they have that their country in a time of peace will continue to receive from 'fraternal Socialist states' the greater part of the economic assistance the country requires to pursue its development goals. But the Lao recognize that in return for such assistance they must be prepared to pay more than lip-service to the concept of international Socialist solidarity. They have faithfully endorsed every foreign policy initiative emanating from Moscow or Hanoi.

While the revolutionary leadership in Laos proclaims its belief in the inevitable victory of Socialism, it is acutely conscious of the opposing forces ranged against it. These take the form of an unholy alliance between US imperialism, Chinese 'great power hegemonism', and Thai militarism. In order to resist this combination the Lao have accepted the Vietnamese position on the need for especially close relations among the states of Indochina. In the Lao view, without such solidarity, the Indochinese states severally could not hope to withstand the threats posed to their respective revolutions. Indo-Chinese solidarity is therefore described as a 'law' of the revolutions of all three states, without which none could succeed. Together the above factors constitute the 'ideological imperative' (Gunn, 1980) underlying Lao foreign policy.

DOMESTIC RESOURCES AND CONSTRAINTS

Actual foreign policy formulation in the LPDR, while it seeks within the ideological context outlined above to pursue the broad objectives of national security and Socialist construction (Stuart-Fox, 1981c), does so within the constraints imposed by domestic resources and the prevailing external environment. In the case of Laos, the domestic resources available to promote either broad objective are quite inadequate to ensure its realization. Laos has the resources neither to ensure its national security nor to carry through its desired program of Socialist construction. Both require international assistance to an extent that places particular demands on Lao foreign policy.

To ensure national security requires, from the point of view of the present regime, both defense of existing frontiers and maintenance of the regime itself. However, the Lao People's Army (LPA) is small in size, numbering some 50 000 poorly equipped, poorly trained, and poorly motivated. Under no circumstances could the LPA withstand major sustained incursion into Lao territory by any of its more powerful neighbors. Neutrality on the Swiss or Swedish model backed by convincingly powerful defense forces is not an option for Laos (Stuart-Fox, 1982b).

It is even doubtful whether the LPA could effectively contain anti-government insurgents supported by neighboring states without Vietnamese military presence in Laos. The weakness of political and administrative institutions, combined with a high degree of *de facto* provincial autonomy, does little to enhance the legitimacy of the regime in much of the country. Nor does it provide an effective basis for containing resistance forces. Thus, Vietnamese troops were stationed on Lao territory not only to defend the LPDR from external threat, but also to defend the regime from internal challenge, until improvement of relations between Laos and its neighbors permitted their withdrawal by early 1989.

The weakness of LPDR leadership control in some areas derives from the ethnic composition of the Lao population, and the strategic location of minority groups (as noted above). Difficulties in communication, shortages of trained personnel, and lack of consumer necessities, all contribute (especially in the far north along the border with China) to limit central Lao government authority. Under such conditions, the regime has no real option but to compromise on questions of sovereignty – not over territory, but over people, their movements and contacts.

Poor administrative control over mountainous regions makes it difficult for the regime to legitimize its exercise of state power (Stuart-Fox, 1983). Where the government provides next to no services, it has little on which to base claims for allegiance. Where attempts are made to interfere with traditional life styles, to abolish 'superstitious' religious practices or modify agricultural methods considered destructive of national resources, the government is even less likely to gain the support of tribal minorities (Wekkin, 1982; Lee, 1982). Foreign policy has thus to assist in creating conditions in border regions which reduce threats to the security of the regime, and reinforce its political legitimacy.

Economic weakness is another internal constraint. Laos is one of the least developed countries. *Per capita* income amounts to only about US$ 140 per annum at free market rates of exchange. Less than 1 per cent of the population is employed in the industrial sector, which accounts for only 7 per cent of GDP (Stuart-Fox, 1986a: 119–20). And Laos is even more economically dependent than it is poor. Hydro-electricity accounts for at least half of all Lao exports. All is sold to Bangkok. So important is this trade to Laos that Vientiane cannot afford to use it as a bargaining counter with Bangkok. Even when Thai-Lao relations were at their nadir during the 1984–85 'three villages' dispute, and Thailand was holding up trans-shipment of fully 273 categories of Lao imports said to be of strategic importance, the flow of Lao electricity to northeast Thailand continued. Meanwhile other exports – notably tin, gypsum, timber, and various forest products – are becoming increasingly tied up in barter agreements with Vietnam and the Soviet Union in return for basic consumer commodities, petroleum products, and to meet the cost of 'aid projects' in Laos. These arrangements limit Lao borrowing from the West by reducing the LPDR's ability to repay interest in convertible currency. They thus limit Lao capacity to purchase Western technology.

In the short term it is unlikely that Lao exports will significantly increase. Mineral resources will be difficult to exploit commercially. Timber provides opportunities for increased exploitation, but access to valuable stands is limited by difficult terrain and poor communications. Thus whereas in the long term, the favourable ratio of population to resources should enable Laos to improve living standards and raise GDP, in the short term the LPDR is entirely dependent on foreign aid to finance even the most basic economic development. Put another way, budgetary receipts in Laos barely meet present administrative costs. Thus even minimal improvements in medical, educational, agricultural or administrative services have to be financed by foreign aid. Lao economic dependency is thus all but absolute.

So fragile is the Lao economy that it is particularly vulnerable to all forms of economic pressure, by Thailand through unilateral closure of the Thai-Lao border and disruption of important cross-border trade, or by China with similar effect. Alternative access via Vietnam to some extent is now able to alleviate closure of the Thai border, but the cost of transportation via Vietnam to the Lao Mekong towns remains high, and the same range of consumer products is not available.

THE RECENT EXTERNAL ENVIRONMENT

Just as it proved impossible to extricate Laos from the Vietnam War, despite the Geneva Conference of 1962, so it has proved impossible for the LPDR to isolate itself from the tensions which have convulsed the region since 1975, particularly the Vietnamese invasion of Cambodia, and China's border war with Vietnam (Stuart-Fox, 1980). The withdrawal of the United States between 1973 and 1975 opened the way for Soviet-Chinese rivalry for influence over the new Communist states of Indo-China. Through no fault of its own, Laos had by 1979 become entangled in this conflict, and had (perhaps a little reluctantly) followed Vietnam into the Soviet camp.

Fully half of all annual economic assistance in the LPDR comes from the USSR. So too does all more advanced military equipment (such as its single squadron of 20 Mig-21s, its transport aircraft, anti-aircraft guns, and SA-7 surface-to-air missiles). The Soviet Union has as many as a thousand political, military, and economic personnel in Laos at any one time, advising Lao ministries, maintaining equipment, and working on aid projects. Soviet experts are responsible for drawing up the Lao five-year plans, for running the television station, for maintaining communications. More than a thousand Lao students are studying in the Soviet Union (Stuart-Fox, 1986a).

The high Soviet profile in Laos worries the Chinese. Beijing has criticized the installation of Soviet military communications and radar facilities at Vientiane, and the construction of a military airfield at Phongsavan on the Plain of Jars in northern Laos. However, the Chinese are not in a position to do much about it. When the Lao government called for the withdrawal of Chinese road construction teams from northern Laos in 1979, Beijing complied. Subsequently the Chinese made some half-hearted moves to destabilize the government through the training and infiltration of Lao insurgents from southern China back into Laos (Stuart-Fox, 1981b). By 1983, however, the Chinese appear to have decided on an alternative longer-term policy – one which sought to restore Chinese influence in northern Laos by more traditional means, through reducing tensions along the border and encouraging cross-border contacts. In June 1988 Laos and China raised their diplomatic relations to ambassadorial level. The friendly relations subsequently prevailing along the Lao-Chinese border thus contrast with the tension along the Vietnamese-Chinese border – a difference officially interpreted in Vientiane as part of a subtle Chinese plot to drive a wedge between Laos and Vietnam (Stuart-Fox, 1986a: 190).

Another external constraint on the present Lao regime has been the continued hostility of Thailand. Much of this hostility has been ideologically based and exacerbated by resentment over the extent of Vietnamese influence in Vientiane. The Thai authorities have taken every opportunity to punish Laos – by holding up delivery of imports, by limiting the number of border crossing points, or by closing the border entirely after some incident on the Mekong. Only briefly during 1979 did Bangkok attempt to improve relations with Vientiane with the aim of increasing Thai influence in the LPDR. But with the overthrow of General Kriangsak Chomanond, author of this alternative approach, Thai policy reverted to its former hostility. Thai military occupation of three disputed border villages in 1984 brought relations to a new low, and renewed ancient Lao fears of pan-Thai irredentism (Ngaosyvathn, 1985; cf. Viraphol, 1985). An even more serious border conflict from December 1987 to February 1988 left hundreds of casualties, but rather surprisingly, much friendlier relations developed once a cease-fire was arranged.

The principal external constraint on Lao foreign policy, however, has been neither the Soviet presence, nor Chinese displeasure, nor Thai hostility, but rather the 'special relationship' that binds Laos closely to Vietnam. Under the terms of the 1977 25-year Lao-Vietnamese Treaty of Friendship and Co-operation, not only can Vietnamese forces be stationed in Laos, but Vietnamese assistance is provided in everything from party organization and cadre training, to economic development and internal security. The very multiplicity of Vietnamese relationships with Laos makes it impossible for the Lao to disregard Vietnamese interests when formulating their foreign policy. Meetings of the foreign ministers of Laos, Cambodia and Vietnam expressly formulate common policy for all three Indo-Chinese states.

The Vietnamese influence in Laos extends far beyond regular meetings of foreign ministers, however. It is exercised on a series of interlocking levels – party to party, government to government, army to army, and even local administration to local administration through the twinning of Lao and Vietnamese provinces (Stuart-Fox, 1987). Add to these channels the influence of Vietnamese advisors attached to the security apparatus of the Ministry of the Interior, and it is at once evident why the present Lao regime cannot but take account of Vietnamese wishes. Party to party relations are particularly close at the highest level, but are consolidated by the exchange of delegations, and by Vietnamese involvement in training Lao cadres. The need for 'unity with Vietnam' has been proclaimed by LPRP Secretary-General Kaysone Phomvihane as the primary criterion for 'fostering the revolutionary qualities of all party members' (*Tap Chi Cong San*, March 1985). All Lao cadres are taught that solidarity between the three states of Indochina constitutes a 'law of history' which no one can oppose. Not surprisingly, no one does.

The importance of the Vietnamese connection as the principal external constraint on the formulation of Lao foreign policy derives from Vietnamese perceptions of the strategic importance of Laos for the defense of Vietnam. The persistence displayed by the Vietnamese in building up a close and enduring relationship with the Lao revolutionary movement throughout the '30-year struggle' provides ample evidence of Vietnamese determination to exercise a dominant influence in Laos. The Vietnamese were not prepared to settle for a neutral Laos, nor even a Communist Laos neutral in the Sino-Soviet dispute once Vietnam had opted for the Soviet side (Stuart-Fox, 1980). Hanoi is determined that Laos will remain a close and faithful ally. There is limited opportunity for the LPDR to do otherwise.

OUTPUT: OBJECTIVES AND STRATEGIES OF LAO FOREIGN POLICY

As noted above, since the present Lao regime came to power in 1975, it has encountered some difficulty in establishing its legitimacy to succeed the Lao monarchy. Not only is the regime administratively and politically weak, but insurgent forces based for the most part in Thailand have directly challenged its authority. Not surprisingly, therefore, maintenance of the regime itself has been a primary objective of Lao foreign policy. Efforts have been made to persuade both Thailand and China to deny the use of their territory to Lao insurgents. At the same time LPDR leadership has cemented relations with its most consistent and determined foreign backer – the Socialist Republic of Vietnam. The closeness of the Lao relationship with Vietnam has therefore to be seen in the light of the regime's need for strong support in the face of continuing threats to its legitimacy and stability. Should these threats diminish, reliance on Vietnam would be less essential.

The alliance with Vietnam has also been of importance in ensuring the security of the state, and the inviolability of its frontiers. To this end some compromise on demarcation of the Lao-Vietnamese border proved necessary, and not too painful. Availability of Vietnamese forces deters not only internal dissent, but also any attempt by what the Lao perceive as a hostile and potentially expansionist Thai state to seize Lao territory (as happened during the Second World War).

The presence of Vietnamese troops in Laos was, however, more of a provocation than a defense where the Chinese were concerned. Deterrence against a possible Chinese thrust through Laos in the event of renewed Chinese-Vietnamese hostilities is of more importance for the defense of Vietnam than of Laos. As the Lao well recognize, the security of the Lao state is better ensured by maintaining, if not cordial then at least correct, relations with Beijing. For this reason, the Lao have encouraged contact with local Chinese authorities across their common border, even while echoing Vietnamese criticism of Chinese attitudes and intentions – a ploy which relies on Chinese willingness to distinguish rhetoric from reality (Stuart-Fox, 1986b). Its success was confirmed by steady improvement in Lao-Chinese relations in the late 1980s.

Recognition of the need to maintain friendly relations with neighboring states has been a constant feature of Lao foreign policy. Lao leaders are acutely aware that a separate Lao political entity survived more through geopolitics (its juxtaposition between Thailand, China and Vietnam; the intervention of the French) than through any capacity of the Lao to defend their state as defined by its present frontiers. As in the case of Cambodia, preservation of the state itself is thus a primary goal. But in the longer term two other factors are essential to ensure the survival of a Lao political entity: national economic development which serves to strengthen the state itself;

and growth of a new sense of Lao national identity. Together these constitute the next most important objectives of Lao foreign policy.

The economic constraints referred to above make Laos entirely dependent on foreign aid for its development program. The Soviet Union and Vietnam provide the bulk of assistance. Other Eastern European states, Cuba, and Mongolia, fund small projects or help by educating Lao technicians. But the LPDR has also actively sought aid from Western donors, notably Japan, Sweden and Australia. Lao policy is to continue to diversify its sources of aid by appealing to other Western donors, particularly the United States and France. It is here, however, that the costs of the Vietnam alliance become evident. For as long as the Cambodia problem remains unresolved, Laos is unlikely to receive substantial American or Western European aid. Nevertheless, the Lao have gone out of their way to improve relations with the US by co-operating in the search for Americans missing-in-action in Laos. In return the US has taken Laos off the list of enemy states. By 1989, therefore, the way was open for a resumption of American aid: only Cambodia remained an obstacle.

A further objective of Lao foreign policy is to create the conditions necessary to build a Lao nation and develop a sense of Lao national identity. The basis for this cannot be ethnic or cultural: there are far more ethnic Lao in Thailand than in Laos, and minority groups cannot be expected to assimilate to the dominant ethnic Lao culture. Nation-building in Laos seeks to include all 60-odd 'nationalities' through the creation of a new socialist culture, free of ethnic prejudice.

For this to occur it is essential for the government to be in administrative control of the entire national territory. Hence the need for a single sufficiently powerful protector to ensure the defense of the state, and to prevent rival powers carving out *de facto* spheres of influence. For the present regime, that protector is Vietnam. The close alliance with the SRV within the 'Indo-China solidarity bloc' both ensures the preservation of the regime itself, and provides it with the opportunity and assistance necessary to build a sense of national identity among the disparate ethnic groups within the frontiers of present-day Laos.

The goal of increasing the sphere of independent action in relations with other states has not been of primary concern to the regime to date – mainly because it clearly conflicts with the above objectives. However, Laos does have diplomatic relations with more than 50 states, 27 of which have representatives based in Vientiane. Also, despite the power rivalries of the post-1975 era, neither the US nor China ever broke off diplomatic relations with Laos. Nor, moreover, did Thailand. This has had the important result of enabling the Lao to keep communications open and thus to maintain a minimal independence of action. Lao negotiations with and policies towards both the US and China since 1983 have differed in small but appreciable respects from those of Vietnam. Laos took the lead over the MIA issue and, as noted above, Lao-Chinese border relations are more harmonious than those between China and Vietnam. In addition, Laos increasingly deals with the Soviet Union outside the context of intra-Indo-China relations.

All the same, it would be a mistake to exaggerate the opportunities Laos has to maximize autonomy in foreign policy decision-making. Important decisions are taken only after discussion at the highest levels of the LPRP with the Vietnamese. Should Lao policies begin to diverge from wider Indo-Chinese (in particular, Vietnamese) interests, strong pressures would be likely to force their appropriate modification. The danger in the longer term to Lao independence comes from progressive institutionalization and integration of Indo-China-wide relations, especially in the fields of communications, commerce, and economic planning and development. The need for financial assistance and advanced technology, neither of which can be supplied by Vietnam, does, however, provide Laos with justification for developing bilateral relations with the Soviet Union, with Western European countries, with Japan, and with the United States. Similarly, the need to minimize friction along the Lao border and eliminate foreign support for anti-government insurgents justifies Lao attempts to improve bilateral relations with both China and Thailand. Fostering the cross-border trade with Thailand that is vital for a developing Lao economy constitutes another important reason to improve relations with Bangkok.

To an appreciable extent, the present Lao regime has successfully pursued its foreign policy objectives. The alliance with Vietnam has served to maintain both the regime and the security of the state. It has also created the necessary conditions for the regime to promote a new Lao national identity. At the same time Laos has been reasonably successful in attracting foreign economic development aid from a range of countries, both Communist and capitalist, and in preparing the way for future programs (notably from the United States). Both the need to ensure sufficient levels of foreign aid, and the need to minimize the hostility of Thailand and China, have led Laos to seek a degree of autonomy in foreign policy, within the constraints permitted by the Lao-Vietnamese alliance. It seems safe to suggest that the principal strategies for future Lao foreign policy will be to maintain a close political and military alliance with Vietnam and at the same time to develop a lively economic relation with Thailand, while moving towards a more 'neutral' position with respect to regional conflicts and rivalries. This would enable the LPDR to promote its development goals by drawing upon not only aid from both superpowers, but also trading opportunities with neighboring states as well. On the success of this strategy will depend the continued existence of Laos as an independent political entity.

BIBLIOGRAPHY

Adams, Nina S. and Alfred W. McCoy (eds) (1970), *Laos: War and Revolution* (New York: Harper & Row).

Gunn, G. C. (1980), 'Foreign Relations of the Lao People's Democratic Republic: The Ideological Imperative', *Asian Survey* 20, 990–1007.

Holsti, Kal (ed.) (1982), *Why Nations Realign: Foreign Policy Restructuring in the Post-War World* (London: Allen & Unwin).

Langer, P. F. and J. J. Zasloff (1970), *North Vietnam and the Pathet Lao: Partners in the Struggle for Laos* (Cambridge, Mass.: Harvard University Press).

Lee, G. Y. (1982), 'Minority Policies and the Hmong', in M. Stuart-Fox (ed.), *Contemporary Laos*, 199–219.

Ngaosyvathn, P. (1985), 'Thai-Lao Relations: A Lao View', *Asian Survey* 25, 1242–59.

Phomvihane, K. (1980), *La Révolution Lao* (Moscow: Editions du Progrès).

Stuart-Fox, M. (1980), 'Laos: The Vietnamese Connection', in *Southeast Asian Affairs 1980* (Singapore: Heinemann), 191–209.

Stuart-Fox, M. (1981a), 'Lao Foreign Policy: The View from Vientiane', *Journal of Contemporary Asia* 11, 351–66.

Stuart-Fox, M. (1981b), 'Laos in China's Anti-Vietnam Strategy', *Asia Pacific Community* No. 11, 83–104.

Stuart-Fox, M. (1981c), 'Socialist Construction and National Security in Laos', *Bulletin of Concerned Asian Scholars* 13, No. 1, 61–71.

Stuart-Fox, M. (ed.) (1982a), *Contemporary Laos: Studies in the Politics and Society of the Lao People's Democratic Republic* (St Lucia, Australia: University of Queensland Press).

Stuart-Fox, M. (1982b), 'National Defence and Internal Security in Laos', in M. Stuart-Fox (ed.), *Contemporary Laos*, 220–44.

Stuart-Fox, M. (1983), 'Marxism and Theravada Buddhism: the Legitimation of Political Authority in Laos', *Pacific Affairs* 56, No. 3, 428–54.

Stuart-Fox, M. (1986a), *Laos: Politics, Economics and Society* (London: Frances Pinter).

Stuart-Fox, M. (1986b), 'Laos in 1985: Time to Take Stock', in *Southeast Asian Affairs 1986* (Singapore: Institute of Southeast Asian Studies).

Stuart-Fox, M. (1987), *Vietnam in Laos: Hanoi's Model for Kampuchea* (Claremont, Calif.: The Keck Center for International Strategic Studies, Essays on Strategy and Diplomacy No. 8).

Viraphol, S. (1985), 'Reflections on Thai-Lao Relations', *Asian Survey*, 25, 1260–78.

Wekkin, G. D. (1982), 'The Rewards of Revolution: Pathet Lao Policy Towards the Hill Tribes since 1975', in M. Stuart-Fox (ed.), *Contemporary Laos*, 181–98.

15 Conclusion
David Wurfel

The broader significance of this volume will depend to a considerable degree on the position of Southeast Asia in the Third World, to what extent it is typical, or distinct, and how such similarities or differences between regions affect patterns of foreign policy. Area specialists are most likely to emphasize the distinctions, whereas students of international relations will tend to note patterns repeated.

THE REGION IN COMPARATIVE PERSPECTIVE

Let us look at the region first in terms of a subordinate state system and then as a series of political economies. Southeast Asia, like Latin America and the Middle East (though unlike Sub-Saharan Africa) sits on the southern border of a great power. Though China is not a superpower, its unmatched size and its historical tendency to try to dominate the region would seem to make of this point more a similarity than a difference. The superpowers have also had roles, but very uneven ones.

In all four Third-World regions under consideration the American role has been dominant and the Soviet one secondary. However, their relationship to the most aggressive actor in each region varies significantly. The greatest threat to regional stability in the Middle East in the view of most states within the region is Israel, an ally of the US – though in recent years Iran has arisen to compete for that role. Likewise the greatest threat in Sub-Saharan Africa is South Africa, also perceived as an American ally. This inhibits American influence in both regions. In Latin America at different times and different places the greatest threat to state autonomy, security and regime has been identified as a Soviet ally, Cuba, or as the US itself. In Southeast Asia, on the other hand, for nearly 40 years the greatest threat to regional stability and ruling élites has been allied with the Soviet Union, first China and now Vietnam. (The lingering fear of Japan was at a much lower level.) To be sure, students and intellectuals frequently perceived an American threat, as did President Sukarno, General Ne Win and Prince Sihanouk in their time – and, of course, the Vietnamese – but this was clearly not the dominant perception of regional élites. The ability to endorse élite fears has been a long-term advantage for the US role in Southeast Asia. The size of the lesser Soviet role has actually been quite similar across regions: a foothold in two countries in Latin America, at least three in Africa and three in Southeast Asia, while its Middle East position has been more precarious, though home base is close at hand. The distinction in Southeast Asia comes in the fact that the two greatest Communist powers have competed most vigorously there. The competition has, of course, given Southeast Asian states some leverage in dealing with the Communist world.

In fact, the regional environment for Southeast Asian foreign policy has moved from the bipolarity (US vs China) of the 1950s to a multipolarity in the 1980s that also includes both Japan and the Soviet Union. While Japan's role has as yet almost no military dimension, in addition to economic it is becoming more political. The active involvement of the four greatest powers along both political and economic dimensions would seem to distinguish Southeast Asia from the other three regions under comparison.

Yet if one looks more carefully at the economic environment, the range of choices which multipolarity suggests may not be as great as first imagined. Southeast Asia presently constitutes two economic blocs, one pro-Western, one pro-Soviet. The countries of Indo-China are heavily indebted to the Soviet Union and thus must send most of their exports there. Even though capitalist penetration of Indo-China is moving apace, and is welcomed by the authorities, Soviet domination will not disappear overnight. ASEAN countries (to which Burma has some similarity, because of the Japanese role) have greater choice in selecting sources of investment capital and markets, but on the increasingly salient issue of debt the capitalist world is co-ordinated by two important institutions, the IMF and the World Bank. And even on other economic issues in Southeast Asia the US and Japan seem to co-operate as much as they compete, thus the concept of a US-Japan condominium. A sharpening of bilateral US-Japan or Japan-China economic conflict and a wider opening of Indochina to the West could, of course, change the current pattern. But for the moment economic autonomy in Southeast Asia is restricted by the domination of each bloc by a well defined center of economic power. The similarities with other regions is obvious, though nowhere else except Cuba is the Soviet economic sphere as clearly delineated as in Indo-China, and in Latin America the degree of American dominance of the capitalist bloc would seem to be greater.

If one excludes Burma, the two Southeast Asian blocs have strategic as well as economic cohesion. One receives military supplies from the US and the other from the Soviets; though China – as well as the Europeans and Israelis – has entered the field on the US side. Each of these blocs has a dominant power: the two most populous countries in Southeast Asia, Vietnam and Indonesia. Indonesia's pre-eminence in ASEAN, however, is hardly to be compared to that of Vietnam in Indo-China. Both Singapore and Thailand are feisty critics of Indonesian attempts at leadership.

While we have suggested that these two blocs are in part sustained by superpower assistance, they also divide – quite independently of superpower influence in the first instance – on an issue within the region, the disposition of Cambodia. Fortunately for intra-regional conflict the dominant power in the capitalist bloc is not the most hostile to the Communist bloc. Vietnam is, in fact, closer to Indonesia than to any other non-Communist power in the region. Thus intra-regional polarization is lessened and the prospects of diplomatic compromise enhanced. To speak of two blocs in the region cannot, therefore, be the same as describing a tight bipolar structure in intra-regional relations. Options for autonomy by exploiting multipolarity, at least within the capitalist bloc, are still considerable. And even in Indochina they are growing rapidly.

When we look inside the region at the characteristics of the national political economies, the dimensions of comparison are multiplied. For one, the number of states in the region is less than in Africa, Latin America or the Middle East. And the variety among them is also unique. The population of the largest state is more than 800 times that of the smallest. And the per capita income of the richest is over 150 times that of the poorest. Variations in level of modernization are almost as sharp with 80 per cent of the workforce in agriculture and fisheries in Cambodia and only 0.7 per cent in Singapore. Southeast Asian states are also split between those which import more than half of their energy needs and those which are energy exporters, self-sufficient or nearly so. Variations in military power are revealed in standing forces ranging from over one million in Vietnam to less than 5000 in Brunei.

Besides these differences that are statistically measurable are the cultural cleavages. Whereas Latin America is dominantly Spanish-speaking and Catholic, the Middle East is dominantly Arab-speaking and Muslim and in Africa élites are mostly Christian, in Southeast Asia only one trio and one pair of countries speak mutually intelligible languages (Malaysia, Brunei, and Indonesia; Thailand and Laos) and all the world's major religions are represented. Three countries are dominantly Muslim, one is Christian, four are Theravada Buddhist, while Vietnam and Singapore both represent a religious mix in which Mahayana Buddhism is prominent. In fact, only Cambodia and Thailand combine religious and linguistic homogeneity in more than 80 per cent of the population. Unlike most of Latin America or the Middle East, Southeast Asia is marked by culturally plural societies. Even compared with Africa the religious pluralism is greater.

While the smaller number makes statistical generalization in Southeast Asia even less meaningful than in other Third World regions, the variety of socio-cultural bases for politics would seem to make it more representative. For instance, a Catholic Philippines has much in common with Latin America; a Muslim sultanate in Brunei has many similarities with the Gulf emirates; and Laos, with half of its population made up of animist tribes, has some characteristics of an African society. Thus comparisons within Southeast Asia have world-wide implications.

To move to a salient political dimension, Southeast Asian states are, by Third-World standards, middle aged. Not nearly as old as the states of Latin America, but one to two decades older than most of those in Africa, Southeast Asian states – except for Thailand – are somewhat younger than those in the Middle East. More time to pursue state-building policies has meant that, on the whole, Southeast Asian states are stronger, more capable than those in Africa, whether in foreign or domestic affairs. As in the Middle East – but rare elsewhere in the Third World – several states are based on powerful ancient kingdoms, namely, Burma, Thailand, Cambodia, Vietnam and Brunei. The other half, like Lebanon or much of Africa, govern a mix of peoples and territories defined as a state in the colonial period. Even in Indonesia, Malaysia and Laos, however, traditional monarchies provided the core of the new state and some modern leadership.

Ancient tradition has sometimes provided legitimacy for postwar rulers and boundaries, but has also fuelled spurts of expansionism in Indonesia, Cambodia and Vietnam. The mix of colonial determination (or lack of determination!) of boundaries and the bitterness of ancient rivalries have produced some intense intra-regional disputes since independence, especially Vietnam-Cambodia and the Philippines-Malaysia, as well as complicating relations with China for Vietnam and Burma. The age of states and their traditional bases distinguish much of Southeast Asia from Africa or Latin America, but make it more similar to the Middle East.

Perhaps the sharpest difference with Latin America, is that Southeast Asian political élites, as in Africa and the Middle East, are racially indigenous, having had almost no admixture with the ethnic strains of the colonial master – except in the Philippines, which, in any case, has a very minor and disappearing Spanish blood line. The only important external ethnic additive to economic and political élites in Southeast Asia is Chinese, a phenomenon which in the past has usually engendered fear of China but more recently has facilitated positive relations. This is a dimension of linkage between the region and the nearest great power which is surely unique to Southeast Asia.

The composition of economic élites also helps to explain the nature of economic performance in Southeast Asia. We have already noted the great contrasts in wealth, as measured by per capita GNP. Growth rates, however, showed rapid progress among most countries. From 1960 to 1982 all but one ASEAN country advanced more than 4 per cent in per capita GNP per year; the exception was the Philippines, having the highest population growth rate in the region. In the same period no African country and only two in Latin America reached 4 per cent growth. Among the five countries growing most rapidly, two, Brunei and Indonesia, were major oil exporters, while the other three, Singapore, Malaysia and Thailand, had economic élites made up of ethnic Chinese, especially skillful and hardworking entrepreneurs. Singapore and Brunei, both with per capita incomes higher than that of Italy, are no longer counted by many analysts to be in the Third-World category.

Whatever the causes, the ASEAN experience – except in the Philippines – disproved the theses of classical dependency theory, and thus has had an impact on the understanding of economic relations in the Third World generally. The strategic – and a degree of economic – multipolarity seems to have given ASEAN states especially a greater opportunity for autonomy than in Latin America, where the dependency concept was spawned. Evans has argued, however, that the later dependency school centered on Cardoso has been more confirmed than challenged in ASEAN experience (Evans, 1987: 221; also F. H. Cardoso and E. Faletto, 1979).

GOALS

Our country studies have paid considerable attention to the relative importance of different state goals which require for their accomplishment both strategy and tactics – the sum of which we call 'foreign policy'. The same goal may require more than one strategy, which could include a particular alliance, and a strategy could serve more than one goal. Furthermore, a strategy well-devised to serve one goal could unintentionally undermine another. Various foreign policy acts or decisions, which are needed to implement strategies, may actually have the same ambiguous relationship to strategies that strategies have to goals. Foreign policy success would mean, in any case, the devising of strategies and the making of decisions which accomplished the intended goal – without undermining other goals to which the state was committed. With these possibilities in mind, let us look at each of the five categories of goals in terms of their relative importance, the strategies designed to achieve them, and explanation of the success or failure in these endeavors. To the extent that we can make generalizations about the region, or about particular types of states or configurations within it, we may have made a contribution towards the formulation of broader hypotheses in the field of comparative foreign policy analysis.

Security

Security is a goal that has been the focus of a large part of the foreign policy literature for many years. It is an objective which encompasses state survival and defense of territorial integrity; most commonly it has been dealt with in military terms. Since the definition of what constitutes a threat to state or territory is in the hands of the political élite, it may be interpreted in such a way as to coincide with what is merely a threat to the regime. Regime maintenance and security goals often overlap. Where political élites have direct responsibility for management of the economy, there may be a greater awareness that long-term state survival requires a certain economic strength; welfare and security goals may also overlap. Yet there is very little evidence that the economic environment affects the pursuit of security goals defined in military terms. The two exceptions seem to be when military expenditures overwhelm the economic development budget, as in Vietnam, or earlier in Indonesia, or when the external actors themselves link strategic and economic policy, notably by the Soviet Union in Vietnam, by Western powers after the invasion of Cambodia, and by the US in the Philippines. For the rest of Southeast Asia one of the two major economic powers, Japan, has largely *de*linked economic and strategic considerations, even though small amounts of technical assistance to military agencies has crept into Japan's foreign aid. (The large Japanese contribution to the projected multilateral aid initiative for the Philippines may be a more important exception.)

The saliency given security objectives in the foreign policies of Southeast Asian states varies considerably, explained in large part by geography and historical experience. Cambodia, flanked by two historic enemies, Thailand and Vietnam, has always given it the highest priority. The search for a large protector first led to the welcome of the French in the nineteenth century; in the 1950s Sihanouk began to recognize the utility of using the Chinese in the same role. Not until the late 1970s, however, did China become the main ally of the Phnom Penh regime against perceived threats from Vietnam. This is the classic strategy of 'the enemy of my enemy is my friend'. Only Vietnam itself followed this strategy with equal vigor, seeking Soviet support against China.

Elsewhere in Southeast Asia as well China was most often the perceived threat, but the standard strategy was to seek US support, even if not a formal alliance. Only Thailand and the Philippines in the 1950s chose the latter path. The Philippines had an Americanized élite which had sought US military and economic aid and investment ever since independence. In the 1950s it was ready to accept American perceptions of threat, and sent troops to fight with the US in the Korean War. Thailand, on the other hand, had no colonial experience, and as a result was less anti-Western than some of its neighbors. Like the Philippines, Thailand had a large Chinese population and an active Chinese Communist Party branch, and thus feared a Chinese 'fifth column'. It too sent troops to Korea. Malaysia was still fighting a Chinese guerrilla force in the 1950s and thus had good reason to fear the Asian 'colossus of the North', but with British support found less need of a formal alliance with the US.

Indonesia had a unique pattern of relations with China, but by the late 1960s followed a policy somewhere between that of Thailand and of Malaysia. In 1958 Sukarno discovered evidence of US backing for a regional rebellion and thus moved closer to China and the Soviet Union, from which he already received military assistance. He found the Indonesian Communist Party, inclined towards the

Chinese side, to be an increasing source of support. (Curiously, at the same time, he opposed the emergence of an autonomous Singapore as a 'Chinese fifth column'.) But as the experience of foreign intervention changed, along with the pattern of domestic politics, by 1966 Suharto saw China as the major threat – under the circumstances a reasonable shift – and turned to the US for both military and economic aid. Indonesia's friendly relations with Vietnam are sustained by a continuing perception of threat from China, augmented by the traditional Indonesian antagonism towards the resident Chinese community. Beijing's support for rebels in East Timor was seen as justification for invading that territory.

Burma's policies were also unique, but with similarities to Indonesia. In a Buddhist country the large Chinese community was not as culturally distinct, was smaller than the Indian minority, and thus was less likely to be regarded as a threat; but China was on the border. In the early 1950s the Burmese government, like Sukarno, believed the US to be involved in supporting an ethnic rebellion, thus breeding distrust for that superpower. Rangoon, continuing to keep the USSR at arm's length, wooed China. Aside from a degree of ideological affinity, Burma's leaders wanted to be assured that China would not invade Burma to attack the KMT remnants that were lurking along the border, and thus offered help (not very effective) in trying to remove this irritant. In the early 1960s Burma's distrust of all great powers – because of the danger of their becoming involved with various ongoing rebellions – led to isolationism.

Despite the widespread identification of China as the major security threat, and the acceptance of aid from the US, it was only the Communist neighbor of China, Vietnam, that saw a military build-up as a necessary part of a policy towards China – not an unreasonable assessment in view of the Chinese invasion of 1979. States receiving US military assistance even at the height of anti-Chinese rhetoric admitted that the primary role of the military was to preserve internal security – though to be sure in the Philippines, Thailand and Malaysia at one time or another the internal security problem was a guerrilla movement supported ideologically and/or militarily by Beijing.

Three smaller states also saw military build-up as an essential part of security policy against the threats of a neighbor not a great power. Laos recently became involved in military clashes with Thailand, as Cambodia in the late 1970s did with Vietnam. Though never having had to use them, Singapore's highly trained (by Israelis) and well equipped forces, including ASEAN's best air force, are clearly designed to hold off an impetuous move by Malaysia or Indonesia. In the early 1980s – after the great power enemy had become the Soviet Union – a larger state, Thailand, did use its armed forces to expel Vietnamese incursions and for a continued manning of the Cambodian and Lao border, but this was a digression from the modern role of the Thai military.

Autonomy

In only two countries in Southeast Asia, Vietnam and the Philippines, did military relations with a great power, justified as part of security policy, pose major dilemmas for autonomy. Two other countries faced this dilemma in relations with Vietnam. Porter suggests, in fact, that after 1979 the leaders of the Heng Samrin regime made a conscious decision to accept temporary loss of autonomy in order to ensure state survival, a particularly cruel choice. For Laos the long-term presence of a much smaller number of Vietnamese troops was less intrusive and the dilemma not so sharp.

Vietnam itself has a similar problem in its relations with the Soviet Union. In 1978, feeling themselves the victims of a squeeze play between China and the Pol Pot regime, the Vietnamese felt compelled to seek massive new Soviet aid. But while they successfully fended off the threat to state survival and territorial integrity from China and its allies, the loss of autonomy in the face of increasing military and economic dependence on the Soviet Union has nevertheless become an increasing concern, even leading to overt tension in the relationship. But the huge Soviet debt and the continuing Chinese probes in the Spratlys have, until recently, made it very difficult for the Vietnamese even to consider any change in the nature of Soviet ties.

Filipino discontent with the strictures on autonomy which arise from the continuing presence of the US military bases is spurred by the recognition that in the 1940s the Philippines had even less choice than did Vietnam in 1978. In effect, the transfer of sovereignty to a war ravaged country in need of rehabilitation aid was made contingent on acceptance of the bases. Since then the threatened loss of economic and military support from the US has been seen as too high a price to pay for national pride. But security policy which undermines another major policy goal cannot be regarded as highly successful. (The economic dimensions of autonomy are discussed below, pp. 300, 306.)

Regime Maintenance

A review of all foreign policies designed to achieve national security reveals considerable overlap with those directed towards the goal of regime maintenance. Of course, regime maintenance has a prerequisite in state survival, something the Brunei sultan or the present Khmer leaders in Phnom Penh have understood fully. But even when state survival has not really been in question, there have often been attempts to conceal regime maintenance goals under the broader umbrella. Sukarno's or Marcos' policies pronounced in the name of national security were particularly well-designed to protect the regime. And where one man has ruled for a generation, as in Burma or Singapore, confusion between the two goals is inevitable. Even in Thailand, with a relatively stable and legitimate political system, the very concept of state survival is linked rhetorically to the protection of monarchy and Buddhism, which is also convenient for a prime minister.

Regime maintenance may be achieved not only through security policy but perhaps even more frequently through noble efforts for economic welfare. Foreign economic assistance has always been understood as a means for propping up a shaky regime – even though in the longer run it could have the opposite effect. Foreign credits are today being sought by Filipino representatives quite explicitly as an endorsement of the Aquino administration. Major foreign investments in Thailand are inaugurated with great fanfare and the presence of high government officials remarking on the advantages of job creation. But there are great differences in the degree to which such prominent symbolism actually contributes to per capita income growth, or better yet, its equitable distribution. Fortunately for most regimes the linkage between incumbent leaders and the announcement of new foreign financed projects is much closer than with their long-term, often faulty and unpublicized implementation. Only Singapore has consistently utilized foreign resources effectively.

Welfare/Development

Though in industrialized societies welfare may be defined largely in terms of equity of benefits and quality of the environment, in developing countries it centers on economic growth. Some authors have, in fact, defined the goal as 'development'. In a discussion on this topic it is easy to lose sight of strategy and tactics which concentrate on dealing with the external environment, that is, foreign policy. Foreign and domestic economic policy interact with each other constantly, and often intensely, yet focus on the former is the *raison d'être* of this volume. Still, the success of foreign economic policy is dependent to a considerable degree on policy with a domestic focus.

The primary task for foreign economic policy appears to have been extracting (or enticing) capital from the external environment, whether investment or credit. Success in this endeavor could – some would say must – undermine autonomy. Yet the defense of autonomy, in turn – as well as the continued flow of foreign resources, may also depend on the success in using foreign resources to promote growth. A strong, healthy economy is in a better position to manage foreign influences that come along with the capital; a weak economy is by definition vulnerable to external penetration.

However, not all Southeast Asian states have seen the attraction of foreign capital as a high priority. In fact, after 1962 Burma followed what was then perhaps the most autarkic policy in the Third World. Fear of the loss of autonomy to foreign capital was greater than the desire for its benefits. Though this might have been a stirring example of the alternative to dependency, it turned out to be a disaster. The greatest irony is that as Burmese leadership in the 1980s began to comprehend the dimensions of the disaster, they turned to foreign capital until Burma now has the highest debt service ratio for publicly guaranteed debt of any country in the region. The other more extreme experiment in autarky, in Cambodia in the late 1970s, was an even greater disaster.

This does not mean that the opposite approach was necessarily an adequate solution to the problems of development. No country in the region courted foreign capital more assiduously than the Philippines from the 1970s. And a conscious decision was soon made to emphasize credit rather than investment both because larger amounts were available and because the state exercised greater control over their use. By the mid-1980s the Philippines ended up with by far the largest foreign debt in the region, as a percentage of GNP, and, like Burma, with negative growth. Neither growth nor autonomy had been attained. What Burma and the Philippines had in common were corrupt rulers presiding over ineffective bureaucracies in a neo-patrimonial system.

In contrast, despite heavy reliance on foreign capital, Singapore's international debt is negligible, and its growth rate has consistently been tops in the region. Its bureaucracy is also the Philippines'

antithesis: well-educated, well-disciplined, well-paid and not suscep-
tible to socio-political pressures. It has provided far-sighted leadership in economic planning as well as effective policy implementation
(see Deyo, 1987).

Yet Vietnam as well has a reputation for a very strong bureaucracy
and since internal peace in 1975 has drawn heavily on foreign capital
– and technology – which in this case was Russian. But the results
have clearly not been the same as in Singapore. What was lacking
was a rational policy that provided incentives to production, allowed
autonomy for decision-makers within the firm, or allocated resources
in response to need. The bureaucratic élite is now aware of the
obstacles to productivity and the loss of international autonomy
which past efforts have produced. But whether a bureaucratic rank
and file morally exhausted after 30 years of war and now runaway
inflation is capable of implementing reform remains to be seen.
Similar problems confront Laos and Cambodia. Nor in Indo-China
can the extent and recency of war damage be forgotten.

The other four states have had varying degrees of economic success, less than Singapore but more than the Philippines. Brunei and
Indonesia, the two major oil exporters, have benefitted much more
from the luck of the world market than from skillful economic policy.
The state most successful economically – Singapore – has the least
natural resources; abundance seems to have inhibited rational policy
decisions in oil-rich states. Indonesia already has a foreign debt as
percentage of GNP which is the third highest in the region, in part
the result of the neo-patrimonial excesses of Pertamina. Both major
oil exporters have been unable to avoid market dependency on
Japan.

The cases of Malaysia and Thailand are less clearcut, and more
interesting. Both have relatively strong bureaucracies and both have
relied heavily on foreign capital. In fact, they have respectively the
second and fourth highest ratio of foreign debt to GNP in the region;
Thailand's debt service ratio is nearing the maximum acceptable
limits. The net negative transfers to creditors are the two highest in
the region as a percentage of GNP. But growth rates have been
strong, Malaysia benefitting from some oil exports. Both have been
able to keep trade sufficiently diversified to avoid trade dependency,
though Japan has been the dominant investor in recent years. Malaysia has very deliberately promoted a Japanese and Korean role in
its 'Look East' policy to balance earlier reliance on Britain and the

US. Thus in terms of both growth and autonomy these two countries have been relatively successful.

Peter Evans (1987) suggests an important reason why the other ASEAN countries have done better than the Philippines in preserving autonomy and promoting development. He believes that dependency approaches which emphasize the economic disadvantages of strong foreign influence provide an insight. As in Latin America, American investment in the Philippines was already dominant before the Second World War; it was protected by 'parity' in the postwar reconstruction. In fact, the ethos of American business in the Philippines did not change greatly even after parity ended in 1974. For many American investors, as well as members of the Filipino élite, foreign intervention in Philippine decision-making was 'natural'. And despite the rise of Japanese investment, Americans have not been dislodged from first place.

Nowhere else in Southeast Asia was American investment dominant at the dawn of independence. In fact, not until the 1960s did US capital begin to come in in large quantities. The context in which it entered was quite different from that in the Philippines. In Thailand in the 1940s and 1950s there was recollection of earlier British dominance and a desire to avoid its consequences. In Malaysia British dominance did not disappear until the 1970s. Indonesia in the 1950s had just experienced an anti-Western revolution; not until after 1965 did US capital find conditions attractive. Thus in all three there was a wariness that did not greet American investors in the Philippines. Furthermore, American unfamiliarity with the other countries inhibited the ability to exercise influence that might have distorted national policy priorities. And by the late 1960s Southeast Asians had a Japanese alternative to almost every American proposition. In any case, the level of total foreign investment has never been as high as in Latin America. Thus the opportunity for investors of any one nationality to corrupt national development policy in ASEAN was never as great as in Latin America, whereas the Philippines largely conformed to the Latin pattern. By the 1970s, however, the influence of foreign creditors legitimized by international institutions was greater throughout the region than that of investors.

While it may be possible to explain the sharp rise in foreign investment in Southeast Asia from the late 1960s in terms of the decisions of capital exporters, part of a world-wide trend, there were also policies of enticement on the ASEAN side which must be explained. Except in the Philippines ASEAN countries were led to independence by leaders with a strong anti-capitalist bias. But by the 1960s there had been an important shift. While the change in Singapore can be explained more in terms of an acculturation of the PAP leadership to capitalist values, there was a different rationale elsewhere. In both Indonesia and Malaysia there came to be an awareness that the best way to break the Chinese stranglehold on the economy was for *pribumi* or *bumiputeras*, to acquire capital and managerial skill through tie-ups with the Americans or Japanese. Even in the Philippines after 1972 a similar rationale motivated Ferdinand Marcos. Fearful of the opposition of the old economic élite Marcos sought to use presidential power to direct new investment and credit to his own oligarchy, the 'cronies'. Nowhere else was the new economic élite so rapacious and so detrimental to the economy, even though similar problems in Indonesia were widely recognized. While the motivation for this strategy was clear, it did not work well, for whenever possible foreign partners sought to tie up with competence and experience. Thus the composition of the economic élites did not change as dramatically as first intended. Condominiums between old and new segments were often struck. Nevertheless, the direction of foreign economic policy had been set. A major consequence of that policy is a mounting foreign debt which could place severe constraints on policy-makers in the next decade. Said Cheryl Payer, 'The complacency about Asia's debt in the 1980s is reminiscent of the complacency about Latin American debts in the 1970s' (1988: 283). Negative net transfers, alongside the capital export that is not recorded, are powerful constraints on economic growth.

Nation and/or State Building

This is a goal which has been identified as being particularly significant among Third-World states. There is no question that soon after independence when state structures and a sense of nationhood were weak that policy-makers sought ways of strengthening them, through both domestic and foreign policy. Malaysia's close relations with Britain in the first decade after independence allowed British colonial administrators to continue working in the civil service so as to avoid a rupture in procedures and to facilitate training. Somewhat the same effect was achieved through foreign aid agreements between the Philippines and the US in the 1950s which helped establish the Institute of Public Administration at the University of the Philippines and furthered other bureaucratic reforms. Even Thailand in this period also accepted American aid to modernize its bureaucracy. This was understandably also an important part of the foreign aid program in South Vietnam in the 1950s.

Military aid programs could also be viewed as efforts towards state building. Since Southeast Asian militaries were more often directed towards defense against internal enemies than foreign even some of that military aid ostensibly for help in fighting external aggressors was used internally, especially from the US in Thailand and from the Soviets in Indonesia. In addition explicit counter-insurgency programs were objects of foreign aid from the US in Thailand, the Philippines, and, of course, South Vietnam, and from Britain in Malaya. The impact of foreign aid on the military as an institution undoubtedly gave it a stronger political role in Indonesia, Thailand, Cambodia and South Vietnam. (That there were also entirely indigenous forces at work was demonstrated, however, by the ascendancy of the military in Burma without substantial foreign aid.) What is apparent, in any case, is that state building through foreign assistance was a phenomenon which seemed to disappear in the 1960s, except implicitly in military aid.

Nation-building through foreign policy has also faded since the 1960s. It was most noticeable under the flamboyant regimes of Sukarno and Sihanouk. One dimension was the politics of sport and foreign support for the building of great stadiums. The positive dimension of nation-building was the promotion of symbols that could be the object of national pride. The Bandung Conference in 1954 was perhaps the most successful of such efforts, giving the impression that Indonesia was at the center of the Asian-African world. Soviet economic aid in Indonesia and Cambodia was also known for projects with more symbolic than instrumental value. In fact, such considerations seemed to have helped distort economic priorities in Vietnam as late as the 1970s, about which the Vietnamese themselves are now complaining. But on the whole, as Southeast Asian states age, they become more confident about national identity and more likely to use foreign resources for economically justified projects. The most recent lapse from this norm was, of course, the antics of Imelda Marcos.

The drive for nation-building could also affect foreign policy in a very different way, what might be called its negative dimension. It made leaders especially sensitive to external threats that seemed to divide the nation, and the most salient divisions derived from regionally focused ethnic or religious groups. Thus for Sukarno American support for a regional rebellion overrode traditional Indonesian distrust of the Chinese as a factor determining alliances. In Thailand, however, indigenous regional rebels came to be Communist-infiltrated in the 1960s and thus reinforced the fear of China. In the Philippines the threat to nation-building came from Colonel Khaddafi, who provided military aid to the Moro National Liberation Front. This required a whole new initiative in Philippine foreign policy to deal with the Islamic world.

PRIORITIES AMONG GOALS

We have recognized that some goals may overlap others but that there may also be inconsistencies, with policies to achieve one goal occasionally undermining those to accomplish another. Policy-makers are thus pushed to set priorities, whether they are conscious of it or not. Country chapters have usually given us some indication of the priorities. Let us now try to fathom how and why they are different.

If an earlier view of Southeast Asia implicit in the 'domino theory' – that it was a power vacuum in which only great powers counted – were still true then we would expect goal priorities and strategies to achieve them to be entirely set by external factors. There is no question but that they are important, in Southeast Asia as elsewhere. The priority for security goals is set by the nature of external threats. For Vietnam or Cambodia with more powerful neighbors poised on the border who were willing to use military force to achieve their objectives failure to put state survival and territorial integrity as the top priority would be quite irrational. For Indonesia and the Philippines, on the other hand, physically remote from a great power threat, security gets a lower priority – unless the distant threat is perceived, reasonably or unreasonably, to have a nearby proxy, as in the case of East Timor.

While security goals have long been considered primary in the foreign policy literature, which originated in the West, careful observation of Southeast Asian practice suggests that regime maintenance more often comes first. As we have noted, the two may overlap, but they often generate distinct strategies and tactics. (For instance, if negotiations on the terms of a bases agreement – as in the Philippines – were for the purpose of strengthening an alliance against external threat, then efficiency of base use by the Americans would be a mutual interest. If, on the other hand, the Philippine President were seeking domestic political support from nationalists as a result of his conduct of the negotiations, as he was in 1978, then he would demand publicly that effective decisions on American base use would remain with the Philippine commander. But allowing the US effective control of the bases, as Marcos ultimately did, was necessary to get maximum compensation, and thus satisfy his military.) The primacy of regime maintenance would depend on the stability and legitimacy of the regime in question and on the availability of foreign resources. If regime legitimacy were lagging, as from the lack of elections in the Philippines after 1972 or poor economic performance in Indonesia before 1965, then looking for compensating resources in the external environment would be urgent, as it was for both Marcos and Sukarno. Both Sukarno and Marcos sought new sources of military aid to placate allies in the military high command. Thai military leaders conveniently found that American aid which satisfied the pride and pocket books of their subordinates, and thus their continued hegemony over the military, fitted nicely within their security doctrine as well.

Nation-building was seldom given top priority unless it encompassed concerns of security or regime maintenance. It was a foreign policy goal to the extent that domestic solutions were costly or distant and externally-oriented decisions seemed more likely of success. Sukarno's cancellation of US aid and turn towards the Communist bloc in the late 1950s because of CIA backing for regional rebellions fit these criteria. Thailand and Malaysia chose more co-operative solutions when both were threatened with armed dissidents using sanctuaries in the territories of the other. Both were insurgencies which, if they had grown, might have found support from outside the region. When foreign threats to national unity subside, as has Khaddafi's support for the MNLF, then domestic solutions become more feasible, as President Aquino's attempts to implement autonomy for Muslims would indicate. Thus the priority of the goal and the strategies chosen to deal with the problem may be a reaction to foreign powers, but also include an assessment of internal developments.

Economic welfare goals were also given higher priority when they were perceived to be coincident with regime maintenance, or security. This was one special reason for the attractiveness of Japanese official development aid; it was often accompanied by private payments to prominent members of the élite – a peculiar kind of 'regime maintenance'. Recent documentation released with the fall of Marcos confirms this pattern in the Philippines. But when the acquisition of foreign resources for economic development seemed to threaten regime maintenance, the latter took precedence. Marcos' refusal for several months to agree to new IMF conditions was because he feared more the unpopularity of the conditions before the May 1984 Assembly elections than he did the delay of IMF funds. The priorities of General Ne Win in 1988 were even more clearcut: he was willing to forego the economic lifeblood of foreign aid rather than accept the conditions and risk losing control of the political system through free elections. (His stubbornness paid off.)

The setting and achievement of welfare goals are affected every bit as much by world powers as are security goals. World market prices, interest rates, the availability of loan or investment capital, or official development assistance all have a profound impact on what foreign economic policies are possible, or even whether heavy reliance on foreign resources is viable at all. But we have already noted that domestic considerations may also be crucial. The cultural identity of the economic élite and the state of its relations with the political élite help determine the quest for foreign resources. The economic interests, ideological orientation and previous military alliances of the political élite determine where foreign resources can be found. Knowing only the external variables would not be an adequate basis for predicting either the priority for or the strategies of foreign economic policy.

Nationalism is associated with the autonomy goal. Thus in a region where most states were born in a burst of nationalism over the last 30 or 40 years one would imagine that the autonomy goal would be a very high priority. But first, even the historical assumption needs examination. To be sure Vietnam, Cambodia, Laos and Indonesia experienced violent nationalist revolutions, and Burma would have if there had not been a last-minute agreement by the British to transfer sovereignty. But that is only half the present number of states. Thailand, of course, never experienced colonialism, so its nationalism was not particularly anti-Western, but initially anti-Chinese, and that has faded. Philippine nationalism which in 1896 was the first in Southeast Asia to rise in revolution had already faded in 1935 when the US promised independence. In 1945 when the date of independence approached and the nation lay wounded after the Second World War, many in the élite contemplated asking the US to delay independence, but the formality was completed in July 1946. In Malaysia and Brunei sovereignty was given by the British to somewhat reluctant recipients. Even Singapore's subsequent break-away from Malaysia was at least as much expulsion as Singapore's desire for nationhood. Thus only half of the states in the region were actually born in a post-war burst of nationalism. Since then, to be sure, spontaneous nationalist movements have grown stronger in Thailand and the Philippines, while nationalism in Brunei, Singapore and Malaysia has received state encouragement.

It is not so surprising, therefore, to find that autonomy as a foreign policy goal has only been given a relatively high priority when the pursuit of neutralism or isolation coincided with security policy or regime maintenance. And since the days of Sukarno and Sihanouk, when it was more common, the latter juxtaposition has been most apparent in Ne Win's Burma and Pol Pot's Cambodia. Since the 1970s the much more common phenomenon has been the willingness to subordinate immediate questions of autonomy to economic development goals. Courting foreign investment and credit has involved the acceptance of limitations on sovereign 'rights' in the spirit of interdependence. Under those conditions the most that can be hoped for is a balancing of foreign influences in order to limit the impact of any one, but in this neither the Philippines, Vietnam, Indonesia, Brunei or Burma (more recently) has been entirely successful. Surely the reality of foreign economic constraints is a powerful factor but, at least in the case of Brunei or the Philippines, because of past experience, interests, and values, the élites' demands for autonomy have not been strong.

We have noted that some goals are given prominence only if they are perceived as reinforcing another, even stronger, goal. Usually compatible goals would appear to include the following pairs: security and regime maintenance, security and state-building, regime maintenance and state building and, under some circumstances, autonomy and nation-building, welfare and regime maintenance, as well as autonomy paired with either security or regime maintenance. But the last four pairs may also exhibit incompatibility and thus create serious dilemmas for foreign policy-makers. Even sharper dilemmas are found in the choice between development and autonomy, development and security, nation-building and regime mainten-ance, and nation-building and security. (The fact that nation- and state-building seem to have different valences when compared with other goals would seem to imply that they should each be regarded as a distinct goal, at least for some purposes.) In each incompatible pair the greater the use of foreign policy to achieve one goal, usually by extracting resources from the external environment, the greater the tendency to fail in achieving the other. Let us look at some examples.

Extracting resources from the external environment as the primary strategy for promoting economic development does not always produce dependency, as the Singapore case indicates, but it commonly does. Singapore, while relying heavily on foreign capital, was careful to diversify sources, and at the same time to avoid heavy foreign debt or trade dependence. The Philippines, on the other hand, long followed a foreign economic policy that produced chronic dependence on the US in investment, debt and to a lesser extent trade, though recent trends could alter this pattern. Despite earlier flings at autarky Burma by the 1980s was increasingly dependent for aid, credit, and investment on Japan.

The compatibility or incompatibility of economic welfare and security goals pursued through foreign policy has been a topic of some controversy among Latin Americanists. To be sure military allies are sometimes a generous source of economic assistance. But a great power decision to abandon a small ally, as Laos learned, can lead to economic bust following the boom. And in the late 1980s economic constraints on the two superpowers make it difficult for them to sustain large economic as well as military assistance programs. Both Vietnam and the Philippines are currently aware of this phenomenon. But perhaps the most fundamental problem is that large foreign military assistance, whether designed to counter an internal or external enemy, strengthens the political role of the military, which usually erodes the prospect of rational economic decisions for either welfare or development. The Saigon regime was perhaps the extreme case, but similar tendencies have been noted in different periods in Thailand, Indonesia and the Philippines.

If nation-building is understood as striving for greater unity in a multi-ethnic society, it requires a considerable responsiveness to ethnic aspirations. A regime which relies heavily on foreign assistance, especially in combating ethnic rebels, has less need of responsiveness or a political settlement but rather assumes the possibility of imposing order. Even if foreign aid is ostensibly for purposes of bolstering external defense, it may have the same consequence. Both Thai and Philippine policies towards uprisings by ethnic minorities were reduced in effectiveness as a result of this phenomenon.

It is in the course of attempting to resolve these dilemmas that policy-makers most clearly reveal their priorities. The pre-eminence for regime maintenance, security and/or economic welfare comes through.

PROCESS AND OUTPUT

Though the authors of this volume have carefully described the nature of the foreign policy decision-making process in Southeast Asia, the foregoing discussion of goals and strategies has not mentioned it. Yet process does affect output at some points. Because the emphasis on particular goals is usually a product of societal, or at least élite, consensus, the characteristics of the foreign policy process usually do not have an effect at this level. However, it may be that the very symbolic gestures that have been described as the foreign policy of nation-building – often associated with a charismatic leader – declined with the increasing institutionalization of the foreign policy process. Bureaucracies are less inclined to emphasize dramatic gestures than more traditional diplomatic activity. In effect, as Southeast Asian diplomats gain experience, they become socialized to the international milieu in which they move. In any case, process seems to have more impact on choice of strategies than on priorities of goals; that choice puts a premium on the availability of information.

The institutionalization of decision-making, which has grown steadily in Thailand, has long been high in Singapore, deteriorated under Ne Win in Burma, was bolstered by Suharto in Indonesia, but suffered lapses in the Philippines by the intervention of Imelda Marcos as well as the personal control of her husband. In Indo-China in recent years the ethos of the diplomatic bureaucrat has been supplanting determinations previously left to party ideologues. On balance the role of the foreign policy professional has expanded, though authoritarian leaders still have a dominant role in some countries, and that of the military remains higher than in the West. In fact, in Thailand, Indonesia, Cambodia, and Vietnam, but especially Burma, military priorities often supersede diplomatic ones. Nevertheless, as foreign policy increasingly involves economic dimensions another corps of decision-makers has been added. Debt negotiations bring in central bankers, guidelines for foreign investment bring in planning agencies, and even foreign aid agreements are often handled outside ministries of foreign affairs. As different bureaucracies tend to formulate and manage different dimensions of foreign policy, the co-ordination function of the President or Prime Minister, democratic or authoritarian, remains crucial.

The non-bureaucratic elements in the policy process are still minor in most Southeast Asian countries. Elected legislatures have real power in only Thailand and the Philippines (a recent revival). In Thailand how to deal with Cambodia and Vietnam is a matter of some public debate in which parliamentarians participate with at least marginal influence on bureaucratic decision-makers. In the Philippines the role of the legislature in 1987–88 has been much greater. A sign that even in liberalizing authoritarian regimes legislatures may play a role in the foreign policy process has recently appeared in Vietnam. A National Assembly which was previously just a rubber stamp debated and amended a foreign investment bill for more than a year before it passed in late 1987. The National Assembly debate apparently reflected the cleavage in the Communist Party over how far and how fast to go in opening to the West.

In any case, what is abundantly clear is that, if it were ever true, foreign policy in most Southeast Asian countries is no longer simply the leader's prerogative. Foreign policy decisions are the result of some consultation, both within and without the bureaucracy. While the perceptions, experiences and even personal whims of the leader have a major impact on the final decision, they are seldom its sole basis.

FOREIGN POLICY RESTRUCTURING

Though our discussion of different national foreign policies has focused on the last decade or two, we have tried to take account of even longer shifts over time. Any minimally successful foreign policy adjusts over the years to changes in the international environment or to the ups and downs of national capability. Rapid changes in goal priority or strategies are more dramatic, noticed not only by journalists but by scholars, for they reveal more clearly cause and effect relationships in the foreign policy process. Holsti, 1982) has called rapid and fundamental change 'foreign policy restructuring'. He reduces all foreign policies to four types – admittedly oversimplified: isolation, self-reliance, dependence, and diversification (non-alignment). These are categories especially useful for Third-World states and with some modification can be applied in Southeast Asia. In any case, the burden assumed by Holsti, which we must also undertake here, was not only to characterize the shifts but to try to explain them.

It would be too early to expect to find restructuring in such a young state as Brunei. Neither is it apparent in the cases of Singapore or Malaysia. This seems to be associated with continuity in the composition of the political élite – each country has been ruled by the same political party since independence – and in the foreign policy bureaucracy as well. In both states the policy process is well institutionalized. Aside from these domestic factors it is also true that unlike Thailand or the Philippines both Singapore and Malaysia were far removed from the great surges and waning of power surrounding the Vietnam War. Both external and internal environments for policy were quite stable.

In contrast, two states underwent partial restructuring and five even more fundamental change. The modest change in Thailand was primarily the result of change in the external environment whereas similar degrees of change in the Philippines were for the most part internally generated. The partial restructuring referred to in the Philippines was the movement from dependence to limited diversification in 1973–75. It occurred after the declaration of martial law in 1972 which made the President the sole policy-maker, unfettered by an elected legislature which in the past had sometimes exercised real power in foreign affairs. Despite rhetorical flourishes after the announcement of the Nixon Doctrine in 1969 or the Paris Agreement in 1973, partial restructuring did *not* involve an abandonment of the American alliance, but rather increased pressure for greater Filipino benefit from it. What it did was take a long overdue initiative to open diplomatic relations with Communist countries, not in defiance of the US but in the wake of an American *rapprochement* with China. It also gave new emphasis to relations with the Third World. The American alliance was, if anything, strengthened. All changes could be linked to a strategy for regime maintenance.

In 1975 Thailand was enjoying the first period of freely elected parliamentary government since the 1940s, and the US had just been expelled from Indo-China. Popular expressions of nationalism – which quickly focused on the negative aspects of US bases – were on the rise and the US had just lost its effectiveness as the front line against Communist expansion. In any case, Thai policy had long had the habit of adjusting to power, and weakness. Thus the American air force was asked to leave, and it did. But the departure was mutually agreeable, part of the post-Vietnam syndrome; neither US economic or military aid was stopped. At a lower level of intensity Thai-American relations remained cordial. The alliance had not ended, and no new one was created to displace it. In fact, some US base operations returned a few years later. The shift had been based on a changed perception of the external environment, facilitated in part by a regime change.

After the 1978–79 Vietnamese invasion of Cambodia, which pushed close to the Thai border, the external environment had dramatically changed, even though there had been no fundamental shift in the character of the Bangkok regime. Discovering that the Chinese had become the most effective counter to the Vietnamese threat, which was clear and present, the Thais made a basic shift in orientation towards China. Diplomatic relations had already been established, but in addition the traditional category of enemy had been changed to ally. Thailand allowed China to provide military supplies to the Khmer Rouge through Thai territory and before long was buying Chinese weapons itself. But given the nature of US-Chinese relations, the new links with China were initially compatible with the older US alliance, thus the term 'partial restructuring'. More recently, however, this Thai policy has produced some tensions with the US.

The five remaining countries all saw more dramatic regime changes and more thorough foreign policy restructuring. The Indo-China countries experienced revolutions while Burma and Indonesia were hit by military coups. (Cambodia and Laos had both. But changes in Laos in the 1960s were so numerous and so shortlived that there will be no attempt to catalog them here.) The year 1975 marked not only the demise of South Vietnam as a 'sovereign' unit, but the displacement of capitalist with Communist regimes in Cambodia and Laos. In Laos the switch was from dependence on the US to dependence on Vietnam, whereas in Cambodia there was a tranformation from US ally to an almost entirely isolated community, a more severe isolation, in fact, than any state in Southeast Asia has known in modern times. In 1970, after the Lon Nol *coup d'état*, Cambodia had moved as abruptly from being non-aligned to a US dependency.

In Hanoi, on the other hand, there had been a Communist regime since 1954. The restructuring of the 1970s was a result of change in the external environment, not regime change. After the army of the North overran the South, China was clearly unhappy about the consolidation of Hanoi's power. Within three years it transformed itself from major ally to major threat, working increasingly through the dominant anti-Vietnamese faction in Cambodia led by Pol Pot. There was, of course, some mistreatment of Chinese businessmen in Vietnam to exploit, but this was just a pretext. By 1978, sensing the magnitude of the Chinese threat, Vietnam signed an economic and military alliance with the Soviet Union, providing markets, tropical produce, and military bases in return. Heretofore Vietnam had learned to play off the two Communist giants against each other to maximize autonomy, but in 1978 Vietnam became truly dependent on the Soviets. In view of China's own dramatic shift, Vietnam felt it had no other option. When it invaded Cambodia to try to remove China's proxy, it established a new protégé regime in Phnom Penh. In both Cambodia and Laos the search for support from the Soviets, Eastern Europe and elsewhere has begun to soften the reality of dependence on Vietnam.

More recently, again without a regime change, despite some new blood in the Politburo, Vietnam may be experiencing a partial restructuring, in the direction of diversification. The search for foreign capital and for capitalist trading partners, in earnest since 1986, is clearly intended to balance the Soviet role. However, since it is associated with economic reforms favored by Gorbachev, it does not constitute in any sense a break with the dominant partner, which may actually seek relief from the burdens of the relationship. Further change is expected after the withdrawal from Cambodia in 1989, when an influx of Japanese – as well as European and ASEAN – trade and capital is hoped to have a major impact. At that point the lessening of dependence on the Soviets could become more substantial.

The restructurings in Indonesia and Burma have received most attention in the literature, the latter by Holsti himself. Holsti does not characterize the Burmese case as a consequence of regime change, but it followed within little more than a year of General Ne Win's takeover in a coup, and within months of the removal of Ne Win's deputy, Brigadier Aung Gyi. Thus regime change must be counted as a major explanatory variable. The somewhat Westernized political élite around U Nu was replaced by the more inward looking Ne Win, and his officers. As a result Burma moved from diversified non-alignment, similar to that of India at the time, to an isolation that was initially only slightly less severe than Cambodia's. Burma withdrew from international organizations and cut off all foreign aid, even closing the country to tourists. Holsti argues that it was more a consequence of the xenophobic nationalism of Ne Win and his coterie than a response to the external environment. But certainly in part it was a passive response to a perceived threat from China which was aiding Communist rebels. Ne Win apparently wanted to remove all pretense for Beijing's hostility. Without another regime change, but in the face of economic disaster, Ne Win has slowly modified his isolation over the last decade, accepting increasing amounts of foreign aid, especially from Japan and international institutions. But the change has been too gradual to describe it as 'restructuring'.

Indonesia, however, did go through two periods of genuine restructuring, the first under Sukarno, 1957–58, and the second under Suharto, 1965–66. The first might be characterized as a shift from non-alignment to quasi-dependence, and the second 'changing partners', from quasi-dependence on the Soviet Union to a similar relationship with the US and Japan. The element of regime change in the first case was mixed with stimuli from the external environment; the second was a more dramatic and complete regime change, but the role of China in that imbroglio was seen as a new sign of threat from that quarter. In any case, it must be recalled that 'restructuring' does not necessarily imply a change of goals but only a shift in their priorities or a change in strategies to achieve them.

The fact that Burma and Indonesia could turn in such different directions in the mid-1960s, both fearing China, would seem to indicate that the international system was not the primary determinant. On the other hand, the international adjustments that followed the Vietnam War had a major impact on foreign policy in Thailand, Vietnam and Cambodia; despite the rhetoric, that was not the major factor in the Philippines.

As we finally conclude this first attempt at a truly comparative study of the foreign policies of Southeast Asian states, it becomes increasingly apparent that it is still inadequate. The precision of terminology, the careful comparability of data and the persistent search for cause/effect relationships that the more theoretical literature so justly demands have often been absent. This book is really only the first of several that should be devoted to foreign policy in the region. The shortcomings of this volume can perhaps best be noted by suggesting the focus of future studies. A more rigorous comparison could have been undertaken if each country study had concentrated on reaction to the same stimulus, for example, the Chinese threat, the debt crisis, or regime change, whether away from or towards democracy. Such a stimulus might be even more narrowly defined, as the Communist victory in Indo-China, Vietnam's invasion of Cambodia in 1978–79, or the *yen* appreciation of 1987. Perhaps a pair of case studies for each country, one from the security category, the other from the welfare category, would make the most interesting comparison. The question of the economic interests of the policy-making élite, so important to political economy, has been only superficially mentioned and should be further studied. Research might also be directed towards compiling the data sufficient to rank the importance of foreign policy goals pursued by each country. Since some countries altered the priorities of goals from time to time, this would require identification of points of transition. A more systematic explanation for the various rankings might then be attempted.

Foreign policy, of course, does not stand still. By the time the above issues have been addressed, Southeast Asia will probably have produced more problems and crises to be analyzed. Hopefully for those subsequent endeavors the tentative hypotheses derived from the foregoing work will help guide the research. The trail towards more comparative study of Southeast Asian foreign policy has been blazed, but we expect the next explorer to go even further.

BIBLIOGRAPHY

Cardoso, Fernando H. and Enzo Faletto (1979), *Dependency and Development in Latin America* (Berkeley: University of California Press).

Evans, Peter (1987), 'Class, state and dependence in East Asia: lessons for Latin Americanists', in Frederic C. Deyo (ed.), *The Political Economy of the New Asian Industrialism* (Ithaca: Cornell University Press).

Holsti, K. J., *et al.* (1982), *Why Nations Realign: Foreign Policy Restructuring in the Postwar World* (London: Allen & Unwin).

Morrison, Charles E. (1988), 'Japan and the ASEAN Countries: The Evolution of Japan's Regional Role', in Takashi Inoguchi and Daniel Okimoto (eds), *The Political Economy of Japan*, Vol. 2 (Stanford: Stanford University Press).

Payer, Cheryl (1988), 'The Asian Debtors', in Altaf Gauhar (ed.), *Third World Affairs, 1988* (London: Third World Foundation for Social and Economic Studies).

TABLE 1 *Demographic, Economic and Military Data on Southeast Asia*

	Burma	Kampuchea	Laos	Vietnam	Brunei	Indonesia	Malaysia	Philippines	Singapore	Thailand
Pop. (000 000)	38.8	6.5	3.8	62.2	0.2	174.9	16.1	61.5	2.6	53.6
% Average Annual Growth ('79–'86)	2.1	2.1	2.5	2.6	2.6	2.1	2.4	2.8	1.1	2.1
Life Expectancy	53	43	50	63	62	58	67	65	71	63
Workforce % in Agriculture and Fishing	64.7	80	75	73	5	54	35.1	49	.8	61
Per Capita Income, US$ '84	172	na	140	na	21,600	566	1,996	603	6,922	646
'86	190	na	159	na	15,556	530	1,636	515	6,431	612
GNP '84 US$ billion	6.2 (GDP)	na	na	na	3.9 (GDP)	90 (GDP)	29.2	31.9	17.7	40.7
'86 US$ billion	7.7	na	0.6	na	3.5	86.5 [1985]	26.3	30.1	18.0	40.2
Av. Annual % GNP Real Growth '80–'84	6.0	na	na	na	-3.3	6.1	6.9	1.3	8.1	5.1
'82–'86	5.5	na	7.0	na	-4.8	3.5	3.2	-1.1	7.0	4.1
Defense as % of GNP	3.1	na	na	na	4.6	2.2	5.8	1.0	6.3	4.2
Size of armed forces (000) '85	186	35	54	1027	4.1	278	110	115	56	235
% of Energy Imported (net)	0	na	5	na	0	0	0	55	100	6.81

SOURCE FEER, *Asia Yearbook*, 1986, 1988.

TABLE 2 *Southeast Asian Debt*

Country	Total External Debt 1980	Total External Debt 1985	Net Transfers from Creditors (1986)	Principal Ratios			
				Total External Debt EDT/GNP (%) 1980	1985	Publicly Guaranteed Debt TDS/XGS (%) 1980	1985
Burma	1 493.4	3 766.3	N/A	25.9	45.2	20.1	55.4
Indonesia	20 888.3	42 089.5	−298.2	27.9	58.5	7.9	29.3
Malaysia*	5 195.9	19 649.8	−123.7	N/A	N/A	3.3	13.7
					DOD/GNP (%)	16.6	65.0
Philippines	17 386.5	28 172.5	−145.0	49.4	93.6	7.2	18.3 (1986)
Singapore	N/A	N/A	N/A	N/A	N/A	1.0	1.4
Thailand	8 257.5	17 958.6	−541.8	25.1	44.7	5.0	16.7

* Long-term debt

XGS = Export of goods and services
EDT = Total external debt
TDS = Total debt service
DOD = Long term debt outstanding

SOURCE World Bank, *World Debt Tables*, Vol. II, 1987–88 ed.

Index